Lecture Notes
in Business Information Processing   **295**

Series Editors

Wil M.P. van der Aalst
Eindhoven Technical University, Eindhoven, The Netherlands
John Mylopoulos
University of Trento, Trento, Italy
Michael Rosemann
Queensland University of Technology, Brisbane, QLD, Australia
Michael J. Shaw
University of Illinois, Urbana-Champaign, IL, USA
Clemens Szyperski
Microsoft Research, Redmond, WA, USA

More information about this series at http://www.springer.com/series/7911

Björn Johansson · Charles Møller
Atanu Chaudhuri · Frantisek Sudzina (Eds.)

Perspectives in Business Informatics Research

16th International Conference, BIR 2017
Copenhagen, Denmark, August 28–30, 2017
Proceedings

 Springer

Editors

Björn Johansson
Lund University
Lund
Sweden

Atanu Chaudhuri
Aalborg University
Copenhagen
Denmark

Charles Møller
Aalborg University
Aalborg
Denmark

Frantisek Sudzina
Aalborg University
Copenhagen
Denmark

ISSN 1865-1348   ISSN 1865-1356   (electronic)
Lecture Notes in Business Information Processing
ISBN 978-3-319-64929-0   ISBN 978-3-319-64930-6   (eBook)
DOI 10.1007/978-3-319-64930-6

Library of Congress Control Number: 2017947754

Printed on acid-free paper

This Springer imprint is published by Springer Nature
The registered company is Springer International Publishing AG
The registered company address is: Gewerbestrasse 11, 6330 Cham, Switzerland

Preface

Business informatics is a discipline that combines information and communication technology (ICT) with the knowledge of management. It is concerned with the development, use, application, and the role of management information systems and all other possible ways of using ICT in the field of management. It is also an important interdisciplinary academic and research discipline. The Perspectives in Business Informatics Research (BIR) conference series was established 16 years ago as a result of a collaboration of researchers from Swedish and German universities in order to create a forum where researchers in business informatics, both senior and junior, could meet and hold discussions. The conference series is led by the Steering Committee, to which one or two persons from every appointed organizer are invited.

To date, BIR conferences were held in: Rostock (Germany – in 2000, 2004, 2010), Berlin (Germany– 2003), Skövde (Sweden – 2005), Kaunas (Lithuania – 2006), Tampere (Finland –2007), Gdańsk (Poland – 2008), Kristianstad (Sweden – 2009), Riga (Latvia – 2011), Nizhny Novgorod (Russia – 2012), Warsaw (Poland – 2013), Lund (Sweden – 2014), Tartu (Estonia – 2015), and Prague (Czech Republic – 2016). This year's 16th International Conference on Perspectives in Business Informatics Research (BIR) was held during August 28 – 30, 2017, in Copenhagen, organized and hosted by the Center for Industrial Production, Aalborg University, Denmark

This year the BIR conference attracted 59 submissions from 23 countries. They were reviewed by 45 members of the Program Committee. As the result, 17 full papers and three short papers were selected for presentation at the conference and publication in this volume. The papers presented at the conference cover many important aspects of business informatics research.

This year, the conference theme was the digital transformation. The challenges and opportunities for the digital transformation driven by the fourth industrial revolution was the central theme for the World Economic Forum summit last year. Industry 4.0 has been used to characterize the shift in society, enabled by connectivity and convergence of physical, digital, and biological technologies. This digital transformation will impact most businesses, organizations, and societies and call for new and radical approaches to how we adopt, use, and manage IT.

The main conference was also accompanied by satellite events: A pre-BIR forum, two workshops, and a doctoral consortium took place during the first day of the conference.

We would like to thank everyone who contributed to the BIR 2017 conference. First of all, we thank the authors for presenting their papers, we appreciate the invaluable contributions from the members of the Program Committee and the external reviewers, and we thank all the members of the local organization team from Aalborg University, for their help in organizing the conference. We acknowledge the EasyChair development team for providing a valuable tool for preparing the proceedings and the Springer publishing team for their excellent collaboration. Last but not the least, we thank the Steering Committee for directing the BIR conference series.

June 2017   Björn Johansson
                                                                   Charles Möller

Organization

Program Co-chairs

Charles Møller	Aalborg University, Denmark
Frantisek Sudzina	Aalborg University, Denmark
Atanu Chaudhuri	Aalborg University, Denmark
Björn Johansson	Lund University, Sweden

Program Committee

Jan Aidemark	Linneaus University, Sweden
Bo Andersson	Lund University, Sweden
Eduard Babkin	LITIS Laboratory, INSA Rouen; TAPRADESS Laboratory, State University - Higher School of Economics (Nizhny Novgorod); Russia
Per Backlund	University of Skövde, Sweden
Rimantas Butleris	Kaunas University of Technology, Lithuania
Sven Carlsson	Lund University, Sweden
Witold Chmielarz	University of Warsaw, Poland
Niclas Eberhagen	Linnaeus University, Sweden
Peter Forbrig	University of Rostock, Germany
Ahmad Ghazawneh	IT University of Copenhagen, Denmark
Jānis Grabis	Riga Technical University, Latvia
Darek Haftor	Linnaeus University, Sweden
Markus Helfert	Dublin City University, Ireland
Stefan Henningsson	Copenhagen Business School, Denmark
Amin Jalali	Stockholm University, Sweden
Gustaf Juell-Skielse	Stockholm University, Sweden
Dimitris Karagiannis	University of Vienna, Austria
Marite Kirikova	Riga Technical University, Latvia
Andrzej Kobylinski	Warsaw School of Economics, Poland
Birger Lantow	University of Rostock, Germany
Michael Le Duc	Mälardalen University, Sweden
Osama Mansour	Linnaeus University, Sweden
Raimundas Matulevicius	University of Tartu, Estonia
Ulf Melin	Linköping University, Sweden
Patrick Mikalef	Norges teknisk-naturvitenskapelige universitet, Norway
Jyrki Nummenmaa	University of Tampere, Finland
Jacob Nørbjerg	Copenhagen Business School, Denmark
Victoria Paulsson	IC4/Dublin City University Business School, Ireland
Tomas Pitner	Masaryk University, Czech Republic
Nava Pliskin	Ben Gurion University of the Negev, Israel

Vaclav Repa	University of Economics, Czech Republic
Kurt Sandkuhl	University of Rostock, Germany
Ulf Seigerroth	Jönköping University, Sweden
Andrzej Sobczak	Warsaw School of Economics, Poland
Janis Stirna	Stockholm University, Sweden
Ann Svensson	University West, Sweden
Torben Tambo	Aarhus University, Denmark
Lars Taxén	Linköping University, Sweden
Olgerta Tona	Lund University, Sweden
Anna Wingkvist	Linnaeus University, Sweden
Jelena Zdravkovic	Stockholm University, Sweden
Alfred Zimmermann	Reutlingen University, Germany

Additional Reviewers

Fernando Bevilacqua
Markus Bockholt
Dominik Bork
Thomas Borup Kristensen
Björn Cronquist
Michael Fellmann
Umberto Fiaccadori
John Gøtze
Marco Nardello
Kestutis Kapocius
Vimal Kunnummel
Markus Lahtinen
Fabienne Lambusch
Kuan-Lin Chen
Audrone Lupeikiene
Carl-Mikael Lönn

Milos Maryska
Jan Ministr
Kaveh Mohajeri
Aurelijus Morkevicius
Przemyslaw Polak
Fatemeh Rahimi
Rahim Rahmani
Solmaz Sajadirad
Azadeh Sarkheyli
Nazli Shahim
Paulius Stulga
Eric-Oluf Svee
Nikolaos Tantouris
Marcus Toftedahl
Tomáš Výrost
Monica Winge

BIR Series Steering Committee

Mārīte Kirikova	Riga Technical University, Latvia (Chair)
Björn Johansson	Lund University, Sweden (Co-chair)
Kurt Sandkuhl	Rostock University, Germany (Co-chair)
Eduard Babkin	State University – HSE, Russia
Rimantas Butleris	Kaunas Technical University, Lithuania
Sven Carlsson	Lund University, Sweden
Peter Forbrig	Rostock University, Germany
Andrzej Kobyliñski	Warsaw School of Economics, Poland
Raimundas Matulevičius	University of Tartu, Estonia
Lina Nemuraitė	Kaunas Technical University, Lithuania

BIR2017_Keynotes

Industry 4.0 and Smart Production

Ulrich Berger[1] and Laurits Andersen[2]

[1] Brandenburg University of Technology, Cottbus, Germany
[2] Aalborg University, Aalborg, Denmark
ulrich.berger@b-tu.de

The industrial world undergoes a paramount change, which is accelerated by massive digitalization. Although the headlines sound different as Industrial Internet of Things (IIoT) in the US, Made in China 2025 or Industry 4.0 in Europe, the challenges and applicable technological solutions with focus on production systems, commonly named Cyber Physical Production Systems (CPPS), are redundant.

Actual tasks are to strengthen the versatility of production equipment and processes in the context of the progressive dynamism of the markets, where approaches like CPPS become in first step necessary regarding the automation of processes. These strategies are intended to increase productivity and efficiency of a company or a business for a long-term period. However, the further changing business conditions will lead to shorter planning cycles and mass customization trends would increase the number of variants down to smallest lot sizes or one-of-a-kind products. Some of these challenges can be solved with the implementation of CPPS. However, in order to comply with more dynamic requirements and also considering cognition and knowledge based aspects, the learning, training and assistance capabilities of the human work force with respect to CPPS has to be significantly upgraded.

As a vision, the combination of CPPS and real-time networking of people, machines, objects and ICT systems would allow a dynamic management and handling of complex production systems. These systems would include software-intensive units and devices (from Big Data to Smart Data), which represent the integration of data, services and comprehensive solutions in order to connect physical and digital systems to each other. In consequence, this vision would lead to a Smart Industrial Ecosystem (SIE).

In order to establish, evaluate and implement such SIE's, there has been established several Industry 4.0 in Europe. They cover research, development and transfer of results aspects. One of them, the Innovation Center Industry 4.0 in Brandenburg (IMI), part of the national Platform Industry 4.0 in Germany, is following this strategy and thus build up on three core elements, which are: 1) The Model Factory, providing showroom and hands on shop floor for advanced technologies; 2) The Innovation Lab, transferring R&D results into practical industrial requirements; and 3) The Knowledge Forum, acting as learning, training and assistance sphere for all staff levels.

During three years of practical work, the IMI has already performed innovation projects with over 100 industrial clients, BIG and SME companies. There have been developed unique consultancy formats as e.g. the Industry 4.0 Check-Up, which analyses and determines the maturity levels in the field of Industry 4.0 and the Industry 4.0 Road Map, which defines the eight migration steps towards Industry 4.0, keeping the individual KPI requirements in mind.

The speech will analyze and describe the building blocks and application sectors of CPPS in industrial environments. It will further reflect the requirements and migration paths towards Smart Industrial Ecosystems and Smart Production systems. The discussion of selected use cases, related from the work of the IMI, including implementation strategies and results will highlight the practical aspects of the speech.

Digital Transformation of Industry Research Challenges and Opportunities in Smart Production

Charles Møller

Department of Materials and Production, Aalborg University, Aalborg, Denmark
charles@make.aau.dk

The central theme of the 16th International Conference on Perspectives in Business Informatics Research is digital transformation. Digital transformation refers to the profound change associated with the adoption of digital models in all aspects of business, society and life in general.

In business, digital transformation opens up to numerous innovative and potential disruptive business models. Industry has traditional been quite conservative, however these years manufacturing and production is undergoing massive digital transformation. The industrial challenges and opportunities for the digital transformation driven by the fourth industrial revolution was the central theme for the World Economic Forum summit last year.

Industry 4.0 has been used to characterize the shift in society, enabled by connectivity and convergence of physical, digital and biological technologies. This digital transformation will impact most businesses, organizations and societies and call for new and radical approaches to how we adopt, use and manage IT. Industry 4.0 is best characterized as a joint research and innovation program designed to support the re-industrialization of Germany. This is an agenda similar to most western European countries, US, and also Japan, Korea, India and China. Also in Denmark, we have seen the emergence of a national industry lead research and innovation initiative on manufacturing: "Manufacturing Academy of Demark (MADE)". What these programs share is the strong focus on IT and automation as an enabler of increased competitiveness. At Aalborg University, we have embrace the change and formed an inter-disciplinary research unit supporting this research agenda, and we have framed the Danish approach as Smart Production enabled by digitalization, automation and new collaborative business models.

Smart Production and Industry 4.0 provide a wealth of new research challenges and opportunities. This talk will present and clarify the concepts, identify some significant areas where business informatics research potentially may contribute with relevant new insights.

Contents

Information Systems Applications

Information Systems Development

Enterprise Architecture

Current State of Governance Roles in Enterprise Architecture Management Frameworks

Matthias Wißotzki[(⊠)], Felix Timm, and Paul Stelzer

Chair of Business Information Systems, University of Rostock,
Albert-Einstein-Str. 22, Rostock, Germany
{matthias.wissotzki,felix.timm,
paul.stelzer}@uni-rostock.de

Abstract. Only if the right people equipped with the necessary competencies fulfill the tasks correctly that should be done in their designated roles, the full concept of Enterprise Architecture Management (EAM) can be deployed. This topic has been discussed quite rarely in the past. Therefore, this work systematically analyzes manifold EAM literature sources like technical literatures and research papers as well as EA frameworks in order to derive a set of roles in EAM. The results were validated by dint of an expert interview with an EAM practitioner. This paper contributes to the EAM discipline by presenting a generalized overview of EAM roles and relates them to certain EAM tasks and required competencies. Finally, the proposed overview is validated by an expert interview.

Keywords: Enterprise Architecture Management (EAM) · Roles · TOGAF · Enterprise Architecture (EA) · Frameworks

1 Introduction

EAM tries to maintain flexibility, cost efficiency and transparency within the EA [1]. Tools are provided to master the complexity and to strategically develop IT landscapes in a business-oriented way [2]. EA in turn provides a holistic view of the enterprise with respect to its elements and dependencies that are required for value creation. Numerous of contributions are dealing with the subject of EAM, but responsible persons and corresponding roles, which are accountable for the development, implementation and optimization of the EAM approach, are rarely taken into account, but exactly these persons determine success or failure. Even EA frameworks, which describe the issue much more accurately through different views and aspects [2], deal with roles only in few cases. Moreover, frameworks, that should help to establish an EA within the enterprise, are described as complex and need to be adapted to the enterprise [2]. In addition, EAM is not only used in large enterprises, but should also be applied in small and medium-sized enterprises [3]. The integration of EAM in the enterprise poses a greater challenge to the staff in this case, because the necessary roles and required competencies are unclear [1]. Moreover, it can be ensured by a precise

© Springer International Publishing AG 2017
B. Johansson et al. (Eds.): BIR 2017, LNBIP 295, pp. 3–15, 2017.
DOI: 10.1007/978-3-319-64930-6_1

role description that a role is right staffed and thus can complete tasks more productive or at lower costs. On that point, the following question should be answered: What tasks must be performed and which competencies are necessary to do so?

To develop a generalized set of role concepts we analyzed more than 50 EA frameworks [4] in order to identify different role concepts, aggregated and pooled them. Why we do so, because this knowledge is of interest for both enterprises introducing EAM to orient themselves in the found role set and existing EAM structures to verify that all task aspects were included in the already established roles.

As already mentioned in the introduction and motivation, knowledge of executive roles in the EAM is important to establish them successfully in the company. This paper will provide a generalized overview of role concepts used in EAM. For this purpose, the concept of a role must be defined first. This raises the question:

RQ1: How is the concept of roles defined in the EAM context?

Furthermore, a classification scheme for the analysis of the roles found in the different resources has to be developed, as this is the only way the roles out of the single EA frameworks can be summarized unified later on. Hence the second research question emerges:

RQ2: Which general roles can be distinguished within an EAM team?

Based on the two questions, the objectives of this paper are defined. In the following, a review of the publications on EAM and an analysis concerning the introduced roles is made. In the second step, the found roles are classified using criteria in order to create an overview of the roles involved in the EAM process. The result has been tested, not validated, in a further step by an expert interview only once. The study investigated whether the identified and classified roles could also be used in EAM practice and whether the names and descriptions have been developed with a practical orientation.

2 Research Approach

To answer our research questions a literature research was performed. Usually two methods could be applied for a literature research: The "systematic method" and the "method of concentric circles" [5].

To find an entry point, the second method was used and it was looked for related work. Therefore, the following search strings have been posted: (1) *"Enterprise Architecture Management"*, (2) *"Enterprise Architecture Management & Rollen"*, (3) *"Enterprise Architecture Management & Roles"*, (4) *"Enterprise Architecture Management & Roles"*, (5) *"Enterprise Architecture" & "Framework"*, (6) *"Unternehmensarchitektur-management"*, (7) *"Unternehmens-architekturmanagement & Rollen"*.

The search in the library catalog of the University of Rostock has shown eleven results for "Enterprise Architecture Management". A wide overview of numerous frameworks and its classifications is given by the work of Matthes in [4]. After that, the literature research was also made with the help of the concentric circles in order to identify the literature that is helpful to answer the research questions (Table 1).

Table 1. Overview search results

Keyword/database	1	2	3	4	5	6	7
UB Rostock	11	0	0	1	1	8	0
WorldCat	651	0	170	264	5	312	0
Scopus	163	0	33	801	1	4	0
Web of Science	53	0	5	470	0	0	0
BSP (EBSCO)	172	0	6	112	0	0	0
GBV	1.014	0	45	350	8	98	0
Google Books	15.900	442	1.200	16.500	44	1.470	13
Google Scholar	1.810	145	692	21.100	48	1.270	34
IEEE Xplore	34	0	1	234	0	0	0
Google.de	149.000	23.700	30.300	695.000	3.900	71.400	875
Bing.de	86.300	3.180	10.200	1.040.000	6.490	12.600	21

The topic of roles rarely appears in the EAM literature. The initial search was conducted by using the stated search terms in databases like *Scopus, EBSCOhost* or *World of Science*, as well as the literature database of the University of Rostock.

After the selection of suitable literature, the application of the method of concentric circles [5] followed, which is visualized by Fig. 1. This required insight into the bibliography and looking up appropriate literature. Special attention was given to sources that occurred in different bibliographies. For validation the method of the expert interview was used. The validated EAM Roles description are presented in Sect. 5.

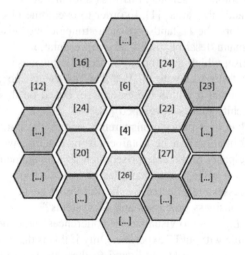

Fig. 1. Method of concentric circles [cp. 5]

3 State of the Art

Before describing the process of identifying EAM roles this chapter focuses on the foundation of EAM and EA Frameworks, on which the role identification is based on. Further, a distinction between the notion of actor and role is made since these terms often are mistakenly used as synonyms. This intends to clarify the authors' understanding of an EAM Role.

3.1 Enterprise Architecture Frameworks

Numerous EA frameworks are available. Dirk Matthes has identified and examined over 50 of them in detail [4]. Usually these are established approaches to accelerate the implementation of EAM in the enterprise, reduce the risk of failure and to increase the efficiency and effectiveness of EAM [1]. EA frameworks define and develop a detailed description of the architecture [1] on the basis of different views and aspects [2]. In general, frameworks help with the development of an EA within the enterprise, using described methods and tools to create coherences between the sub-architectures [2, 6]. These tools and methods help with the analysis, design and implementation of an EA [4]. However, the focus of EA frameworks concerning scope and purpose can be set differently, as they are mostly based on experience gained through realized projects [4].

3.2 Enterprise Architecture Management

EAM is an interdisciplinary management approach, building on techniques and practical approaches from computer science, business administration, change management, process management and other areas [1]. In order to overcome IT complexity tools are provided. "EAM develops the IT landscape in a strategic and business oriented way" [2]. TOGAF and Niemann describe an EA as a representation of the processes and all systems of an enterprise, which aim for supporting the business objectives in combination. EAM has the tasks to create an EA that represents the current state in the enterprise and to implement it within the enterprise. Based on this, a catalog of measures for the target architecture is developed [7].

The aim of EAM is to produce transparency across the entire IT landscape. In addition, a lot of information can be obtained from the EA, which help to answer questions of the participants in the enterprise, such as management, project managers and others [2]. Hanschke gives some examples of how such questions can look like: "Which business processes are affected by the failure of an IT system?" or "Who is responsible for which business processes and IT systems?"

Furthermore, it is important to visualize the coherences and dependencies so that an understanding is possible without IT expertise. Only if this is the case, the interaction of business and IT is possible. The IT is aligned to the objectives of the enterprise that way [2].

EAM aims for meeting the information needs, increasing transparency and reducing risks. On the one hand, it makes gathering information easier, as there is a common database through the sub-architectures in the EA. On the other hand, discretion to act is shown. Furthermore, coherences between processes and systems can be understood better and the preparation time for new projects is reduced [2].

3.3   Notion of Role and Actor

Often, the term "actor" is used alongside the term "role", but they should not be used as synonyms. Especially sociology often deals with action and actors theories [8]. Still, a generally accepted definition of the term "actor" does not exist. Schimank examines four sociological actor models [32]. An actor always performs an action within a certain context. Actors are people or organizations that are composed of several people. Human actors have certain characteristics: they have a meaningfully oriented behavior, exist in their environment and act objective-oriented [32]. Their objectives are determined by them or their environment. He or she is the holder of tasks with several competencies to fulfill them [9].

This reveals the difference towards the notion of roles, which are seen as logical functions with the aim to fulfill a task by conducting certain activities [9, 10]. An actor can be assigned to numerous roles whose required competencies he or she meets. Thus, each role is related to a certain set of required competencies necessary to conduct the relevant activities (cf. [11]) while an actor possesses these required competencies.

This is in line with the perception of the concepts business role and business actor from the perspective of the EAM research discipline. In the newest version 3.0 of the ArchiMate standard – the modelling language for the TOGAF Framework – a business actor is defined as "...*business entity that is capable of performing behavior*" [12]. A business role is understood as "...*the responsibility for performing [...] behavior, to which an actor can be assigned*" [12]. Further, the standard points out, that this responsibility is always related to behavior (e.g. a business function) and competencies. Table 2 represents our understanding about both concepts based on these elaborations.

Table 2. Distinction between role and actor

	Role	Actor
Definition	A role describes a certain behavior for which a specific set of competencies is required	An actor holds competences and performs behavior by being assigned to one or more roles
Describes	Behavior/tasks, responsibility, set of required competencies	Human person, organizational entity, competencies

4   Role Identification Process

The identification of roles was performed based on the identified literature on EAM and EA Frameworks. Each source was analyzed regarding mentioned EAM roles. These descriptions must include at least one task, responsibility or required competencies. The mention of the role without one of these facts will be considered as a not existing description. This chapter is separated by the type of sources utilized for role identification.

Enterprise Architecture Frameworks Analysis
Starting point for finding roles in the EA framework is the "Enterprise Architecture Framework Compendium" listing over 50 EA Frameworks [4]. Furthermore, EA Frameworks not considered in [4] have been analyzed, e.g. the General Enterprise Framework (GEF) [13].

The categorization of the frameworks by [4] was applied, which distinguished (1) management, (2) military and (3) government frameworks. For each EA framework the same analysis approach was conducted. Initially, each framework was checked for free availability, it was excluded from the analysis. Accessible documentation was analyzed for whether the terms "role" or "actor" were used and a precise description was given. In the (1) management category twelve EA frameworks were not freely available and thus, had to be excluded. Some frameworks, such as the Architecture of Integrated Information Systems (ARIS), focus on methods for the optimization of processes [14] without examining which roles are related to these activties. In summary, only the toolbox for Enterprise Architecture Management (t-eam), TOGAF, Virtual Enterprise Reference Architecture and Methodology (VERAM) and the Zachman EA Framework defined roles related to EAM [15].

In most cases of the (2) military field access was not possible. Some of these were written neither in German nor in English (e.g. the "Atelier de Gestion de l'Architecture" was only available in French [16]) or the download was not publicly released (such as the Australian Defence Architecture Framework [4]). From nine identified frameworks four meet the requirements for role identification. For instance, the NATO Architecture Framework could not be investigated in the latest version since it is not completed yet [17]. However, it should be based on UK Ministry of Defence Architectural Framework (MoDAF) and TOGAF [18], which were be analyzed.

In the area of (3) government seven EA Frameworks were identified, which cover area like public transport and healthcare. In two frameworks identification was not possible because of accessibility reasons. For the Treasury Enterprise Architecture Framework (TEAF) secondary literature was available [19], but without going into roles. In three other frameworks, however, no roles with the meaning of Sect. 3 could be found. The National Institutes of Health Enterprise Architecture Framework, for example, covers only the persons who perform a task in the processes [20]. In the end two frameworks provided information regarding EAM roles, namely the Federal Enterprise Architecture (FEA) and the Queensland Government Enterprise Architecture Framework.

To summarize, it can be stated that only a fractional part of the EA framework was freely available, while access to most documents was not possible. Furthermore, only few approaches concretely investigated EAM roles as we define them. TOGAF provides the most comprehensive overview of roles and their required competencies. Table 3 shows the analysis at a glance. It demonstrates how many EA frameworks have been identified, how many could be investigated and how many enabled the identification of roles. Hence, 21 out of the total 33 EA Frameworks had a matching documentation. Roles were identified in only 7 of these 21 frameworks.

Table 3. Analyzed EA frameworks

Type	EA frameworks	Accessible	Chosen frameworks
(1) Management	17	12	4
(2) Military	9	4	1
(3) Government	7	5	2
Overall	33	21	7

Literature Analysis

During the literature review five contributions have been identified dealing with the EAM structure and its roles. Hanschke covers necessary roles multiple times in [2, 21]. However, the same roles are named in this case and the role description is nearly identical. For this reason only [21] because of currency reasons.

Moreover, in [1] Glen Hobbs deals with the EAM structure, although most roles are only named and not explained in more detail. In [22] Niemann examines individual areas, where the roles are not explicitly mentioned, but divided into the single areas business architecture [22], application architecture [22] and more. Roles like business architect or application architect can be derived from them. Dern describes the roles related to the management of EA in high detail in [23], where the understanding of a role has been added to each role. In [24] the role of the "Enterprise Architect" [24] was examined more closely. In this case, roles and responsibilities were explained and practical examples were given. In [25], Mannmeusel describes how EAM can be established even in small and medium-sized enterprises. At it, there is an enterprise architect (also called EA manager), who gets the information from roles that are already present in the enterprise. Thus, the process owners, the IT controlling, project managers and the IT infrastructure provide the necessary information, but are not part of the EAM structure themselves [25].

In total, roles for EAM could be identified in 12 sources. However, the detail of the role descriptions, tasks, competencies and abilities varies widely in literature. While TOGAF describes the roles and the needed competencies in detail [6], Veram only provides short statements about the respective roles [26]. Table 4 clearly shows the number of sources in the two types of literature, how many roles were identified in total in each area and how many of them have been described. After the analysis of the individual sources, 70 roles with description were finally identified and listed. After the roles out of the various sources have been identified and analyzed, a classification of these roles is made in the following chapter. The aim is to develop a classification scheme that helps to assign the roles out of the various sources to specific role classes.

Table 4. Identified roles in literature

	Sources	Identified roles	Roles with description
EA Frameworks	7	42	40
Literature	5	39	29
Overall	12	81	69

5 Role Analysis

Based on a literature review, a total of eleven roles were identified, which may be included in EAM. In addition to the literature review, an expert interview was conducted, which was used for designation and the contentual homogenization of the aggregated roles. The following eleven roles are the compact result of the analysis of the found 70 roles and its validation by dint of the expert interview.

The *Enterprise Architect* is one of the most common roles. This role describes the tasks of the head of EAM who ensures the completeness and quality of the architecture from a cross-departmental perspective. Thus, it requires profound technicals as well as strategical knowledge [6]. In small and medium-sized enterprises, the tasks can also be performed by other roles, with other people/roles of the enterprise supporting the architecture development [25]. In larger enterprises, the role can be assigned to several actors working together in an EAM team and perform the development and design of the EA [21]. The Enterprise Architect also looks for synergies between the sub-areas (business, information, application, and infrastructure architecture). Solutions developed by the role of a Solution Architect is tested for compliance with standards and specifications.

The *Standard Manager* is responsible for developing and maintaining of standards, which new projects or initiatives need to comply with. Furthermore, he or she supports the usage of standards [21]. These tasks could also be assigned to the actor performing the Enterprise Architect – depending on the EAM initiative's size.

The *Business Architect* is responsible for the design, documentation and development of the business architecture and reports to the Enterprise Architect. He or she also takes care of the analysis of business processes [27]. In addition, he or she conducts information demand analyses for each business process.

The *Information Architect* designs, documents and develops the information architecture [21, 23]. He or she determines its interfaces to business and technology architecture [21] to connect them to the business architecture. That way, it is shown which business processes are supported by which information systems [28]. The Information Architect is responsible for the design, maintenance and implementation of a consistent data model. Moreover, the Information Architect checks where the business objects are created and processed in the system.

The application landscape is maintained by the *Application Architect*. He or she is responsible for its documentation [27] and addresses the stakeholders involved in the applications.

The *Infrastructure Architect* takes over responsibility for the technologies, certain services and operating systems and their optimization. For this purpose, he or she creates the system architecture of an enterprise [22]. The Infrastructure Architect is also charged with the development of the infrastructure [22] and the documentation of the system environment such as operating systems or networks [27]. He or she ensures an active reuse of systems and technologies in new projects.

Planning software solutions for concrete projects is the task of the *Solution Architect*. He or she supports the Business Architect, who hence has not to deal with the technologies and systems used [6]. The Solution Architect also examines the project requirements in order to use technologies and systems that are already existing in the enterprise. This task is based on the infrastructure architecture, which is managed by the Infrastructure Architect.

Another member of the EAM team is the *Demand Manager*. This role sets clearly structured requirements for each department, which are later transformed into concrete plans by the Solution Architect through.

Furthermore, the role of the *Security Manager* considers safety aspects within the EA and addresses the process security [27]. He or she monitors the safety matters of the enterprise, the models and performs security assessments.

The *Risk Manager* performs risk assessment and evaluation in terms of the probability of occurrence and amount of damage. Additionally, precautions for the event of loss are taken.

Finally, the *Process Owner* takes responsibility over certain processes within the enterprise and thus holds the knowledge about them [23]. He or she documents, plans and implements the processes in the enterprise. This includes the training of actors who are affected by a new process [29]. According to the expert, the Process Owner does not directly belong to the EAM team, but is an important counterpart for the other roles.

The required competencies of the roles differ from each other only in a few points. In this regard, the Enterprise Architect must have leadership competencies [6, 24], since he or she is responsible for the complete overview of the architecture [6]. All roles require high communication competencies for technical matters and teamwork, as the architects work with the enterprise's employees, both in IT, as well as in the several departments [6, 21]. Comprehensive IT knowledge is in demand especially for the Information Architect, Application Architect, Infrastructure Architect and Solution Architect [6]. Necessary competencies are only discussed for the Enterprise Architect in detail in different sources, whereas this aspect of the other roles is only examined by TOGAF. While background knowledge of a specific competence is sufficient for some roles, another role must have an expert status to fulfill the tasks with the required quality. A summary of the roles of an EAM team in terms of their main tasks and the required competencies is provided in Table 5.

Table 5. Identified roles in Enterprise Architecture Management

Role	Main Tasks	Required Competencies
Enterprise Architect	Ensures completeness of the EA; identifies synergies between the subdomains; communicates results	Leadership, teamwork, project experience, profound IT and business knowledge, communication
Business Architect	Design, documentation, development of business architecture; formulates which information is required in each business process	Teamwork, communication, knowledge of business processes and business models

(continued)

Table 5. (*continued*)

Role	Main Tasks	Required Competencies
Information Architect	Design of the information architecture; review of the business objects in terms of their creation and processing in the system	Teamwork, communication competencies, knowledge of business processes and excellent IT
Application Architect	Documentation of the application environment with the aim of creating plans for the construction of new software systems and components	Teamwork, communication competencies, knowledge of business processes and good IT
Infrastructure Architect	Documentation of the system environment for re-use of systems and technologies	Teamwork, communication and extensive IT knowledge
Solution Architect	Planning the concrete implementation of solutions based on existing systems and technologies	Teamwork, communication, extensive business and IT knowledge
Standard Manager	Development and maintenance of standards	Teamwork, communication, project experience
Process Owner	Plans, maintains and optimizes certain processes in the company	Leadership, teamwork, communication
Security Manager	Monitoring of security issues; performing security reviews	Expert in the field of IT security, knowledge of legal requirements and regulations, knowledge of the model
Risk Manager	Risk assessment and evaluation in terms of probability and extent of damage; making precautions for the damage event	Knowledge of IT risks, knowledge of the model
Demand Manager	Creating clearly structured requirements in each department	Knowledge of business processes, understanding of the business

6   Conclusion and Outlook

The aim of EAM is to master the complexity in the IT environment and to align it simultaneously to the enterprise's objectives [2]. According to that, the tasks that an EAM team has to deal with are extensive and important [2]. One of the research questions was therefore: RQ1: *What is a role in EAM?* To answer this question, the definition of the term role was elaborated, isolated to the notion of actor and related to EAM in chapter 3 and 4. A role describes an activity and tasks for which certain competencies are required [10], while an actor is a human person who is able to execute one or more roles [7]. On this basis, the roles in EAM were identified. At that, the literature was divided into EA frameworks and scientific literature and analyzed regarding the presence of roles. Of the total 33 EA frameworks, 21 contained a documentation that were freely available. However, roles could be identified only in seven of these 21 frameworks. This underlines the statement that in spite of the knowledge about the importance of roles they are rarely discussed. In the field of professional literature, roles in EAM were treated in five sources and finally, a scientific contribution that names roles in EAM was identified.

Overall, 70 roles with description were found (cf. Sect. 5). The 70 role descriptions were analyzed and aggregated in the next step. In chapter 5, the results were discussed to answer RQ2: *Which general roles can be distinguished within an EAM team?* For generalization, the role descriptions were analyzed for their tasks and clustered according to task types. As criteria for the different roles of an EAM team the result clusters were used. Each role type had to be associated with at least two types of tasks. Further applies that at least two roles of the initial set can be assigned. Ultimately, eleven different roles for EAM have been created on the basis of the task descriptions, from which especially the Enterprise Architect gains attention from research. This role was examined in eleven out of 70 roles, while the roles Process Owner or the Security Architect only appeared twice.

In summary it can be said that the classification into role classes allows a first overview of the range of tasks of EAM. Especially for the introduction of EAM, statements about the roles that have to be assigned can be made faster. At the same time, the tasks of the roles and competencies required for them are shown. In this regard, an employee can perform several roles or it can be distributed among several actors. Thus there are several Enterprise Architects, Business Architects and Demand Managers in large enterprises, which are responsible for only one particular business area then.

There is already extensive literature on the subject of EAM that pays close attention to the subject. In addition, many EA frameworks were developed over time. Such were clearly shown by [4] for example. A need for further reviews is the reexamination of EA frameworks that have not yet been investigated. Moreover, we are aware that this kind of review procedure comes along with limitations. The systematic literature review was conducted based on conferences and journals available over the University of Rostock library network in the defined period of time. The number of the relevant papers should rise when taking other journals, conferences, books and time spans into account. However, concrete EAM roles are considered only rarely, although its importance is recognized in the literature [1].

This paper provides a first approach for roles an EAM team may consist of. A first validation was applied by dint of an expert interview. Further validations need to be applied. Another critical aspect of the study is the fact that not all books and articles were freely available. Many EA frameworks are not freely available. While TOGAF can be downloaded for evaluation purposes immediately after a short registration, an activation through the vendor was necessary for t-eam, which lasted about a week. Other EA frameworks anon, such as the CLEAR Framework [4], could be downloaded not at all. For this reason, this paper provides only an extract of literature and identified roles. A starting point for further work is given by the information supply of the identified roles. The information demands depend on the tasks of a particular role [30]. Since the information demands in EAM are large and the roles have to be provided constantly with current information, it is recommended to create information demand patterns for the eleven roles so that the right information can be given to the right person at the right place at the right time [30]. Thus, the information demands of the role have to be determined, the quality criteria of the information needs have to be ascertained considering the time aspect [31].

Finally, a need for research concerning the connection of roles with certain committees is possible [21]. For example, Hanschke describes the IT Board, the EAM Board, the Project Portfolio Board and the Blueprint Board [21]. In [1] Hobbs defines the Enterprise architecture council, Architecture review board and Architecture forum. Even in TOGAF the Architecture board is discussed [6]. Thus, a classification of these committees could be done and, based on that, an assignment of role classes to individual committees could take place.

References

1. Ahlemann, F., Stettiner, E., Messerschmidt, M., Christine, L.: Strategic Enterprise Architecture Management: Challenges, Best Practices, and Future Developments. Management for Professionals. Springer, Heidelberg (2012)
2. Hanschke, I.: Enterprise Architecture Management - einfach und effektiv: Ein praktischer Leitfaden für die Einführung von EAM. Hanser, München (2012)
3. Wißotzki, M., Sonnenberger, A.: Adoption of enterprise architecture management in small and medium enterprises – a comparison of theory and practice (unpublished)
4. Matthes, D.: Enterprise Architecture Frameworks Kompendium: Über 50 Rahmenwerke für das IT-Management. Xpert.press. Springer, Heidelberg (2011)
5. Sandberg, B.: Wissenschaftlich Arbeiten von Abbildung bis Zitat: Lehr- und Übungsbuch für Bachelor, Master und Promotion, 2nd edn. Oldenbourg, München (2013)
6. The Open Group: TOGAF Version 9.1, 1st edn. Van Haren Publ, Zaltbommel (2011)
7. Wißotzki, M., Sonnenberger, A.: Enterprise architecture management - state of research analysis & a comparison of selected approaches. In: Short Paper Proceedings of the 5th IFIP WG 8.1 (2012). CEUR-WS.org
8. Lüdtke, N., Matsuzaki, H.: Akteur - Individuum - Subjekt: Fragen zu, Personalität' und, Sozialität'. VS Verlag für Sozialwissenschaften. Springer Fachmedien Wiesbaden GmbH Wiesbaden, Wiesbaden (2011)
9. Rohloff, M.: Integrierte Gestaltung von Unternehmensorganisation und IT. Gito, Berlin (2009)
10. Tsolkas, A., Klaus S.: Rollen und Berechtigungskonzepte: Ansätze für das Identity- und Access Management im Unternehmen. Vieweg+Teubner (GWV), p. S.1 (2010)
11. Asprion, P.M.: Funktionstrennung in ERP-Systemen: Konzepte. Methoden und Fallstudien. Springer, Wiesbaden (2012)
12. The Open Group: Archimate 3.0 Specification. Van Haren Publishing, Zaltbommel (2016)
13. Mottal, G., Sacco, D., Barroero, P.: General Enterprise Framework (GEF). In: IEEE (Herausgeber) IEEE International Conference on Service Operations and Logistics, and Informatics (SOLI), 2012, Piscataway, NJ, pp. 54–59. IEEE (2012)
14. Software AG: ARIS-Methode: Methodenhandbuch Version 9.6 (2014)
15. Zachman, J.: A framework for information systems architecture. IBM Syst. J. 26(3), S.276–S.292 (1987)

16. Délégation Générale pour l'Armement: Manuel de référence AGATE V3 (2005). http://www.achats.defense.gouv.fr/IMG/zip/Guide_S-CAT_n10002_Ed_01_sans-.NET.zip. Accessed 09 Apr 2015
17. NATO: NATO Architecture Framework v4.0 Documentation (draft) (2014). http://nafdocs. org/. Accessed 10 Apr 2015
18. NATO: Methodology|NATO Architecture Framework v4.0 Documentation (draft) (2014). http://nafdocs.org/methodology/. Accessed 10 Apr 2015
19. Rob, T., Beamer, R., Sowell, P.: Civilian application of the DOD C4ISR architecture framework: a treasury department case study. Paper of the 5th International Command and Control Research and Technology Symposium (2000). dodccrp.org. Accessed 08 Apr 2015
20. National Institutes of Health: Guide to NIH Enterprise Architecture (2011). https:// enterprisearchitecture.nih.gov/Pages/guide.aspx. Accessed 10 Apr 2015
21. Hanschke, I.: Strategisches Management der IT-Landschaft: Ein praktischer Leitfaden für das Enterprise Architecture Management, 3rd edn. Hanser, München (2013)
22. Niemann, K.D.: Von der Unternehmensarchitektur zur IT-Governance: Bausteine für ein wirksames IT-Management, Edition CIO. Vieweg+Teubner (GWV) (2005)
23. Dern, G.: Management von IT-Architekturen. Springer Fachmedien, Wiesbaden (2009)
24. Koch, C.: A new blueprint for the enterprise. CIO 1 and 18(10), 39–50 (2005)
25. Mannmeusel, T.: Management von Unternehmensarchitekturen in der Praxis: Organisatorische Herausforderungen in mittelständischen Unternehmen. In: Suchan, C., Frank, J. (eds.) Analyse und Gestaltung leistungsfähiger IS-Architekturen, pp. 35–57. Springer, Heidelberg (2012). doi:10.1007/978-3-642-27700-9_2
26. Kazi, A., Hannus, M., Laitinen, J., Nummelin, O.: Distributed Engineering in Construction: Findings from the IMS GLOBEMEN PROJECT (2011). http://www.itcon.org/2001/10/ paper.pdf. Accessed 10 Apr 2015
27. Chief Information Officer Council: A practical guide to federal enterprise architecture (2001)
28. Braun, C.: Modellierung der Unternehmensarchitektur: Weiterentwicklung einer bestehenden Methode und deren Abbildung in einem Meta-Modellierungswerkzeug. Dissertation, Universität St. Gallen, Hochschule für Wirtschafts-, Rechts- und Sozialwissenschaften, St. Gallen (2007)
29. Fischermanns, G.: Praxishandbuch Prozessmanagement, ibo-Schriftenreihe, vol. 9, 9th edn. G. Schmidt, Gießen (2010)
30. Lundqvist, M.: Information demand and use: improving information flow within small-scale business contexts. Licentiate thesis, Department of Computer and Information Science, Linköping University, Linköping, Sweden (2007). http://liu.diva-portal.org/smash/get/diva2: 24074/FULLTEXT01.pdf. Accessed 01 Apr 2015
31. Sandkuhl, K., (ed.): Information demand patterns: capturing organizational knowledge about information flow. In: Patterns 2011: The Third International Conference on Pervasive Patterns and Applications (2011)
32. Schimank, U.: Literatur. In: Schimank, U. (ed.) Differenzierung und Integration der modernen Gesellschaft, pp. 277–297. VS Verlag für Sozialwissenschaften, Wiesbaden (2005)

How Enterprise Architecture Maturity Enables Post-Merger IT Integration

Robert Lorenz Törmer[(✉)] and Stefan Henningsson

Department of Digitalization, Copenhagen Business School,
Howitzvej 60, 2000 Fredriksberg, Denmark
{rlt.digi, sh.digi}@cbs.dk

Abstract. While world-wide Mergers and Acquisitions (M&As) activity continues to accelerate, a substantial proportion of deals fails to yield the expected value. The inability to plan and implement post-merger integration of information technology contributes substantially to these failure rates. This paper advances the argument that a company's pre-existing Enterprise Architecture decisively shapes the capability to implement post-merger IT integration and subsequently realize benefits from M&A. Our multiple-case study investigates three acquisition cases and develops an explanatory theory of how Enterprise Architecture maturity enables the implementation of distinct integration strategies. The results do not only enrich the academic literature on M&A, but also show the strategic value of Enterprise Architecture maturity.

Keywords: Mergers & Acquisitions · Enterprise Architecture · Post-Merger IT Integration

1 Introduction

Companies are using Mergers and Acquisitions (M&As) more than ever before as a regular instrument in the pursuit of overall corporate strategic goals [1]. Most commonly, however, these investments do not create value for acquirers per-se, but require acquisition targets to be integrated into the buying company to reap intended business benefits, such as synergies or enhanced capabilities [2]. Recent market research and case evidence reveal that the inability to do so effectively has led to an acquisition failure rate of beyond 50 percent in the past decade [3, 4].

In this context, one of the most complex challenges of the post-merger period remains the integration of information technology (IT) between the merging parties, commonly referred to as post-merger IT integration (PMITI). As IT is entangled with companies' operational as well as strategic business processes [5], its integration turns into a crucial task to keep business running during mergers, avoid short-term business disruptions and reach long-term acquisition goals [6]. Business slowdown due to turbulences in IT integration does not only imply forgone earnings, but can also result in extremely costly long-term consequences, such as permanent loss of customers [c.f. 7]. During integration projects, "companies have a critical window of time to get the most out of the merger or acquisition" [8, p. 10]. Under tremendous time pressure ideal solutions to integration cannot be constantly ensured and the integration period itself

© Springer International Publishing AG 2017
B. Johansson et al. (Eds.): BIR 2017, LNBIP 295, pp. 16–30, 2017.
DOI: 10.1007/978-3-319-64930-6_2

becomes accordingly in many cases a best effort endeavor. Therefore, "being ready at that juncture, at the close, provides a great platform for integration success" [8, p. 10].

The current state of academic literature recognizes this need for preparation not only through careful planning of individual integration projects, but also in terms of long-term capability development to become "ready-to-acquire" for any possible future merging partner [9, 10]. In that vein, the accumulation and exploitation of capabilities to diagnose and implement appropriate integration strategies allows acquirers to reach short-term acquisition benefits and long-term acquisition goals [11]. The current state of the literature furthermore suggests that these capabilities should be complemented by the development of a standardized, scalable, and flexible IT platform [10–13]. However, by focusing on the technical IT infrastructure, existing research only considers the lower layers of Enterprise Architecture (EA) and neglects that IT systems are nowadays highly intertwined with organizational business processes. Additionally, current studies do not elaborate in detail, how these virtues are implemented architecturally or why they enable companies to overcome inherent challenges of distinct PMITI strategies.

EA, on the other hand, is solely addressed by existing work on PMI in terms of management capabilities and their effect on integration success [14]. Given the fact that these structures are, along with people, the main elements to be integrated, a sharper focus on the design of EA, as such, is necessary. This paper therefore sheds light on the following research question: How does a company's existing EA enable the implementation of different PMITI strategies?

To answer these research questions, we embark on a multiple-case study on three acquisition cases. Within a resource-based perspective, we analyze to what extent the constituent resources and capabilities of different EA maturity stages [15] enable acquirers to overcome challenges of distinct PMITI strategies and reach desired acquisition outcomes. As a result, an explanatory theory [16] on how EA maturity enables the implementation of distinct PMITI strategies is established.

2 M&A and the Integration Challenge

M&As are most commonly motivated by either the quest for "cost economies and market power" or the access to "strategically important resources and capabilities" [2, p. 398]. Even though they comprise two distinct forms of organizational junction, mergers as well as acquisitions entail the transfer or combination of company ownership and a differentiation is not relevant for the purpose of this paper.

M&A by themselves to not necessarily imply a need for integration of organizational structures between the involved parties after the transaction. Instead, "the degree and mode of integration should be dependent on synergies expected as a higher level of integration is resource demanding" [17, p. 26]. Therefore, scholars as well as practitioners have emphasized the need carry out in-depth pre-merger planning before the deal is signed to align the overall integration strategy as well as the IT integration strategy with overall acquisition goals [9, 18].

In the academic literature, four generic PMITI strategies have emerged that cater for distinct degrees of integration required and can be implemented as manifold combinations or in their singular form. The *Absorption* strategy assumes that one company's

IT resources can support the operations of both entities and expands these resources into the other company, whose previous systems are shut down and replaced. The *Co-Existence* strategy maintains both companies' IT resources partially or entirely and connects them via bridges to exchange data or functionality. The *Best-of-Breed* strategy, in turn, aims for process enhancements and postulates the deliberate selection of individual IT-based business processes from both companies based on their superiority. Commonly, this strategy is implemented by rebuilding one company's superior processes on the other company's IT platform, which is subsequently rolled out in the merged organization. In contrast to these three path-dependent strategies, the *Renewal* strategy is path-breaking and triggers an organizational transformation by retiring both organization's IT resources as well as substituting them by the development of completely new ones [10].

After closing the deal, the subsequent implementation of the singular or manifold strategy is executed by combining both organization's IT resources to achieve the intended business benefits [10]. Based on distinct mechanisms, each strategy requires the completion of different implementation tasks to reach the desired target state.

As a result from previous M&A, but most importantly as an enabling factor during PMITI, the literature proposes different concepts of organizational PMITI capabilities that effect the outcome of individual PMI projects [11, 12, 19]. In that vein, *Diagnostic* and *Implementation Capabilities* are put forward that entail the "ability to select the appropriate mix of IT integration strategies" and "the ability to redeploy the combined IT resources post-acquisition contingent on the [...] strategies selected" [11, p. 9ff]. These capabilities do not only enable superior short-term M&A benefits, but also long-term strategic IT alignment and organizational performance [11].

Yet, becoming "ready to acquire" is not limited to capabilities in the form of knowledge, but also requires appropriate underlying resources for integration to be in place. For this purpose, the adoption of a standardized, scalable, and flexible IT platform is postulated in the literature [10, 12, 13]. However, a more fine-grained analysis of how such a platform can be implemented architecturally and how its inherent characteristics can enable an acquirer during the inherent PMITI challenges of distinct integration strategies is still missing. The "next step in theory development would include an analysis of the interaction between organizational IT integration capabilities and the nature of the specific IT integration challenge" [20, p. 14].

Therefore, this paper fills the identified research gap by investigating on a more fine-grained level, which integration challenges merging companies face during the architectural implementation of Absorption, Co-Existence, Best-of-Breed, and Renewal strategies. The analysis reveals concrete requirements that distinct integration strategies pose on merging companies' EA. These demands allow for inferences on virtues of an EA that enable companies to successfully implement the elaborated PMITI strategies architecturally and reap short- as well as long-term acquisition benefits. By relating these virtues to the concept of EA maturity, we elaborate in-depth, how a mature EA enables companies to implement distinct PMITI strategies successfully.

3 Enterprise Architecture and Maturity

To achieve superior performance, companies should build a solid foundation for the execution of their strategy that efficiently carries out core processes by digitizing them in IT systems [15]. The establishment of this foundation is a tough strategic decision that requires high levels of attention during definition, but afterwards allows for the automatic and effective exploitation of core capabilities as well as routine business activities [15].

3.1 Operating Model

The operating model represents "a general vision of how a company will enable and execute strategies" [15, p. 38]. All enterprises adopt an overarching operating model at the corporate level, but might at the same time also define distinct operating models at lower levels, such as the business unit or divisional level [15].

During its definition, management teams have to decide on "the necessary level of business process integration and standardization for delivering goods and services to customers" [15, p. 8]. In this context, integration "links the efforts of organizational units through shared data" and allows for end-to-end processing of transactions, the presentation of a single face to customers, and accurate information for managerial decisions [15, p. 27]. Process Standardization refers to their equal execution independently from location or performer. This reduces variability in execution and can imply "dramatic increases in throughput and efficiency" [15, p. 27].

Based on the two presented dimensions, four different types of operating models can be adopted [15]. A *Diversification* operating model is characterized by low levels of business process standardization and integration. A *Unification* strategy comprises high levels of both. *Coordination*, on the other hand, leverages high integration and low standardization. Finally, *Replication* works the other way around [15].

3.2 Enterprise Architecture

Once an operating model has been defined, it is to be implemented in the form of an effective EA. For that purpose, EA is defined as "the organizing logic for business processes and IT infrastructure reflecting the integration and standardization requirements of the company's operating model" [15, p. 47]. Graphical representations are commonly used for the elaboration as well as communication of results [15]. These designs contain just enough detail on business processes and data sharing to understand company operations. For the implementation of EA, however, a deeper understanding of the interplay between people, processes and IT is necessary [15]. For that reason, EA is in the IT context often divided into four layers from the bottom to the top: the technology architecture (IT infrastructure), the application architecture, the data or information architecture, and the business process architecture. Lower layers provide the foundation for higher layers to operate on. The composition of the lower three levels makes up a company's IT architecture.

3.3 EA Maturity

During the implementation and posterior advancement of EA, companies commonly experience a journey from initial ventures to build their foundation for execution via the emergence of new technologies, and changes in economic boundary conditions. In the course of this voyage, enterprises usually experience similar challenges that require the modification, and implementation of new systems as well as processes without disrupting on-going business. At the same time, they harvest increasing benefits, such as lower IT cost and greater strategic agility. [15] reveal that companies generally traverse consistent patterns during the advancement of their EA, which the authors label the "four stages of architecture maturity": *Business Silos, Standardized Technology, Optimized Core,* and *Business Modularity* [15, p. 70].

While companies in the Business Silos stage do not standardize nor integrate processes end-to-end, the Standardized Technology stage is characterized by an increasing acceptance of standard IT solutions to enable cost savings and reliability. In the Optimized Core stage, companies move from local applications and shared infrastructure to the adoption of enterprise resource planning (ERP) systems, a centrepiece of optimized standard processes as well as shared data. Finally, in the Business Modularity architecture stage, companies gain strategic agility by modularizing previously digitized business processes and their supporting IT systems.

4 Research Method

This study adopts a case study approach [21, 22] to develop an explanatory theory of how the existing EA enables (or constrains) PMITI. Explaining and predicting theories are closely related to prescriptive design theories. A multiple-case study is chosen to develop general explanations that fit the varying details of each singular case [21]. By showing the influence of changing contextual factors, multiple-case studies "yield more general research results than single cases" [22, p. 609].

A total number of seven semi-structured interviews with key informants were conducted as a primary source of evidence [23]. The case companies had been selected by using the M&A database Zephyr to search for large, multi-national companies headquartered in Denmark or Germany. For that purpose, an interview guide containing open-ended questions was created that investigated on the state of EA in each case company as well as its role during PMITI. With exception of one interview, all others were recorded, transcribed, and added to a case database (Yin, 2009). For the purpose of triangulation, secondary data in the form of newspaper articles, press releases, company websites, detail information from the Zephyr database, share prices, and architecture plans was used as additional sources of evidence.

Due to the fact that the three case companies exhibit bold differences in size, industry, and EA setups, contextual factors vary severely between the cases, which supports the generality of the eventual findings [22].

Data analysis subsequently applied paragraph-level coding by concepts known from the literature. Based on within-case analysis and cross-case comparisons, the eventual research model was established and substantiated [22]. Following the coding, case stories were developed containing plenty of individual quotes by the informants to support the line of reasoning.

5 Case Evidence

In this section, the multiple-case study involving three cases with companies of different size as well as industry is introduced to elaborate our theoretical model. First, the acquisition and Best-of-Breed integration of BiotechComp by the ChemicalCorp is presented. Then, the case of EngineeringCompA acquiring WaterTechCompA provides insights into what drives a Renewal strategy. Eventually, the merger between FinancialBankA and KreditBankB extends the context of this study to M&A in general.

5.1 ChemicalCorp

ChemicalCorp is a large global chemical company that serves business-to-business (B2B). In addition to chemical products, the closely related business segments also include crop protection products. ChemicalCorp's IT is managed centrally from its competence center for information services and the entire organization's IT infrastructure is provisioned by an external contractor.

Particularly since the beginnings of the 21st century, ChemicalCorp has become a serial acquirer, purchasing mostly several companies per year. ChemicalCorp relies on a Unification operating model to enable operational efficiency through high degrees of standardization and integration. A Business Integration Manager (BIM) explains: "I would say [processes are] probably about 75 percent standardized" and "data is probably close to 100 percent integrated". This operating model is implemented through an EA that builds on a one-instance SAP system. ChemicalCorp's processes and modules are standardized on this platform and used by all business units worldwide. Local exceptions to standard processes are only allowed, if they are critical to business continuity. Moreover, the SAP platform is based on a Service-Oriented Architecture (SOA) and implements a Business Process Engine that enables the flexibility to reconfigure and reuse business processes steps without the need for code customizations. "It's more based upon a process engine [...] we do very little hard-coding within the system [...] to keep [it] flexible" (BIM - ChemicalCorp).

ChemicalCorp's crop protection business specializes on the development of seed treatment technologies that protect agricultural crops from diseases, weeds, or pests. Since its establishment, the division has been growing organically as well as through M&A. To gain capabilities in biological crop protection and refocus on the North-American market, the division decided to acquire the US-based global provider of biological crop protection products BiotechComp in 2012.

Major synergies should result from providing the acquired unit access to ChemicalCorp's global R&D platform as well as new markets and customers. Via ChemicalCorp's sales force, BiotechComp could sell products in significantly larger numbers and harvest economies of scale. These acquisition goals drove the integration project's strategy and implementation. As the Lead of Integration (LOI) explains, the concept was already clear during the later stages of due diligence: "We wanted to integrate the business to 100 percent. So a standalone was not an option."

For ChemicalCorp's IT experts, due diligence allowed for a first inspection of the acquisition's IT landscape and revealed an eminently immature EA. BiotechComp had been growing through M&A in the past and ChemicalCorp was now "dealing with three basic non-connected ERP systems." (LoI - ChemicalCorp).

Following the overall integration concept and basing on the acquirer's stringent Unification strategy, a Best-of-Breed strategy was chosen for IT integration. On the one hand, ChemicalCorp's superior IT systems were entirely rolled out in BiotechComp, replacing existing systems and spreading standardized ChemicalCorp processes throughout the acquisition. "I told them [...] there will be a full integration. No discussion! [...] Their processes have been a nightmare. So their IT unit actually came to us: 'Whatever you give us, it will be better than what we have!'" (LoI – ChemicalCorp). On the other hand, the acquisition also targeted the adoption of some unique superior capabilities from BiotechComp that were rebuilt as processes on ChemicalCorp's platform. According to the BIM, integration consisted of "90 percent data migration and probably 10 percent unique process-driven integration".

From an IT perspective, the Best-of-Breed strategy's implementation required the completion of four main tasks: data migration, process migration, system rollout, and change management. "Data management is actually the biggest component when you are transforming a company into a ChemicalCorp system" (BIM – ChemicalCorp). Hence, as one of the first work streams, dedicated master data specialists for the agricultural business were sent to all BiotechComp sites to collect and manually enter master as well as product data into ChemicalCorp's ERP platform. "We looked at every single data point by hand, approved it and put it [...] in our organizational structure. [...] So it was roughly 20 to 40 [fixed duration employees] only doing master data. And they did this for half a year" (LoI - ChemicalCorp). ChemicalCorp's strict adherence to a central data scheme enabled division to successfully migrate all business-critical master data and avoid posterior business disruptions. "If you do not set up strict rules, you come into trouble relatively quickly. And the consequence out of that are non-shipments. [...] Our failure rate was extremely good [...], because we paid so much attention to master data" (LoI - ChemicalCorp). Transactional data was only migrated, if it was needed for legal reasons, such as tax regulations.

Additionally, also some of BiotechComp's business processes, which were not covered by ChemicalCorp standards, had to be defined on the platform. The process migration covered "a part of the business that [ChemicalCorp] did not utilize before" (BIM - ChemicalCorp). For that matter, the SAP system's Business Process Engine allowed the team to define new processes rapidly. This saved time as well as cost of the project and kept the system flexible for future modifications or updates.

Technical infrastructure components, such as desktop computers and network connections, were rolled out in the acquisition in collaboration with retained IT personnel. Since all components are standardized and provisioned by one global provider, their connection to enable communication was not an issue.

Although the scalability of ChemicalCorp's ERP platform is a necessary requirement that needs to be managed in general, the concrete integration was "just [about] rolling out that infrastructure to a new building, to a new site, and that's it [...] it's more based upon how your back-office is handling the performance of the system and enhancing it to be utilized at its high peak" (BIM - ChemicalCorp). In this context, the inherent fragmentation of SAP systems into a three-tier architecture does enable the IT experts at the ChemicalCorp to manage system scalability centrally.

When technical integration was completed four weeks prior to go-live, the systems were tested in parallel to the legacy systems and measured against ChemicalCorp's internal 'report card' approach to ensure platform robustness. Also, beta testing gave system users the chance to understand and internalize system functionality.

When the system finally went live country by country, dedicated staff was available on site for the subsequent two months to provide effective change management. According to the report card measurement, the integration project was remarkably successful in terms of business continuity. Worldwide, only two customer deliveries were not being shipped. The integration was delivered in the architectural to-be state three months ahead of schedule and did not produce any misalignments that limited the division ex-post or required subsequent consolidation efforts. Two months later, the integration team retreated and let the business run by itself.

Eventually, the BIM reveals that "having this [stable structure] in place with the processes and the business units on one platform [...] allows us to integrate acquisition businesses a lot easier because the processes are already there. [...] And from that aspect, I think it makes it very easy to onboard a company nowadays".

5.2   EngineeringCompA

EngineeringCompA is a large European conglomerate with main business activities in civil and industrial engineering, but an overall highly diversified business portfolio. Since the company targets customers in both, the B2B and the consumer market, in a variety of different industries, business segments are grouped in divisions that act as holdings for the individual subdivisions. Although their industries might differ tremendously, the majority pursues customer intimacy strategies. Hence, products are created in close collaboration with customers and to a large extent in on-site projects. In close alignment with the divisional governance structure, EngineeringCompA's IT governance is set up in a hybrid mode. Consequently, some global systems, such as email or financial reporting, are standardized across the company and provided by corporate IT. Other solutions, such as managerial reporting systems, are delivered from local entities. Some divisions maintain local ERP systems, while others are using one of several centralized platforms.

Particularly as of the turn of the millennium the conglomerate embarked on an intensive growth-by-acquisition strategy purchasing several companies per year. Yet, the levels, to which acquired targets have been integrated into the company, have differed tremendously in distinct cases. According to process heterogeneity, acquisition size, acquisition geography, and market volatility, a full integration is not always expedient for EngineeringCompA. Nevertheless, some of the past decisions to refrain from integration have also suffered from inappropriate diagnosis and overly generous concessions to acquisition targets' management.

Consequently, EngineeringCompA's Chief Information Officer (CIO) underlines that "there is not one EA. It's good to have one, [...] to have this target system", but in reality, the conglomerate possesses several EAs at different levels. Processes are only to a very low degree standardized and integrated throughout the entire company. Also, the existence of hundreds of legal entities with individual ERP systems has created 'data silos' around the world. Some administrative processes are standardized on global platforms, but most IT is heterogeneously provided at the local level.

On the level of individual business divisions, by contrast, the pictures can differ tremendously from each other. Here, processes are more similar and higher degrees of standardization and integration might be desirable. Whereas some divisions run standardized and integrated processes on global platforms, others exist in holding structures with little degrees of process standardization.

By the end of 2012, one of the architecturally more immature business divisions was EngineeringCompA's legacy water technology segment. The business area was focused on the production of water as well as waste treatment technologies and had grown through a previous acquisition some years earlier. The division's operations mostly took place in projects in close collaboration with customers and the segment's legal entity structure equally implied partitioned ERP systems of different units.

During the corporate growth-by-acquisition strategy, EngineeringCompA decided to acquire WaterTechCompA to increase net income. Additionally, the acquisition should generate synergies in the form of economies of scope in production technology as well as economies of scale through the access to new customers in untapped geographical markets. The need for full integration to reap these synergies became evident early and a completely new water technology division was formed.

According to a Senior Enterprise Architect (SEA) in EngineeringCompA however, the acquisition "was mostly a production company" and "[EngineeringCompA] had no experience and no business with the production modules. [...] The order from the customer [was] always really a customer-related, specific order and one piece [did] not match the next one piece. So we [did] not have serious production here." Consequently, neither the acquirer's nor the acquisition's existing ERP systems could be scaled to the entire division. A Renewal strategy was the only option to harmonize all processes of the new water technology division on one global ERP platform.

Once this decision was made, the actual challenges of strategy implementation did not differ greatly from the ones of a common ERP introduction. The main difficulties arose from defining new harmonized processes and managing the change. Additionally, infrastructure rollout, data migration, and system customizations were to be completed. The SEA explains: "When we decided to integrate the whole company on one ERP system, then we also decided to harmonize all the processes. [...] From the beginning on, we had both parties in workshops in here to create a common template for both." In this context, the main challenge was to bring people from different countries together, manage cultural differences, and make them agree on common business processes. After the template had been elaborated, the technical implementation of the system was comparatively straightforward. An SAP ERP platform was selected, business-specific templates from a consultant company were used and mildly customized to the target state that had been defined.

The platform first went live in the acquisition and subsequently in all existing water technology sites of the acquirer. During the rollouts, existing infrastructure components, were reused as much as possible, while some hardware components needed to be added to connect sites to the new parent company's infrastructure. The continuous adding of new users and legacy data to the SAP platform did not result in scalability issues. "[With] SAP, it doesn't really matter. Scalability is endless [because] the database [...] is fantastic." (CIO - EngineeringCompA).

Data migration solely required the definition of a standardized format in spreadsheets and data transformation was subsequently largely in the hands of the corresponding legal entities. Since legacy data was available in each ERP system's standardized format, data migration was largely seen as a commodity service.

Eventually, "the biggest [challenge] was change management – to get all people to understand each other, to work together [and] to really accept and use the system, this is far more difficult" (SEA - EngineeringCompA). Change management was an ever-ongoing process that started with managing cultural and site-specific differences during process definition, included setting up divisional support structures for go-live, and reached far beyond system rollout.

One year after the first rollout in the acquisition, the last site was brought onto the new platform successfully, finishing the integration project within budget and on time. The Renewal integration did not produce any misalignments or leftovers that had to be fixed in subsequent consolidation projects. Correspondingly, the CIO praises the project success: "We managed in time and budget to create this SAP system, migrate first of all the newly acquired [...] entities into the SAP system, and then afterwards all the old [...] companies in the same division. So that is the, I think, ideal approach: You have something that you acquired, you look at it [...], make the decision – architectural wise – [to] create something new [...], and also migrate the older legacy company to that. And it went perfectly well".

5.3   FinancialBankA

FinancialBankA is a large Danish bank that offers financial products in retail, private, and corporate banking in several European countries. The bank's IT organization consists of three main organs. Whereas the internal IT department supplies IT services, IT operations, infrastructure, and a large extent of applications development are outsourced to two partially owned external providers.

In the 20th century, FinancialBankA has grown equally through organic growth and external M&A, which mostly targeted the access to new customers by purchasing banks with existing compounds of branch offices.

By the beginning of 2014, FinancialBankA was following a Unification operating model. Business processes were accordingly standardized and integrated to a large degree throughout the company. FinancialBankA's core banking system is a legacy mainframe system that implements all common daily banking processes, transactions, as well as products. The system is provided by one of the partially owned external vendors and used by multiple of its customers. Individual differences in requirements are mostly handled through parameters of corresponding software modules. Thereby, the system gains some limited flexibility to change products and processes without altering its source code. FinancialBankA's self-developed applications reuse the core system and enable strategic differentiation.

The bank "has a long tradition for integration" (IT Architect - FinancialBankA) and has created several standardized mechanisms to allow for data exchange between its system components. For that purpose, the core banking system has been wrapped into several layers to provide different technology-independent services in application programming interfaces (APIs) to the outside while encapsulating core functionality. These integration mechanisms and the adherence to the Single Responsibility principle [24] enable high degrees of business process standardization and integration. By providing different levels of service interfaces, FinancialBankA is targeting a SOA, but the core banking system itself is a pure monolith. Furthermore, the use of a business process engine is planned, but not adopted yet.

By the beginning of 2014, FinancialBankA acquired KreditBankB to officially complete a merger that both parties had agreed on in advance. On the one hand, FinancialBankA could complete its product portfolio with mortgage loans. On the other hand, KreditBankB could broaden its sales channels by gaining access to an extensive branch network. Moreover, the deal aimed for cross-selling opportunities, risk spreading from diversification and cost synergies from consolidation.

Except for a small retail bank, which made up five to ten percent of KreditBankB's business, both product portfolios were almost perfectly complementary and business processes heterogeneous. Given these differences, a partial Co-Existence strategy was chosen. The small retail bank was fully absorbed into FinancialBankA, KreditBankB's mortgage loan business was kept as a separate brand and an IT consolidation was launched to reduce system redundancies between the two entities.

The Absorption of the retail bank's IT systems was relatively straightforward to implement. An IT Architect explains: "It was the same approach we're using when we acquire a bank. […] Either they're on the same core banking system [of the external supplier] or they're on one of the other two or three core banking operators. And then we set up a minor project to move their data and their whole customer portfolio. […] It's a quiet normal procedure". As most Danish banks have outsourced their core banking systems to one of three IT operators, the data schemes are known and "these three bank centrals are quiet good at that. […] Moving banks in-between these three centrals is […] being done several times a year".

Even though system scalability was not an issue in the context of the Absorption, it is a necessary precondition and the main reason, why banks are still using legacy mainframe systems nowadays. For FinancialBankA, the separation of the entire architecture into several tiers enables scalability by allowing for the targeted addition of appropriate resources at the corresponding tier and the implementation of request optimization mechanisms, such as load balancing or resource pooling.

The major implementation challenges from leaving KreditBankB's mortgage loan business in Co-Existence, by contrast, emerged from the merger's initial goals. To be able to sell each other's products and identify cross-selling opportunities, business processes, applications and data from the two parties needed to be connected.

This process benefited tremendously from the pre-existence of web service interfaces in both institutions to expose functionality to other applications. A key component was FinancialBankA's integration platform. "It's a Java application facing our core system from all our applications. [...] It's kind of an integration [Enterprise Service Bus]-like architecture. And [KreditBankB's systems] are accessing this [...] platform" (IT Architect - FinancialBankA). The integration platform adds a layer of abstraction above all services and unifies interfaces for internal and external reuse.

As these mechanisms facilitated integration efforts, the more demanding challenges of integration for FinancialBankA were subsequently business-critical security requirements of the financial industry. The IT Architect explains that "having user authentication or authorization is actually quiet complex when you merge two organizations". Again, FinancialBankA could draw on previous experience to implement a certificate-based approach to establish trust between distinct systems.

While consolidation projects are still ongoing nowadays, the IT integration is considered a success. Although the achievement is not measured in any metrics, the bank's IT Director is satisfied with the progress so far. "We could have gone even further, but [...] we are where we're supposed to be. So I would call it a success." By consolidating IT operations and systems, the new financial institution could already realize IT-based cost synergies, while avoiding disruptions to daily business operations. However, some ex-post misalignment exists and a lot of potential for synergies through consolidation of processes as well as functions remains.

6 Analysis

The three cases provide evidence for how the constituent resources and capabilities of distinct EA maturity stages enable a company's PMITI implementation capabilities.

For once, the acquisition of WaterTechCompA by EngineeringCompA illustrates an acquirer in the Standardized Technology maturity stage that was forced by its EA immaturity to embark on a Renewal strategy to integration. After closing, the legally unified company aimed for a Unification operating model, which required complete integration of the acquisition. However, business processes were neither standardized nor integrated throughout the division, data was embedded in local ERP systems, and technology was only standardized to a limited extent. The division was therefore in the lower areas of the Standardized Technology stage. This immaturity impeded the adoption of any path-dependent strategy and forced the division to embark on a Renewal strategy. The case justifies the first proposition of our theoretical model:

Proposition 1: Companies or business units in either the Business Silos architecture stage or the Standardized Technology architecture stage do not posses an adequate EA to enable the implementation of any path-dependent PMITI strategy. They are therefore forced to conduct a Renewal strategy in order to achieve acquisition benefits and sustain strategic IT alignment.

Moving on, the merger between FinancialBankA and KreditBankB exposes how a company in the Optimized Core stage was enabled by its mature EA to implement a partial Co-Existence strategy successfully.

Prior to the merger, FinancialBankA's processes were highly standardized as well as integrated. Moreover, the bank's EA exhibited limited degrees of flexibility by allowing for core system modifications through parameter substantiation. Its EA was therefore located in the upper areas of the Optimized Core stage.

During the Absorption of KreditBankB's bank, FinancialBankA's EA largely had to support data migration, which was highly facilitated by having core banking outsourced to a provider that guides industry standards and interoperability. If data and processes had not been standardized on a central, scalable platform, migration would have been a lot costlier and may have forced FinancialBankA into a Renewal.

During the implementation of the Co-Existence with KreditBankB's mortgage loan business, FinancialBankA's main challenges resolved around application and data integration. When connecting applications from KreditBankB, FinancialBankA highly benefited from pre-existing integration, because appropriate components, such as the integration platform, were already in place to provide technology-independent interfaces that could be applied for the creation of connections to the merging partner. In combination with standardized and integrated business processes, the existence of such "interfaces to critical corporate data" [15, p. 76] constitute the Optimized Core architecture stage. The merger case therefore justifies Proposition 2:

Proposition 2: Companies or business units in the Optimized Core architecture stage posses an adequate EA to enable the implementation of the Absorption as well as the Co-Existence strategy during PMITI. Thereby, they are in the position to achieve acquisition benefits while sustaining strategic IT alignment.

Eventually, ChemicalCorp's acquisition of BiotechComp elucidates the enablement of a successful Best-of-Breed strategy by the Business Modularity stage.

ChemicalCorp follows a Unification operating model and the company's processes are largely standardized as well as integrated on an advanced ERP platform, which follows a SOA and implements a Business Process Engine. This enables the company to reconfigure and reuse business processes without the need for source code customizations and places the company's EA in the Business Modularity stage.

The challenges faced during the integration of BiotechComp were data migration, process migration, system rollout, and change management. While effective data migration was critical to the realization of acquisition benefits, ChemicalCorp's standardized data scheme clearly enabled the acquirer to succeed. Platform scalability [c.f. 12] did not become an issue during the integration, but is seen as a precondition for system rollout. Having a scalable platform of standardized and integrated business processes in place clearly enabled the acquirer to roll these out in the acquisition.

While these challenges could have been equally overcome by a company in the Optimized Core stage, it is the process migration requirement that underlines the value added by Business Modularity: The agility to onboard new business processes from BiotechComp by modelling them in a Business Process Engine, reusing existing system components and only introducing low-level functionality if it is an absolute novelty. This capability enables ChemicalCorp to avoid costly source code modifications and keeps the platform flexible for future changes. Companies without this ability may also be able to conduct a Best-of-Breed strategy, but the implementation will be costlier or result in increasing platform complexity as well as misalignment. Particularly serial acquirers would eventually face a situation of excessive platform complexity that requires consolidation. We therefore conclude Propositions 3 and 4:

Proposition 3: Companies or business units in the Optimized Core architecture stage do not posses an adequate EA to enable the implementation of the Best-of-Breed strategy during PMITI without suffering deficiencies in acquisition benefits or the emergence of ex post strategic IT misalignment.

Proposition 4: Companies or business units in the Business Modularity architecture stage posses an adequate EA to enable the implementation of all four PMITI strategies and subsequently achieve acquisition benefits while sustaining strategic IT alignment.

7 Conclusion

The case evidence and our theoretical model reveal how higher levels of EA maturity enable companies during the implementation of distinct PMITI strategies. By elaborating in detail, how a mature EA endows a company to overcome architectural integration challenges during PMITI, we substantiate our claim that the existing EA of a company is part of its PMITI implementation capabilities and shapes its capacity to implement the four integration strategies. This reasoning also shows how EA management and EA maturity create strategic value in the context of M&A.

The case evidence explains on a great level of detail how distinct EA maturity stages are implemented and how they afford a company to overcome the challenges that are inherent in the four PMITI strategies. The implication for practitioners is that companies should prepare their EA to become ready for intended PMITI strategies and select appropriate strategies according to the prevalent level of EA maturity. The developed theory additionally exposes that the desirable degree of PMI eventually depends on the choice of operating model and underlines the strategic importance of this decision.

Naturally, this paper is subject to several limitations. Firstly, conclusions are drawn based on case evidence that has largely been collected using the interview method. Although the threats to validity and reliability are addressed during the research process, internal and external validity remain disputable due to selection bias and method bias [25]. Particularly acquisition success is an ambiguous concept and key informants pose the thread of rendering project success in a biased way. Secondly, the propositions are based on merely three cases. Future research should collect concrete evidence to support the claims and foster validity. In this context, investigations on acquisition failures should contribute analyses of what went wrong. Finally, this study embarks on a qualitative research approach to examine the phenomena under consideration in greater detail. This should be complemented by quantitative research to examine the validity of the model.

References

1. Thomson Reuters: Mergers & Acquisitions Review - Financial Advisors - Full Year 2015 (2016). http://share.thomsonreuters.com/general/PR/MA-4Q15-(E).pdf
2. Grant, R.M.: Contemporary Strategy Analysis: Text and Cases Edition. Wiley, Hoboken (2016)

3. Deloitte: M&A trends report 2014 (2014)
4. Weber, Y.: A Comprehensive Guide to Mergers & Acquisitions: Managing the Critical Success Factors Across Every Stage of the M&A Process. FT Press, Upper Saddle River (2013)
5. El Sawy, O.A.: The IS Core IX: The 3 faces of IS identity: connection, immersion, and fusion. Commun. Assoc. Inf. Syst. **12**, 39 (2003)
6. Sarrazin, H., West, A.: Understanding the strategic value of IT in M&A. McKinsey Q. **12**, 1–6 (2011)
7. Bank, D.: Press Release - Decline in profit due to integration expenses (2008)
8. Deloitte: Integration report 2015 - Putting the pieces together (2015)
9. Wijnhoven, F., Spil, T., Stegwee, R., Fa, R.T.A.: Post-merger IT integration strategies: an IT alignment perspective. J. Strateg. Inf. Syst. **15**, 5–28 (2006)
10. Henningsson, S., Yetton, P.: Post-acquisition IT integration: the sequential effects in growth-by-acquisition programs. In: 24th Australasian Conference on Information Systems (ACIS 2014) (2013)
11. Henningsson, S., Yetton, P.: Towards a Theory of Post-Acquisition IT Integration (Working Paper) (2016)
12. Tanriverdi, H., Uysal, V.B.: Cross-business information technology integration and acquirer value creation in corporate mergers and acquisitions. Inf. Syst. Res. **22**, 703–720 (2011)
13. Benitez-Amado, J., Ray, G.: Introducing IT-enabled business flexibility and IT integration in the acquirer's M&A performance equation. In: Proceedings of the 33rd International Conference on Information Systems (ICIS 2012) (2012)
14. Toppenberg, G., Henningsson, S., Shanks, G.: How Cisco Systems used enterprise architecture capability to sustain acquisition-based growth. MIS Q. Exec. **14**(4), 151–168 (2015)
15. Ross, J.W., Weill, P., Robertson, D.: Enterprise Architecture as Strategy: Creating a Foundation for Business Execution. Harvard Business Press, Brighton (2006)
16. Gregor, S.: The nature of theory in information systems. MIS Q. **30**, 611–642 (2006)
17. Henningsson, S., Carlsson, S.: The DySIIM model for managing IS integration in mergers and acquisitions. Inf. Syst. J. **21**, 441–476 (2011)
18. Haspeslagh, P.C., Jemison, D.B.: Managing Acquisitions: CREATING Value Through Corporate Renewal. Free Press, New York (1991)
19. Robbins, S.S., Stylianou, A.C.: Post-merger systems integration: the impact on IS capabilities. Inf. Manag. **36**, 205–212 (1999)
20. Henningsson, S., Yetton, P.: Managing the IT integration of acquisitions by multi-business organizations. In: Proceedings of the 32nd International Conference on Information Systems (ICIS 2011) (2011)
21. Yin, R.K.: Case Study Research Design and Methods. Sage, Thousand Oaks (2009)
22. Dubé, L., Paré, G.: Rigor in information systems positivist case research: current practices, trends, and recommendations. MIS Q. **27**(4), 597–636 (2003)
23. Ritchie, J., Lewis, J., Nicholls, C.M., Ormston, R.: Qualitative Research Practice: A Guide for Social Science Students and Researchers. Sage, Thousand Oaks (2013)
24. Martin, R.C.: Agile Software Development: Principles, Patterns, and Practices. Prentice Hall PTR, Upper Saddle River (2003)
25. Yin, R.K.: Case Study Research: Design and Methods. Sage publications, Thousand Oaks (2013)

The Information Infrastructures Design Space:
A Literature Review

Stefan Henningsson[✉], Charikleia Rapti, and Thomas Emil Jensen

Copenhagen Business School, Copenhagen, Denmark
{sh.itm, cr.itm, tej.itm}@cbs.dk

Abstract. This paper develops a framework for characterising the design space of Information Infrastructures (IIs). Existing research has generally sought to unravel the convergent characteristics and mechanisms uniting IIs across a wide range of manifestations. In this research, we explore this divergence within the II design space. We do so by reviewing the II literature, focusing on the two domains of design situation and design resolution. Design situation refers to the relevant dimensions of the context in which an II is employed. Design resolution covers the dimensions along which the socio-technical constituents can be assembled to form an effective solution. The resulting framework allows for the comparing and contrasting of II initiatives, and contributes towards a cumulative knowledge process aimed at a more refined understanding of how an II can be configured to address the specific problem at hand.

Keywords: Information infrastructures · Digital infrastructures · II design space · Literature review

1   Introduction

Information infrastructures (IIs) or digital infrastructures [1–3] are today present in areas as disparate as health care, payments and law enforcement. Paralleling the growth in practical manifestations, IIs have received increasing attention in the academic literature. Here it is argued that II needs to be conceptualised as a specific class of IT artefacts, characterised by the number and heterogeneity of the interconnected socio-technical components, which are typically co-managed by a wide range of diverse organisational entities [1, 3].

However, previous literature on II is limited in that research has generally searched for the *convergent* themes and the 'essence' of the II artefact [4]. Implicitly or explicitly, research has theorised about IIs based on an assumption of IIs as a homogenous group of artefacts. In strong contrast, a comparison of practical manifestations also shows important differences the artefacts denoted as II. The II concept covers a wide range of adopters such as regional bank networks, national health authorities and global research initiatives, among others. IIs can also differ in scales of implementation, as well as various levels of the maturity and heterogeneity of the constituent IT components. A comparison of the internet with a national patient registry shows important differences in the problem situations that warrant different configurations of effective II resolutions.

© Springer International Publishing AG 2017
B. Johansson et al. (Eds.): BIR 2017, LNBIP 295, pp. 31–44, 2017.
DOI: 10.1007/978-3-319-64930-6_3

The existence of variety in the II artefact is frequently recognised in passing. For example, Tilson et al. [2] suggest that IIs should be defined with respect to the entity being supported or enabled as global, national, regional, industry, or corporate infrastructures. Similarly, Henningsson and Zinner-Henriksen [5] as well as Constantinides and Barrett [6] explicitly recognise that their theoretical contributions pertain to IIs with collaborative governance structures. *Divergence* has, however, never moved to the forefront of II theorisation. Therefore, the objective of this paper is to unfold the divergence in the class of IT artefact commonly referred to as II and to develop a conceptualisation of II that encompasses the variety that exists within this artefact class.

To do so, we undertake a developmental review [7] of the II literature with the focus on construct divergence. Specifically, we focus on divergence within the two domains of *design situation* and *design resolution*. Design situation refers to the relevant dimensions of the context in which an II can be employed. The domain of design resolution covers the dimensions along which an II can be configured to be effective in a given situation. The II design space then refers to the combined possibility of matching both situation and resolution dimensions.

Under the assumption that there is no single best way to configure an II, but that the many possibilities to configure an II must be adapted to the problem situation at hand, the framework developed here allows researcher and practitioners to understand and define the specificity of a given II manifestation. In this capacity, the framework allows for cumulative knowledge-building about divergence in II challenges as well as the articulation of forward-looking agendas covering the development of granular II approaches tailored to subsets of artefacts.

2   Research Design and Method

The study design of this review rests on a view of II management based on contingency theory. Contingency theory [8–10] argues that there is no best way to organise a corporation, to lead a company, or to make decisions. Instead, the optimal course of action is contingent (dependent) upon the situation at hand.

A contingency view of II entails a fundamental assumption that there is no single best way to assemble the socio-technical II artefact. Instead, the way in which the II should be assembled in order to be effective is contingent on the problem it is intended to address. As argued in the introduction, the contingent course of II assemblage has largely been overlooked in the literature that has searched to establish the distinctiveness of the II artefact compared to traditional IS.

Following a contingency view of II, the literature review presented in this paper is conceptualised as a review of the relevant dimensions in two domains: *design situation* and *design resolution* (Fig. 1). In the review of the design situation we aim to unearth the findings of previous research in terms of relevant characteristics to consider when shaping an II, including, for example, the number of actors and the geographical dispersion. In reviewing the design resolution, we aim to capture the findings of previous literature in terms of relevant alternatives to configuring the socio-technical components of the II.

Fig. 1. Research design: the II design space

Article search took place in two supplementary phases. The first articles search included a keyword search within the leading IS journals, often referred to as "the basket of eight". The keyword-driven search provided a collection of twenty articles from seven sources. The keyword search was supplemented with backward (scanning of references) and forward (examination of citations) searches in order to identify further high impact research material [11]. Within this search, only articles with more than 35 citations in subsequent publications were also subject to review. The backward search rendered 10 more articles and the forward search identified two additional articles of relevance. In total, 32 articles were included in the final sample (see the table of results in Sect. 3).

The analysis involved a parallel mapping of the features of the situation and resolution of an II described by the authors. This process led to the identification of 43 variables within the areas of situation and resolution. Following a consistent method of comparison, the variables were specified by uniting overlapping features. The result of this process was the creation of a concept matrix representing which concepts are examined in each of the reviewed articles [11].

3 Review Results: The II Design Space

The dimensions of the II design space are graphically depicted in Fig. 2. Table 1 maps the dimensions to the reviewed literature. Since IIs are socio-technical constructs, the relevant dimensions span both social and technical aspects in both design situation and design resolution.

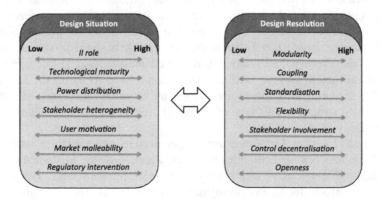

Fig. 2. The II design space

Table 1. Results

Variable / source	Aanestad and Jensen, 2009	Angelides and Agius, 2000	Ardagna and Francalanci, 2005	Bietz et al., 2010	Broadbent and Weill, 1997	Chung et al 2003	Ciborra, 2000	Constantinides and Barrett, 2014	Damsgaard and Lyytinen, 1998	Edwards et al., 2007	Garfield and Watsor, 1998	Grisot et al., 2014	Hanseth, 2000	Hansteh et al., 1996	Hanseth and Lyytinen, 2010	Henfridsson and Bygstad, 2013	Henningsson and Henriksen, 2011	Hsu et al., 2015	Iannacci, 2010	Monteiro, 1998	Monteiro and Hanseth, 1997	Nielsen and Aanestad, 2009	Pollock and Williams, 2010	Reimers et al., 2004	Reimers et al., 2014	Ribes and Finholt, 2009	Rodon and Silva, 2015	Sahay et al., 2009	Sanner et al., 2014	Star and Ruhleder, 1996	Tilson et al., 2010	Vaast and Walsham, 2009
Design Situation																																
II role				x	x										x																	
Technological maturity																		x						x	x							
Power distribution																														x		
Stakeholder heterogeneity			x	x	x	x		x	x			x					x				x			x					x	x		
User motivation																										x						
Market malleability																								x	x							
Regulatory intervention	x									x	x						x	x						x	x						x	
Design Resolution																																
Modularity			x	x		x								x	x										x		x			x		
Coupling			x									x				x											x	x		x		
Standardisation				x	x		x			x		x	x			x					x				x	x	x					
Flexibility	x		x	x	x	x		x		x	x	x		x	x		x			x			x				x		x	x		
Stakeholder involvement	x			x	x		x			x				x															x			x
Control decentralisation				x		x									x																x	
Openness				x	x																											

3.1 Situation Domain

The situation domain describes the context in which the II is built. Literature discusses a variety of dimensions in this sense, as well as their possible effects on the design and development of an II.

II Role. This variable concerns the type of need that the II is intended to cover. The role that the II is expected to play within the organisation (or any other broader user community) can reveal the "position" of the technology. Broadbent and Weill [12] describe IT infrastructures as serving a utility, dependent or enabling role. More specifically, a utility infrastructure is intended to facilitate economies of scale leading to cost efficiencies. Ciborra et al. [13] explains that although this II aims to achieve efficiency in processing and transmission activities, it is not likely to interfere with the attached applications or processes. A dependent infrastructure is created to address particular strategic needs, such as the support of specific business processes, meaning that the relevant investment is closely linked with business strategy [12, 13]. Finally, an enabling infrastructure aims to facilitate innovation with a focus on the longer-term horizon [12], preparing the ground for new applications and business processes through architecture and structure. This type of II also highlights the issue of alignment with business strategy [13].

Hanseth and Lyytinen [1] discuss another perspective with a different terminology, distinguishing between vertical infrastructures which provide functionality that is directly deployable by users and horizontal support infrastructures which include protocols or interfaces for further deployment of applications. The latter group can be further divided into transport and support infrastructure, based on the specific functionality that the protocol or interface aims to provide.

IT Maturity. This variable investigates the concepts identified in the literature and expresses both the familiarisation with IT and, in a broader sense, the maturity of the users regarding technology. The IT maturity of the user base also constitutes a factor that should be examined in order to understand the technological background of an II. For example, Reimers et al. [14] suggest that national culture regarding the use of IT plays a role in the design and the adoption of an II. Their study investigates e-business systems in China, where the particular cultural characteristics increased the requirements for local adaptation and reduced the ease of adoption. The findings of the empirical study by Hsu et al. [15] also suggest that the level of IT knowledge impacts relevant decisions, with IT-savvy organisations tending more towards innovative and promising solutions.

Power Distribution. The structure and relationships between the users and the broader stakeholders can have a dominant position regarding the situation for an II development. The hierarchical balance of stakeholders defines the ways in which power relations and roles are formed. Reimers et al. [14] examine the structure of the value network and more particularly the forms of fragmentation and collaboration in its component parts. This type of approach can be extended to the internal environment for the case of IIs in order to investigate the relationships between the various stakeholders. More particularly, this variable examines how they are structured and how they interact, for example whether they are equal, or whether there is one stakeholder with a leading role who is individually responsible for decisions without participation from the rest of the actors.

Stakeholder Heterogeneity. The definition by Star and Ruhleder [3] describes IIs as embedded in social structures, meaning that they entail a "taken-for-grantedness" within organisational structures, in terms of being inherent resources for the user community that new participants are acquainted with. Ciborra et al. [13, p. 32] explains that IIs represent "an alliance between humans and non humans where the latter (architectures, operating systems, standards) seem to have a say as important as the humans". The human component has been referred to as human infrastructure, and includes the knowledge and skills for managing IT resources [12, 13, 16]. On these grounds, while the utilisation of an II usually extends the boundaries of a certain group of users, this is shared within a wide reach involving a broad community consisting of diverse stakeholders [17]. For this reason, this variable may have a variety of parallel manifestations. Firstly, heterogeneity can be examined in terms of the geographical reach; i.e. the geographical territory that the II covers. This reach can be regional, national or global [2, 14]. Edwards et al. [18] also refer to this II categorisation and consider the possibility of a national cyber-infrastructure to extend national borders and achieve global adoption. Moreover, Garfield and Watson [19] discuss the effects of national differences in mindset, values and culture on II policies, while Hsu et al. [15] highlight the challenges related to institutional factors and social norms which are embedded within efforts to establish global IIs.

Besides the geographical aspect, the range of the intended user base is a key feature of the heterogeneity of II users. Reimers et al. [14] refer to the boundaries within which the II is used, involving firms, industry segments, or value systems. In addition to this, the authors also point out the difference in needs among the variety and type of actors involved; for example, business-to-customer and business-to-business infrastructures are expected to have distinctive characteristics. Nielsen and Aanestad [20] also mention the different scales an II can serve, involving corporate, business sector and universal levels, while Tilson et al. [2] differentiate between corporate and industry infrastructures.

The variable of heterogeneity also refers to the level of uniformity of the intended users' needs and intentions. The variety of actors involved in the establishment and development of an II create a complex network of relationships which entails a particular balance of powers [13]. Consistency can be examined through a variety of lenses as the relevant research suggests. Examples for assessing this involve the degree of business process alignment, variability in IT sophistication [14] and cultural and organisational differences [6, 18].

User Motivation and Support. User motivation towards the II project and can therefore enhance the image of the organisational setting in which an II is built. Ribes and Finholt [21] also note this, focusing on the field of scientific IIs in which the unique and individual needs of scientists can have an influence on the development of an II. More particularly, they argue that the competing interests and ambitions of the scientists involved (e.g. in terms of publications or academic position) may hinder the development of a community and thus prevent contribution to a shared infrastructure. On these grounds, the authors recognise the value of the contribution of II developers/users and, more importantly, the need for management to motivate them in order to ensure that their contribution is aligned with the overall II objectives.

Market Malleability. Examining market conditions can help to illustrate the particularities of various II problems and the level of fit of the respective solution. The state of the market or industry, and, more particularly, its malleability, can reveal the tendency towards stability or innovation to be enabled by an II. In this context, Reimers et al. [14] refer to the age or level of maturity of the industry, while Reimers et al. [14] elaborate further by referring to the level of industry consolidation. According to these authors, consolidation and IIs have a dual relationship in this case; that is, higher levels of consolidation lead to higher collaboration and therefore the emergence of IIs, while at the same time the emergence of IIs contributes to higher consolidation. Furthermore, Reimers et al. [14] suggest an examination of the level of competitive pressure based on Gibbs et al. [22] who consider it a key factor determining e-commerce diffusion.

Regulatory Intervention. Government or regulatory intervention is also a variable in this group. Given that IIs can be of public or private interest or even a combination of both, the role of government intervention can considerably influence their environment. For example, certain infrastructures are initiated and supported by public bodies in order to enhance national security or to contribute to economic growth [18].

Reimers et al. [14] examine the effect of government policies on standards. The authors find that in cases where standards are imposed at a government level, the need for collaboration at organisational level is higher than in the case where standards are developed by the companies themselves. In addition to the area of standards, Reimers et al. [14] also suggest that governments can influence aspects such as industry structure, IT use and dynamics among industry associations. Although these are not directly connected with the design of an II, they certainly affect the closer context and the stakeholders involved, and can determine the following stages and ultimately the outcome of the II. Reimers et al. [14] describe highly regulated industries as having high demand for inter-organisational IS, affecting, among other things, their need for uniformity. This can be easily leveraged to the II level and to the role of regulatory requirements in key decisions affecting their design characteristics and reach [23]. Regulation has also been characterised as a restriction on or requirement for standards adoption [15, 24, 25] as well as relevant to flexibility in the design of IIs [2].

3.2   Resolution Domain

A generally agreed-upon element of II research is the fact that IIs constitute combinations of technical and social components [1, 2, 18, 26]. For this reason, the design resolution domain comprises variables concerning the design and implementation of an II from a technical and social perspective. These aspects constitute the object of interest of a considerable proportion of the literature examined, since they are directly linked with the IIs under study.

The technical design refers to the architecture of the II and involves variables that describe how the technical components are interlinked. These variables concern the modularity, looseness of coupling, standardisation and flexibility of an II. The social aspect of the design refers to the governance of the II. This begins with the level of participation of users during the development of the II and continues with the way it is managed and controlled, although it also refers to the public or private image it adopts. The relevant variables are stakeholder involvement, control decentralisation and openness of an II.

Modularity. One of the key features of an infrastructure is that it does not instantly develop to its full extent but is built through modular increments to independent systems and networks which are gradually integrated, leveraging the existing dynamics of the installed base [3, 14, 18]. Hanseth et al. [27] and Hanseth and Lyytinen [1] discuss the concept of modularity as a scheme of connected and interrelated ecologies, where sub-infrastructures are built in layers on top of one another, linking networks and connecting separate components and thus creating an interdependent structure. Additionally, Chung et al. [16] describe this modularity as being based on processing programming routines in separate modules, which enables the management of software applications and Bietz et al. [28] point out that contrary to IS, a key characteristic of IIs is that they are embedded and therefore operate using networks of linked nodes and webs.

Another perspective on modularity relates to cost efficiency. Ardagna and Francalanci [29] suggest that distributing a system computing load to multiple machines, and positioning them according to certain communication patterns, can influence network costs.

Looseness of Coupling. This essence of networked architecture gives rise to the need to build connectivity between the various components. This connectivity is realised through coupling, a feature that can define one of the key dimensions of an II's architecture. In contrast to physical infrastructures, which have tight coupling between technical and service delivery components, the modularity and recursive organisation of IIs enables generativity and the creation of new capabilities [2]. The authors underline that "disconnecting" these two dimensions leads to a reallocation of control and thus enables other users (non-owners of the physical parts) to use and develop the services and application in alignment with their own needs and interests. For example, two technological components can be aligned in order to interoperate through an application programming interface (API) which provides a very high potential for customisation and innovation [28]. Furthermore, Rodon and Silva [30] refer to APIs as a means of fostering external innovation within an II.

Moreover, Henfridsson and Bygstad [26] consider loose versus tight coupling to be a key distinction for IIs, arguing that it can significantly affect their evolution. The issue of connecting components and networks has also been addressed through the concept of gateways, which act as links consolidating the infrastructures [18]. Gateways provide a means for adaptation or conversion between different formats, in order to enable communication among isolated systems or modules and allow them to act as integrated systems [31].

Standardisation. The concept of standardisation has been widely discussed in the relevant literature and is considered one of the key factors not only for an II's stability but also for its capability for expansion. The connection and integration of the modular elements requires technical effort, which creates the need for specifications in order to facilitate these endeavours. Hanseth et al. [27] refer to standards as indispensable tools allowing infrastructure partners to communicate. The authors comment that in the absence of standards, this communication can be enabled via bilateral agreements or proprietary protocols, although such alternatives are harder to manage and usually more costly.

Rodon and Silva [30] also present the various options in terms of integration. In particular, they refer to stratification, which constitutes a means for integrating and standardising behaviour in a consolidated hierarchical structure, while the option of meshworking does not involve standardisation but instead a more distributed and independent assembly of parts.

Moreover, as Chung et al. [16], Hanseth et al. [27] and Sahay et al. [32] argue, standardisation enables compatibility between components via the ease of adherence to the interface specifications. More particularly, the use of standardised features and components enables attachment to other infrastructures, thereby increasing the quality of transparency and the broader reach of an II [3].

Edwards et al. [18] discuss three types of gateways and their meaning in terms of standardisation. Dedicated gateways are designed for the unique needs of a system and signify a low level of standardisation. Generic gateways show a moderate level of standardisation, applying widely accepted standards concerning system interconnection. Finally, meta-generic gateways show the highest level of standardisation, by defining a protocol or framework for the formulation of standards, rather than the standards themselves.

Monteiro and Hanseth [33] refer to standards as the technical foundations regulating the communicative patterns of an II. This is particularly useful given the increasing trend in favour of decentralised operations and their need to customise different features, since this increases the need for standardised integration tools as well as for flexible technologies, as further elaborated below [3]. On these grounds, Hanseth [17] describes the use of standardised interfaces integrating different elements such that modularity is not visible, although the II can be seen as "irreducible".

Flexibility. Flexibility has been described as a feature of the technical design of an II that not only enables but often determines its possibility for growth, since a lack of flexibility, or "irreversibility", may act as a barrier to evolution [27]. This is because an II can allow innovation in business processes and capabilities, and this potential is illustrated through the flexibility of the infrastructure's components [16].

In other words, flexibility is argued to be a necessary feature for embedding in the technical design of an II, with the aim of enabling continuous growth so as to meet user needs [14, 32], thus offering a major competitive advantage to organisations within the rapidly evolving and highly competitive business environment [16]. Despite this, the digital nature of IIs suggests that, in principle, the only boundaries to an II's capability for application or service development are set by its own technical design and configuration [2].

Ciborra et al. [13] discusses the dilemma between high flexibility, enabling unforeseeable business redesign in the future, and low flexibility, based on consistency with ongoing strategic needs. From a more technical perspective, Tilson et al. [2] refer to "upward flexibility" as the ability to create applications or services using the II's basic communication and storage capacity. Grisot et al. [34] describe this phenomenon as "innovation in infrastructures" which can be experienced when IIs are designed in a generic way.

This concept is parallel to modularity; Chung et al. [16] and Hanseth et al. [27] mention the latter as a means of enabling the flexibility of an II. This is possible because modularity accelerates the development and modification of applications and at the same time allows interoperability with other systems. Similarly, Tilson et al. [2] explain the concept of "downward flexibility", which signifies that interconnectivity can be provided by a variety of digital or physical networks. Such flexibility is provided by "the malleability of software implementing the logic laid down in layers over the physical layer of interconnected hardware" [2, p. 6], which is linked to the concept of modularity as described above.

One of the primary challenges in designing and implementing a successful II lies in achieving a balance between the contradictory aspects of an II. Flexibility and stability have both been widely argued to be key features of an II; however, it is possible that their coexistence creates a controversial relationship or dilemma. Star and Ruhleder [3] point out that the inherent flexibility of an II can act as an enabler of innovation, although such innovation and evolution might be hindered in the case of an incumbent infrastructure facing lock-in situations. Impediments to evolution can also be induced by increased standardisation and a focus on stability, which might prevent decentralised initiatives. For example, applying technical specifications that are not available for public use can limit the possibilities for evolution through external sources [5]. Ciborra et al. [13] also acknowledges this paradox and suggests that the optimal solution would combine decentralised generativity capabilities with centralised control over resources and processes.

Stakeholder Involvement. The socio-technical nature and, more particularly, the role of the stakeholders involved create a challenge regarding the connection and coordination of the range of stakeholders, which may have diverse needs and interests [1]. Constantinides and Barrett [6] also discuss user heterogeneity as a challenge which leads to a need for extensive coordination and collective action, and underline that the motivation of lower-layer levels can be significantly affected by their degree of inclusion in relevant decisions.

This issue has also been discussed by Hanseth and Lyytinen [1] on the grounds that traditional top-down design approaches pose challenges regarding the fulfilment of the needs of an II's wide user base. Following a top-down approach based on critical stakeholders' agreement might provide some stability; however, such an approach disregards the complexities and possibility of evolution of an II, thus limiting its flexibility [34].

Control Decentralization. Henfridsson and Bygstad [26] discuss the options of management rights given to the user institutions, or a centralised position usually held by a state authority. Tilson et al. [2] examine the level of centralisation in terms of control of the services deployed, critical resources, data ownership and data management. Data management, and especially decisions about sharing, storage and preservation, is also discussed by Edwards et al. [18]. More particularly, the authors argue that the emergence of true infrastructures happens when locally built and centrally governed systems are connected into networks involving decentralised coordination and control. Constantinides and Barrett [6] describe a "polycentric" governance approach in which individual centres or units are entitled to independence within their specific area, thus distributing governance into wider networks. The authors support the argument that flexibility is higher when governance is decentralised, but also argue that such an approach can lead to increased complexity and divergence from the initial vision. Moreover, they suggest that decentralised autonomy should be authorised to all stakeholders to the extent that their autonomy does not disturb the other independent units.

Openness. Ciborra et al. [13] uses another categorisation based on the categorisation of the infrastructure as open or closed. Closed infrastructures are suitable for restricted and controlled environments, such as specific organisations. On the other hand, open infrastructures have a public nature, and are available for use and further development by broader user communities. Constantinides and Barrett [6] also examine an II as a private or public good with regard to its properties and more particularly the benefits it provides.

4 Discussion and Conclusion

The main argument of this paper is that within the class of II artefacts, there are important differences in both the problems addressed and the II solutions crafted to address these problems. Based on this position, we have reviewed the high quality and high impact literature on II to unearth the relevant dimensions of the II design space. We found that the problem side of II design, the design situation, has been framed in terms of seven dimensions: II role, technological maturity, power distribution, stakeholder heterogeneity, user motivation, market malleability and regulatory intervention. We also found seven dimensions that had been reported as relevant in framing the solution side of II design, the design resolution, and these were modularity, coupling, standardisation, flexibility, stakeholder involvement, control decentralisation and openness. Here, we report on all 14 dimensions as continuums where any given II artefact can, at least in theory, assume any value and characterise a unique II design. Taken together, these 14 dimensions also illustrate the aspect of divergence within the artefact class of II, a divergence that needs to be taken into account to understand the many struggling II projects throughout the world.

As in any research, our findings are subject to limitations and validity constraints. Although we have employed a broad and comprehensive approach to the article search, it cannot be guaranteed that we have been able to identify every relevant article and every relevant variable in the selected articles. The research also involves certain limitations and acknowledges certain weaknesses. One of these is linked to the filtering of literature sources, which was performed in order to ensure the identification of high quality literature but which may have hindered the finding of additional sources which could have enriched the content of the literature review. Regarding the formation of the framework, although the concepts used as variables have been selected as being commonly referenced aspects of IIs, they could be considered rather broad and theoretical, with potential for being significantly enhanced with more detail, especially concerning the technical aspects of the II design. Furthermore, as research in this area develops, more relevant dimensions will be discovered. We are, however, convinced that the main argument of the paper, that within the class of II artefacts there is important divergence, rests on a solid foundation.

The design of the conceptual research means that we identify two important limitations on the scope of the review. One is that we do not intend here to say anything about which attributes of resolution match which attributes of situation. Second, we also omit the process view of II development. Both of these limitations are important areas for exploration in future research.

The main academic contributions of this paper are the critical argument that the way in which the II artefact is conceptualised needs to be reconsidered, and the multi-dimensional framework characterising the II design space, presented in Fig. 2. Although previous research has discussed a variety of settings and problems in which IIs arise, it has only provided general guidelines on how IIs should be built, overlooking the diversity of potential conditions around them. In view of this, the most important implication of this research concerns the expression of the need to examine the unique context and environment surrounding each II individually, rather than treating all cases in the same way.

Our multi-dimensional characterisation of the II design space allows for further theorisation of the II artefact resting on a view of divergence within the artefact class. For further research, the framework provides a tool to characterise a specific II and to contrast it with other known examples in order to find patterns linking scenarios to outcomes. This is particularly useful in areas where efforts to establish effective IIs have shown to be especially difficult for II development, such as in international trade, health care and finance [35–38].

Further theorisation would also include a search for an explanatory and design theory that matches distinct subsets of the II artefact class and to find archetypical II designs. That is, in theory, the positioning along the dimensions in the framework can be freely combined. In reality, however, it seems that certain choices within these dimensions go more naturally together. These 'natural fits' in dimensions indicate that there might possible archetypical II set-ups of design attributes that align with each other. The implication of this finding is that anyone interested in the shaping of an II cannot make independent choices regarding the dimensions, but have to recognise the systemic dependencies between the choices. That is, one specific choice will influence the possibility for choices in the other decision points. It also follows that these archetypical designs may have specific configurations between situation and resolution dimensions. For example, what would be the design principles for the success of an II built nationally with high regulatory involvement? Would these principles be different in a setting with a low distribution of power and a homogenous user base?

A final academic possibility granted by the framework is to develop process theory based on certain process-defining characteristics. While the II process has generally been described as cultivation, recognising divergence may reveal additional insights as to why this process takes different paths in different attempts.

In practice, the framework in this paper has at least two valuable areas of use. The obvious lesson to be learnt is that there is no single best way to build an II. At the same time, it becomes more evident that there is more than one situation in which the need for an II arises. The theoretical framework presented above can aid practitioners in the analysis of the design space of their IIs and support them in their decision-making processes.

Practitioners can also use the framework as a starting point to analyse the critical 'must-win' battles of their II designs. For example, for an II built on a high degree of openness the must-win battle might be fast user enrolment for expansion of the II, while an II with high regulatory support might have more stamina in user enrolment. Similarly, a low or high level of user heterogeneity or power distribution entails different critical battles to be managed in the socio-political dimensions of the II design space.

References

1. Hanseth, O., Lyytinen, K.: Design theory for dynamic complexity in information infrastructures: the case of building Internet. J. Inf. Technol. **25**, 1–19 (2010)
2. Tilson, D., Lyytinen, K., Sørensen, C.: Research commentary - digital infrastructures: the missing IS research agenda. Inf. Syst. Res. **21**, 748–759 (2010)
3. Star, S.L., Ruhleder, K.: Steps toward an ecology of infrastructure: design and access for large information space. Inf. Syst. Res. **7**, 111–134 (1996)
4. Henningsson, S., Hanseth, O.: The essential dynamics of information infrastructures (2011)
5. Henningsson, S., Henriksen, H.Z.: Inscription of behaviour and flexible interpretation in information infrastructures: the case of European e-Customs. J. Strateg. Inf. Syst. **20**, 355–372 (2011)
6. Constantinides, P., Barrett, M.: Information infrastructure development and governance as collective action. Inf. Syst. Res. **26**, 40–56 (2014)
7. Rowe, F.: What literature review is not: diversity, boundaries and recommendations. Eur. J. Inf. Syst. **23**, 241–255 (2014)
8. Donaldson, L.: The Contingency Theory of Organizations. SAGE, Thousand Oaks (2001)
9. Hofer, C.W.: Toward a contingency theory of business strategy. Acad. Manag. J. **18**, 784–810 (1975)
10. Fiedler, F.E.: A contingency model of leadership effectiveness. Adv. Exp. Soc. Psychol. **1**, 149–190 (1964)
11. Webster, J., Watson, R.: Analyzing the past to prepare for the future: writing a litterature review. MIS Q. **26**, xiii–xxiii (2002)
12. Broadbent, M., Weill, P.: Management by maxim: how business and IT managers can create IT infrastructures. Sloan Manag. Rev. **38**, 77–92 (1997)
13. Ciborra, C., Braa, K., Cordella, A., Dahlbom, B., Failla, A., Hanseth, O., Hepsø, V., Ljungberg, J., Monteiro, E., Simon, K.A.: From Control to Drift: The Dynamics of Corporate Information Infastructures. Oxford University Press, Oxford (2000)
14. Reimers, K., Li, M., Xie, B., Guo, X.: How do industry-wide information infrastructures emerge? A life cycle approach. Inf. Syst. J. **24**, 375–424 (2014)
15. Hsu, C., Lin, Y.-T., Wang, T.: A legitimacy challenge of a cross-cultural interorganizational information system. Eur. J. Inf. Syst. **24**, 278–294 (2015)
16. Chung, S.H., Rainer Jr., R.K., Lewis, B.R.: The impact of information technology infrastructure flexibility on strategic alignment and application implementations. Commun. Assoc. Inf. Syst. **11** (2003)
17. Hanseth, O.: The economics of standards. In: Ciborra, C. (ed.) From Control to Drift. The Dynamics of Corporate Information Infrastructures. Oxford University Press, Oxford (2000)
18. Edwards, P., Jackson, S., Bowker, G., Knobel, C.: Understanding infrastructure: dynamics, tensions, and design. NSF report of a workshop: history and theory of infrastructure: lessons for new scientific cyberinfrastructures (2007)
19. Garfield, M.J., Watson, R.T.: Differences in national information infrastructures: the reflection of national cultures. J. Strateg. Inf. Syst. **6**, 313–337 (1997)
20. Nielsen, P., Aanestad, M.: Control devolution as information infrastructure design strategy: a case study of a content service platform for mobile phones in Norway. J. Inf. Technol. **21**, 185–194 (2006)
21. Ribes, D., Finholt, T.A.: The long now of technology infrastructure: articulating tensions in development. J. Assoc. Inf. Syst. **10**, 5 (2009)
22. Gibbs, J., Kraemer, K.L., Dedrick, J.: Environment and policy factors shaping global e-commerce diffusion: a cross-country comparison. Inf. Soc. **19**, 5–18 (2003)

23. Angelides, M.C., Agius, H.W.: Eight scenarios of national information superhighway development. J. Inf. Technol. **15**, 53–67 (2000)
24. Damsgaard, J., Lyytinen, K.: The role of intermediating institutions in the diffusion of electronic data interchange (EDI): how industry associations intervened in Denmark, Finland, and Hong Kong. Inf. Soc. **17**, 195–210 (2001)
25. Iannacci, F.: When is an information infrastructure? Investigating the emergence of public sector information infrastructures. Eur. J. Inf. Syst. **19**, 35–48 (2010)
26. Henfridsson, O., Bygstad, B.: The generative mechanisms of digital infrastructure evolution. MIS Q. **37**, 907–931 (2013)
27. Hanseth, O., Monteiro, E., Hatling, M.: Developing information infrastructure: the tension between standardization and flexibility. Sci. Technol. Hum. values **21**, 407–426 (1996)
28. Bietz, M.J., Baumer, E.P., Lee, C.P.: Synergizing in cyberinfrastructure development. Comput. Support. Coop. Work (CSCW) **19**, 245–281 (2010)
29. Ardagna, D., Francalanci, C.: A cost-oriented approach for the design of IT architectures. J. Inf. Technol. **20**, 32–51 (2005)
30. Rodon, J., Silva, L.: Exploring the formation of a healthcare information infrastructure: hierarchy or meshwork? J. Assoc. Inf. Syst. **16**, 1 (2015)
31. Sanner, T.A., Manda, T.D., Nielsen, P.: Grafting: balancing control and cultivation in information infrastructure innovation. J. Assoc. Inf. Syst. **15**, 220–243 (2014)
32. Sahay, S., Monteiro, E., Aanestad, M.: Configurable politics and asymmetric integration: health e-infrastructures in India. J. Assoc. Inf. Syst. **10**, 399 (2009)
33. Monteiro, E., Hanseth, O.: Social shaping of information infrastructure: on being specific about the technology. In: Orlikowski, W., Walsham, G., Jones, M.R., Degross, J. (eds.) Information Technology and Changes in Organisational Work, pp. 325–343. Chapman & Hall, Boca Raton (1996)
34. Grisot, M., Hanseth, O., Thorseng, A.A.: Innovation of, in, on infrastructures: articulating the role of architecture in information infrastructure evolution. J. Assoc. Inf. Syst. **15**, 197–219 (2014)
35. Henningsson, S., Rukanova, B., Hrastinski, S.: Resource dependencies in socio-technical information systems design research. In: Communications of the AIS 27 (2010)
36. Henningsson, S., Hedman, J.: Industry-wide supply chain information integration: the lack of management and disjoint economic responsibility. In: Information Technologies, Methods, and Techniques of Supply Chain Management, pp. 98–117. IGI Global (2012)
37. Hedman, J., Henningsson, S.: Competition and collaboration shaping the digital payment infrastructure. In: Proceedings of the 14th Annual International Conference on Electronic Commerce, pp. 178–185. ACM (2012)
38. Henningsson, S., van Veenstra, A.F.: Barriers to IT-driven governmental transformation. In: European Conference of Information Systems (ECIS) (2010)

Identifying Quality Factors of Information Systems Integration Design

Iyad Zikra[✉], Janis Stirna, and Jelena Zdravkovic

Department of Computer and Systems Sciences (DSV), Stockholm University,
Stockholm, Sweden
{iyad,js,jelenaz}@dsv.su.se

Abstract. The Information Systems (IS) community has long recognized the importance of studying quality at various stages of the IS design process. Many studies target the quality factors at various stages of design and development. However, research about the factors that specifically affect the quality of IS integration remains largely fragmented. Existing quality frameworks fail to cover integration-specific factors. This motivates the need for a holistic model of integration quality. The paper proposes two artefacts to address this need. It explores the literature of related domains, including systems, model, and process quality to elicit the quality factors that are relevant in the context of IS integration. The factors can be used to evaluate the quality of integration solutions during design and development. The paper also proposes a quality model to describe the quality of the design components of integration solutions following the principles of model-driven development. The model enables the quality factors to be associated with other parts of the IS integration design. The proposed factors are evaluated with the help of expert feedback using a questionnaire, and the quality model is demonstrated with an example business case.

Keywords: Information systems integration · Quality factors · Quality model · Meta-model

1 Introduction

Modern organizations rely on a wide range of Information Systems (IS) to support their operations and deliver products and services. The systems need to work together in harmony despite their reliance on different data formats, implementation technologies, and communication protocols. Integration solutions facilitate communication between IS and guarantee that they can work together seamlessly. Nevertheless, IS integration lacks a clear and unambiguous definition. The study of integration-related problems is dispersed across loosely related and diverse domains [13], including strategic management, systems design and development, and the different research areas, including Enterprise Modelling, Enterprise Architecture, Business Process Management, Interoperability, Web and cloud services.

Quality has long been recognized as an important ingredient for the success of IS design and development [27]. A large body of research addresses the quality of data, systems, models, and business processes. However, it is considerably more limited

© Springer International Publishing AG 2017
B. Johansson et al. (Eds.): BIR 2017, LNBIP 295, pp. 45–60, 2017.
DOI: 10.1007/978-3-319-64930-6_4

when it comes to the impact of quality on the overall integration design [7]. Quality is traditionally studied independently at each stage of the integration process. Existing quality frameworks are unable to account for factors that specifically affect the quality of integration. Improving how the integration solution is positioned within the overall organizational design requires understanding and formalizing the integration quality factors. This, in turn, will improve alignment between organizational design and IS design, thereby increasing the added value for the organization [10].

This paper addresses the need for a holistic view of IS integration quality. The objective of the paper is two-fold: (1) to identify the quality factors that affect the various stages of integration design and development; and (2) to develop a general quality model that enables the systematic definition and evaluation of integration quality factors. The paper applies the principles of design science research [37] to develop two artefacts that address the objectives, namely (i) is the *integration quality factors*, compiled from related literature and evaluated with the help of expert feedback, and (ii) the *Integration Quality View*, a quality model that serves as a vehicle to create formal representations of the quality factors. The overall aim is to use the formally described factors to describe other components in an integration solution, e.g. as part of a model-driven development project. The factors presented in this paper focus on quality of integration. Nevertheless, other quality attributes need to be considered, as described in relevant literature, to provide a complete quality view of the integration solution, being itself an IS.

The remainder of the paper is structured as follows. Section 2 describes the method that drives the research presented herein. Section 3 gives an overview of the literature concerned with the quality aspects in domains associated with IS integration. Section 4 elaborates on and motivates the elicited integration quality factors. Section 5 describes the details of the proposed quality model, and ends with an example case that demonstrates how the model can be used in the context of integration design. Finally, concluding remarks and future research directions are presented in Sect. 6.

2 The Research Method

This paper adheres to the Design Science Research Methodology (DSRM) [37] for research in IS. The results presented herein are part of on-going research on IS integration. Figure 1 illustrates the stages of two traversals of the design cycle. Italic text describes the DSRM stage name, and normal text describes how the stage is applied in the research presented herein. Arrows represent progression between stages. Dashed arrows denote the overlap between the design cycles.

The paper is initiated as problem-centred research: Studying the literature of IS integration reveals the lack of a holistic conceptualization of the factors affecting integration quality. The objective of the first design cycle is to create an artefact that captures quality as part of integration design. To this end, an integration quality model is proposed as an extension to the Unifying Meta-Model (UMM) [46]. Developing the model is challenged by the lack of clear understanding of what constitutes IS integration [13] and, as a result, integration quality. A second design cycle is initiated to survey the quality factors in integration-related domains. The artefact developed in this

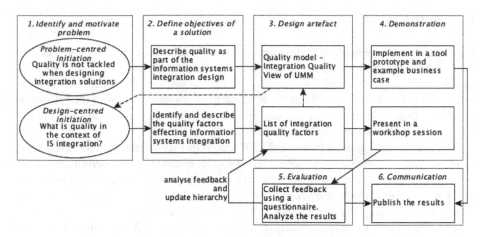

Fig. 1. The stages of the DSRM [37] as they are applied in the paper.

cycle is a list of integration quality factors. Overlapping definitions of factors are reconciled, in an interpretivist stance, to account for contextual differences [2, 4] and arrive at a conceptualization that is generally applicable in the overarching integration context. Therefore, this part of the research can be characterized as behavioural. Furthermore, the elicited integration-specific factors provide input for improving the quality model. The factors were presented (i.e. demonstrated) at a session of the annual workshop of the Swedish Requirement Engineering Research Network (SIREN). The ensuing discussion generated input to improve the description of the factors.

Evaluation of the quality factors is conducted with the help of a questionnaire. The questions are organized into four sections to reflect the proposed categories of factors (see Sects. 4.1–4.4). A description is given for each factor, and the respondents are queried on the necessity and motivation of the factor. 18 respondents answered the questionnaire: 9 researchers, 7 practitioners, and 2 who identify themselves as both. The respondents are active in a range of domains, including requirements engineering, conceptual modelling, verification, banking, healthcare, and automotive industry. All respondents have experience in working with integration-related problems, ranging from less than 2 years to more than 10 years. Analysis of the answers provided further guidance for amending and improving the quality factors, and consequently influencing the proposed quality model. Factors that were deemed inapplicable specifically to integration were removed, and new factors were introduced. Some factors were reconciled and encapsulated as one, because their interpretations within the integration context were found to be tightly overlapping. The mixed feedback from respondents with different backgrounds highlights the lack of a common understanding of integration and its quality.

The prototype tool for UMM is extended to support the quality model artefact, and an example case (Sect. 5.1) demonstrates the use of the model with the help of a prototype tool. Finally, the results of the two design cycles are communicated to the research community via this paper.

3 Related Work

There are many frameworks that describe quality in IS in terms of the aspects of design and development. Some frameworks focus on the quality of the conceptual models of the IS, while others consider the quality of the modelling process as well. Some frameworks also include guidelines for defining qualities and evaluating the fulfilment of desired quality levels. However, surveying research works on quality reveals the lack of an integration-specific quality framework.

The quality management framework [29] groups quality aspects in three categories: syntactic quality referring to the adherence of model instances to the definitions of the modelling language; semantic quality covering the relationship between the model and the domain from which the model contents are elicited; and pragmatic quality addressing the perception of the model by the intended audiences.

The conceptual modelling quality framework (CMQF) [33] organizes the statements that affect quality in groups, called cornerstones, that correspond to physical or socials aspect of the domain and its model. The cornerstones are arranged in four layers to reflect the progression of the modelling process from the physical world to the representation model. 24 quality types describe the relationships between statements from different cornerstones, and quality is described as the fulfilment of these relationships. The CMQF combines the quality framework of [27], which is extended as SEQUAL in [24], with the representational framework of [42], which adopts an ontological view of the conceptual modelling process.

In IS development, desired qualities are typically described as non-functional requirements (NFRs). They include constraints that the IS must adhere to and conditions that must fulfilled. The NFR Framework [14] enables IS developers to capture NFRs using soft-goals and to refine the definition of abstract (or vague) NFRs into more concrete ones. The NFR Framework includes mechanism to capture the relative effect of NFRs on each other as positive/negative and implicit/explicit interdependencies. Requirement operationalization in the NFR Framework enables the identification of functional mechanisms to fulfil the NFR. The shift from qualitative requirements to functional mechanisms represents a gap, and further analysis is required to demonstrate that the proposed mechanisms indeed fulfil the NFR that they operationalize.

The Architecture Tradeoff Analysis Method (ATAM) [22] is a technique for developing software architectures by analysing quality requirements. Utility trees are used to identify and motivate architectural design decisions that contribute to the fulfilment of the quality attributes. The utility trees are constructed by studying the external stimuli and internal parameters that affect the architecture, as well as the expected responses of the architecture. Leaf nodes in the utility trees describe tactics [3], i.e. concrete measures for fulfilling the quality attributes. Examples of architecture quality attributes that can be analysed using utility trees include performance, availability, modifiability, and security.

Providing concrete values for quality factors is a difficult task. The NFR Framework acknowledges the need to conduct fulfilment analysis. However, it is neutral with regards to the quantitative measures necessary to estimate degree of fulfilment through operationalizations. Similarly, the tactics proposed in the ATAM to construct solutions to quality issues without measuring the actual fulfilment of the qualities.

The list of quality attributes that affect an IS can grow to a level that is hard to manage [38]. Therefore, the study of quality needs to be contextualized. For pragmatic reasons, many studies focus on identifying the quality attributes that are relevant in a specific application domain or development stage. In such studies, the meaning of a quality attribute depends on its application context [2, 4]. Some studies include guidelines for evaluating the attributes and correcting quality flaws. E.g., SEQUAL [24] has specialized versions that address, among others, aspects of business process modelling, enterprise modelling, and model-driven development. Concerning IS integration, research studies focus on the quality of the integration constituents, as described by the integrated data, systems/services (as data sources), and processes.

The quality of data can be studied by analysing properties of the data sources or the structure (i.e. schema) of the data. The study in [2] surveys the data quality attributes that are covered in major quality management methodologies. The result is a unified list that includes 50 attributes, divided into 28 dimensions, with most of the surveyed methodologies supporting less than three attributes. Quality driven integration of heterogeneous IS is explored in [32] with a focus on information quality. The study in [8] identifies 24 attributes of data quality in business process modelling, and proposes strategy for mitigating quality problems in a process model using data quality blocks as control activities in the model.

Business process quality can be studied by analysing variables associated with process performance (e.g. using KPIs [6] or balanced scorecards [21]), or by evaluating quality attributes associated with the process model or the data being input or manipulated by the process [18]. The study in [28] surveys existing approaches to business process quality management, and develops a quality framework that extends the traditional, mechanistic, data-oriented (i.e. data as input to the process) view of process quality to account for the relationship to the organizational goals that the process serves. The framework identifies four basic quality domains for business processes: efficacy, efficiency, design and implementation quality, and enactment quality. The framework proposes capturing quality with the help of a triad: quality attributes, quality criteria, and quality predicates. The relationships between the triad elements cover the interactions between the business process and the organizational targets affecting and affected by the process. [41] offers an alternative approach to process quality that focuses on the technical properties of process models, including coupling, cohesion, complexity, modularity, and size. The metrics proposed by the approach can assist in improving the quality of processes by helping designers identify potential errors and problem areas, and guide them towards effectively resolving the problems.

Quality of Service (QoS) is a collective term that describes the quality attributes of software service delivery and the measures used for evaluating the qualities [9]. The details of what constitutes QoS vary amongst researchers, but generally include cost, reliability, execution time, and security [23].

4 Quality Factors for IS Integration Design

Designing an integration solution that can serve the organization in fulfilling its goals depends on maintaining quality at all stages of the integration process. This section presents the quality factors that are identified as having direct effects on integration. Quality is interpreted in terms of each factor's relationship to the design and development of integration solutions. The factors are elicited from literature on quality in domains associated with IS integration, including the quality of IS, models, and the organizational factors affecting the success of integration. The factors are organized into four groups that reflect the following aspects of integration: the integrated systems, integration design model, integration process, and the IS integration solution itself. The resulting groups are presented below. They include the final, revised list of quality factors.

4.1 Candidate System-Related Factors

Choosing IS that can fulfil the integration goals is essential for the success of the integration project. Quality of IS has been long recognized as a cornerstone for successful adoption and use [38]. In the context of integrating systems, the following factors help in deciding whether or not to include a candidate IS in the integration solution, or whether an alternative system needs to be identified:

- Freshness: describes the age of the data, i.e. how the importance and relevance of the data are affected by time [2, 5, 32]. A candidate system must be able to provide data that meets freshness requirements as describe by the integration goals.
- Reliability: the system's ability to provide uninterrupted and correct data (or service) within the expected response time [44]. A candidate system must be reliable when being included in an integration solution. Reliability is affected by available failure mitigation mechanisms [11], as well as with the availability [15] and reputation [1] of the candidate system.
- Data Completeness: a candidate system is able to provide a portion of the required data to fulfil the integration goals. Nevertheless, assessing completeness can help in determining which sources to access and how the data can be integrated [31].
- Accuracy: the percentage of errors in the data [32]. In the integration context, errors are any deviations in the data from what is required to fulfil the integration goals. Accuracy, viewed in the integration context, can be seen as subsumed by the broader system completeness, as defined by [27]. A candidate system may provide unprocessed (i.e. raw) data or offer mechanism for pre-processing (i.e. cleaning and organizing) the data to fit integration needs better.
- Price: the financial cost of accessing the system [44], affecting the decision to integrate the system or not [9]. A candidate system must be possible to access for a price that fits within the budget for developing, running, and maintaining the integration solution.
- Type of System Interface: affects the ease of integration, i.e. the effort required to implement a connection to the interface. A candidate system may have a standard

interface (e.g. relational databases, RESTful services [36]), which may simplify integration, or a custom one that requires additional analysis to integrate with [26].

- Compatibility: refers to the system belonging to the same or different platform than other candidate systems. A candidate system may be easier to integrate if it belongs to the same platform or complies with similar technologies or standards as the remaining candidate systems, because the knowledge required for integration can be reused [43].

- Security Mechanism: integration-related security is a subset of the security usually considered for IS [34]. A candidate system must strive to balance simplicity of access, which improves ease of integration, and complexity of security mechanisms, which improves protection against unpermitted automated access in the integration context.

4.2   Integration Models-Related Factors

The list of model quality factors in the literature is extensive and covers diverse perspectives [19, 27]. This section focuses on the factors that affect the quality of IS integration. The factors represent attributes of the modelling language chosen for designing the integration. They include:

- Expressiveness: refers to the (objective) ability of the modelling language to capture the design details [16, 17, 29]. The modelling language needs to provide constructs for describing all aspects of the integration, including the integrated systems, the integration processes, and the data exchanged between the systems.

- Audience Interpretation: refers to the (subjective) ability of the models to be correctly interpreted by the audience (i.e. owners of integrated systems, and analysts, designers, and developers of integration solution). The modelling language may indirectly influence this factor by accounting for the relationship between the model semantics and the contextual domain knowledge [24, 27].

- Model Completeness: refers to the state at which the model is said to contain all the relevant design details [27]. This factor is evaluated while the solution is under development. It characterizes the integration design model rather than the modelling language. However, evaluating syntactical consistency, i.e. conformance of the model to the language rules [24], may help uncover missing integration details [2]. Language expressiveness affects the ability to address model completeness.

- Conflict Resolution: refers to the ability to identify and resolve inconsistencies in models [2]. Conflicts arise when attempting to integrate heterogeneous systems. The modelling language needs to be able to capture and identify conflicting design details, thereby facilitating their resolution.

4.3   Integration Process-Related Factors

Improving the quality of the process for developing a model (or an IS) contributes to improving the quality of the model (or the IS) itself [30, 33]. Applied to integration design, this underlines the need for addressing the quality of the integration methodology. Well-designed methodological guidelines can contribute to the quality of the solution. The methodology needs to be complete, i.e. covering all the necessary steps for designing an integration solution. The guidelines need to be logically consistent and progress in a systematic, modular manner. They need to be prescriptive and carefully explain the activities that should be carried out. Furthermore, the integration methodology needs be demonstrably effective for developing integration solutions of high quality, and account for the integration-specific factors described in Sects. 4.1, 4.2, and 4.4. The factors need to be built into the methodological guidelines to drive the progress of the solution's design and development. A model-driven methodology can especially employ model-related quality factors (both general and integration-specific ones) to improve the solution's quality. It is necessary to adopt a holistic view of quality in relation to integration methodology. However, the details of such a methodology are outside of the scope of this paper.

4.4   Solution-Wide Factors

The quality factors presented thus far apply to the components of integration. A holistic view of the integration solution's quality needs to consider solution-wide factors as well. Integration solutions typically accompany wider efforts of organizational integration. Therefore, solution-wide factors need to adopt an organizational perspective on quality. The work presented in [25] identifies four groups of integration success factors that relate to business, organization, technology, and project areas. The factors cover diverse issues such as the integration strategy, management support, cultural fit, use of appropriate, current, and mature technologies, and project planning and monitoring. Added value represents the most important solution-wide factor, describing the value that the organization gains from developing and using the integration solution [10]. Added value is also called net benefits [38], and refers to the perceived value when the solution's quality is reviewed during design and development.

Addressing quality issues that holistically affect the solution can contribute to better alignment between the organizational goals of integration and the developed solution. Furthermore, it is necessary to consider solution-wide factors alongside the factors discussed in the previous sections. However, the solution-wide factors reside on a high level of abstraction, making it hard to measure the extent of their fulfilment. A mechanism is needed to relate the solution-wide factors to the design details of the solution. The following section proposes using a quality model to describe quality factors and their measurements, as well as capturing their relationships to to other components of the integration design.

Calculating measurements for solution-wide quality factors is a complex task. Suitable frameworks need to be identified and used, including guidelines for how the measurements can be calculated. These organizational quality factors are affected by the factors discussed in previous sections. Further investigation is necessary to understand the relationships between the factors and reveal how they influence each other.

5 A Model for Designing Integration Quality Factors

A quality model is proposed in this section to support the formal definition of quality factors. The quality model is defined as an extension to the Unifying Meta-Model (UMM) for enterprise and systems design [46]. The UMM is comprised of complementary views that capture organizational and systems design knowledge. The views cover organizational goals, concepts, business processes, and IS architecture, thereby providing a holistic view of the organization and bridging the gap between enterprise models and system design models. Figure 2 illustrates the views that comprise the UMM, including the newly added *Integration Quality View*.

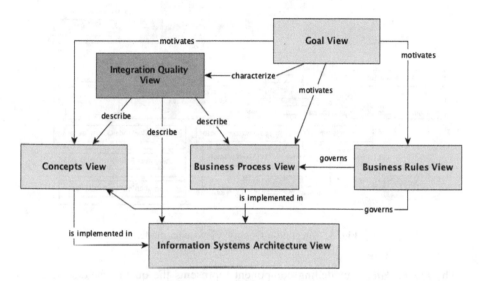

Fig. 2. Overview of the Unifying meta-model.

Inside each view's meta-model (c.f. [46] for details), relationships are defined as top-level modelling components, i.e. as classes in the meta-model. Relationship are either intra-model, i.e. associating modelling components within a single view, or inter-model, i.e. crossing over view boundaries to associate components from different views and guarantee that traceability is inherently built into the meta-model. Relationships in Fig. 2 are coarse representations of inter-model relationships between the modelling components of the views.

Defining the quality model as a view of the UMM enables associating the quality factors to other components of the integration design, as described using the remaining views of the UMM. The newly added quality factors are associated with modelling components from existing views with the help of inter-model relationships. This positions the integrated systems within the scope of organizational design. After all, an integration solution needs to be consistent globally with the overall organizational design and serve the organizational goals [12] in order to provide added value to the organization. The details of the meta-model of the Integration Quality View are illustrated in Fig. 3. The meta-model uses MOF notation [35], which closely resembles UML's class diagram notation. The little arrows on some modelling components indicate that the component is defined in another view of the UMM. Red boxes in Fig. 3 describe intra-model relationships, and blue boxes describe inter-model relationships.

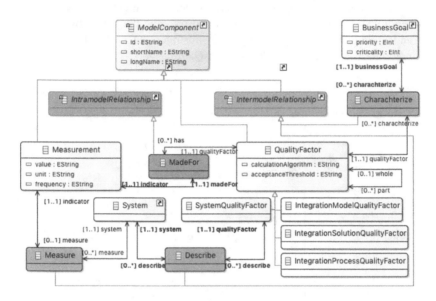

Fig. 3. Integration Quality View meta-model.

The *QualityFactor* modelling component represents the quality factors discussed thus far. It also represents any custom, project-specific factors. The wide scope of the quality factors makes it difficult to prescribe a uniform set of measurements for estimating the values of all factors. The integration designer must select a suitable evaluation framework to apply. However, the Integration Quality View enables the definition of desired *Measurements*. The *MadeFor* intra-model relationship illustrates how a quality factors can have multiple measurements, while a Measurement can participate in the measuring of one quality factor. Furthermore, The *calculationAlgorithm* and *acceptanceThreshold* attributes of QualityFactor pertain to the qualitative and diverse nature of the factors. They are used to document the algorithm for acquiring a value for the factor, and the acceptable value or range, respectively.

Business goals, defined in the UMM as part of the Goals View, guide the selection of relevant quality factors. They also guide the selection of appropriate measurements for the factors at different stages of the integration design. *BusinessGoal* is therefore associated to QualityFactor using the *Characterize* inter-model relationship.

SystemQualityFactor represents the quality factors that describe a candidate IS for integration (see Sect. 4.1). It is associated to *System*, which is defined in the UMM as part of the Information Systems Architecture View, using the *Describe* inter-model relationship. Furthermore, Measurements that are made for a SystemQualityFactor are associated with the specific System they measure, using the *Measure* relationship. Each candidate IS has its own SystemQualityFactors and related Measurements. The integration designer may choose from the factors described in Sect. 4.1, or define custom ones that are required by the project at hand. The measurements are calculated while the solution is being designed.

The modelling components *IntegrationModelQualityFactor*, *IntegrationProcessQualityFactor*, and *IntegrationSolutionQualityFactor* represent the factors related to integration models (Sect. 4.2), integration process (Sect. 4.3), and entire solution (Sect. 4.4), respectively. These three types of factors affect the quality of the integration solution differently from SystemQualityFactor. They are not associated with specific modelling components in an integration design, but rather denote qualities of the whole integration design and the resulting integration solution.

5.1 Example Business Case

This section demonstrates the use and utility of the integration quality model for describing quality of an example integration case. Demonstration is a first step of evaluation in DS research [37]. It serves to evaluate one traversal of the design cycle in the larger research context. The newly added Integration Quality View is instantiated with the help of a prototype UMM tool [45], which is developed in Eclipse [39]. The tool relies on the Eclipse Modelling Framework (EMF), an Eclipse plugin that implements the MOF standard [35] and supports the definition of MOF-based meta-models. The tool also relies on the Graphical Modelling Project (GMP), another Eclipse plugin that supports creating graphical interfaces for graphically designing instance models of the UMM.

The scenario of the example case describes an international aid organization that is looking to improve its public perception in order to increase its funds, a large part of which comes from public donations. Therefore, the organization is looking to develop an integration solution that monitors its online social presence, consolidates data from different social media platforms, and generates summaries and reports. The online social presence is described as the mentions (e.g. likes, tags) of the organization's name or projects. Analysis of the collected data is done using a cloud-based service.

The UMM is used to design the integration solution. The focus of this example is on using the Integration Quality View for capturing and measuring the quality of the solution during design. Other parts of the design model of the solution are omitted.

Figure 4 illustrates an instance model of the Integration Quality View. The candidate systems for integration, i.e. the social media platforms and the cloud-based analysis service, are associated with relevant quality factors. "Freshness", "Price", and "Data Completeness" are system quality factors that describe the Twitter social media platform [40]. "Freshness" and "Price" also describe another candidate system for integration, namely Instagram [20], however using different instances of the factors. The model describes how AnalyzeThis, the cloud-based service, is described by the "Accuracy" quality factor. The quality factors are selected by the integration designer, who deems them suitable for the respective system.

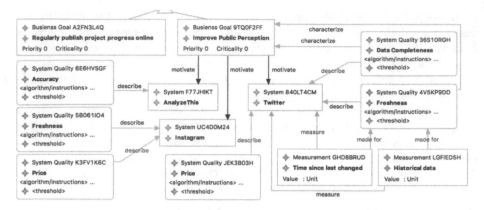

Fig. 4. Part of the design model (UMM instance model) of the integration solution for an international aid organization, focusing on quality factors of the candidate systems.

"Freshness" of Twitter is measured with the help of two measurements: "time since last changed" describes the intervals at which Twitter can provide the data, and "historical data" refers to Twitter's ability to provide historical usage data. The two measurements rely on different value ranges and unit types. Furthermore, "Freshness" of Instagram may rely on different measurements than those applicable to Twitter. Similarly to the quality factors, the integration designer identifies and creates the necessary measurements for each factor. The calculationAlgorithm attribute of quality factors, represented graphically as "algorithm/instructions", is used for describing how the factor's measurements can be consolidated. The algorithm may also cover how different factors affect each other. The integration designer is able to rely on a quality framework, e.g. the freshness framework described in [5], to describe the algorithms.

Acquiring values for the measurements enables the identification of problems attributed to quality factors. The proposed quality model allows the integration designer to register values for the measurements. However, measuring the values themselves lies outside the scope of the model, and the integration designer needs to identify the suitable means for acquiring the measurements. The "threshold" attribute of the factor for which the measurements can help determine whether a system fulfils acceptable quality requirements. The model supports a scenario where the measurements of the quality factors of Twitter are found to be below the acceptable threshold. In such cases, the integration designer is able to find an alternative platform that provides higher quality while the solution is under development. Similarly, the cloud-based analysis service may turn out to be unsuitable for the fulfilment of the integration goals, prompting the designer to replace it with an alternative service of higher accuracy. Design decisions are thereby informed by the quality of the integrated systems.

6 Conclusion

This paper presents a set of quality factors pertinent to designing and maintaining IS integration solutions, which are a contemporary trend as more information systems are built based on the principle of integrating existing IS. The study of quality in the context of IS integration, however, is fragmented and lacks the necessary holistic view. It remains dispersed in studies concerning the quality of models, processes, modelling, and systems. Integration-specific quality factors are under-studied. The proposed set of quality factors is elicited and reviewed with the help of feedback from domain experts. The effects of each factor on integration design are discussed.

The paper also presents a quality model that can be used to describe the quality of the integration design. The quality model extends the UMM with a new view, called the Integration Quality View, to enable the quality factors to be systematically associated with the components of the integration design. The model captures measurements for the factors to facilitate identifying quality problems, and the integration designer is able to mitigate them while the solution is under development.

The particular focus of this paper has been the quality of IS integration. Other quality factors that are generally applicable to IS or that target specific domains (e.g. model quality or service quality) are omitted from the proposed list, notwithstanding their importance. Integration designers should have the ability to define new factors deemed necessary in a given project, as well as the ability to reuse factors that proved useful in previous projects. The proposed quality model facilitates defining custom qualities. Work is planned to extend the tool prototype with a repository of quality factors to provide reuse capabilities.

The quality factors discussed herein form the basis for devising methodological guidelines for the design and development of integration solutions. The methodology can explain how and when the factors should be defined, how they affect each other, and how to rectify any quality problems that are identified. Furthermore, the methodology can aid in systematically identifying suitable measurements or choosing a quality framework. This is especially important considering how the same quality factor may be measured differently when describing different systems, as demonstrated in the previous section. For example, when a candidate system is a service, applicable Quality of Service models [23] may cover some of the integration quality factors.

References

1. Ardagna, D., Pernici, B.: Adaptive service composition in flexible processes. IEEE Trans. Softw. Eng. **33**(6), 369–384 (2007)
2. Batini, C., Cappiello, C., Francalanci, C., Maurino, A.: Methodologies for data quality assessment and improvement. ACM Comput. Surv. (CSUR) **41**(3), 16 (2009)
3. Bass, L., Clements, P., Kazman, R.: Understanding quality attributes. In: Software Architecture in Practice, 3rd edn. SEI Series in Software Engineering, pp. 63–78. Addison-Wesley (2013)

4. Bianchi, T., Santos, D.S., Felizardo, K.R.: Quality attributes of systems-of-systems: a systematic literature review. In: Proceedings of the Third International Workshop on Software Engineering for Systems-of-Systems, pp. 23–30. IEEE Press, Piscataway (2015)
5. Bouzeghoub, M.: A framework for analysis of data freshness. In: Proceedings of the 2004 International Workshop on Information Quality in Information Systems, pp. 59–67. ACM, New York (2004)
6. Camp, R.C.: Benchmarking: The Search for Industry Best Practices that Lead to Superior Performance. Quality Press, Welshpool (1989)
7. Capilla, R., Babar, M.A., Pastor, O.: Quality requirements engineering for systems and software architecting: methods, approaches, and tools. Requir. Eng. **17**(4), 255–258 (2012)
8. Cappiello, C., Caro, A., Rodriguez, A., Caballero, I.: An approach to design business processes addressing data quality issues. In: Proceedings of the 21st European Conference on Information Systems, paper 216 (2013)
9. Cardoso, J., Sheth, A., Miller, J., Arnold, J., Kochut, K.: Quality of service for workflows and web service processes. Web Semant.: Sci. Serv. Agents World Wide Web **1**(3), 281–308 (2004)
10. Chapman, C.S., Kihn, L.A.: Information system integration, enabling control and performance. Account. Organ. Soc. **34**(2), 151–169 (2009)
11. Chauhan, M.A., Babar, M.A.: Migrating service-oriented system to cloud computing: an experience report. In: IEEE International Conference on Cloud Computing (CLOUD), pp. 404–411. IEEE (2011)
12. Chen, D., Doumeingts, G., Vernadat, F.: Architectures for enterprise integration and interoperability: past, present and future. Comput. Ind. **59**(7), 647–659 (2008)
13. Chowanetz, M., Legner, C., Thiesse, F.: Integration: an omitted variable in information systems research. In: Proceedings of the 20th European Conference on Information Systems, paper 227 (2012)
14. Chung, L., Nixon, B.A., Yu, E., Mylopoulos, J.: The NFR framework in action. In: Basili, V.R. (ed.) Non-Functional Requirements in Software Engineering. International Series in Software Engineering, vol. 5, pp. 15–45. Springer, Heidelberg (2000). doi:10.1007/978-1-4615-52 69-7_2
15. Dustdar, S., Pichler, R., Savenkov, V., Truong, H.L.: Quality-aware service-oriented data integration: requirements, state of the art and open challenges. ACM SIGMOD Rec. **41**(1), 11–19 (2012)
16. Engelsman, W., Wieringa, R.: Understandability of goal-oriented requirements engineering concepts for enterprise architects. In: Jarke, M., Mylopoulos, J., Quix, C., Rolland, C., Manolopoulos, Y., Mouratidis, H., Horkoff, J. (eds.) CAiSE 2014. LNCS, vol. 8484, pp. 105–119. Springer, Cham (2014). doi:10.1007/978-3-319-07881-6_8
17. Genon, N., Heymans, P., Amyot, D.: Analysing the cognitive effectiveness of the bpmn 2.0 visual notation. In: Malloy, B., Staab, S., Brand, M. (eds.) SLE 2010. LNCS, vol. 6563, pp. 377–396. Springer, Heidelberg (2011). doi:10.1007/978-3-642-19440-5_25
18. Gharib, M., Giorgini, P., Mylopoulos, J.: Analysis of information quality requirements in business processes, revisited. Requir. Eng. 1–23 (2016)
19. Green, P., Rosemann, M.: An ontological analysis of integrated process modelling. In: Jarke, M., Oberweis, A. (eds.) CAiSE 1999. LNCS, vol. 1626, pp. 225–240. Springer, Heidelberg (1999). doi:10.1007/3-540-48738-7_17
20. Instagram Developer API. https://www.instagram.com/developer/
21. Kaplan, R.S., Norton, D.P.: The balanced scorecard: measures that drive performance. Harv. Bus. Rev. **70**(1), 71–79 (1992)

22. Kazman, R., Klein, M., Clements, P.: ATAM: method for architecture evaluation. Technical report, no. CMU/SEI-2000-TR-004. Software Engineering Institute, Carnegie-Mellon University, Pittsburgh, PA (2000)
23. Kritikos, K., Pernici, B., Plebani, P., Cappiello, C., Comuzzi, M., Benrernou, S., Brandic, I., Kertész, A., Parkin, M., Carro, M.: A survey on service quality description. ASM Comput. Surv. **46**(1), Article 1 (2013)
24. Krogstie, J.: Model-Based Development and Evolution of Information Systems: A Quality Approach. Springer, London (2012)
25. Lam, W.: Investigating success factors in enterprise application integration: a case-driven analysis. Eur. J. Inf. Syst. **14**(2), 175–187 (2005)
26. Lemos, A.L., Daniel, F., Benatallah, B.: Web service composition: a survey of techniques and tools. ACM Comput. Surv. (CSUR) **48**(3), 33 (2016)
27. Lindland, O.I., Sindre, G., Solvberg, A.: Understanding quality in conceptual modeling. IEEE Softw. **11**(2), 42–49 (1994)
28. Lohrmann, M., Reichert, M.: Understanding business process quality. In: Glykas, M. (ed.) Business Process Management, SCI, vol. 444, pp. 41–73. Springer, Heidelberg (2013). doi:10.1007/978-3-642-28409-0_2
29. Moody, D.L., Shanks, G.G.: Improving the quality of data models: empirical validation of a quality management framework. Inf. Syst. **28**(6), 619–650 (2003)
30. Moody, D.L., Sindre, G., Brasethvik, T., Sølvberg, A.: Evaluating the quality of information models: empirical testing of a conceptual model quality framework. In: Proceedings of the 25th International Conference on Software Engineering, pp. 295–305. IEEE Computer Society, Washington (2003)
31. Naumann, F., Freytag, J.C., Leser, U.: Completeness of integrated information sources. Inf. Syst. **29**(7), 583–615 (2004)
32. Naumann, F., Leser, U., Freytag, J.C.: Quality-driven integration of heterogeneous information systems. In: Atkinson, M.P., Orlowska, M.E., Valduriez, P., Zdonik, S.B., Brodie, M.L. (eds.) VLDB 1999 Proceedings of the 25th International Conference on Very Large Data Bases, pp. 447–458. Morgan Kaufmann, San Francisco (1999)
33. Nelson, H.J., Poels, G., Genero, M., Piattini, M.: A conceptual modeling quality framework. Softw. Qual. J. **20**(1), 201–228 (2012)
34. O'Brien, L., Merson, P., Bass, L.: Quality attributes for service-oriented architectures. In: Proceedings of International Workshop on Systems Development in SOA Environments, p. 3. IEEE Computer Society, Washington (2007)
35. Object Management Group Inc.: OMG's MetaObject Facility. http://www.omg.org/mof/
36. Pautasso, C., Zimmermann, O., Leymann, F.: Restful web services vs. "big" web services: making the right architectural decision. In: Proceedings of the 17th International Conference on World Wide Web, pp. 805–814. ACM, New York (2008)
37. Peffers, K., Tuunanen, T., Rothernberger, M.A., Chattarjee, S.: A design science research methodology for information systems research. J. Manag. Inf. Syst. **24**(3), 45–77 (2007)
38. Petter, S., DeLone, W.H., McLean, E.R.: Information systems success: the quest for the independent variable. J. Manag. Inf. Syst. **29**(4), 7–62 (2013)
39. The Eclipse Foundation. https://eclipse.org/
40. Twitter Developer API. https://dev.twitter.com/rest/public
41. Vanderfeesten, I., Cardoso, J., Mendling, J., Reijers, H.A., van der Aalst, W.M.: Quality metrics for business process models. BPM Workflow Handb. **144**, 179–190 (2007)
42. Wand, Y., Weber, R.: An ontological model of an information system. IEEE Trans. Softw. Eng. **16**(11), 1282–1292 (1990)
43. Yahia, E., Aubry, A., Panetto, H.: Formal measures for semantic interoperability assessment in cooperative enterprise information systems. Comput. Ind. **63**(5), 443–457 (2012)

44. Zeng, L., Benatallah, B., Dumas, M., Kalagnanam, J., Sheng, Q.Z.: Quality driven web services composition. In: Proceedings of the 12th International Conference on World Wide Web, pp. 411–421. ACM, New York (2003)
45. Zikra, I.: Implementing the unifying meta-model for enterprise modeling and model-driven development: an experience report. In: Sandkuhl, K., Seigerroth, U., Stirna, J. (eds.) PoEM 2012. LNBIP, vol. 134, pp. 172–187. Springer, Heidelberg (2012). doi:10.1007/978-3-642-34549-4_13
46. Zikra, I., Stirna, J., Zdravkovic, J.: Bringing enterprise modeling closer to model-driven development. In: Johannesson, P., Krogstie, J., Opdahl, Andreas L. (eds.) PoEM 2011. LNBIP, vol. 92, pp. 268–282. Springer, Heidelberg (2011). doi:10.1007/978-3-642-24849-8_20

Business Process Management

Hybrid Weaving in Aspect Oriented Business Process Management

Amin Jalali[(✉)]

Department of Computer and Systems Sciences,
Stockholm University, Stockholm, Sweden
aj@dsv.su.se

Abstract. Business processes need to conform with many regulations. These regulations usually cross over many business processes, so a change in one regulation can affect many business processes. To apply such a change, the systems that support these processes need to be audited and changed accordingly. Aspect-Oriented Business Process Management is a paradigm that aims to solve this problem by encapsulating these regulations separately from the core process models. To enact these models, two approaches are defined, named static and dynamic weaving. These approaches support enactment of these models effectively, yet they cannot address the management of non-retroactive regulations effectively. This gap hinders the management of business processes in organizations. Therefore, this paper proposes a third approach called hybrid weaving to fill this gap. The operational semantics of this approach is defined formally, and it is verified using state space analysis technique. This approach enables management of retroactive and non-retroactive regulations by weaving them into core process models at configuration time and run time. The result also enabled us to distinguish a new sort of process flexibility that can be offered when managing business processes.

Keywords: Business process management · Aspect oriented · Weaving · Flexibility · Process versioning · Non-retroactive regulations

1 Introduction

Managing business processes is a challenge in organizations that aim to perform their activities in an effective and efficient way. Business processes usually need to comply with many regulations which are defined to ensure the compliance of processes with some laws. The regulations can be defined in two ways, i.e. (i) they should be applied for actions that will happen after the time of establishment (non-retroactively), or (ii) they should be applied for actions that also happen before the time of establishment (retroactively). The ex-post-facto law prohibits introducing retroactive regulations in many contexts, e.g. criminal, tax, etc. Thus, there are many regulations in businesses which should only be applied non-retroactively.

© Springer International Publishing AG 2017
B. Johansson et al. (Eds.): BIR 2017, LNBIP 295, pp. 63–78, 2017.
DOI: 10.1007/978-3-319-64930-6_5

Regulations in an organization usually cross over many business processes, so they have *cross-cutting* relations to process models [18]. A change in a regulation can affect many business processes, so the systems supporting the affected processes need to be audited and changed accordingly. Thus, managing these regulations is a challenge in organizations.

Aspect-Oriented Business Process Management (AOBPM) [18] is an area of research that aims to address this challenge by encapsulating these regulations. The retroactive regulations can be supported by an approach that enforces changing the behavior of process instances at runtime, known as *dynamic weaving* [22]. The non-retroactive regulations can be supported by an approach that weaves regulations and core process models into an integrated model, known as *static weaving* [17], so a new version of the process model can be used for new cases that should comply with non-retroactive regulations.

Although the weaving approaches in AOBPM support modeling and enactment of the regulations, they are not effective in managing business processes. The problem is that processes need to comply with many regulations, and we need to produce a new version for each process model for each new cases in order to comply with non-retroactive regulations. In this way, the configuration of the system is an ongoing activity in the organization that should be performed for each case, which is neither effective nor efficient for managing business processes.

Therefore, there is a need for a new approach that supports organizations to address this problem. Thus, this paper proposes a third approach called hybrid weaving to fill this gap. This approach is introduced as a new business process use case, and its operational semantics is defined formally. The formalization is implemented as a model in CPN Tools, and it is verified using state space analysis technique. The model can be used as a blueprint to extend the functionality of different business process management systems. This approach enables management of retroactive and non-retroactive regulations by weaving them into core process models at configuration time. Thus, it also enabled us to distinguish a new sort of process flexibility that can be offered when managing business processes.

The remainder of this paper is organized as follows. Section 2 introduces the problem using a motivating example. It also gives an overall picture of current approaches in an abstract level. Section 3 defines the hybrid weaving use case, the operational semantics and the summary of the analysis result. Section 4 extends the process flexibility taxonomy based on our result and discusses the related work. Finally, Sect. 5 concludes the paper and introduces future works.

2   Background

In this chapter, we explain basic terms and definition which are required to explain and discuss our approach. These terms will be explained through a motivating example.

2.1   Motivating Example

The left side of Fig. 1 illustrates the cross-cutting relations between several regulations and processes in a bank as a fictitious example. The vertical and horizontal rectangles show the regulations and core process models respectively. Regulation should be considered in a process model if it is visually crossed over the process models in this figure. For example, a regulation like security is applicable for all processes, while Anti-Money Laundering (AML) regulation is applicable for those in which the customer can deposit a large amount of money.

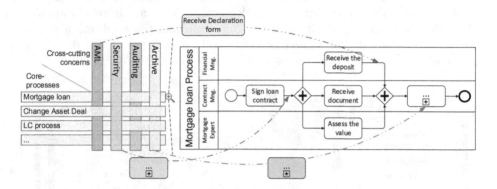

Fig. 1. The motivating example

The dependency between these regulations and processes depends on the law that defines such relation. For example, consider a new anti-money laundering regulation that enforces the bank to freeze large deposits of customers unless they fill the deposit declaration form. Such a regulation can affect many business processes in the bank including the mortgage loan process, LC process, etc., because a large deposit is usually required in these processes. The mortgage loan process requires complying with AML, Security and Archive regulations in our example. Each of these regulations mandates a set of activities to be performed in this process.

The mortgage loan process is shown in the right side of Fig. 1. This process starts when a contract manager signs a loan contract with a customer. This contract indicates the regulations that should be considered for each case, which will be signed by both the customer and the bank's employee. Then, the financial manager should receive the deposit from the customer. In parallel, two other activities need to be performed, i.e. contract manager needs to receive documents from the customer, and mortgage expert needs to assess the mortgage value. The rest of process is not depicted in details for the sake of simplicity.

Traditionally, all regulations should be captured by related process models, which results in scattering the realization of the regulations in many business process models. For example, the *receive declaration form* should not only be included in the *mortgage loan process* but also in other applicable processes.

The inclusion of this activity (as a realization of the regulation) results in the scattering problem.

Aspect-Oriented Business Process Modeling overcomes this problem by supporting separation of each concern [6,10,23]. This approach enables encapsulation of the regulations and enforces them in the relevant processes when they are needed.

Figure 2 shows an abstraction that explains how this approach supports this sort of encapsulation. Each core process is encapsulated by a process model called *core concern*, and each regulation is specified in a separate model *called advice*. The relation between these two models are specified by a third model *called pointcuts*. This is very effective modeling since a change in regulation will only affect its model. In addition, if the rule regarding the application of the regulation is changed, the related pointcut will be changed. Thus, it will be much easier to manage both processes and regulations in the bank.

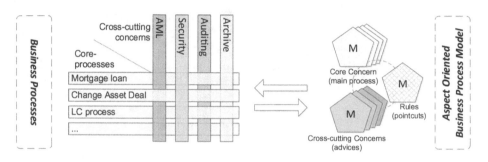

Fig. 2. Aspect oriented business process modelling, adopted from [18]

There are two approaches that support the enactment of aspect-oriented business process models, called static and dynamic weaving.

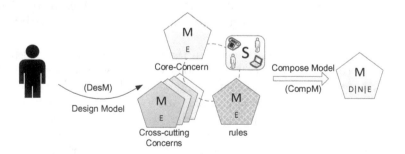

Fig. 3. The static weaving use case

In static weaving [17] (depicted in Fig. 3), all fragments of an aspect-oriented business process model that are designed by a process designer are composed together to produce a traditional model. Thus, it does not support the change in cross-cutting regulations or their rules at runtime. Neither does it support the adjustment of business processes to the new regulations at runtime. This technique can be used for introducing regulations that should be applied non-retroactively by producing new versions of a process model for each case, but it is not an efficient way since it put an ongoing configuration cost when enacting business processes. This means that the development team needs to constantly produce a new version for each process model for each case - which is not desirable nor practical. This technique is a kind of "composite model" use case [1], where a model is composed from several existing models.

In dynamic weaving [25] (depicted in Fig. 4), the Business Process Management Systems (BPMSs) should be aware of the semantics of these models [24], and it adapts the process instances at runtime by enforcing the execution of advice based on interpreting pointcuts [22]. Thus, it supports changing cross-cutting regulations or their rules at runtime. A change in regulations will be applied to all cases. This technique is a kind of "Adapt while running" use case [1], where the system knows the semantics of models to execute them correctly.

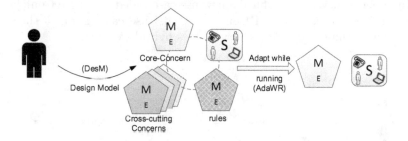

Fig. 4. The dynamic weaving use case

Although these two approaches can support different use cases, they cannot solve the problem of managing regulations that should be applied non-retroactively in an effective and efficient way.

For example, if we want to introduce the AML regulation in our example, these two approaches are not helpful. The static weaving cannot help since the development team should configure a new process model for each loan application, which is not feasible. Note that there are many regulations in real processes, and the process participants will not know about a change in regulations, so static weaving needs to be performed for every case to guarantee the conformance of processes to regulations. The dynamic weaving cannot help since the new AML regulation will be applied for all cases.

3   Approach

We propose a new approach in this section, called hybrid weaving, which can support management of regulations in business processes in an effective and efficient way. In this approach, we divide regulations which are a sort of cross-cutting concerns into two categories, non-retroactive and retroactive. Non-Retroactive cross-cutting concerns are those concerns which should not be applied to the cases that are created before introducing the concern. Retroactive cross-cutting concerns are those concerns which should be applied for all cases.

First, we explain our approach by introducing a business process use case for hybrid weaving. Then, we specify the formalization of the operational semantics of the systems that aim to support hybrid weaving to solve the problem.

3.1   The Hybrid Weaving Use Case

Hybrid weaving is a combination of both static and dynamic weaving that can address this gap. We introduce this approach as a business process use case by combining several use cases which are introduced by van der Aalst [1], i.e. Design Configurable Model, Configure Configurable Model and Adapt While Running use cases. We also defined a new use case called Compose Configurable Model which is an extension of Compose Model use case. Figure 5 shows the combination of these use cases, which enables hybrid weaving.

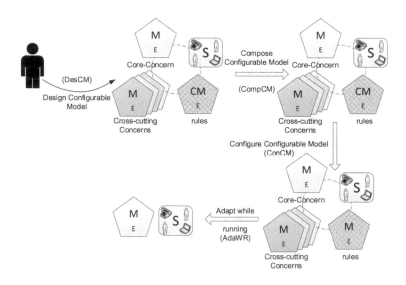

Fig. 5. The hybrid weaving use case

In the hybrid weaving use case, the process designer needs to define a configurable aspect-oriented business process model that distinguishes between retroactive and non-retroactive cross-cutting concerns (DesCM). As it can be seen in the figure, the pointcut needs to be configurable in these models. Then, the designed models can be composed into a new configurable model (CompCM) by the hybrid weaver. This is a new use case that we introduced since the static weaving needs to be done on a configurable version of aspect-oriented business process models and the result is still configurable. The result needs to be configurable since the pointcuts need to be configured and be associated with the new model in the next step (ConCM). Finally, the generated configured model will be used by a system which is aware of the semantics of dynamic weaving (AdaWR).

As it can be seen in the figure, the process is complex, and it needs to be formalized in order to investigate its soundness. The result can be used by different workflow management systems to extends their functionality. We will further explain these use cases when describing the operational semantics in this section.

3.2   The Operational Semantics

This section specifies the formalization of the operational semantics of hybrid weaving use case. The formalization can be used as a blueprint to implement these systems. In addition, it enables us to verify the solution to make sure it is sound. We used Coloured Petri Nets (CPN) [26] to formalize the semantics, because it is a widely-used formalization technique in system design and verification. This technique is also supported by a tool called CPN Tools that enables verification of the result through different technique [27]. This technique is also widely used in the domain of workflow management systems, e.g. Adams specifies the semantics of worklet service using Coloured Petri nets [3], or Jalali et al. define the formalization of dynamic weaving using Coloured Petri nets [24] which is later implemented and applied in a banking case [22,25].

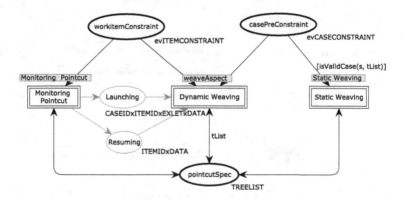

Fig. 6. The hybrid weaving net

Figure 6 shows the top net of the CPN model for Hybrid Weaving. It contains three subnets, called monitoring pointcuts, dynamic weaving and static weaving:

- Monitoring pointcut net is responsible for monitoring business process instances. A strong monitoring service needs to capture different business process perspectives [20].
- The dynamic weaving net is responsible for enforcing cross-cutting concerns at runtime. The dynamic weaving and monitoring nets define how the Adapt While Running (AdaWR) use case is defined in the hybrid weaving use case. The semantics is defined by Jalali et al. [24].
- The static weaving net is responsible for performing the Compose Configurable Model (CompCM) and Configure Configurable Model (ConCM) use cases.

The service starts when a case is created in the workflow management systems. For every case, the service will investigate if there is non-retroactive cross-cutting concern that should be weaved into the model. The detailed method which is defined as a model is explained bellow.

Compose Configurable Model

In this sub- use case, we need to compose a new model that composes non-retroactive advice with the core process specification in a new model.

To perform such operation, the system reacts for each instance of a business process model that is created as a case in the system. The creation of each case is recognized by an event represented as a token appears in the *casePreConstraint* place. The process is depicted in Fig. 7.

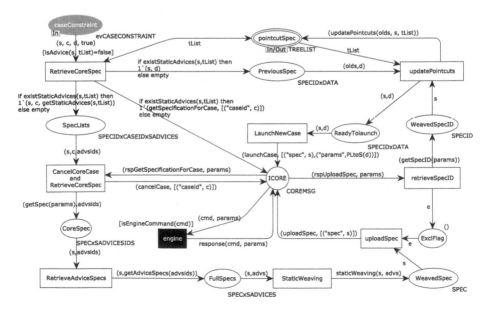

Fig. 7. The configuration steps in hybrid weaving

The service starts when an instance of a business process model is created in the system as a case. This service reads the pointcuts models and investigates if any non-retroactive advice is defined for this case. If no non-retroactive advice is related, then the service will not change the configurable model, and it can be enacted as a model with the help of dynamic weaving semantics, specified by Jalali et al. [24].

However, if some non-retroactive advice is defined for such a case, the service needs to retrieve the specification of process model from the server by sending a request. Note that the request is sent as a message through an channel called *ICore* in our model, and the response will be given from the same channel. Next, the system can cancel the initiated case. The cancellation cannot be performed at the first place since it might happen before retrieving the case specification due to concurrent nature of message passing with workflow management systems.

Then, the service needs to retrieve non-retroactive advice, and it should perform static weaving [17]. The result is a woven model as a new specification.

The system needs to upload the new specification, which is performed by the *uploadSpec* transition.

Configure Configurable Model
At this point, the retroactive advice is related to the previous process model. Thus, the system needs to configure pointcut model to be related to the new generated model. Thus, the system get the *ID* of uploaded specification using the *retrieveSpecID* transition. It will update the pointcut repository using the *updatePointcuts* transition.

Adapt While Running
At this point, all configuration is applied appropriately. Thus, the system will create a new instance of the new process model by *LaunchNewCase* transition. Note that the creation of such a case will raise a new case constraint event by the workflow management system. This event will make the service active again. However, it will skip the static weaving part since there is no non-retroactive advice related to the new case. Hence, the new case will only go through the dynamic weaving service [24], which handles the Adapt While Running sub- use case.

The result can enable management of both non-retroactive and retroactive cross-cutting concerns in an effective manner.

3.3 Analysis

The presented CPN model allows us to verify the design of our artifact using state space analysis technique. The verification is a complicated task due to the numerous types of advice and their possible combinations that may be triggered by an activity. We divide all the possible situations into three groups and define three abstract scenarios to characterize them.

We aimed to support both retroactive and non-retroactive advice using our approach. Therefore, these scenarios are defined to investigate the correctness of our approach:

These are the scenarios:

- Scenario 1: Introducing a non-retroactive advice for a business process model while some of its instances are currently executing.
- Scenario 2: Introducing a retroactive advice for a business process model while some of its instances are currently executing.
- Scenario 3: Introducing both a retroactive and a non-retroactive advice for a business process model while some of its instances are currently executing.

We applied the state space analysis technique to investigate if:

- In Scenario 1, the non-retroactive advice is only applied for new cases, and old cases are not affected.
- In Scenario 2, the retroactive advice is applied for both new and old cases.
- In Scenario 3, the non-retroactive advice is only applied for new cases, and old cases are not affected; while the retroactive advice is applied for both new and old cases.

The result shows that all these requirements are held by the model. In addition, the number of nodes and arcs for both State Space results and Strongly Connected Component (SCC) graphs are the same, which indicates the lack of cycle in our model. In each scenario, there is only one dead marking, which is equivalent to the home marking. This indicates that there is only one final state in this model from which no other states can be reached, which is the end marking. In addition, the reports state that there is no infinite occurrence sequences neither any live transition instances. The result of general state space analysis technique shows that our approach does not have any deadlock nor livelock, and the net will be properly ended.

4   Discussion and Relate Works

We discuss how our approach can help to extend the taxonomy of process flexibility in BPM in this section. We also discuss related work as well.

4.1   Discussion

This paper introduced a new business process use case that configures the process specification at runtime. It provides a unique sort of flexibility by altering process specification at both configuration and runtime. To position this sort of flexibility, we realized that flexibility in configuration time is not considered in the taxonomy of flexibility in BPM area [33]. Thus, we extend the taxonomy of process flexibility based on which we will discuss hybrid weaving.

The Taxonomy of Process Flexibility
Schonenberg et al. categorize process flexibilities into different types based on two criteria, i.e. (i) if the process specification is complete, and (ii) if the flexibility needs to be handled at design time or runtime [33].

Flexibility by design is a sort of flexibility where all deviations and possibilities of variations for a process instance is known by process designer and are incorporated in the process model at design time. In reality, it might be hard to know all possibilities beforehand. Workflow patterns [34] are examples of how this flexibility can be incorporated in a process model.

Flexibility by underspecification (late binding) is a sort of flexibility where the point of flexibility in process instances and the solutions are known by process designer at design time. This point is defined by a placeholder in process models which can be bound later to defined solutions.

Flexibility by underspecification - late modeling is a sort of flexibility where the point of flexibility in process instances are known by process designer at design time, but the solution is not completely known. The flexible point is defined by a placeholder in process models, and the solution can be later defined at runtime. Thus, it is called late modeling. Worklet selection service [3] is an example of flexibility by underspecification.

Flexibility by deviation & Flexibility by change are sorts of flexibility where the point of flexibility is not known by process designer at design time, so the process specifications are complete. These flexibilities are needed to be handled at runtime. If the flexibility is only limited to one process instance, it is known as flexibility by deviation. Otherwise, it is known as flexibility by change, where the flexibility will change the process specification. Worklet exception service [3] is an example of flexibility by deviation.

The Extension of Taxonomy of Process Flexibility

Figure 8 shows the extended version of taxonomy of process flexibility which is defined in [33]. In addition to design time and runtime for flexibility configuration, we also consider configuration time. Thus, two sorts of new flexibility can be defined.

- If the flexibility in a business process is configured in the configuration time and the process model is complete, it is called *flexibility by variation*.
- If the flexibility in a business process is configured in the configuration time and the process model is not complete, it is called *flexibility by underspecification - late configuration*.

Configurable process models [28] can be considered as an example of *flexibility by variation*. These models incorporate many alternations and variations of a family of a business process in one model, which can be configured to be suitable for one business process. To use these models, process admin can configure them before using them at runtime. They contain all alternations that can happen, so the process specification is complete, and they can be configured for different variations of a business process in different situations.

Theoretically, the underspecification can also be adjusted at configuration time, so it is feasible to consider *flexibility by underspecification - late configuration* as a type of process flexibility.

The Hybrid Weaver is a sort of combinations of *flexibility by underspecification - late configuring & binding*, *flexibility by deviation*, and *flexibility by variation*. It is a sort of *flexibility by underspecification - late configuring* because

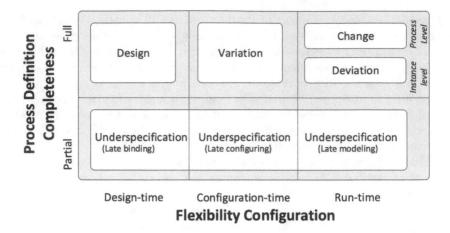

Fig. 8. The extended version of flexibility types in BPM

it produces pointcuts which configure placeholders of advice to core concerns at configuration time. It is a sort of *flexibility by underspecification - late binding* because it has a placeholder in advice which will be used to be bound at runtime to core processes. It is a sort of *flexibility by deviation* because it enforces enactment of advice by altering the behavior of core process instances. It is a sort of *flexibility by variation* because it configures the pointcuts at configuration time after performing the static weaving algorithm.

4.2 Related Work

In this section, we discuss related work. Different researchers proposed different approaches to supporting separation of cross-cutting concerns when management business processes. The idea is introduced to the BPM area based on the lesson learned by introducing aspect orientation to service composition [7–9]. To enable effective and efficient management, the management of business processes requires different sort of supports in different phases.

To support the design phase, the idea of aspect-oriented business process modeling is proposed by Charfi et al. [10] and Cappelli et al. [6]. Cappelli et al. [6] developed a tool to support modeling of such models, called CrossOryX, which is based on Oryx [11] framework. The definitions of aspect-oriented business process modeling are formalized by Jalali et al. [23]. These works focus on BPMN notation, which is an imperative business process modeling. Thereafter, Jalali et al. proposed two different approaches for declarative [19] and hybrid [21] aspect-oriented business process modeling.

In addition to these works, some researchers proposed some approaches to support the discovery of aspect-oriented business process models, e.g. [12–14, 31]. The list of some open issues in modeling aspect-oriented business process modeling is listed by Santos et al. [32]. Jalali proposed a framework that enables comparison of these approaches [16].

To support the analysis phase, Jalali formalizes the definition of aspect-oriented business process modeling using the Petri nets notation [17]. He also defined a static weaving algorithm that merges these models into a traditional process models. In this way, the traditional model can be analysed using existing analysis technique such as place invariants [36], transition invariants [30], reachability graph [29], Woflan [35], etc.

To support the configuration/implementation phase, Jalali et al. [24] defines the operational semantics of dynamic weaving using Coloured Petri Nets. This approach only supports definition and management of the retroactive cross-cutting concern. We extended this definition to support non-retroactive approaches in this paper.

To support the run/adjustment phase, Jalali et al. implemented a service in Yet Another Workflow Language (YAWL) [2], called Aspect Service [22,25]. They also explained how this approach could support agile business process development in organizations [4].

To support the data-based analysis phase, Jalali A. proposed an approach to do aspect mining in BPM [15]. The discovery part of the approach is further investigated by Brandão et al. to identify cross-cutting concerns automatically from event logs using cloning and clustering methods [5].

All of these approaches only focus on managing retroactive cross-cutting concerns, and they cannot handle non-retroactive ones. This work extends the area of Aspect-Oriented Business Process Management by defining a new approach to fill this gap.

5   Conclusion

In this paper, we proposed a new weaving approach to support management of non-retroactive and retroactive cross-cutting concerns in business process management. This approach is a combination of static and dynamic weaving approaches that support execution of aspect-oriented business process models, so it is called hybrid weaving. The approach is defined based on business process uses cases, and we formalized the operational semantics of this approach using Coloured Petri Nets. We developed the semantics using CPN Tools, which enabled us to verify the model by applying state-space analysis technique.

This approach also helped us to identify a gap in the taxonomy of process flexibility, so we extended this taxonomy by distinguishing the configuration time as another factor in supporting process flexibility. Then, we elaborated on how the hybrid approach can be position based on this taxonomy.

As future work, we aim to use this model as a blueprint for implementing a service in YAWL to support management of retroactive and non-retroactive regulations in the enactment phase. It is also interesting to investigate how non-retroactive concerns can be supported by other approaches in business process management like exception handling, process configuration, etc.

References

1. van der Aalst, W.M.P.: Business process management: a comprehensive survey. ISRN Softw. Eng. **2013**, 37 p. (2013). https://www.hindawi.com/journals/isrn/2013/507984/
2. van der Aalst, W.M.P., Aldred, L., Dumas, M., Hofstede, A.H.M.: Design and implementation of the YAWL system. In: Persson, A., Stirna, J. (eds.) CAiSE 2004. LNCS, vol. 3084, pp. 142–159. Springer, Heidelberg (2004). doi:10.1007/978-3-540-25975-6_12
3. Adams, M.J.: Facilitating dynamic flexibility and exception handling for workflows. Ph.D. thesis, Queensland University of Technology Brisbane, Australia (2007)
4. Bider, I., Jalali, A.: Agile business process development: why, how and when-applying Nonaka's theory of knowledge transformation to business process development. Inf. Syst. e-Bus. Manag. **14**(4), 1–39 (2014)
5. Brandão, B.C.P., Santoro, F., Azevedo, L.G.: Towards aspects identification in business process through process mining. In: Proceedings of the Annual Conference on Brazilian Symposium on Information Systems: Information Systems: A Computer Socio-Technical Perspective, vol. 1, p. 99. Brazilian Computer Society (2015)
6. Cappelli, C., Santoro, F., do Prado Leite, J., Batista, T., Medeiros, A., Romeiro, C.: Reflections on the modularity of business process models: the case for introducing the aspect-oriented paradigm. BPM J. **16**, 662–687 (2010)
7. Charfi, A.: Aspect-oriented workflow languages: AO4BPEL and applications. Ph.D. thesis, der Technischen Universitat Darmstadt, Darmstadt, November 2007
8. Charfi, A., Mezini, M.: Aspect-oriented web service composition with AO4BPEL. In: Zhang, L.-J., Jeckle, M. (eds.) ECOWS 2004. LNCS, vol. 3250, pp. 168–182. Springer, Heidelberg (2004). doi:10.1007/978-3-540-30209-4_13
9. Charfi, A., Mezini, M.: Ao4bpel: an aspect-oriented extension to BPEL. World Wide Web **10**(3), 309–344 (2007)
10. Charfi, A., Müller, H., Mezini, M.: Aspect-oriented business process modeling with AO4BPMN. In: Kühne, T., Selic, B., Gervais, M.-P., Terrier, F. (eds.) ECMFA 2010. LNCS, vol. 6138, pp. 48–61. Springer, Heidelberg (2010). doi:10.1007/978-3-642-13595-8_6
11. Decker, G., Overdick, H., Weske, M.: Oryx – an open modeling platform for the BPM community. In: Dumas, M., Reichert, M., Shan, M.-C. (eds.) BPM 2008. LNCS, vol. 5240, pp. 382–385. Springer, Heidelberg (2008). doi:10.1007/978-3-540-85758-7_29
12. Di Francescomarino, C., Tonella, P.: Crosscutting concern mining in business processes. Softw. IET **5**(6), 552–562 (2011)
13. Di Francescomarino, C., Tonella, P.: Crosscutting concern documentation by visual query of business processes. In: Ardagna, D., Mecella, M., Yang, J. (eds.) BPM 2008. LNBIP, vol. 17, pp. 18–31. Springer, Heidelberg (2009). doi:10.1007/978-3-642-00328-8_3
14. Ghidini, C., Di Francescomarino, C., Rospocher, M., Tonella, P., Serafini, L.: Semantics-based aspect-oriented management of exceptional flows in business processes. IEEE Trans. Syst. Man Cybern. Part C Appl. Rev. **42**(1), 25–37 (2012)
15. Jalali, A.: Aspect mining in business process management. In: Johansson, B., Andersson, B., Holmberg, N. (eds.) BIR 2014. LNBIP, vol. 194, pp. 246–260. Springer, Cham (2014). doi:10.1007/978-3-319-11370-8_18

16. Jalali, A.: Assessing aspect oriented approaches in business process management. In: Johansson, B., Andersson, B., Holmberg, N. (eds.) BIR 2014. LNBIP, vol. 194, pp. 231–245. Springer, Cham (2014). doi:10.1007/978-3-319-11370-8_17

17. Jalali, A.: Static weaving in aspect oriented business process management. In: Johannesson, P., Lee, M.L., Liddle, S.W., Opdahl, A.L., López, Ó.P. (eds.) ER 2015. LNCS, vol. 9381, pp. 548–557. Springer, Cham (2015). doi:10.1007/978-3-319-25264-3_41

18. Jalali, A.: Aspect-oriented business process management. Ph.D. thesis, Department of Computer and Systems Sciences, Stockholm University, December 2016

19. Jalali, A., Bider, I.: Towards aspect oriented adaptive case management. In: 2014 IEEE 18th International Enterprise Distributed Object Computing Conference Workshops and Demonstrations (EDOCW), pp. 143–151, September 2014

20. Jalali, A., Johannesson, P.: Multi-perspective business process monitoring. In: Nurcan, S., Proper, H.A., Soffer, P., Krogstie, J., Schmidt, R., Halpin, T., Bider, I. (eds.) BPMDS/EMMSAD -2013. LNBIP, vol. 147, pp. 199–213. Springer, Heidelberg (2013). doi:10.1007/978-3-642-38484-4_15

21. Jalali, A., Maggi, F.M., Reijers, H.A.: Enhancing aspect-oriented business process modeling with declarative rules. In: Johannesson, P., Lee, M.L., Liddle, S.W., Opdahl, A.L., López, Ó.P. (eds.) ER 2015. LNCS, vol. 9381, pp. 108–115. Springer, Cham (2015). doi:10.1007/978-3-319-25264-3_8

22. Jalali, A., Ouyang, C., Wohed, P., Johannesson, P.: Supporting aspect orientation in business process management. Softw. Syst. Model. **16**(3), 1–23 (2015)

23. Jalali, A., Wohed, P., Ouyang, C.: Aspect oriented business process modelling with precedence. In: Mendling, J., Weidlich, M. (eds.) BPMN 2012. LNBIP, vol. 125, pp. 23–37. Springer, Heidelberg (2012). doi:10.1007/978-3-642-33155-8_3

24. Jalali, A., Wohed, P., Ouyang, C.: Operational semantics of aspects in business process management. In: Herrero, P., Panetto, H., Meersman, R., Dillon, T. (eds.) OTM 2012. LNCS, vol. 7567, pp. 649–653. Springer, Heidelberg (2012). doi:10.1007/978-3-642-33618-8_85

25. Jalali, A., Wohed, P., Ouyang, C., Johannesson, P.: Dynamic weaving in aspect oriented business process management. In: Meersman, R., Panetto, H., Dillon, T., Eder, J., Bellahsene, Z., Ritter, N., Leenheer, P., Dou, D. (eds.) OTM 2013. LNCS, vol. 8185, pp. 2–20. Springer, Heidelberg (2013). doi:10.1007/978-3-642-41030-7_2

26. Jensen, K.: Coloured petri nets. In: Brauer, W., Reisig, W., Rozenberg, G. (eds.) Petri Nets: Central Models and Their Properties. LNCS, vol. 254, pp. 248–299. Springer, Heidelberg (1987). doi:10.1007/BFb0046842

27. Jensen, K., Kristensen, L.M., Wells, L.: Coloured petri nets and CPN tools for modelling and validation of concurrent systems. Int. J. Softw. Tools Technol. Transfer **9**(3–4), 213–254 (2007)

28. La Rosa, M.: Managing variability in process-aware information systems. Ph.D. thesis, Queensland University of Technology Brisbane, Australia (2009)

29. Murata, T.: Petri nets: properties, analysis and applications. Proc. IEEE **77**(4), 541–580 (1989)

30. Reisig, W.: Petri Nets: An Introduction. Monographs in Theoretical Computer Science. An EATCS Series, vol. 4. Springer, Heidelberg (1985)

31. Santos, F., Cappelli, C., Santoro, F., do Prado Leite, J., Batista, T.: Analysis of heuristics to identify crosscutting concerns in business process models. In: Proceedings of the 27th Annual ACM Symposium on Applied Computing, SAC 2012, pp. 1725–1726. ACM, New York (2012)

32. Santos, F., Cappelli, C., Santoro, F., do Prado Leite, J., Batista, T.: Aspect-oriented business process modeling: analyzing open issues. Bus. Process Manag. J. **18**(6), 964–991 (2012)
33. Schonenberg, H., Mans, R., Russell, N., Mulyar, N., van der Aalst, W.M.P.: Towards a taxonomy of process flexibility. In: CAiSE Forum, vol. 344, pp. 81–84 (2008)
34. van der Aalst, W.M.P., Ter Hofstede, A.H., Kiepuszewski, B., Barros, A.P.: Workflow patterns. Distrib. Parallel Databases **14**(1), 5–51 (2003)
35. Verbeek, H.M., Basten, T., van der Aalst, W.M.P.: Diagnosing workflow processes using Woflan. Comput. J. **44**(4), 246–279 (2001)
36. Yamalidou, K., Moody, J., Lemmon, M., Antsaklis, P.: Feedback control of petri nets based on place invariants. Automatica **32**(1), 15–28 (1996)

Business Processes Modelling Assistance by Recommender Functionalities: A First Evaluation from Potential Users

Michael Fellmann[1]([⊠]), Novica Zarvić[2], and Oliver Thomas[2]

[1] Institute of Computer Science, University of Rostock, Rostock, Germany
michael.fellmann@uni-rostock.de
[2] Information Management and Information Systems Group,
Osnabrück University, Osnabrück, Germany
{novica.zarvic,oliver.thomas}@uni-osnabrueck.de

Abstract. Recommender systems are in widespread use in many areas, the most prominent being e-commerce solutions. In this contribution, we apply recommender functionalities to business process modelling (BPM) and investigate their potential to improve process modelling. To do so, we have implemented two prototypes. With the help of the prototype systems that have been demonstrated to and used by participants at a fair, we have conducted a first evaluation from potential users. Our results indicate that increased modelling speed is the most prominent advantage according to the participants' expectation and that recommender functionalities should be complemented by collaboration features.

Keywords: Recommender systems · Semantic Modelling · Process-oriented Information System · Empirical evaluation

1 Introduction

Recommender systems are generally characterized by the fact that they "generate meaningful recommendations to a collection of users" [14]. Such recommender functionalities are features that simplify and ease the work and interaction of a user with the system under consideration. They are "providing suggestions for items to be of use" and for "supporting their users in various decision-making processes" [20]. This is a very relevant issue in today's world and information society, because humans are often overwhelmed with the increasing amount of available information. Recommender functionality is for instance a well-known feature from search engines and/or market places on the internet (e.g. amazon.com), where online users are supported in dealing with the existing information overload.

However, recommender functionality is next to internet usage and electronic commerce also capable in supporting users in other fields of activities, like for example in the context of business process management (BPM). Organizations can benefit of using tools that are supporting the users, or more specifically the modellers of business processes. Such a support might help to more conveniently create models conforming

© Springer International Publishing AG 2017
B. Johansson et al. (Eds.): BIR 2017, LNBIP 295, pp. 79–92, 2017.
DOI: 10.1007/978-3-319-64930-6_6

to specified naming conventions and that stick to a well-defined abstraction level [4]. Regarding the former, terminological problems are amongst the main problems when using conceptual (process) models [24]. Regarding the latter, it might help to figure out where to start and stop modelling and on which abstraction level [25, 26].

The BPM market is estimated to have about four billion U.S. dollars volume in 2011 and is therefore considered to be a relevant market [18]. In more detail, Gartner [16] estimates the market for business process management platforms in 2015 to 2.7 billion U.S. dollars per year. The market for BPM systems with business process modelling and analysis functionality is estimated by Gartner to have a volume of 1.9 billion U.S. dollars [21]. In this paper we present a recommending-based BPM approach, which is supported by two prototypical tools. The SEMPHIS (Semantic Modelling of Process-oriented Information Systems) tools put recommender functionalities for modelling business processes into execution. More specifically, we are investigating the usefulness of our solution on the basis of a preliminary evaluation from potential users' responses and which is based on a recent survey. Hence, the goal of this article is to get first empirical evidence based on an estimation of how well the prototypes might be able to ease daily work of modellers in the BPM domain and what kind of additional functionalities would probably represent "a nice to have"-feature.

Our paper is structured as follows: the second section provides some important background information on recommender systems in general and on our prototypical solution in particular. Then, the third section briefly describes the research approach taken, before we present our evaluation results in Sect. 4. Section 5 outlines our future activities and research actions to be taken before we finally conclude our paper in Sect. 6.

2   Background Information

2.1   On Related Research Directions

The fundamental idea of our approach is to support the modeller with a recommendation feature that makes use of existing process knowledge. Therefore, research regarding modelling support leveraging knowledge representations in a broad sense is related to our work. Such research can be found in several areas.

Reference-based Model Construction. The construction of models leveraging existing models is focused in the area of reference modelling. New models are constructed by adapting existing models which may be selected from a reference model catalogue [6], a repository of process fragments [19], a community portal [8] or which may be included in a modelling tool such as the IT Infrastructure Library which is included in several modelling tools [11]. Although reuse is intended, recommendation features have not yet gained much attention in this research direction.

Reuse-based Model Construction. Reuse is recently discussed in BPM as a more holistic approach in comparison to reference modelling in the sense of spanning different abstraction levels from process oriented systems. IT-support plays a central role e.g. to assemble models [23], enable the reuse of best practice IT-processes [15] or manage extensions [1]. However, as in the Reference-based model construction area, approaches offering recommendations are rarely implemented since the attention is more geared towards reusing configuration knowledge and IT-assets attached to process definitions.

Query-based Support for Model Construction. Another field of research is concerned with finding models or model fragments which can be used to complete the model under construction. Koschmider [12] describes an approach and a tool to determine the similarity of the model currently under construction compared to models which already exist in a repository. In this approach, queries are generated "behind the scenes" in the tool which automatically translates the model under construction to a query against the repository. The described approach as well as other approaches based on query languages are invoked manually and tend to offer more coarse grained modelling support such as lists of ranked similar models.

Pattern-based Model Construction. Patterns originate from the discipline of architecture and have been introduced as analysis patterns in conceptual modelling by Fowler [7]. They represent knowledge in the form of abstract templates used to apply well-known solutions to similar problems. Up to now, research has mainly focused on pattern detection (e.g. [3, 13]), although a few approaches support modelling [22]. In comparison to other construction support techniques, patterns are more abstract in nature and usually require a thorough interpretation by the modeller, in contrast to element suggestions implemented by recommender systems.

2.2 On Recommender Systems

Since the early 1990s, recommender systems have been used to recommend items such as news group messages, videos or music to users based on their individual taste or preferences. Videos and e-commerce products are still the primary type of recommended items in the recommender systems research community due to the availability of huge data sets used for system comparisons [10]. In practice, the application of recommender systems extends well beyond these traditional areas and nowadays also encompasses domains such as travelling, accommodation or social networks. Predominant recommendation paradigms are collaborative filtering, content-based filtering, knowledge-based recommendation and hybrid approaches ([10], p. 81). Whereas collaborative filtering means that recommendations are based on the preferences of similar users, content-based recommendations are based on the properties of items. Knowledge-based approaches require some extra codified knowledge such as a product taxonomy in conjunction with recommendation rules.

In general, there is a plethora of approaches for combining these paradigms and calculating recommendations. There is no single superior approach for achieving best recommendations in all use cases. Rather, the quality and usefulness of the recommendations is highly dependent on the respective domain. It thus has to be evaluated for each use case separately. A further characteristic of recommender systems is that complex systems do not always perform better in evaluations than simpler systems. Combining several recommendation paradigms and performing complex (and computationally expensive) calculations may not automatically lead to better recommendations than e.g. simple top-k rating recommendations (see e.g. Jannach et al. [9], p. 207). Consequently, an incremental research approach in which at first a system is built which is improved according to empirical evaluations seems to be an adequate way to explore the use of recommender systems in BPM. We follow also such a research approach. Therefore, we have implemented a first recommendation tool combing item- and knowledge-based recommending augmented with implicit user rating.

2.3 Recommender Functions in the SEMPHIS-Project

Models of business processes are more important than ever as multiple objectives can be achieved by them: The documentation of the business processes, the optimization of these processes as well as the development, customization and integration of the involved IT systems. But process models are not easy to create. Especially for novice modellers, it is often difficult to maintain a uniform level of abstraction and to detect the relevant procedures without gaps. Therefore, in SEMPHIS an adaptive and intelligent modelling tool is developed, which simplifies and accelerates business process modelling via predefined semantic building blocks and patterns, which are offered to the user through an intuitive and easy to use assistant function. Specifically, we support the modeller in deciding which activity should be inserted next in the process model. This functionality has been implemented in two preliminary prototypes.

Firstly, a traditional modelling tool has been extended with modelling assistant allowing to refine model elements with more detailed information (see Fig. 1) [5]. To do this, the user can right-click on elements marked with an info-symbol, retrieve the detailed information and can insert this information automatically into the model.

However, the detailed information is fixed and can only slightly be modified e.g. by omitting elements from insertion. Therefore we plan to design and implement a more advanced recommender functionality that offers a ranked list of model element suggestions. Thus, a prototype of this recommender service is already implemented as a web-based prototype (see Fig. 2). It offers the user suggestions which are ranked according to the industry (e.g. health or automotive), the process category (e.g. sales or production) and in particular with the frequency with which suggestions have actually been inserted into the model during past modelling activities of the user.

Using the parameters described, which can be weighted according to the user preferences, it is possible to adapt the guidance in process modelling according to different requirements. This, in turn, calls for empirical investigation since the established parameters and their weight cannot be determined using existing theories of business process modelling. Therefore we are gathering first feedback from potential users and experts in order to validate our assumptions and design choices.

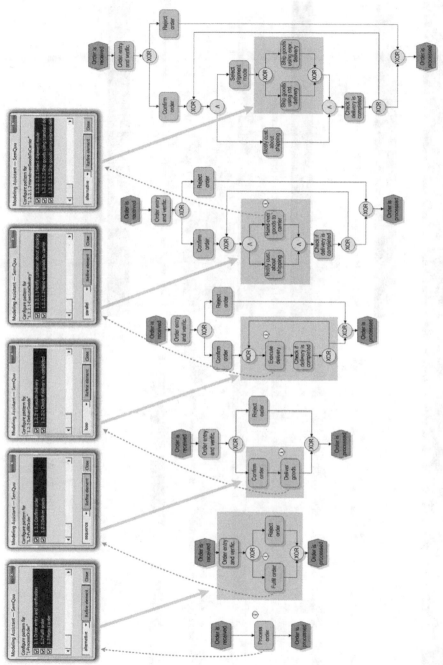

Fig. 1. Extension of a modelling tool (Microsoft Visio) with a modelling assistant feature

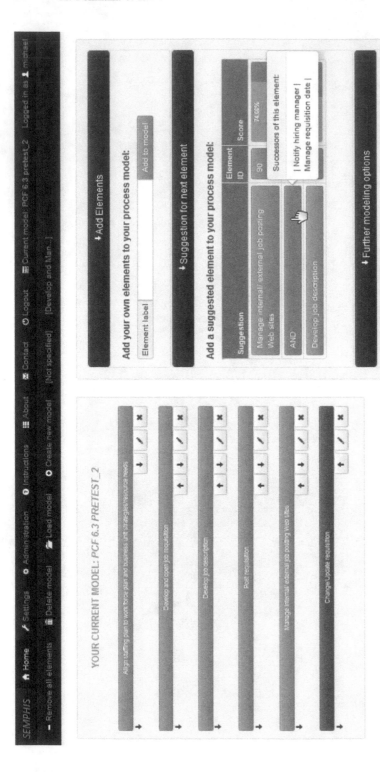

Fig. 2. Web-based recommender demo for business process modelling

3   Research Process

To get a first feedback, we have prepared a questionnaire for gathering empirical evidence on those issues that seem to be relevant in the current stage of our prototypical SEMPHIS solutions. We considered several options of how to perform the data collection that is needed in this context, most notably sending the questionnaire or demonstrating the prototype followed by a survey. We opted for the latter strategy since first, we aimed at presenting the interviewees the SEMPHIS prototypes personally in order to get a richer and more immediate feedback. Such a presentation would not be possible, when sending the questionnaires to potential interviewees via mailing lists or via ordinary post. We believe that live-demonstrations with interactive discussions lead to a better understanding and to qualitative responses. Moreover, and as far as the tools are currently not publically available, we wanted to give the interviewees after our presentation also the chance to try our tools out. Secondly, convenience sampling – as performed in this study – is especially suited for preliminary studies concerning e.g. pilot testing [2]. It belongs to the group of non- probability sampling and is a sampling technique where the samples are gathered in a process that does not give all the individuals in the population equal chances of being selected [17]. Therefore, it is also considered to be not generalizable [2]. Nonetheless, we are of the opinion that it might be useful for getting first feedback at an early stage.

Fig. 3.   Research process

The applied sequential research process is depicted in Fig. 3 above and consists of five major activities. The first activity implied the creation of the questionnaire (1) The questionnaire itself was organised in three parts: (a) personal information about the interviewees, (b) evaluation of the functionalities presented, and (c) gathering additional requirements that seem to be useful for being additionally implemented. The next activity implied the presentation of the exhibit (2) at the world's leading high-tech event CeBIT[1] in Hannover, Germany, where interested fairgoers where recruited and the filled-out forms (3) have been collected again. The analysis of the responses (4) took place at our university and the results (5) are presented in detail in the following section. Note that as part of another work, a very high-level overview of some selected results has already been described in [4, 27] as part of a triangulation strategy, but neither at the level of detail provided in this work nor to the extent and depth provided in the paper at hand.

---

[1] See http://www.cebit.de/.

4 Evaluation Results

4.1 Information About the Interviewees

The first part of our survey dealt – as mentioned earlier – with personal information about the interviewees. The first goal of this part was to get an overview of the people that participated. The second goal was to eventually identify correlations with respect to the other parts of the survey by calculating correlation coefficients. We were able to attract 78 visitors in total and to present them our prototypical implementations. All 78 visitors have been asked to fill out our survey, of which 66 were willing to do so. Since the survey was the last step after our presentation, visitors not interested in process modelling already escaped our presentation before we could ask them to fill out the survey. Therefore, all visitors that finally filled out the survey had at least moderate knowledge on process management or process modelling.

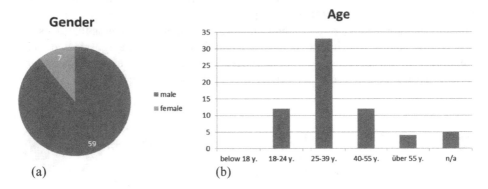

Fig. 4. Gender and age of the respondents

As can be seen from Fig. 4a above most of the respondents that were interested in the presentation of our prototypes were male visitors. This can probably be explained by the fact that we were presenting our exponate at a technology-intensive fair, which had also in past years a much higher percentage of male visitors[2]. It is also interesting to have a look at the age of the respondents. Figure 4b depicts that most respondents were between 25 and 39 years of age. The two categories 40–55 years and 18–24 years were represented equally by 12 respondents each. One can conclude from this data that most respondents have a relevant working age, including with the latter category also people that are up to finish their studies and to start their working career. This brings us to the following two criteria that have been analysed, namely the educational background and the working experience.

It can be seen from Fig. 5a that a high majority of 44 respondents have a university degree, accompanied by five PhDs. A university-entrance diploma was possessed by 12

---

[2] For instance, 90% of the fairgoers at CeBIT 2002 were male: http://www.zdnet.de/2106960/cebit-18-prozent-weniger-messebesucher-in-2002/ (accessed on 30.05.2017).

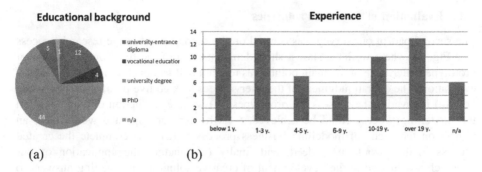

Fig. 5. Educational background and working experience of the respondents

respondents, which exactly corresponds to the category 18–24 years from Fig. 4b. Additionally only a small number of four people had no university education, but possess a vocational education. This information is quite relevant, because it shows that the high majority of respondents are highly educated and probably do have specific skills. By moving to the working experience expressed in years we can observe that 23 respondents have more than 4 years of working experience. However, we can see a similar number of people that have working experience of less than three years. In the following we are going to present two further criteria that were analysed in the first part of our survey: the type of industry and the size of the organisation/company where the respondents are affiliated with.

The most represented types of industry are information and communication technology (ICT) and research and education. There was also a big category that did not fit into one of the above industry types, as can be seen on the very right of Fig. 6a. The size of company/organisation showed that the biggest category is made up of so-called small and medium sized enterprises (SMEs). The rest of the respondents were affiliated to bigger companies and organisations.

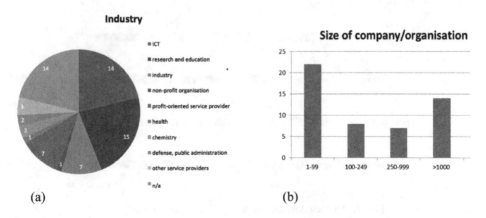

Fig. 6. Industry type and company/organization size of the respondents

4.2 Evaluation of Current Prototypes

The second part of our survey was centred on the second point in the research process (see Fig. 3), where we have shown short demonstration of the functionalities that our prototypes offer. One of the main points was to get a first feedback in form of a "light"-evaluation. The overall judgment of the interviewees tackled five points, namely to rate how (a) innovative they assess the prototypes, (b) whether reduction of complexity in the modelling process could be achieved, (c) whether our approach would have an impact on the speed of modelling business processes, (d) how complete the created process models would be indeed, and finally (e) whether the application of our approach would lead to the development of creative solutions. For getting answers to these points we applied a four-level Likert-like scale. A value of ++ is used to represent complete agreement whilst a value of −− is used to represent complete disagreement with the above mentioned points.

Figure 7 shows the results of the second part of our survey at a glance. It can be seen that all points were evaluated from a vast majority in a positive way. This provides us a first justification of our work. In particular the respondents had the highest consent on the increased speed (c), i.e. a faster creation of business process models, where only two respondents disagreed. As can be seen, a similar high affirmation holds for (e) the creation of innovative solutions, (b) the reduction of complexity while performing modelling tasks, and (a) the creation of innovative solutions. The highest number of disagreements can be observed with respect to (d) the complete-ness of the resulting business process models, where we have a two-digit number of disagreements. Many fairgoers stated that the completeness of the created models depends on the lexical knowledge in form of semantic building blocks and not on the prototypical solution itself. Additionally, to the analysis shown in Fig. 7, we also calculated correlations between the personal information of the respondents and the results of this subsection. Following correlations have been found (Table 1):

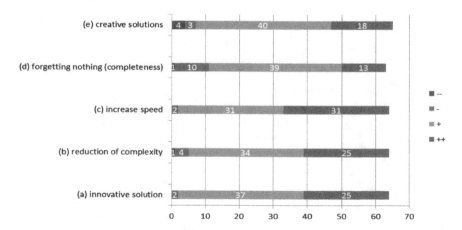

Fig. 7. Expected benefit of using recommender features

Table 1. Correlations between first and second part of survey responses.

Correlation 1	Male respondents thought that the solution is innovative (Correlation coefficient: *0,249**)
Correlation 2	Female respondents thought that the solution is not innovative (Correlation coefficient: *−0,249**)
Correlation 3	The respondents feel with increasing age and hence normally with increasing work experience that the solutions will not contribute to the reduction of complexity (Correlation coefficient: *−0,210**)
Correlation 4	Respondents affiliated to companies/organisations from 100–249 employees think that the resulting solutions are innovative (Correlation coefficient: *0,309**)
Correlation 5	Respondents affiliated to companies/organisations with more than 1000 employees think that the resulting solutions are not innovative (Correlation coefficient: *−0,236**)

*The correlation is significant at 0,05 levels (two-tailed).

4.3   Additional Requirements

The third part of our survey was concerned with the elicitation of (additional) requirements and needs that the fairgoers would like to see implemented in future. This is an important issue, because we want to respond adequately to the needs of potential users.

As can be seen from Fig. 8, the first question was concerned with the tool provision. A Software-as-a-Service (SaaS) solution is here on first place. Many respondents opted also for the installation on an own server in the firm or a pure desktop solution – mainly for reasons of security [4]. Another important question with respect to business process modelling is the provisioning of a collaboration function, which would enable the modellers to work from different places and probably at different times together in a project. This issue was desired by the vast majority of respondents, whereas nine respondents did not express such a desire.

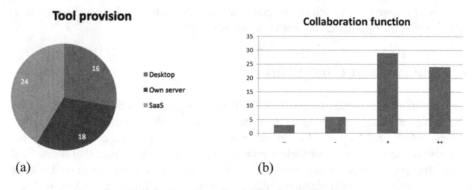

Fig. 8. Elicitation of (additional) requirements

The third part of the study was also accompanied by an open question section, where the respondents were able to express further requirements or comments. These requirements include for example to suggest next to the process steps also information objects and key performance indicators.

Additionally, we have also documented conversation contents. One important comment – raised by multiple fairgoers – was concerned with the applicability of the approach in different industries, because each industry has next to generally existent processes also its industry-specific processes.

5 Future Research

Regarding future research, we are especially interested in criteria like the influence of suggestions on the model quality and speed of model construction. We therefore plan to analyse data we collect in an experiment where the participants have to construct a model both with and without suggestions switched on. We then plan to compare the manually constructed models with the models constructed using our tool-based recommendations with each other and against a standard solution. Performing the comparisons, we intend to get sets of model elements that allow a more detailed analysis. A first set would be the elements included in the standard solution. A second set of elements would be those present in the model that has been manually constructed. A third set of elements is constituted by the elements included in the model constructed with recommendations. Using basic set operations such as union, intersection and complement, we can calculate interesting new sets out of the basic ones. An example for this is a set of elements that are present in the standard solution and in models that have been constructed using recommendations, but not in models constructed manually (recommendation gain). Further, the set of elements that are present in models that have been constructed using recommendations but that are not required according to the standard solution would be of interest (recommendation ballast). Comparing these sets as well as the required time for model construction and other metrics, such as syntax errors in the models, we plan to gain interesting insights on the impact of recommendations on process model construction regarding the quality of the result and time consumption. Finally, also the influence of the process type to be modelled (e.g. for which user category, at which abstraction level) as well as the modelling situation (e.g. reengineering or optimization) should be investigated.

6 Summary and Conclusions

Our preliminary analysis of recommender functionalities applied to BPM shows interesting results. Even though the results are not really generalizable and representable, because the interviewees have been chosen simply because it happened that they visited the fair, they nevertheless give first useful insights by potential users. First of all, the participants of our tool-demo, survey and discussions seem to be quite optimistic that tool-based recommendations during modelling can in fact increase modelling speed as well as reducing the complexity and fostering innovative process designs. Surprisingly, completeness of the models (i.e. not forgetting important elements) is not regarded as an area where improvements can be achieved. A reason for this lies in the nature of knowledge-based recommending approaches itself. The interviewees said that if the extra codified knowledge is not complete, then the resulting process model can also not be complete. Regarding the tool provision, the most voted option would be to provide the tool online as SaaS. Also, collaboration functions are considered important. Our analysis thus provides interesting insights into the expectations of potential customers and opens us many directions for future research (cf. Sect. 5).

Acknowledgements. The authors are thankful to the European Regional Development Fund (ERDF) for supporting the project SEMPHIS (Semantische Modellierung prozessorientierter Informationssysteme) under number ZW 6-80131109.

References

1. Balko, S., Ter Hofstede, A.H.M., Barros, A.P., La Rosa, M., Adams, M.J.: Business process extensibility. Enterp. Model. Inf. Syst. Archit. J. **5**(3), 4–23 (2010)
2. Boxill, I., Chambers, C.-M., Wint, E.: Introduction to Social Research: With Applications to the Caribbean. Canoe Press, University of the West Indies, Kingston (1997)
3. Delfmann, P., Herwig, S., Lis, L., Stein, A.: Pattern matching in conceptual models – a formal multi-modelling language approach. In: Mendling, J., Rinderle-Ma, S., Esswein, W. (eds.) Proceedings of the 3rd International Workshop Enterprise Modelling and Information Systems Architectures (EMISA 2009), 10–11 September, Ulm, Germany, pp. 13–27 (2009)
4. Fellmann, M., Zarvic, N., Metzger, D., Koschmider, A.: Requirements catalog for business process modeling recommender systems. In: Thomas, O., Teuteberg, F. (eds.) Proceedings of Wirtschaftsinformatik (WI 2015), 4–6 March, Osnabrück, Germany (2015)
5. Fellmann, M., Thomas, O.: Process model verification with SemQuu. In: Nüttgens, M., Thomas, O., Weber, B. (eds.) Enterprise Modelling and Information Systems Architectures (EMISA 2011), Hamburg, Germany, 22–23 September 2011, pp. 231–236 Bonn: Köllen (2011). (GI LNI, P-190)
6. Fettke, P., Loos, P.: Methoden zur Wiederverwendung von Referenz-modellen – Übersicht und Taxonomie. In: Becker, J., Knackstedt, R. (eds.) Arbeitsberichte Nr. 90, Institut für Wirtschaftsinformatik, Westfälische Wilhelms-Universität Münster (2002)
7. Fowler, M.: Analysis Patterns: Reusable Object Models. Addison-Wesley Longman, Amsterdam (1996)
8. Frank, U., Strecker, S., Koch, S.: "Open Model" – ein Vorschlag für ein Forschungsprogramm der Wirtschaftsinformatik. In: Oberweis, A., et al. (eds.) Proceedings of 8th International Tagung Wirtschaftsinformatik (WI 2007), Karlsruhe, Germany, vol. 2, pp. 217–234 (2007)
9. Jannach, D., Zanker, M., Felfernig, A., Friedrich, G.: Recommender Systems – An Introduction. Cambridge University Press, Cambridge (2011)
10. Jannach, D., Zanker, M., Ge, M., Gröning, M.: Recommender systems in computer science and information systems – a landscape of research. In: Huemer, C., Lops, P. (eds.) EC-Web 2012. LNBIP, vol. 123, pp. 76–87. Springer, Heidelberg (2012). doi:10.1007/978-3-642-32273-0_7

11. Kopperger, D., Drawehn, J.: Qualitätsmanagement, Referenz-und Reifegradmodelle. In: Spath, D., Weisbecker, A. (eds.) BPM Tools 2008 – Eine evaluierende Marktstudie zu aktuellen Werkzeugen, pp. 71–91. Fraunhofer-Verlag, Stuttgart (2008)
12. Koschmider, A.: Ähnlichkeitsbasierte Modellierungssunterstützung für Ges-chäftsprozesse. Dissertation an der Universität Karlsruhe, Fakultät für Wirtschaftswissenschaften (2007)
13. Lau, J.M., Iochpe, C., Thom, L.H., Reichert, M.: Discovery and analysis of activity pattern co-occurrences in business process models. In: Proceedings of the 11th International Conference on Enterprise Information Systems (ICEIS 2009), 6–10 May 2009, Milan, Italy, pp. 83–88 (2009)
14. Melville, P., Sindhwani, V.: Recommender Systems. Encyclopedia of Machine Learning. Springer, Berlin (2010). doi:10.1007/978-0-387-30164-8_705
15. Motahari-Nezhad, H.R., Graupner, S., Bartolini, C.: A framework for modeling and enabling reuse of best practice IT processes. In: Muehlen, M., Su, J. (eds.) BPM 2010. LNBIP, vol. 66, pp. 226–231. Springer, Heidelberg (2011). doi:10.1007/978-3-642-20511-8_22
16. Moore, S.: Gartner Says Spending on Business Process Management Suites to Reach $2.7 Billion in 2015 as Organizations Digitalize Processes, Gartner Newsroom Press Relese. Gartner Inc., Stamford, USA (2015)
17. Oates, B.J.: Researching Information Systems and Computing. SAGE Publications, London (2006)
18. Pelkmann, T.: Wertschöpfung findet firmenübergreifend statt. In: Neuer Bitkom-Leitfaden BPM und SOA (2010). URL: http://www.cio.de/strategien/analysen/2237539/. Accessed 17 May 2013
19. Remme, M.: Konstruktion von Geschäftsprozessen: Ein modellgestützter Ansatz durch Montage generischer Prozeßpartikel. Schriften zur EDV-orientierten Betriebswirtschaft. Gabler, Wiesbaden (1997). doi:10.1007/978-3-322-84500-9
20. Ricci, F., Rokach, L., Shapira, B., Kantor, P.B.: Recommender Systems Handbook. Springer, Berlin (2011). doi:10.1007/978-0-387-85820-3
21. Sinur, J., Hill, J.B.: Magic Quadrant for Business Process Management Suites. Gartner Inc, Stamford (2010). Gartner Research Note G00205212
22. Thom, L.H., Iochpe, C., Reichert, M., Weber, B., Matthias, D., Nascimento, G.S., Chiao, C. M.: On the support of activity patterns in ProWAP: case studies, formal semantics, tool suppor. Revista Brasileira de Sistemas de Informação (iSys) 1(1), 27–53 (2008)
23. Zlatkin, S., Kaschek, R.: Towards amplifying business process reuse. In: Akoka, J., et al. (eds.) ER 2005. LNCS, vol. 3770, pp. 364–374. Springer, Heidelberg (2005). doi:10.1007/11568346_39
24. Sarshar, K., Weber, M., Loos, P.: Einsatz der Informationsmodellierung bei der Einführung betrieblicher Standardsoftware: Eine empirische Untersuchung bei Energieversorgerunternehmen. Wirtschaftsinformatik. 48, 120–127 (2006)
25. Nielen, A., Költer, D., Mütze-Niewöhner, S., Karla, J., Schlick, C.M.: An Empirical Analysis of Human Performance and Error in Process Model Development. In: Jeusfeld, M., Delcambre, L., Ling, T.-W. (eds.) ER 2011. LNCS, vol. 6998, pp. 514–523. Springer, Heidelberg (2011). doi:10.1007/978-3-642-24606-7_42
26. Wilmont, I., Brinkkemper, S., Weerd, I., Hoppenbrouwers, S.: Exploring intuitive modelling behaviour. In: Bider, I., Halpin, T., Krogstie, J., Nurcan, S., Proper, E., Schmidt, R., Ukor, R. (eds.) BPMDS/EMMSAD -2010. LNBIP, vol. 50, pp. 301–313. Springer, Heidelberg (2010). doi:10.1007/978-3-642-13051-9_25
27. Fellmann, M., Metzger, D., Thomas, O.: Data model development for process modeling recommender systems. In: Horkoff, J., Jeusfeld, Manfred A., Persson, A. (eds.) PoEM 2016. LNBIP, vol. 267, pp. 87–101. Springer, Cham (2016). doi:10.1007/978-3-319-48393-1_7

Towards Supporting Business Process Compliance with Policies

Ludmila Penicina[⊠]

Institute of Applied Computer Systems, Riga Technical University,
1 Kalku, Riga LV-1658, Latvia
ludmila.penicina@rtu.lv

Abstract. This paper discusses early findings of the research in progress to create an approach to support an organization in bridging the gap between existing business processes and policies. Business processes are valuable assets of any organization, and business process modelling has become the key activity for capturing and analysing business processes. However, advances in technology, growing expectation of openness by research funders, competition, regulations in IT security and privacy, and overall economic situation facilitate emergence of new policies, and urge enterprises to change their business processes to be compliant with the new requirements. The goal of the research is to propose the approach for closing the gap between business process models and legal states of business objects described in policies by means of using Bunge-Wand-Weber model. The approach includes means for explicit definition of legal and illegal state spaces of business objects in (1) policies, and (2) as-is business process models, and compliance checking between state spaces of (1) and (2) to indicate the gap. It is an initial input for building to-be business process models that are complaint with newly imposed policies. As a running example to illustrate the approach a publishing business process of a scholar journal is used. New policies from research funders require Open Access (OA) to all outputs from publicly-funded research, and business processes of publishing scholar journals require changes.

Keywords: Business process modelling · BWW model · BPMN · States · Compliance

1 Introduction

Business processes are valuable assets of any organization. In organizations business process modelling has become the main activity for capturing, analysing, and improving business processes. At the same time there is an increased pressure on organizations to guarantee compliance of their business processes with various legislative and regulatory requirements, other externally imposed constraints, and other policies [1] (further in the text – policies). One domain where new policies are actively adopted is research; e.g., Open Access and Open Data policies (further in the text – OA policies) are introduced to facilitate the transition to Open Science. In the EU member countries introduction of OA policies are mainly based on the European Commission's Recommendation to Member States of July 2012 that they develop and implement

© Springer International Publishing AG 2017
B. Johansson et al. (Eds.): BIR 2017, LNBIP 295, pp. 93–107, 2017.
DOI: 10.1007/978-3-319-64930-6_7

policies to ensure OA to all outputs from publicly-funded research [2]. As a result funders and research institutions have introduced new expectations and requirements, and organisations (e.g., scholar publishers) must have in place services and resources to allow compliance with funder policies [3]. According to [4] academic community will experience rapid changes in the way research is conducted, published, and results are shared. Both policies to enable OA to publications and, more recently, to research data are commonplace at European universities and around the globe, however there are other ingredients to Open Science: such as Open Reviewing and Open Software [4]. Based on that it can be predicted that new policies facilitating Open Science will be introduced in the near future, e.g., as Open Research Data pilot was introduced in Horizon 2020 [5], and organizations will have to provide compliance by introducing changes to the existing business processes.

On the other hand, nowadays organizations employ industry modelling standards like Business Process Model and Notation (BPMN) and ArchiMate to understand and improve business processes. BPMN is the de-facto standard for representing in a very expressive graphical way the processes occurring in virtually every kind of organizations [6]. However, BPMN has its limitations when it comes to modelling other aspects of organizations such as organizational structure and roles, functional breakdowns, data, strategy, business rules, and technical systems [7]. Information about Enterprise Architecture (EA) is needed to create real-world business process models. To provide a uniform representation for diagrams that describe EA, ArchiMate modelling language has been developed [8]. The core of ArchiMate language consists of three main types of elements: active structure elements (subjects), behaviour elements, and passive structure elements (objects).

Business process modelling comprises two aspects – the control-flow perspective and data-flow perspective [9]. Control-flow perspective defines possible execution paths of a business process, while data-flow perspective represents how business objects are manipulated and change states during a process. Control flow perspective is represented in business process models using BPMN. Data in business process models are usually declared in terms of business objects (physical or virtual). Business objects and subjects are represented in EA models using ArchiMate (active and passive structure). Policies impose legal (further in the text also lawful) states of business objects. The previous research has shown that BPMN lack in ability to describe flow of business objects in business process models, and explicitly declare states of business objects and state transition laws imposed by regulations (see [10–12]). This gap hinders compliance of business processes with policies because lawful and unlawful states of business objects are not explicitly defined in business process models, models might contain meaningless states, since a set of conceivable states is not depicted, and, as the result, business process models do not represent real-world processes and can lead to business process incompliance with policies. Also, since BPMN proclaims to be directly executable, omitting states and state transition laws may hinder correct automated execution.

The goal of this research is to propose an approach to support organizations in checking compliance of existing business processes against new policies by means of Bunge-Wand-Weber model. Wand and Weber [13] built a set of models for the evaluation of modelling techniques based on an upper ontology defined by Bunge [14].

They extended Bunge's ontology and applied it to the modelling of information systems (BWW model). BWW model consists of constructs present in the real world that must be represented in information systems. BWW model allows straightforwardly addressing (further in the text BWW elements are in italics): (1) *states* of *things*, (2) *lawful state space* and *lawful event space* of *things*, (3) *conceivable state space* and *conceivable event space* of *things*, (4) *state law* that restricts values of the properties of *things* to a lawful subset, and (5) *lawful transformations* that define which events in *things* are lawful. BWW model provides an explicit representation of business objects, states of business objects, and state transition laws, and allows to monitor whether a business object has assumed an unlawful state. That is the reason why in this research the BWW model is used as a framework to represent in a structured way the policy and the business process for canonical comparison of both to indicate the existing gaps between the process and the policy.

Monitoring states of business objects in business processes against policies: (1) can assist organization in compliance to ensure that organization will not violate laws and there will be no potential legal problems for the organization, and (2) can contribute to consistency in collaborative business processes and customer satisfaction. A number of studies exist that show the importance of addressing states of business objects in business process models, e.g., in [15] authors indicate the importance of object states in large engineering processes such as assembling of a car or an airplane, and according to [16] in order to achieve safe execution of a process model it must be ensured that every time a task attempts to access a business object, the object is in a certain expected state (legal state). And, since not all possible transitions of states are meaningful, restrictions on object state transitions are also required. In this paper the author intentionally uses the term "business objects" and not "data objects", since active structure elements (such as actors or application components) are also capable of assuming a state which can be illegal and should be also monitored.

The research methodology is a design science method using deductive research approach. The validation of the proposed solution is out of the scope of this paper. It will be conducted using Delphi estimation method combining expert judgement. Delphi estimation will include individual estimates, sharing the estimates with experts, and having several rounds until consensus is reached.

The paper is structured as follows. In Sect. 2 the related work is outlined. In Sect. 3 the proposed approach is described. The example of applying the proposed approach is outlined in Sect. 4. Brief conclusions are presented in Sect. 5.

2   Related Works

The lack of consistent theoretical foundation for building information systems urged Wand and Weber to build a set of models for the evaluation of modelling techniques [13]. Wand and Weber have extended the ontology presented by Bunge [14] and developed a formal foundation called BWW model for modelling information systems. Elements in BWW model (in the text shown in italics) can be organized in the following groups (adapted from [17]):

1. *Thing* – including *Properties, Classes* and *Kinds* of *Things*. *Thing* is an elementary unit in BWW. *Things* possess *Properties*, which defines *States* of a *Thing*. *Things* can belong to *Classes* or *Kinds* depending on a number of common *Properties*. A *Thing* can act on another *Thing* if its existence affects the *History* of the other *Thing*. *Things* are coupled if one *Things* acts on another.

2. *State of Thing* – *Properties* of *Things* define their *States*. *State Law* restricts *Values* of *Properties* of *Things*. *Conceivable State Space* is a set of all *States* a *Thing* can assume. *Lawful State Space* defines *States* that comply with *State Law*. *Stable State* is a *State* in which a *Thing* or a *System* will remain unless forced to change by a *Thing* in the *System Environment*. *Unstable State* is a *State* that will be changed into another *State* by the *Transformations* in the *System*. *History* is the chronologically-ordered *States* of a *Thing*.

3. *Transformation* – transformation between *States of Things*. *Transformation* is a mapping from one *State* to another. *Lawful Transformation* defines which *Events* in a *Thing* are lawful.

4. *Event* – event is a change in *State* of a *Thing*. *Conceivable Event Space* is a set of all *Events* that can occur to a *Thing*. *Lawful Event Space* is a set of all *Events* that are lawful to a *Thing*. *Events* can be *Internal Events* and *External Events*. *Events* can be *Well-Defined* - an *Event* in which the subsequent *State* can be predicted - or *Poorly-Defined* – an *Event* in which the subsequent *State* cannot be predicted.

5. *System* – a set of coupled *Things*. *System Composition* are *Things* in the *System*. *System Environment* is *Things* outside the *System* interacting with the *System*. *System Structure* is a set of couplings that exists among *Things*. *Subsystem* is a *System* whose composition and structure is a subset of the composition and structure of another *System*. *System Decomposition* is a set of *Subsystems*. *Level Structure* is an alignment of the subsystems.

This paper continues the research presented in [11, 12] where the evaluation of BPMN and ArchiMate against BWW model was presented. Majority of BPMN and ArchiMate core elements can be mapped to BWW constructs. However, it is necessary to supplement BPMN and ArchiMate modelling languages with the missing elements in order to be able to maintain a set of object states in business process models. In BPMN and ArchiMate there is no explicit representation for object's *State, Conceivable State Space, Lawful State Space, State Law, Conceivable Event Space, Lawful Event Space,* and *History* – the resulting BPMN and ArchiMate models may be irrelevant and modellers may need to incorporate additional modelling techniques to overcome these defects. It may be impossible to detect from BPMN and ArchiMate models which states should be expected to occur and which states can occur but are illegal (unlawful). Another important aspect is lacking of element *History* which chronologically describes state changes of business objects. This deficiency can lead to problems regarding maintaining system's log and recovery.

The authors of [5] propose a notion of "weak conformance" which checks conformance of a process model with respect to data objects. This notion can be used to tell whether in every execution of a process model each time a task needs to access a data object in a particular state, it is ensured that the data object is in the expected state or can reach the expected state and, hence, the process model can achieve its goals.

In [18] authors identify that consistency between business process models and object life cycle is required, however, their relation is not well understood. Authors clarify this relation and propose an approach to establish the required consistency by explicitly defining object states in business process models and then generating life cycles for each object type in the process. The authors of [18] indicate that object life cycle modelling is valuable at the business level. However, we propose to consider states of objects also at the application and technology levels of enterprise architecture since objects can be hidden and specified in sub-process structures at different levels of an enterprise. The authors of [19] use object life cycle as a common means for explicitly modelling allowed state transitions of an object during its existence and propose a technique for generating a compliant business process model from a set of given reference object life cycles. The notion of a "legal state" is also mentioned in [20] where authors indicate that the representation of legal states in a model of a trade procedure is essential because organizations should be able to derive their obligations, rights, and duties at each point during the execution of the trade procedure and propose to annotate the states in Petri nets.

In [1] authors investigate the use of temporal deontic assignments on activities as a means to declaratively capture the control-flow semantics that reside in business regulations and business policies. In object-oriented paradigm, state machines are extensively used for representation of states of objects [21]. In [22] the authors propose logic based formalism for describing the semantics of business contracts and the semantics of compliance checking procedures and close the gap between business processes and business contracts.

This research differs from the related work in that it uses BWW model as a missing part or a bridge to close the gap between: (1) legal states represented in policies, (2) BPMN business process models, (3) active and passive structure elements represented in ArchiMate EA models (business objects and subjects).

3 The Proposed Approach

The proposed approach requires the following prerequisites:

1. There is a policy describing legal and illegal states of business objects that an organization must be complaint with.
2. There is a BPMN business process model that needs to be monitored against the policy to indicate the gap.
3. There is an ArchiMate EA model that describes business objects and subjects (active and passive structure elements) depicted in the BPMN business process model.
4. There is an expert from the represented business domain using the approach that is familiar with BPMN, ArchiMate and BWW model (further in the text – the modeller).

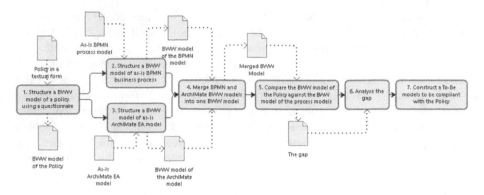

Fig. 1. The steps of the proposed approach.

The proposed approach includes the following steps (see Fig. 1):

1. Structure a BWW model of a policy using a questionnaire – the input to the activity is an existing policy in a textual form. The questionnaire is presented to the modeller online in the form of questions to answer. The questionnaire is built specifically to answer the questions about the policy in the context of the BWW model to be able to construct the BWW model automatically with the values of the BWW model elements recorded against questions. The output of the activity is the constructed BWW model of the policy. The BWW model of the policy is constructed in a canonical way by means of an XML document. Below are examples of the questions from the questionnaire:
   a. How many *Things* the policy describes?
   b. What *Things* are passive elements?
   c. What *Things* are active elements?
   d. Describe *Properties* of each *Thing* (*Property* name and *Property* value).
   e. Describe *State Law* of each *Thing* (*Values* of the *Properties* that are lawful).
   f. Describe *Lawful States* based on the *State Law*.
2. Structure a BWW model from an as-is BPMN business process – the input to the activity is the as-is BPMN business process model that describes the existing business process. The purpose of the approach is to check the existing business process model against the policy to indicate the gap. This step uses the BPMN model to construct the BWW model to be able to compare it with the BWW model of the policy. This step uses the mapping of BPMN to the BWW model presented in [17, 21] to construct the BWW model from the BPMN business process model. The output of the activity is the BWW model of the BPMN business process model.
3. Structure a BWW model of an as-is ArchiMate EA model – the input to the activity is the as-is ArchiMate EA model that describes the existing enterprise architecture that refines the existing BPMN business process model. This step uses the Archi-Mate model to construct the BWW model to be able to compare it with the BWW model of the policy. This step uses the mapping of ArchiMate to the BWW model

presented in [12, 21] to construct the BWW model from the ArchiMate model. The output of the activity is the BWW model of the ArchiMate EA model.

4. Merge the BWW models constructed from the BPMN and ArchiMate models into one BWW model – the input to the activity are both BWW models constructed from the BPMN business process model and the ArchiMate EA model. The BWW models are represented as XML documents and merged into one XML document to represent one BWW model that will be compared with the BWW model of the policy.

5. Compare the BWW model of the policy against the BWW model of the existing business process models – two canonical representations of the BWW models are compared to indicate the gap between the existing business process models and the policy. The BWW models are represented as XML documents and two XML documents are compared to indicate the differences between the two. The gap represents elements that are missing in the existing business process models compared to the policy. If the gap exists, this means that the business process models are not compliant with the policy and might contain illegal business objects states. The gap is represented as a set of differences between two XML documents.

6. Step 6 and 7 are outside of the scope of the approach, however these steps are recommended for organizations since the goal of the compliance checking is to build a to-be business process model that is compliant with the policy and describes all the necessary business objects and states represented in the policy. Step 6 is performed by the modeller to analyse the indicated gap as an initial step to construct the to-be business process model. Step 7 is creating the to-be business process model (BPMN and ArchiMate models). The to-be business process model can be monitored against the policy using the previous steps.

The construction of the BWW model from BPMN and ArchiMate models includes the following:

1. Explicitly defining *Things* from the models – both active and passive structure elements.
2. Explicitly defining *Properties* of *Things* (business objects and subjects) using formal definitions presented in [22] and indicating whether business object is an input or output parameter of an activity.
3. Explicitly defining *Conceivable State Space* based on the *Properties* of the *Things*.
4. Explicitly defining *State Law* of *Things* and *Lawful State Space* of business objects and subjects based on the *State Law*.

Compliance can be checked during or after the execution of the business process, called compliance by detection; or compliance can be checked while modelling the business process, called compliance by design [23]. The proposed approach in this paper employs the compliance by design approach. The proposed approach for monitoring compliance of business processes with policies requires a repository-based modelling tool that accommodates BPMN, ArchiMate, and BWW.

4 Example

This section describes an example to explore how the proposed approach can be applied to a scholar publisher business domain and support the publisher's needs to change its journal publishing business process to be compliant with the OA initiative. The scholar publisher presented in this section is the university press that publishes the journal of the history of medicine. Existing business process of the scholar publisher is based on a traditional printed and subscription-based publishing business model, and it is clear that the publisher does not support OA. However, a deeper analysis is needed to understand the gap between the OA policy and the existing business process models. The proposed approach in this paper can be used to indicate the gap between the OA policy and the existing publishing process.

The goal of the scholar publisher is to change its publishing business process to become more visible and discoverable online, and to improve bibliometric indicators, e.g., citations. Also the research published in the journal is publicly-funded and according to the European Commission guidelines must be OA [2].

To achieve the goal the editorial team of the scholar publisher has made a decision to launch a project for inclusion in the Directory of Open Access Journals (DOAJ) [24]. DOAJ is a community-curated list of open access journals and aims to be the starting point for all information searches for quality, peer reviewed open access materials [24]. To be included in the DOAJ any publisher must be compliant with the basic requirements for inclusion in DOAJ. These requirements are available online [25], here are some examples of the DOAJ requirements:

1. All content (full texts of journal articles) should be available for free and be Open Access without delay (i.e. no embargo period).
2. User registration is not acceptable and journals requiring users to register to read full text will not be accepted.
3. All articles must have a publication date. DOAJ encourages the use of unique article identifiers, such as the DOI.
4. DOAJ considers the application of a Creative Commons license [26], or its equivalent, as the best practice.

In the context of this paper these requirements are considered as a policy that the publisher's business processes must be compliant with. Now it is possible to proceed to the first step of the approach – to make a canonical description of this policy based on the BWW model. The constructed BWW model will be used as a framework to monitor compliance of the business process. To construct the BWW model, the formal definitions of the BWW model are used described in [22]. Below (see Tables 1 and 2) is presented a fragment of BWW model of the DOAJ inclusion policy. Table 1 shows *Things* and all possible *Properties* of *Things* described in the DOAJ policy, and also the *Property* "Type of Thing" is added for the purpose of differentiating active and passive structure elements based on ArchiMate. A *Thing* is the elementary unit in the BWW model. *Things* possess *Properties*. A *Property* is modelled via a function that maps the *Thing* into some value. Table 2 shows *State Law* and *Lawful State Space* based on the *State Law*. A *State Law* restricts the values of the *Properties* of a *Thing* to a subset that

Table 1. The BWW model of the DOAJ inclusion policy (1)

Thing	Properties			
	Property	Values		
Article	Type of thing	Active	Passive	
	Full text OA?	Yes	No	
	Separate URL per article	Yes	No	
	Publication date	Year	Date	Not available
	Review type	Not available	Peer review	Editorial
	Review date	Not available	Date	
	Copyright and licensing	Creative commons	Other	
	Unique Identifier	DOI	Other	Not available
Full texts	Type of thing	Active	Passive	
	Open access	Yes	No	
	Embargo	Yes	No	
	Price	For free	Charges apply	
	Copyright and licensing information	Embedded	Not embedded	
	Format	PDF	HTML	other
Readers	Type of thing	Active	Passive	
	Need to register to read full texts?	Yes	No	

is deemed lawful, e.g., an article cannot be an active type of thing. *Lawful State Space* is the set of *States* of a *Thing* that comply with *State Law* of the *Thing*.

According to the approach, the BWW model of the policy can be represented in a formal way, e.g., as XML document, see Code Fragment 1 of the XML code below.

Code Fragment 1: The fragment of the XML code of the DOAJ policy BWW model

```
<xs:element name="Article">
        <xs:complexType>
            <xs:attribute name="Type_of_Thing" type="xs:string"/>
            <xs:attribute name="Full_text_OA" type="xs:boolean"/>
            <xs:attribute name="Separate_URL_per_article"
type="xs:boolean"/>
            <xs:attribute name="Publication_Date" type="xs:date"/>
            <xs:attribute name="Review_type" type="xs:string"/>
            <xs:attribute name="Review_date" type="xs:date"/>
            <xs:attribute name="Copyright_and_licensing"
type="xs:boolean"/>
            <xs:attribute name="Unique_Identifier" type="xs:string"/>
        </xs:complexType>
    </xs:element>
```

The next step of the approach is to construct a BWW model from the existing BPMN process model based on the BPMN-BWW mapping presented in [17, 21].

Table 2. The BWW model of the DOAJ inclusion policy (2)

Thing	Property	State law	Lawful state space
Article	Type of thing	Passive	
	Full text OA?	Yes	Full texts are OA
	Separate URL per article	Yes	URL per article
	Publication date	Year, Date	Publication year or date is available
	Review type	Peer review	Reviewed by peer review
		Editorial	Reviewed by editorial review
	Review date	Date	
	Copyright and licensing	Creative commons	Copyright and licensing information available
	Unique identifier	DOI	DOI unique identifier
		Other	Other unique identifier
Full texts	Type of thing	Passive	
	Open access	Yes	Full texts OA
	Embargo	No	Full texts are not embargoed
	Price	For free	Full texts are free
	Copyright and licensing information	Embedded	Copyright and licensing info embedded in full text
	Format	PDF	Full texts are PDFs
		HTML	Full texts are HTML
Readers	Type of thing	Active	
	Need to register to read full texts?	No	Not asked to register to access full texts

A fragment of the existing publishing business process BPMN model is depicted in Fig. 2. The existing ArchiMate EA model is presented in Fig. 3. The BWW models of both models are constructed based on the previous work described in [17, 21].

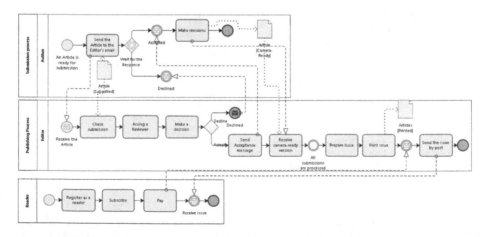

Fig. 2. The fragment of the as-is BPMN business process model of the publisher.

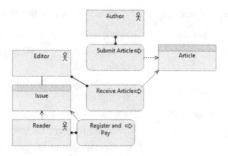

Fig. 3. The fragment of the ArchiMate model of the publisher.

A fragment of the BWW model from both models are presented below (see Table 3).

The next step is to compare two canonical descriptions of the constructed BWW models to indicate the gap between the policy (Tables 1 and 2) and the existing business process models (Table 3). Below is presented a fragment of the comparison between lawful states of the policy and lawful states depicted in the existing models (comparison between Tables 2 and 3 is presented, see Table 4).

Table 3. The fragment of the BWW model of the existing models.

Thing	Property	State law	Lawful state space
Article	Type of thing	Passive	
	Submitted	Yes	Article submitted
	Checked by editor	Yes	Article checked by editor
	Reviewer assigned	Yes	Reviewer assigned
	Reviewed	Yes	Reviewed by peer review
	Review date	Date	
	Decision made	Accepted	Article accepted
		Declined	Article declined
	Printed	Yes	Article printed
	Publication date	Date	Publication date is available
Issue	Type of thing	Passive	
	Prepared	Yes	Issue prepared
	Printed	Yes	Issue printed
	Sent by post	Yes	Issue sent
Editor	Type of thing	Active	
Readers	Type of thing	Active	
	Need to register to read full texts?	Yes	Reader is registered
	Need to pay to read full texts?	Yes	Reader has paid

From the Table 4 it can be concluded: (1) that existing business process models are not compliant with the policy and (2) which lawful states of business objects and

Table 4. The fragment of the comparison between the BWW models.

Lawful state space from the policy	Corresponding lawful state space from the models
Full texts are OA	No corresponding lawful state description in the existing models
URL per article	No corresponding lawful state description in the existing models
Publication year or date is available	Publication date is available
Reviewed by peer review	Reviewed by peer review
Reviewed by editorial review	No corresponding lawful state description in the existing models
Copyright and licensing information available	No corresponding lawful state description in the existing models
DOI unique identifier	No corresponding lawful state description in the existing models
Other unique identifier	No corresponding lawful state description in the existing models
Full texts OA	No corresponding lawful state description in the existing models
Full texts are not embargoed	No corresponding lawful state description in the existing models
Full texts are free	No corresponding lawful state description in the existing models
Copyright and licensing info embedded in full text	No corresponding lawful state description in the existing models
Full texts are PDFs	No corresponding lawful state description in the existing models
Full texts are HTML	No corresponding lawful state description in the existing models
Not asked to register to access full texts	No corresponding lawful state description in the existing models

subjects from the policy are not represented in the existing business process models. This gap is an input for constructing a to-be business process model that is compliant with the policy. This example does not fully represent the proposed approach, only the main idea behind the approach is illustrated. The presented work is a research in progress.

5   Conclusions

This paper presents an ongoing research towards supporting organization in monitoring compliance of business processes with policies. The BWW model is used as the foundation, since it allows straightforwardly addressing the lawful and conceivable state spaces of business objects. The previous research has shown that BPMN and ArchiMate lack in ability to describe flow of business objects in business process models and explicitly declare states of business objects imposed by regulations (see [10–12]). This gap hinders compliance of business process models with different policies. There are 6 BWW model elements that are not supported by these modelling languages, namely, *State Law*, *Conceivable State Space*, *Lawful State Space*, *History*, *Conceivable Event Space*, and *Lawful Event Space*.

This research differs from the related work in that it uses the BWW model as a missing part or a bridge to close the gap between: (1) legal states represented in policies, (2) BPMN business process models, and (3) active and passive structure elements represented in ArchiMate EA models (business objects and subjects). The proposed approach supports organization in defining a canonical representation of policies using the questionnaire that is based on the BWW model. Based on the questionnaire answers the BWW model of policy is constructed. The proposed approach includes construction of the BWW model for existing BPMN and ArchiMate models to compare it with the BWW model of the policy to indicate the gap between existing business processes and policies. Comparison between the structured representations of (1) the policy, and (2) the business process models provides organization an explicit method to see what states are missing and with what elements the existing business process must be refined in order to be compliant with the new policy. The paper describes how the proposed approach can support scholar publishers in achieving compliance with the OA policies. However, the proposed approach is developed to be universal and can be used in other business domains.

Definition of object states in business process models are especially required in data-driven processes – in any process model that is based on data and manipulates with business objects. The main contribution of the research will be a formalized solution prototype that will support organizations in facilitating monitoring of the compliance of business processes with policies.

Acknowledgments This research is funded in part by the Latvian Council of Science grant for project No. 342/2012, and in part by the Latvian National research program SOPHIS under grant agreement Nr.10-4/VPP-4/11.

References

1. Goedertier, S., Vanthienen, J.: Designing compliant business processes with obligations and permissions. In: Eder, J., Dustdar, S. (eds.) BPM 2006. LNCS, vol. 4103, pp. 5–14. Springer, Heidelberg (2006). doi:10.1007/11837862_2
2. European Commission: Communication from the Commission to the European Parliament, the Council, the European Economic and Social Committee and the Committee of the Regions. Towards better access to scientific information: boosting the benefits of public investments in research, pp. 1–12 (2012)
3. Fina, F., Proven, J.: Using a CRIS to support communication of research: mapping the publication cycle to deposit workflows for data and publications. Procedia Comput. Sci. **106**, 232–238 (2017)
4. van der Aalst, W., Bichler, M., Heinzl, A.: Open research in business and information systems engineering. Bus. Inf. Syst. Eng. **58**, 375–379 (2016)

5. European Commission: Guidelines on open access to scientific publications and research data in Horizon 2020, p. 10 (2016)
6. Chinosi, M., Trombetta, A.: BPMN: an introduction to the standard. Comput. Stand. Interfaces **34**, 124–134 (2012)
7. Silver, B.: BPMN Method and Style with Implementer's Guide. Cody-Cassidy Press, Aptos (2011)
8. The Open Group ArchiMate Forum: An Introduction to ArchiMate, an Open Group Standard (2012)
9. Weske, M.: Business Process Management. Springer, Heidelberg (2012)
10. Rosemann, M., Recker, J., Indulska, M., Green, P.: A study of the evolution of the representational capabilities of process modeling grammars. In: Dubois, E., Pohl, K. (eds.) CAiSE 2006. LNCS, vol. 4001, pp. 447–461. Springer, Heidelberg (2006). doi:10.1007/11767138_30
11. Penicina, L., Kirikova, M.: Towards completeness and lawfulness of business process models. In: Kobyliński, A., Sobczak, A. (eds.) BIR 2013. LNBIP, vol. 158, pp. 63–77. Springer, Heidelberg (2013). doi:10.1007/978-3-642-40823-6_6
12. Penicina, L.: Linking BPMN, ArchiMate, and BWW: perfect match for complete and lawful business process models? In: Short Paper Proceedings of the 6th IFIP WG 8.1 Working Conference on the Practice of Enterprise Modeling (PoEM 2013), Vol. 1023, pp. 156–165 (2013)
13. Wand, Y., Weber, R.: On the ontological expressiveness of information systems analysis and design grammars. Inf. Syst. J. **3**, 217–237 (1993)
14. Bunge, M.: Treatise on Basic Philosophy: Ontology II: A World of Systems, vol. 4. Springer, Heidelberg (1979)
15. Müller, D., Reichert, M., Herbst, J.: A new paradigm for the enactment and dynamic adaptation of data-driven process structures. In: Bellahsène, Z., Léonard, M. (eds.) CAiSE 2008. LNCS, vol. 5074, pp. 48–63. Springer, Heidelberg (2008). doi:10.1007/978-3-540-69534-9_4
16. Meyer, A., Weske, M.: Weak conformance between process models and synchronized object life cycles. In: Franch, X., Ghose, Aditya K., Lewis, Grace A., Bhiri, S. (eds.) ICSOC 2014. LNCS, vol. 8831, pp. 359–367. Springer, Heidelberg (2014). doi:10.1007/978-3-662-45391-9_25
17. Recker, J., Indulska, M., Rosemann, M., Green, P.: Do process modelling techniques get better? A comparative ontological analysis of BPMN. In: Campbell, B., Underwood, J., Bunker, D., (eds.) 16th Australasian Conference on Information Systems (2005)
18. Ryndina, K., Küster, Jochen M., Gall, H.: Consistency of business process models and object life cycles. In: Kühne, T. (ed.) MODELS 2006. LNCS, vol. 4364, pp. 80–90. Springer, Heidelberg (2007). doi:10.1007/978-3-540-69489-2_11
19. Küster, J.M., Ryndina, K., Gall, H.: Generation of business process models for object life cycle compliance. In: Alonso, G., Dadam, P., Rosemann, M. (eds.) BPM 2007. LNCS, vol. 4714, pp. 165–181. Springer, Heidelberg (2007). doi:10.1007/978-3-540-75183-0_13
20. Bons, R.W.H., Lee, R.M., Wagenaar, R.W., Wrigley, C.D.: Modelling inter-organizational trade using documentary petri nets. In: Proceedings of the Twenty-Eighth Hawaii International Conference on System Sciences, vol. 3. pp. 189–198. IEEE Computer Society Press (1996)
21. Penicina, L., Kirikova, M.: Towards controlling lawful states and events in business process models. In: IEEE 16th Conference on Business Informatics (CBI 2014), pp. 15–23 (2014)
22. Penicina, L., Kirikova, M.: Towards compliance checking between business process models and lawful states of objects. In: 2nd International Workshop on Ontologies and Information Systems (WOIS 2014), pp. 30–41 (2014)

23. Lohmann, N.: Compliance by design for artifact-centric business processes. In: Rinderle-Ma, S., Toumani, F., Wolf, K. (eds.) BPM 2011. LNCS, vol. 6896, pp. 99–115. Springer, Heidelberg (2011). doi:10.1007/978-3-642-23059-2_11
24. Directory of Open Access Journals. https://doaj.org/about
25. DOAJ: Publishing best practice and basic standards for inclusion. https://doaj.org/publishers#advice
26. Creative Commons. http://creativecommons.org/

Process Driven ERP Implementation: Business Process Management Approach to ERP Implementation

Tarik Kraljić$^{(\boxtimes)}$ and Adnan Kraljić

Ghent University, Ghent, Belgium
{tarik.kraljic,adnan.kraljic}@ugent.be

Abstract. One of the most indicated reasons for ERP implementation failure is that the organization failed to recognize the impact the system would have on business processes. A possible solution to this could be to use an approach focusing on process change when implementing ERP systems. In this research paper, we take a look at Enterprise Resource Planning systems implementation from a Business Process Management point of view. It attempts to improve ERP implementations, which are frequently unsuccessful, with insight provided through the BPM Paradigm. The focus lies on the phases and activities in the two concepts as well as defined success factors which targeting the similar objectives. The data collection was conducted in the form of interviews with respondents from two companies in Bosnia and Herzegovina and Croatia that conducts ERP implementations. It was concluded that the first four phases of BPM fit the frameworks of ERP implementation. What authors found interesting is findings suggesting the main enabling activity to be process modelling. Also CFS for ERP and BPM were compared, and the conclusion is that both are targeting similar aspects–operational business processes.

Keywords: Enterprise Resource Planning · Business process management · ERP implementation · BPM life cycle · Business process modelling · ERP and BPM critical success factors

1 Introduction

The role of Enterprise Resource Planning (ERP) systems in managing business processes has expanded significantly over the past decade from an emphasis on specific business areas such as sales, manufacturing or purchasing, to broader use throughout the company.

ERP systems are standardized software that includes modules for practically every aspect of an enterprise. Comes with best practice (an in-built process suggestion) of how a business should work and how data should flow within the organization. On the other hand, while the built-in processes in an ERP often can be considered best practices, there is no guarantee that they will work better than the current processes in an organization [1]. Instead of making a system completely adapted to the company's processes, an ERP system offers a set of processes for the organization to follow [2]. While the main job of the system is to improve the flow of information in an

© Springer International Publishing AG 2017
B. Johansson et al. (Eds.): BIR 2017, LNBIP 295, pp. 108–122, 2017.
DOI: 10.1007/978-3-319-64930-6_8

organization, it's inevitable that the business processes are affected as well [3]. In fact, using an ERP as a solution to solve operational problems such as ineffective business processes is frequently stated as motivation for the implementation [4]. But, we are witness of high numbers ERP projects which do not satisfies initial customer expectations. As Fig. 1 shows, less than 50% of implementations achieve expected benefits, while only 17% of the companies experienced more than eighty percent of their projected benefits.

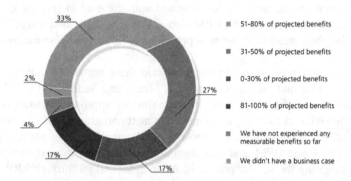

Fig. 1. Expected benefits for ERP projects (Panorama Consulting Solutions Report 2012)

Research done by the consulting group Panorama Consulting Solutions shows that one of the reasons that ERP implementations take longer than expected or fail to achieve their expected benefits can be attributed to the high degree of code customization used to tailor ERP systems to business requirements (business process requirements) (see Fig. 2). The research shows that 60% of companies perform some degree of customization which can contribute to longer implementation times and higher costs. (Panorama Consulting Solutions Report 2012).

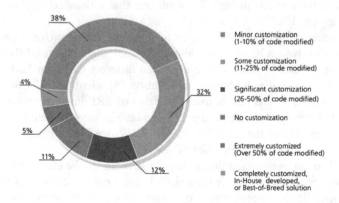

Fig. 2. Degree of customization in ERP projects (Panorama Consulting Solutions Report 2012)

As we see in Fig. 2. ERP systems implementations tend to be conservative, regarding the scope of customization and change. And this is the issue for the most customers – they are not satisfied with the extend of system modification in favor of their own business processes. In order to better manage and improve business processes, BPM (Business process management) become one of the crucial point to every competitive business.

As it is stated by [5], BPM takes a softer approach to process change and instead of being rapid and radical the change is seen as an evolutionary procedure. BPM with a focus on evolutionary change, collaboration and with the goal to give the control over IT back to the business people [5]. BPM also advocate a focus on change of business processes rather than creation of business processes to fit the changing nature of today's business.

Since it's highly recognized we can conclude there are strong linkages between ERP implementation and process change (e.g. Shang and Seddon [1]; Aladwani [6]), and there should also be a possibility to combine an approach focused on process redesign (BPM) with an ERP implementation. In next paragraphs, we will go deeper in explanation of similarities/differences between ERP and BPM. First we will give brief description of ERP and BPM, and then compare their Critical Success factors in other see are they targeting the similar problems. After it we will go through ERP and BPM implementation methodologies.

1.1   ERP, ERP CFS and SAP ERP Implementation Methodology

ERP systems are standardized software that includes modules for virtually every aspect of an enterprise. Comes with best practice (an in-built process suggestion) of how a business should work and how data should flow within the organization. It's however important to critically examine what these processes look like and not take for granted that they are best practice for the implementing company's specific business [6]. Klaus et al. [7] suggest that this is one of the causes of ERP implementation failures, because the view of functions is too limited. They suggest that a broader view must be used when implementing ERP.

Critical success factors can be created to compare and improve implementation methods. For this research, we have also compared the CSFs of ERP and BPM implementations. Multiple studies have identified different CSFs for ERP implementations. One of these studies by Somers and Nelson [8], identified 22 CSFs. Their list was compiled from a meta-study of over 110 cases of ERP implementations. This list was used by Akkermans and van Helden [9] who let 52 managers rate these CSFs and compiled a ranked list of the 22 CSFs. In our study, we will use this ranked list to compare it with our list of BPMS CSFs (Table 1).

In this ranked list, we can see that there is little focus on the effect of ERP systems on the business processes in the organization, but we can conclude that all CFS targeting the operational improvement of companies, which indirectly suggesting improvement of business processes.

Table 1. List of BPMS CSFs

1.	Top management support	8.	Project champion	15.	Education on new business processes
2.	Project team competence	9.	Vendor support	16.	BPR
3.	Interdepartmental co-operation	10.	Careful package selection	17.	Minimal customization
4.	Clear goals and objectives	11.	Data analysis and conversion	18.	Architecture choices
5.	Project management	12.	Dedicated resources	19.	Change management
6.	Interdepartmental communication	13.	Steering committee	20.	Vendor partnership
7.	Management of expectations	14.	User training	21.	Vendor's tools

SAP ERP Implementation Methodology

As the ERP implementation methodology we chose to investigate SAP ERP methodology, which is one of the most widely used The SAP ASAP 8 methodology comprises of six phases as highlighted in Fig. 4., which is a disciplined approach to managing complex projects, organizational change management, solution management, & industry specific implementations. The SAP ASAP 8 methodology is the enhanced Delivery model with templates, tools, questionnaires, and checklists, including guide books and accelerators. ASAP 8 empowers project teams to utilize the accelerators and templates built in to SAP solutions. The Agile add-on is available in SAP Solution Manager. Figures 2, 3 and 4 explains various phases of SAP ASAP 8 Methodology.

SAP Solution Manager in SAP Activate on-premise project

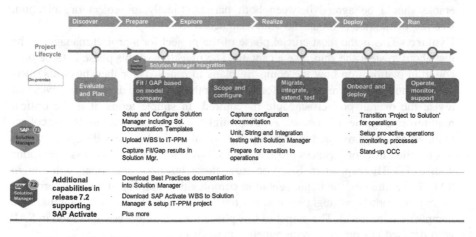

Fig. 3. New SAP methodology – SAP activate on premise project (SAP 2017)

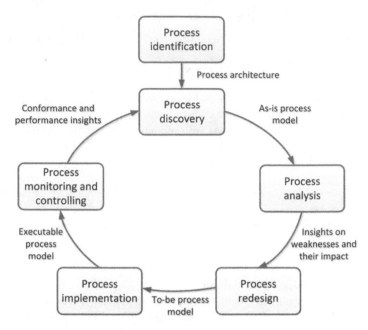

Fig. 4. BPM lifecycle

1. **Prepare** - This phase encompasses the entire project preparation and planning activities with infrastructure, hardware/network sizing requirements completed. It involves setting up the infrastructure, team, project goals, charter, and agree upon schedule, budget, risk baseline, proof-of-concept planning if applicable with implementation sequence. The project manager on the ground will discuss with the customer project manager to identify risks early on with a mitigation plan. The PM will be responsible for drafting a high-level project plan with all milestones with a detailed task level plan chalked out with critical dependencies. Each phase deliverable should be agreed between both parties. Finally, a project organization, steering committee is organized with assigned resources.

2. **Explore** - This is the most crucial phase of the project for a project manager as he just about to steer the ship, like a captain. The objective of this phase is to be on a common platform on how the company plans to run SAP for their business operations. Thus, a PM is responsible for analyzing the project goals and objectives and revise the overall project schedule if required. In simple terms, it is the critical requirements gathering phase, A PM might use appropriate tools to collect requirements with required traceability. The result is the Business Blueprint, which is a detailed flow of business process AS-IS, how they run the business operations with a TO-BE mapped in SAP, on how these business operations will run in SAP. Depending on the implementation complexities, number of business process, Blueprint workshops might span for a few days or weeks or even months, in a complex environment. The output of this phase is the baseline configuration in SAP with detailed custom code requirements analysis done.

3. **Realize** - In simple terms, realization is the actual development phase of the project, where you'd configure, develop custom code and conduct required testing. It involves coding-unit testing-integration testing-User acceptance testing (UAT). As per the business blueprint and mapping the SAP system as agreed with business, all the business process requirements will be implemented. In reality, there are two major work packages: (a) Baseline (major scope); and (b) Final configuration (remaining scope). The success of any implementation project relies on how closely you're able to develop custom code, test and release it to the UAT phase, in order to support adequate testing by the users. Also, the challenge is to adopt changes as indicated during the UAT. This phase is resource intensive and the team is at peak team size to ensure all deliverables are met and sign-off. Often times Integration fail due to lack of test data, and testing in a "PRD" like environment to be able to test all critical business scenarios. A good practice is to copy a "PRD"-like environment and start testing if the system already exists. If it is GreenField environment, ensure adequate test data is available to test it rigorously.
4. **Deploy** - **Final preparations** before cutover to production ensure that that the system, users, and data are ready for transition to productive use. The transition to operations includes setting up and launching support, then handing off operations to the organization managing the environment.

1.2   BPM, BMP CFS and Implementation Methodology

BPM is a series of methods, techniques and tools to analyze, design and improve processes that take place in a company [10]. BPM resolves around processes and implementation of IT systems around these processes. Lee and Dale [10] suggest that multiple paths have to be taken when implementing IT-systems, a method that can handle the implementation of IT-systems in every situation is impossible.

BPM CFS

Through literature research of scientific papers we have searched for keywords like CSF BPM, CSF BPMS implementation, critical success factors of business process management and critical success factors of business process management implementation. We found a list of CSFs concerning BPM implementations. These CSFs originated from different BPMS methods like Cordys@work, BPMS implementation method, Goal driven BPM, and Nine-step approach. For a complete overview of different BPM related implementation methods we refer to Ravesteyn and Versendaal paper [11]. From their list of CSFs we determined which factors are process- orientated.

We aim for process oriented CSFs to constrain the scope of this research, and to keep to the core of BPM, which are processes. Also, other CSFs are more function-orientated, meaning the use of these CSFs will not broaden the view of ERP implementations. The CSFs are extracted from the research of Ravesteyn and Versendaal work (Table 2).

The following critical success factors of BPM implementations have been found:

Table 2. Critical success factors of BPM implementaion

1.	Understanding the processes of the company	6.	Know-how and experience with Project Management	11.	Well organized maintenance and (quality) control of the process models
2.	Understanding how processes and data are linked together	7.	Experience with Change Management	12.	Having a set of key performance indicalurs and measuring the change (improvement)
3.	Understanding the Business Process Management concept	8.	A well organized design phase (modeling)	13	Understanding how to use web services
4.	Ensuring that the BPM project is part of a continuous optimization effort	9.	Using the 'best' modeling standards and techniques	14.	Involving the right people in the project
5.	Proper information systems integration	10.	Understanding interdependencies and integration of data sources	15.	Creating a culture of attention to quality within the organization

BPM Implementation Methodology

It's divided into eight parts and stretches from discovery to analysis in a continuous cycle. Similar life cycles have been presented by van der Aalst et al. [12] as well as Netjes et al. [13]. The two-latter compressed the life cycle to only being four and five phases respectively. However, the extra phases in Smith and Fingar [5] are often present in the other life cycle definitions as well, but then as activities instead of full phases.

We will go in detail explanation of each phase of BPM lifecycle.

1. *Discovery*. The discovery of a process means finding out how something is done or can be done and should provide a clear picture of how the process works, both internally and externally. This process mining can be done either manually by mapping out the business or automatically by introspection of legacy system code. The goal is the same, to make ingrained processes explicit and provide an understanding of the business as a whole.

2. *Design*. The input in this phase is either a need for a new process or an already existing process that through the diagnosis phase has shown weaknesses. If it's the latter, the objective is to create an alternate process where improvements have been done to those areas of the process the diagnosis found weak (Netjes et al. [13]). The emphasis lies on the performance of the process and what the internal structure looks like. The activities in the design phase are modelling, manipulating and redesign of the processes after they've been discovered. All the elements of the process, the actors, resources, rules and relationships are determined and tested in different scenarios with the help of simulation. Process metrics should be set in order for business analysts to be able to spot any variances and quickly react to

competitive pressure or opportunities in the market. Smith and Fingar [5] point out that the modelling notation used should include behavioral aspects of the process and be compact in nature to be able to include abstract business concepts. The modelling in BPM is meant to be done by business analysts rather than software developers who usually create models to interpret the business in order to create a system that supports it [5]. The output of the phase is a process definition that states process structure, resource structure, allocation logic and interfaces.

3. *Deployment.* The deployment phase means that the process is rolled out to the involved people, applications and connected processes. The process is moved from the modelling board to the real business and the necessary resources are distributed. Smith and Fingar [5] claim that in the new era of BPM, all this can be done with minimal manual intervention and without additional technical steps. They state that IT is capable of doing this through in advance using a projection of the process to integrate application components. The process can also be mapped and bound to standardized interfaces to work between organizations, business units and management systems.

4. *Execution.* When the conditions for the process are set in the deployment phase, the process goes live and is carried out by the participants. Generally, the execution is performed by a process management system that controls the flow of data, translates where needed and stores data about a process. In the execution phase the attention shifts from the internal structure of the process to how it works in a specific context and what factors in the context that can change [13]. Some of these environmental aspects are information on arriving cases and availability and behavior of the internal as well as external resources involved in the process. By the van der Aalst et al. [12] this phase is called the enactment phase and represents the launch or execution of the process through a chosen tool, often an IT tool.

5. *Interaction.* Process portals and process desktops are used to let people interact with business processes. The tools act as a gateway between manual work and automation, and lets people manage, observe, monitor and intervene within processes. BPM represents processes as data and it is Smith and Fingar's [5] presumption that techniques will emerge that lets users create, read, write, modify and extend process description in a manner similar to how HTML editors work today.

6. *Monitoring and Control.* This phase represents the maintenance of the process in a way similar to how maintenance of an Information system works. Activities include making sure sufficient resources are allocated, dealing with unexpected errors and making sure the technical environment works as it should. By identifying variances in the flow and alerting process owners, temporary bottlenecks can be prevented by the adding of extra resources. Minor changes to the internal structure are done in the form of adding, removing or changing participants. The monitoring involves tracking of the input throughout the whole process in order to see that it works as smooth as possible. Both data on individual cases and aggregate performance of the workflow is recorded [13]. The data collected can then be used as input for the diagnosis in the analysis phase in order to identify any improvement possibilities.

7. *Optimization.* The optimization aspect means a process of continuous improvement of single processes, classes of processes and the business as a whole. It's the activity that closes the BPM life cycle since it takes the feedback from process performance

analysis and returns it as input for a new design phase. Process optimization becomes possible when the result of the monitoring is used to determine whether changes can be made to reduce costs, increase effectiveness or similar [12]

8. *Analysis*. The measuring of process performance and the analysis of the results is what really makes a difference when it comes to business improvement [5]. The data from the control phase makes it possible to diagnose processes and decide whether they can be improved in any way. The aggregate data becomes the subject of process mining, business process intelligence and data mining techniques to identify factors that makes the process not function optimal [13]. Business Intelligence in the form of business metrics like activity-based costing or key performance indicators should be extracted directly from processes in order to see exactly what affects them. This data can be compared to history, benchmarked to best practice or compared to other similar processes. Once again simulation becomes an important technique, since it can help in providing information on how changes can improve a process.

2   Theoretical Framework

The theoretical framework builds upon three keystones of articles and books; those focusing on providing ERP and BPM implementation frameworks, those debating the relationship between Process Management and ERP and BPM critical success factors.

This paper sets out to investigate what possibilities exist to combine the strategic approach of BPM with ERP implementation. In order to do this the two concepts must be thoroughly explored, the phases in ERP implementation must be determined as well as what activities these phases consist of. Achieving a detailed description through quantitative means is a possibility but then the holistic picture of an implementation could be missed. In a quantitative survey for example, much of the researcher's control is lost once the survey is sent out, meaning that if the data wasn't sufficient to show the full picture of an implementation another complementary survey would have to be sent. In qualitative research, it's on the other hand possible to quickly and freely move between collection of data and theoretical analysis [14].

Furthermore, a qualitative approach is best used when variables not easily can be identified and when there is a need to present a detailed view of the topic [15].

Out of the five methodologies described by Creswell [15] the study has the most similarities with a case study. First, the setup of the research matched the description of case studies by Yin [16]. The research question is an exploratory "what"- question, there is no need for control over behavioural events and it focuses on contemporary events. We decided to use interviews in other to collect data. Methodologically, the strength with interviews is that they are targeted and focuses directly on the researched topic [16].

Choosing few respondents can be beneficial when the problem is not thoroughly explored and in need of indepth analysis (Kvale, 1996) We had a choice between approaching businesses that had recently implemented an ERP system, seek contact with consulting firms that conduc them more often or to collect data from both sides. It was decided that respondents from consulting companies would be the most suiting for the research paper, since it would give access to a wider spectrum of data that still were as detailed as if a "normal" business would be chosen for the study. Methodologically, the strength with interviews is that they are targeted and focuses directly on the researched topic [16].

2.1 Case Studies: JP Elektroprivreda BiH (Company A) and B4B (Company B)

Company A: JP Elektroprivreda BiH d.d.

JP Elektroprivreda Bosne i Hercegovine d.d. Sarajevo (Public Enterprise Electric Utility of Bosnia and Herzegovina) is a joint stock company in which 90% of the capital is owned by the Federation of BiH, and 10% is owned by minority shareholders.

Electric utility activities performed by the Company as public services are:

- Generation of electricity for unqualified (tariff) customers
- Electricity distribution
- Electricity supply for unqualified (tariff) customers.

JP Elektroprivreda BiH has about 15.000 employees which are supported by internal IT organization. Integral part of IT organization is SAP internal team with over 15 people supporting about 1000 users.

Company B: B4B d.o.o. Zagreb

b4b d.o.o is the leading regional SAP consulting company with the head office in Zagreb and since April 2001 it has been a SAP partner for Croatia, Slovenia, Bosnia and Herzegovina, Serbia and Montenegro, Albania, Romania and Slovakia. b4b d.o.o has around +100 employees and more than +90 consultants with rich business and IT experience gained and proven by numerous SAP implementations in Croatia and in the region. b4b d.o.o belongs to the elite society of Croatian "knowledge exporters".

We chose 3 participants from both companies. All participants are the ERP consultants, with over 10 years of experience in SAP ERP implantations. Also, they are all Manager levels in their companies (from junior consultants to mangers) which should indicate solid knowledge in both technical and process aspects.

2.2 Discussion on Interviews with Expert from Company A and Company B

Some might argue that combining ERP implementation and BPM isn't possible due to the difference in organizational level they are conducted at. BPM calls itself a strategic approach while an ERP is meant to enhance the operational functionality of a business. However, by looking at the concepts in the form of phases, both concepts can be found on a tactical level. The specific activities in each phase relates to tasks performed on a day to day basis, either by participants in an implementation project or a process manager.

In BPM, the actual management and monitoring of processes is on a tactical level where process owners can make adjustments to solve short-term problems like temporary bottlenecks. BPM initially focuses on the discovery, design, deployment and execution of one of organizations core operational aspects, its business processes. These processes are the same that is going to be affected by the ERP system, therefore making it possible to use BPM in an ERP implementation. The life-cycle match can *be shown by describing the similarities between the phases in BPM and the phases in ERP implementation:*

Discovery. To find out how something is done or how it can be done can be seen as one of the earliest activities in the preparation for implementing an ERP system. This phase can therefore only really be connected to ERP if an ERP system is decided as the way of putting the process change into practice.

This means activities like setting up preliminary goals for the implementation and evaluating different ERP vendors.

In company B's methodology the business processes are communicated to the consultants in the first phase in order for them to understand what the business really is. Since the activities aren't included in Company A method and not found in Ross and Vitale [3] or Markus et al. [18] the connection of this phase to ERP implementation is questionable. However, the introspection of the business most likely means that the project has started, at least from the business point of view. For an integration of the concept to function, the process mining and discovery must be done by business first and then communicated to the consultants.

Design. Smith and Fingar [5] state that the main activities in the design phase are modelling, manipulation and redesign of business processes. This is to be done using a modelling notation understandable by business analysts and thereby cutting of the long chain from requirement specification to executable code. The design phase in BPM in many ways corresponds to the design phase described in ERP frameworks and to the GAP-phase presented in the paper. It can be argued that since an ERP system comes with a predefined set of processes, why and how should these then be modelled? The answer lies partly in what Parr and Shanks [4] describes in their "Re-engineering"-phase where a mapping should be done between the current business processes and the functions of the ERP (GAP analysis).

This means the modelling is three-tiered and becomes essential in ensuring a fit and making sure the business learns what the change will be like.

The choices proposed by Ross and Vitale [3] about process change and process standardization very much affect what modelling effort is needed in the implementation. These decisions will determine to what extent the system needs to be customized. The taxonomy by Parr and Shanks [4] is useful when determining if BPM can play a beneficial role in ERP implementations. Vanilla implementations, which involves few sites and adoption of the process suggestion embedded in the ERP require less modelling since there is no mapping and no major design of the system solution needed. It is hard to believe that Vanilla implementations will be sufficient for companies with well-developed legacy system.

Also, implementations that falls under the "Comprehensive" category that involve multiple sites in different countries and a lot of modules mean a much bigger change with more people and business units affected. The need for customization increases in order for the ERP to work with existing core processes. In large implementations there are usually a need for integrations, either with necessary legacy systems or with clients and suppliers. This adds up to all three modelling activities being needed; design of processes, mapping of processes to the system and design of the system itself.

Deployment. While the description of deployment by SAP implementation methodology is that the process is rolled out automatically to all participants, they also mention it to be a preparation for the execution. By preparing integration with legacy systems or external systems the transition to the new process goes through with little friction. Company A uses the SAP implementation methodology that include a phase of final preparation, where the business makes the last adjustments before the system goes live. Also as interviewee mentioned integration with old systems or other stakeholders systems aren't uncommon when implementing ERP systems. The deployment activities in BPM could be used to make sure these integrations work when the system finally goes live. A step in that direction can be seen in the Business process management suite in Company B's ERP system, where an enterprise collaborator is used to communicate with other systems in the organization. By using such a tool, all other systems could prepared for the launch of the ERP system.

Execution. When all preparation is complete, the new process is executed with the help of a process management system according to Smith and Fingar [5]. However, the execution itself is all about setting the process in motion and making sure all participants can fulfil their tasks and have the necessary resources allocated to them. The execution is the equivalent of the go live of an ERP system, which in effect means that all the new processes are used.

While the comparison shows that the initial four steps of BPM can be combined with an ERP implementation, there is no match between the remaining steps and the project of implementing an ERP system. Interaction, monitoring and control, optimization and analysis emphasizes the "management" in BPM and has to do with the ongoing work of supervising and enhancing business processes. It can be argued that the Shakedown and Onward and upward phases of Markus et al. [18]) describes these activities in an ERP context but what it does is really stating the obvious, that there is a time of ups and downs after implementing an ERP. Both the Ross and Vitale [3] and Parr and Shanks [4] frameworks include similar phases labelled Continuous improvement, Transformation and Enhancement but also they lack specific description of activities. The last step in both Company A and Company A (since they used the same methodology) method is Go Live support, where adjustments to the system or extended training for the users are the main activities.

When it comes to maintenance and management of the processes that is not a part of the implementation. The rest of the phases in BPM can therefore not be said to fit in an ERP implementation. However, that is not to say that an ERP system can't facilitate these activities of managing business processes. It's beyond the scope of this thesis to investigate that further, but the fact that most ERP system has a workflow module and that BPM is based on Workflow Management makes it a possibility worth investigating. If it should prove to be possible, the third wave of Process Management could be built upon the ERP technology of today. The Process flow integrator module in Company B has the functionality for process modelling and process description as described by BPM theory. It however lacks the functionality for management, monitoring and diagnosis which also is stated as the difference between WfMS and BPMS by van den Aalst et al. [12]. The match between the phases of ERP implementation and BPM relies on one big assumption. While Smith and Fingar [5] continuously couples BPM with specified technology in the form of BPMS, that kind of technology is not a necessity for the discovery or the design parts of BPM. In fact, van den Aalst [12] and Netjes et al. [13] do not involve IS until after the design, in the enactment phase and execution phase respectively. What this means is that in order for the proposed match to hold, the decision to use ERP as the IT solution of choice must be taken already in the discovery phase of the BPM life cycle.

As the all participants concluded the main enabler of connecting ERP and BPM methodologies would be intermedia – such as business process modelling tool/notation.

By using a modelling language like BPMN (or other) in the process modelling, users can more easily understand and have more control over how the ERP system will impact business processes.

Process Modelling
Process Modelling and the use of BMPN is an essential part of the use of BPM in ERP implementations. Using BPMN means that the new processes becomes understandable by the business and individuals from the business side can take bigger part in the designs of the processes, customization of the system and the mapping between them. It can greatly help in reducing the errors in the GAP document, which later becomes a source of resistance according to interviewee from Company B. This could be resolved since there no longer would have to be a consultant trying to understand what it is the business really want the new system to do. Instead, the business side could themselves learn BPMN and model the way they want their business to work with the new ERP system. The mapping of the current processes to the system could be done by the business and the consultants together. After those two design activities, the consultants could then design the system solution with the help of BPMN, making the final solution understandable by the business that then better could target their training and prepare for the transition. The process flow integrator in Company B's product claims to have a functionality for process modelling where a notation is used that requires no computer language skills.

To fully enable the BPM approach, the next step would be to use the BPM module from the start in an ERP implementation. In doing this, it becomes a tool for the implementation of the ERP system by providing modelling possibilities as well as a tool for managing processes after the system has gone live. Since it's already a part of the ERP system, the BPM module would handle the deployment of the new processes in the way a BPMS would do, as suggested by Smith and Fingar [5].

3 Conclusion

This paper researched how an ERP implementation could be improved by using a BPM based strategy. The resulting conclusions of the study are as follows - there is a fit between the activities in the first four phases of BPM and ERP implementation. The discovery, design, deployment and execution of processes are possible to integrate with activities in an ERP implementation. The final step of an ERP implementation is taken a short time after the system has gone live and is in many ways similar to the execution of processes in BPM.

Also, the CFS of BPM and ERP are not the same, but targeting the similar aspects – business process, which are the key focuses of both implementations.

The main activity that can connect the concepts is Process Modelling using a notation understandable by individuals in the business and that corresponds to immediate changes to the system. By using a modelling language like BPMN in the process modelling, users can more easily understand and have more control over how the ERP system will impact business processes.

To let the business be a part of the actual process modelling and customization of the system could make sure the end result matches the expected result. It also means that the gap between business and configuration of IT systems is eliminated, a central idea of BPM.

References

1. Shang, S., Seddon, P.B.: Managing process deficiencies with enterprise systems. Bus. Process Manag. J. 13(3), 405–416 (2007)
2. Somers, T.M., Nelson, K.G.: A taxonomy of players and activities across the ERP project life cycle. Inf. Manag. 41, 257–278 (2004)
3. Ross, J.W., Vitale, M.R.: The ERP revolution: surviving vs thriving. Inf. Syst. Front. 2(2), 233–241 (2000)
4. Parr, A., Shanks, G.: A model of ERP project implementation. J. Inf. Technol. 15, 289–303 (2000)
5. Smith, H., Fingar, P.: Business Process Management: The Third Wave. Meghan-Kiffer Press, Florida (2007)
6. Harris, J.: The road to ERP optimization. Gov. Finance Rev. 20(6), 18 (2004)
7. Klaus, H., Rosemann, M., Gable, G.G.: What is ERP? Inf. Syst. Front. 2(2), 141–162 (2000)
8. Somers, T.M., Nelson, K.G.: The impact of strategy and integration mechanisms on enterprise system value: empirical evidence from manufacturing firms. Eur. J. Oper. Res. 146, 315–338 (2003)
9. Akkermans, H., van Helden, K.: Vicious and virtuous cycles in ERP implementation: a case study of interrelations between critical success factors. Eur. J. Inf. Syst. 11, 35–46 (2002)
10. Lee, R.G., Dale, B.G.: Business process management: a review and evaluation. Bus. Process Manag. J. 4(3), 214–225 (1998)
11. Ravestyn, P., Versendaal, J.: Constructing a situation sensitive methodology for business process management systems implementation. In: Proceeding of the Pacific Asia Conference on Information Systems (2009)

12. Van der Aalst, W.M.P., ter Hofstede, A.H.M., Weske, M.: Business process management: a survey (2003)
13. Netjes, M., Reijers, H.A., van der Aalst, W.M.P.: FileNet's BPM life-cycle support. Eindhoven University of Technology, Department of Technology Management (2006)
14. Mark, R.: Research Made Simple: A Handbook for Social Workers. SAGE, Thousand Oaks (1996)
15. Creswell, J.W.: Qualitative Inquiry and Research Design: Choosing Among Five Traditions. SAGE, Thousand Oaks (1998). Euro-Par 2006. LNCS, vol. 4128, pp. 1148–1158. Springer, Heidelberg (2006)
16. Yin, R.K.: Case Study Research: Design and Methods, 3rd edn. SAGE, Thousand Oaks (2003)
17. Gulledge, T.R., Sommer, R.A.: Business process management: public sector implications. Bus. Process Manag. J. **8**(4), 364–376 (2002)
18. Markus, L.M., Axline, S., Petrie, D., Tanis, C.: Learning from adopter's experience with ERP: problems encountered and success achieved. J. Inf. Technol. **15**, 245–265 (2000)
19. Idorn, N.: A Business process management approach to ERP implementation. A study of ERP implementation in the light of the third wave of Process Management (2008)
20. Curran, T., Ladd, A.: SAP R/3 Business Blueprint: Understanding Enterprise Supply Chain Management. Prentice Hall, Upper Saddle River (2000)

Business Analytics

Navigating in the Land of Data Analytics

Katrina Kronberga[1], Marite Kirikova[1(✉)], and Daiga Kiopa[2]

[1] Department of Artificial Intelligence and Systems Engineering,
Riga Technical University, 1 Kalku, Riga 1658, Latvia
{katrina.kronberga,marite.kirikova}@rtu.lv
[2] Lursoft IT, 8 Matisa, Riga 1001, Latvia
daiga@lursoft.lv

Abstract. The increasing popularity of data analytics comes together with the many approaches, methods, algorithms, and tools used in different tasks of analytics. When facing a new example of an application of analytics methods with its particular requirements, it would be useful to have an open repository where the experience of the use of different analytical tools is amalgamated. This research in progress paper presents the first results and challenges in the creation of such a repository. The challenges are related to variability in classification, granularity, field of application, purpose of research and other factors. The proposed structure of the repository meets these challenges to some extent and builds the foundation for further development of the repository.

Keywords: Data analytics · Information retrieval · Big data · Data cleansing · Social network analysis · Business intelligence · Data mining · Machine learning

1 Introduction

Data analytics has become a mainstream topic in the field of information systems and business informatics research, but seeing how the number of different analytical methods has grown since the last century (as outlined in Chap. 1 of *Introduction to Artificial Intelligence* [1]), finding the appropriate analytical methods for researchers and analysts can be difficult if not overwhelming. Therefore it is necessary to find a way to navigate this range of available experiences, documented in peer reviewed sources, in order to ease the selection process of analytical methods and minimize the possibility of choosing a method that many have already established as not suited for a particular task or field.

A very good example of amalgamated experiences is Weka – a collection of machine learning algorithms for data mining tasks maintained by the University of Waikato [2]. However, this still refers only to a small part of all the different tasks that occur in various data analytics application cases. Machine learning is not the only data processing method that is used in data analytics and in many cases, – combinations of different methods (e.g., algorithms [3, 4]) are applied. Therefore, additional information is necessary to decide which methods to apply, how to prepare the data, and which tools (dedicated software) to use, or to create, for executing the chosen algorithms.

© Springer International Publishing AG 2017
B. Johansson et al. (Eds.): BIR 2017, LNBIP 295, pp. 125–132, 2017.
DOI: 10.1007/978-3-319-64930-6_9

Currently there are a number of surveys available, for example [5–7], that offer some structured insight into methods of analytics. The challenge with surveys is that they differ in their purposes and grouping methods and thus cannot be extended and used as a backbone for a maintainable knowledge repository of approaches, methods, algorithms, and tools.

The purpose of this research was to survey different works on analytics methods and to build a preliminary structure of a repository which would provide the knowledge of analytics approaches, methods, algorithms, and tools; enabling easy navigation in the "land of analytics", so that the experience gained in research and practice in this area, would be easily accessible and appropriate solutions would be found in the shortest time possible. In the first phase of this research, primarily algorithms have been investigated.

The remainder of the paper is structured as follows. Section 2 discusses related surveys of approaches, methods, algorithms, and tools used in solving tasks of analytics. Section 3 describes the method of creating the initial structure of the repository of analytics-related knowledge. This section also demonstrates how the current structure of the repository has been populated and discusses the challenges that have not been met so far. Section 4 presents brief conclusions and indicates the direction of future work.

2 Related Work

Data analytics is applied in many different areas, such as business intelligence [8], software and network analytics [9] and numerous others. According to Cao [10] data analytics has emerged as an important paradigm for driving the new economy and domains such as Internet of Things, social and mobile networks, and cloud computing; and reforming the classical disciplines. According to [5], data analytics includes data gathering, finding information from the data, and displaying the knowledge to the user. The areas of application of data analytics differ according to the type of data used; for example: amount of data, structure of the data, data actuality (with respect to the time), etc. These differences influence the ways that surveys of data analytics have been created and are used [6, 7].

Authors of [5] distinguish between the following three types of analytics: *Data analytics* – like traditional enterprise data analytics; *Big Data analytics* that requires taking care of data processing time because of volume, velocity, and variety of data; and *Self-learning analytics*, which is not further discussed in [5].

Authors discuss data analytics methods mainly via data mining approaches. Most of these approaches relay on so called structured data, i.e., data which can be analyzed based on their semantic organization that can be used by the data mining algorithms. Structured data is a type of data which is subject to a strictly defined structure; most often a table or a matrix structure in which each row represents an instance of the element, and each column – a descriptive characteristic or a part of the instance [5]. Images can also be seen as structured data. Besides structured data we shall consider also semi-structured data (e.g. text organized under a particular semantically distinguishable structure); and unstructured data such as plain text.

Semi structured and unstructured data are to be considered especially in social media analytics [7], but structured data can be considered the most useful in data analytics because it provides the most varied and useful results, through automated large-scale data analysis. Large-scale data analysis is a complex process in which the following four tasks are most often performed [5]: Clustering, Classification, Discovery of association rules, and Discovery of sequential patterns.

Clustering is a process in which the object instances are grouped so that the instances of the same cluster are more similar to each other than to any other instance of another cluster. Classification is the process in which the instances are grouped into two (or more) groups by one (or more) pre-determined criteria. Association rules is a machine learning method, with the help of which the relationships between the records in the database can be found [11]. Sequential patterns (hereinafter – SP) is a task that aims to find (statistically) significant patterns between the data examples, in which the values are discrete and sequential. As distinct from association rules that characterize object instances that are implemented during the same time, SP is about instances that are carried out at different periods of time.

It should be noted that none of the abovementioned tasks is an algorithm itself, but they are only principles on which the specific algorithms are based. Although each of the listed tasks is often mentioned in the literature, a source [12] claims that all the tasks carried out by algorithms can be classified into two groups – pattern recognition and forecasting; and all other tasks are types of tasks within these groups. The difference between these two categories is the algorithm's output in the particular case. Everything else depends on usage and interpretation. Algorithms performing pattern recognition usually have more than one exit, thus, separating a single group of data into several subgroups. Pattern recognition enables classification of tasks, modeling tasks, and, depending on the context, noise removal from data; because all these tasks are based on recognition of some type of correlation. Algorithms that perform forecasting tasks are characterized by only one output, and their results depend either on the output size, or, alternatively, the generation of a binary yes/no exit [12].

With respect to the algorithms, one of the most successful sources, where the algorithms are amalgamated and made available, is the Weka repository of machine learning algorithms [2]. Machine learning algorithms are often used in data analytics, e.g. in data mining. In this paper Weka will be regarded as the related repository of knowledge that can be referenced from the broader repository of analytics related knowledge. We performed a wider analysis of approaches, methods, algorithms and tools because we aimed at contextual knowledge of usage of them, i.e. we wanted to build a repository of experiences gained in data analytics to ensure an easier and faster selection process of appropriate approaches, methods, algorithms, and tools for specific tasks of analytics. Different lists of algorithms and tools (e.g. platforms [5]) are available in the surveys done by different researchers and this information was valuable for the building of the repository. However, the surveys usually do not report the context of use of algorithms and tools, thus, some of this information had to be traced back in our study.

We analyzed a number of sources of information, to identify what approaches, methods, algorithms, and tools are most commonly used for particular analytics tasks, so as to enable the informed choice of these, from the repository, i.e. to provide an easier navigation in the analytics area. The method of literature analysis and initial structure of the repository are discussed in the next section.

3 Towards Data Analytics Experience Repository

When designing the structure of the repository we first tried to see how different authors approached specific tasks; what are the relationships between the methods and algorithms, and what pros and cons of application of particular methods and algorithms can be found in the literature. One of the challenges that we did not fully resolve was that there is no clear distinction between the methods and algorithms in the literature, so, in many cases, we had to seek for appropriate interpretation by visiting Weka and looking for additional information in related work. The excerpt of preliminary results obtained by this literature analysis is presented in Table 1. Altogether 65 sources were analyzed and 22 methods considered.

After this preliminary analysis (first iteration, Table 1), in the second iteration the initial structure of the repository was decided. It consisted of the following items:

- The *title* of the method, model, or algorithm: the attempt to distinguish explicitly between approaches, methods, and algorithms was not successful, because the authors of related research seemingly had different assumptions regarding how to define an approach, method, and algorithm. The notion "model" was introduced as in many sources the term "model" was used when referring to the approaches used in data analytics. Currently the tools were left out of the scope of the repository as their proper addressing required additional research.
- *Abbreviation* of the method, model, or algorithm, which was further used in other parts of the repository to refer to the method, model, or algorithm.
- *Usage area* describes the area of application of the method, model, or algorithm. The usage is described at two levels of abstraction:
  - General – referring to the type of application in general, e.g. natural language processing;
  - Specific – referring to the particular usage, e.g. recognition of writer names [13].
- *Application case* describes particular application cases of the method, model, or algorithm as described in the analyzed source.
- *Data* describes what kind of data is needed to apply the method, model, or algorithm, e.g., text or images.
- *Used together with* – describes together with what other methods, models, or algorithms the current one has been used in a particular case. This is further detailed as follows: *Before*: referring to what methods, models, and algorithms have been applied to the same data before the use of the current one (to prepare the data); *In parallel*: methods, models, and algorithms which have been used in parallel with the current one for the same task, e.g. for comparison of the behavior of the algorithms; *Together*: sometimes methods, models, and algorithms are integrated or joined together to achieve better functionality [1]; and *After*: the methods, models, or algorithms that have been used to process the data, obtained by the current method, model, or algorithm.
- *Critique/conclusions*: Comprehensive conclusions about the use of the method, model, or algorithm (if such were available in the related work).

Table 1. Methods and algorithms and their usage (1st iteration).

Method	What it does	Algorithms	The basic concept	Pro's	Con's
Bayes approach	Classification	Naive Bayes approach (Naïve Bayesian classification) NBC [8]	Defines a model for the probability distributions in the classes and formulates the classification problem in the context of Bayes decision theory [2] NBC is based on the notion of word independence - the conditional probability of a word in a category is assumed to be independent from the probabilities of other words in that category [9]	- NBC is a popular document classification method because of good performance in a variety of cases [9] - a simple and effective machine learning method in text classification [9]	- not adequate for handling real-time stream data [9]
K-Nearest-Neighbor Classification	Classification	K-Nearest-Neighbor (NN) Classification	An object is classified by a majority vote of its neighbors, with the object being assigned to the class most common among its *k* nearest neighbors [2]	- does not need an explicit training phase [2] - suitable for classification problems of time series [2] - good accuracy, is suitable for multiple classification problems, widely used in the field of document classification [10]	- is sensitive to the local structure data [2] - problematic to measure the distance between non-quantitative variables [2] - when dealing with a training data set with a class imbalance problem, classification results tend to be biased towards majority class; accuracy of classifier is reduced [10]
Logistic regression	Classification		Measures the relationship between the categorical dependent variable and one or more	- Linear regression is useful for data with linear relations or applications for which a	- is slow for high-dimensional problems, but [9] provides a (non-standardized) solution to this problem

(continued)

Table 1. (*continued*)

Method	What it does	Algorithms	The basic concept	Pro's	Con's
			independent variables by estimating probabilities using a logistic function, which is the cumulative logistic distribution. [9]	first-order approximation is adequate [9] - interpretability of the parameter estimates [9]	
Neural Netw.	Classification, pattern recognition	Several NN algorithms	Learns to classify and/or recognize patterns from test data and recognize and classify similar data accordingly [8, 21]	- suitable if one must find models for problems with limited knowledge about the relation between input and output variables [2]	- difficult to calculate weights [8]

Currently the repository is organized as a table in Excel. To illustrate some of the records in this paper, we chose the Vector Space Model (abbreviation – VSM) that is used for information filtering, indexing, and relevance rankings. For this model, the following general usage areas were detected: social network analysis [9, 14]; natural language processing [15]; and image analysis. In the *general usage* area for social network analysis two specific areas were recorded, namely, tweet analysis in Twitter [14] and analysis of other social networks [9]. The application case for Twitter analysis is the analysis of the set of tweets to produce a graph of the most important concepts. The data used in this case is text. In this application case the tokenization is used before the application of VSM, and the data obtained using VSM is processed by Latent Discrete Allocation (LDA) and Markov Clustering (MCL). In natural language processing the following specific usage cases were recorded:

- Analysis of similarity of sentences [16] (data type – text), with the application case "semantic similarities based text similarity analysis" used in parallel with dependency trees and WordNet database [17]; and with the critique that this model is not applicable for short sentences.
- Plagiarism detection [18], with the application for text similarity analysis based on the similarity of words used, data type – text. Used in parallel with the Jaccard similarity measure, together with the unigram approach, bigram approach and trigram approach, the results are further processed by the Cosine similarity measure.
- Name recognition [15], applied for name recognition in cases where several authors have the same name or one and the same author has published work under different names, data type – text. The data obtained is post-processed by CSM.
- Document classification, which is based on ontology concepts and their location in the ontology [19], data type – text, pre-processed by Markov algorithms and used

together with Decision trees; and applied for specific criteria-based document classification [20], with the data types: text and image.

The current structure of the repository has the following advantages: (1) it is possible to search the methods by different criteria; (2) it is possible to group the methods, models, and algorithms in bigger granules, based on proven results of other researchers; (3) it is easy to extend the repository; and (4) it is easy to have several different views on the repository.

However there are also several challenges that have not yet been resolved, namely (1) it has not been found how to correctly distinguish between the titles "method", "model", "algorithm", and "approach" as different authors refer to one and the same things in various ways; (2) the tools the authors used when performing data analytics were often omitted or just mentioned without providing sufficient information to make conclusions and thus have not been included; (3) the structure of the repository chosen in the 2nd iteration does not fully include the knowledge obtained when developing its first version illustrated in Table 1; and (4) the maintenance strategy of the repository has not yet been designed.

4 Conclusions

The paper discusses the research in progress which aims at developing a repository that amalgamates experiences in the use of data analytics approaches, methods, algorithms, and tools. The initial structure of the repository was elaborated in two iterations – first by focusing on methods and trying to relate them to the algorithms and tools, and than finding pros and cons of the methods; and, second, by elaborating the findings so that the relationships between different methods, models, and algorithms would be seen and each application case could be traced separately.

The repository that has been created helps to navigate the knowledge on data analytics and it was successfully applied for algorithm selection for a multi-agent system of identification of politically exposed persons. Its further development will concern meeting the challenges that were discussed at the end of Sect. 3. One of the possible approaches to be taken is situational methods engineering [21].

Acknowledgment. The research was supported by the funding from the research project "Competence Centre of Information and Communication Technologies" of EU Structural funds, contract No. 1.2.1.1/16/A/007 signed between ITCC and CFCA, project No. 1.14. "Development of optimization model for the flow of data processing algorithms to be used for the identification of politically exposed persons".

References

1. Mariusz, F.: Introduction to Artificial Intelligence, 1st edn. Springer International Publishing, Switzerland (2016)
2. Witten, I.H., Frank, E., Hall, M.A., Pal, C.J.: Data Mining, Fourth Edition: Practical Machine Learning Tools and Techniques (Morgan Kaufmann Series in Data Management Systems), 4th edn. Morgan Kaufmann, Burlington (2016)

3. Wang, Y., Xu, L.: Research on text categorization of KNN based on K-means for class imbalanced problem. In: 2016 Sixth International Conference on Instrumentation & Measurement, Computer, Communication and Control, pp. 357–583 (2016)
4. Jung, Y.G, Kim, K.T., et al.: Enhanced Naive Bayes classifier for real-time sentiment analysis with SparkR. In: 2016 International Conference on Information and Communication Technology Convergence (ICTC), pp. 141–147 (2016)
5. Tsai, C.W., Lai, C.F., Chao, H.-C., Vasilakos, A.: Big data analysis: a survey. J. Big Data 1, 2–21 (2015)
6. Singh, D., Reddy, C.K.: A survey on platforms for big data analytics. J. Big Data 2, 1–8 (2014)
7. Batrinca, B., Treleaven, P.C.: Social media analytics: a survey of techniques, tools and platforms. AI & Soc. 30, 89–116 (2015)
8. Grossmann, W., Rinderle-Ma, S.: Fundamentals of Business Intelligence. Springer, Heidelberg (2015). 361 p.
9. Khotimah, H., Djatna, T., et al.: Tourism recommendation based on vector space model using composite social media extraction. In: Proceedings of the International Conference on Advanced Computer Science and Information Systems (ICACSIS), pp. 303–308 (2014)
10. Cao, L.: Data science and analytics: a new era. Int. J. Data Sci. Anal. 1, 1–2 (2016)
11. Margaret, R.: Search business analytics, Association rules (in data mining) (2010). (updated February 2011). http://searchbusinessanalytics.techtarget.com/definition/association-rules-in-data-mining. Accessed 15 Dec 2016
12. Kattan, A., Abdullah, R., Geem Z.W.: Feed-forward neural networks. In: Artificial Neural Network Training and Software Implementation Techniques, pp. 3–10. Nova Science Publishers, New York, United States of America (2011)
13. Brando, C., Frontini, F., Ganascia, J.-G.: REDEN: named entity linking in digital literary editions using linked data sets. Complex Syst. Inform. Model. Q. CSIMQ (7), 60–80 (2016). doi:10.7250/csimq.2016-7.04. ISSN 2255-9922
14. Azam, N., Abulaish, M., et al.: Twitter data mining for event classification and analysis. In: Proceedings of the Second International Conference on Soft Computing and Machine Intelligence, pp. 79–83 (2015)
15. Arif, T., Ali, R., Asger, M.: Author name disambiguation using vector space model and hybrid similarity measures. In: Seventh International Conference on Contemporary Computing (IC3), pp. 135–140 (2014)
16. Gunasinghe, U.L.D.N., De Silva, W.A.M., et al.: Sentence similarity measuring by vector space model. In: Proceedings of the International Conference on Advances in ICT for Emerging Regions (ICTer), pp. 185–189 (2014)
17. Liu, D., Liu, Z., et al.: A dependency grammar and WordNet based sentence similarity measure. J. Comput. Inf. Syst. 8(3), 1027–1035 (2012)
18. Jahan, J.A., Ragel, R.: Plagiarism detection on electronic text based assignments using vector space model. In: Proceedings of the 7th International Conference on Information and Automations for Sustainability, pp. 1–5 (2014)
19. Kastrati, Z., Imran, A.S., Yayilgan, S.Y.: An improved concept vector space model for ontology based classification. In: Proceedings of the 11th International Conference on Signal-Image Technology & Internet-based Systems, pp. 240–245 (2015)
20. Premalatha, R., Srinivasan, S.: Text processing in information retrieval system using vector space model. In: Proceedings of the International Conference on Information Communication and Embedded Systems ICICES2014, pp. 1–6 (2014)
21. Henderson-Sellers, B., Ralyté, J.: Situational method engineering: state-of-the-art review. J. Univ. Comput. Sci. 16(3), 424–478 (2010)

Model for Identification of Politically Exposed Persons

Zane Miltina[1], Arnis Stasko[1], Ingars Erins[1], Janis Grundspenkis[1],
Marite Kirikova[1(✉)], and Girts Kebers[2]

[1] Riga Technical University, Riga, Latvia
{zane.miltina, arnis.stasko}@edu.rtu.lv,
{ingars.erins, janis.grundspenkis,
marite.kirikova}@rtu.lv
[2] SIA "Lursoft IT", Riga, Latvia
kebers@lursoft.lv

Abstract. Due to increasing strength of regulatory requirements in area of money laundering and terrorism financing prevention, financial institutions are looking for ways to retrieve, analyse and interpret relevant information on politically exposed persons (PEPs). Task addresses complex decision making over distributed data. Manual PEP identification is labour and time consuming, therefore, IT solutions are necessary to support and enhance the process. This paper highlights the complexity of regulatory demands inherent in the PEP definition, reveals a number of requirements for PEP identification and proposes a model for PEP status identification. The model follows a multi-agent paradigm enabling several scenarios of PEP identification with involvement of software and human agents. Although the proposed PEP status identification model is created in accordance with the regulatory requirements and countries specific data sources for the Republic of Latvia, still, the model can be adjusted for use also in other EU countries.

Keywords: Politically exposed person · Multi-agent approach · Data and business analytics · Conceptual modelling

1 Introduction

With strengthening of the precautionary and control activities regarding the prevention of money laundering and financing of terrorism in the world and also in the Republic of Latvia, special attention should be paid to identification of politically exposed persons (hereinafter – PEPs). The strengthened requirements and subsequently identification and monitoring of PEPs are requiring the financial institutions to set up an internal control system to actively analyse and identify the PEPs [3].

Financial institutions are currently grounding their PEP status identification effort either on manual searches from various databases and lists, or on PEP status identification solutions based on pre-fed PEP lists. These solutions are efficient in PEP status identification for PEPs, but are largely failing on PEP family member or person closely related to PEP identification. There is no holistic solution for efficient PEP status

© Springer International Publishing AG 2017
B. Johansson et al. (Eds.): BIR 2017, LNBIP 295, pp. 133–147, 2017.
DOI: 10.1007/978-3-319-64930-6_10

identification that would be able to analyse, extract and interpret information combined from various data sources. The purpose of this paper is to amalgamate and structure the requirements for PEP identification and to develop the PEP status identification model that meets these requirements.

In the study underlying this paper the design science approach was followed, which provides both new knowledge and new artefact(s) [1, 2]. Identification, collection and systematic analysis of the scientific works have been carried out to get new knowledge of the existing possibilities of PEP status identification. This knowledge forms the basis for the development of a new artefact – a PEP status identification model.

This paper proposes PEP status identification model based on the multi-agent approach, which enables combining various approaches, methods and algorithms depending on their specialisation and available data sources. PEP status identification model offers high degree of practical applicability in solving complex problems, ensured by flexible combination of specialised agents.

The paper is structured as follows. The scope definition is provided in Sect. 2. The problem definition is given and related work is discussed in Sect. 3. In Sect. 4 the requirements relevant in PEP status identification model development are presented. The multi-agent PEP status identification model is proposed in Sect. 5. The model enables a holistic and systematic approach to PEP status identification. The proposed solution includes PEP status identification and validation mechanisms, points out the needed data sources for obtaining PEP identification information, and defines the knowledge and research areas necessary for the PEP status identification and validation. The proposed model is evaluated in Sect. 6. Conclusions are stated in Sect. 7.

2 Scope Definition

In order to ensure compliance with the requirements of the Law on the Prevention of Money Laundering and Terrorism Financing [3] financial institutions are expected to develop an internal control system that covers customers identification, customers evaluation for their financial transactions and behaviour pattern fitting the type and the specifics of the business that the particular customer is operating in as well as monitoring and reporting suspicious transactions to the relevant regulatory authorities.

Law [3] stipulates obligation for financial institution not only to identify the PEPs, but also to identify the PEP related parties, family members, friends and relatives who could affect actions done by PEP. In this paper, for simplicity, where appropriate, the statuses of "PEP family members" and "persons closely related to PEP", as noted in the Law [3], are commonly referenced as PEP related persons or PEP related parties.

Various sources define and elaborate on PEP identification requirements thus expanding the PEP definition and related requirements. The Financial Action Task Force (FATF) defines the PEP as an individual who is or has been entrusted with a prominent public function [4]. Due to their position and influence, it is recognised that many PEPs are in positions that potentially can be abused for the purpose of committing money laundering offences and related predicate offences, including corruption and bribery, as well as conducting activity related to terrorism financing [4].

The PEP status identification model is designed considering the PEP definition and the governing regulatory requirements in force as of April, 2017. Three types of PEP are specified in details by the Law [3, Sect. 1, Clause 18], namely: PEP, PEP family member and Person closely related to PEP. Additional complexity to the PEP identification task was added by the obligation to apply complementary measures and in-depth customer research for the PEP, his/her family member, and a person who is closely related to the politically exposed person [4, 5]. This means that the research to be done by financial institution is not limited to analysis of easily accessible information sources such as public data registries, but also demands additional effort of investigating supplementary data sources to identify missing information and also to cross check and verify the information found. This in requires verification of data source credibility and evaluation of information retrieved by combining multiple data sources.

Considering the full set of requirements embedded in definition of a PEP, family members of a PEP and persons closely related to a PEP, there can be multiple search criteria for each requirement placed in PEP definition and preferred data sources identified where to search for the needed information. In order to ensure thorough assessment of PEP and their related persons' status identification, the following relationship categories were defined:

- PEP entity and its associated entities;
- PEP relationship types (to determine the family and close relations);
- Transaction types (in order to identify mutual business relationships and a motive).

PEP status identification model design was created purely basing it on the PEP status definition in statutory requirements. Based on the requirements, information needed for PEP status identification was determined and the available data sources were matched into created model along with specialised agents for information extraction, fusion, interpretation and decision-making. In order to ensure consistency, the PEP status identification model is designed considering that the data source is a variable – it is assumed that individual data sources can be added or removed, depending on their availability. Technical retrieval of the information from data sources with various data retrieval algorithms, web crawlers, and manually obtained and interpreted data are out of the scope of this paper. PEP status identification model has been created also on the assumption that the entity using the solution complies with all relevant data protection law requirements.

3   Problem Definition and Related Work

Identification of PEPs is one of the major challenges in the field of national and financial security. Researchers and analysts have endeavoured to meet this challenge mostly by trying to create a comprehensive PEP and PEP related party status identification models. Recommendations for Credit Institutions and Financial Institutions to Establish and Research Politically Exposed Persons, their Family Members, and Closely-related Persons and to Monitor Transactions issued by Financial and Capital Market Commission of Latvia [5] provide definition of PEP and their related parties, define the information sources for PEP identification, which affect the status of the related parties, the use of personal data and other legitimate factors. These Recommendations [5] provide more specific interpretation of PEP definition and application guidelines of the Law [3] and The Financial Action Task Force (FATF) guidance [4].

There is very limited information on PEP status identification related issues in scientific sources, nevertheless, there are several patents and commercial tools found. CaseWare Analytics [6, 7] describes an IT solution for global identification of the PEP. CaseWare Analytics study offers division of PEP status into four classes, depending on the likelihood (risk) that a person is a PEP, as well as providing insight into the PEP identification solution development, i.e. the principal (the necessary) components – a possible solution for automation, integration and use of the solution in real-time; as well as describing the solution use and maintenance of the process and PEP status visualization. CaseWare Analytics also highlights a number of issues that require more detailed research in connection with the PEP status identification, such as same person being listed in several government lists – needing to recognise that it is the same person; having the name transcribed in ways; alternative names being used – mechanism for matching the person in several sources thus decreasing the number or duplicates in PEP list and other issues.

Possible solutions of the PEP identification problem and related data retrieval risks are provided in a number of patents. Schiffer patents titled "Method of ranking politically exposed persons and other persons and heightened risk entity" [8] describes a method in which a person is assigned with an index, which determines the likelihood that a person is politically exposed; visual graphs of related parties are created and persons are indexed based on their political, financial or social impact in their related parties graph.

David Lawrence (David Lawrence) patents titled "Automated Political risk management" [9] describe the risk management methods and analytical system that based on the person's position, transaction history, political opinions and other factors (such as interpretation of world events) analyses and quantitatively expresses risks associated with PEP.

Patent related to [9] "Method, system, apparatus, program code and means for the identifying and extracting information" [10] develops further the ideas proposed by Lawrence [9] and defines the information retrieval on PEPs from a more technical point of view, providing with an in-depth description of the PEP risk factors, solution design and architecture and related business processes.

Patent "Evaluating customer risk" [11] provides a different approach to the PEP and the associated risk identification. A system, aimed to identify customers with an increased money laundering or terrorism financing risks is described. Solution described in the patent contains questionnaires that customer is expected to respond and based on the customer's responses the solution establishes the risk factor of a customer (value from 0 to 100) and quantifies it based on a risk model [11].

Each of the described solutions above relies upon an explicit or tacit interpretation of PEP definition. If this interpretation is not unambiguously provided, the possibility to reuse the solution is low, as the mechanism might return the results that do not correspond to the interpretation applied in the reuse situation.

4 Requirements for the PEP Status Identification Model Development

As a result of the study of PEP status identification problem the following main challenges and their possible solutions were identified:

- **Ambiguously interpretable data:** not always the information available in data sources is sufficient for clear/unmistaken identification of the unique person. It refers especially to information in such data sources as social networks, portals, newspapers, etc.; and to information on relationships with closely related persons of a PEP. According to the regulatory requirements of Latvia [12] the only way to uniquely identify a person is by using a personal identification number as well as name and surname combinations. However, such data is not always available in one particular data source; therefore, different combinations of data (or data fusion) should be used to obtain needed information.
- **Duration of PEP status:** The Law states that the PEP status expires in either of two events: a PEP dies or a PEP does not hold a major public position for at least 12 months and his/her business relationships no longer create an increased risk of money laundering [3, Sect. 25, Paragraph 5]. This means that after 12 months PEP status identification should be repeated and if there are no other evidences found that a person is a PEP, then the PEP status can be removed. Therefore, when designing PEP status identification model, the time factor needs to be incorporated along with the PEP status and repeated status checks scheduled.
- **Identification of a motive:** besides the list of clearly defined family members, the Recommendations [4, 5] stipulate that persons, which are substantially considered to be family members (such as an actual cohabiting partner), but formally are not included in the list of family members; persons outside the family (such as friends, girlfriends, lovers) can be PEP related persons, as well. This complicates the model design as these persons are difficult or even impossible to detect as these relationships are not registered. Moreover, the motive has to be identified: "There is the trust and commitment between such persons, which can serve as grounds for the PEP to hide his/her abuse of public power for personal benefit by the help of such person" [4, 5]. Since there are no registers of cohabitation partners, such information has to be searched in social networks or media, which are both low reliability data sources.
- **Identification of close relationship with PEP:** Recommendations [5] stipulate that a person, who has business relationships with the PEP, has to be granted with a status of a "person closely related to PEP". Several areas are to be of particular interest: real estate deals, procurement deals of state, business partners of the PEP, as well as those who share participation in a company's board or council with the PEP. For the purpose of the model creation, business relationships, business areas, transaction types, transaction parties and the data sources for obtaining such information have been identified. In order to identify high-risk transactions, the criteria can be used for the transaction amount. Existing regulatory requirements do not stipulate a specific transaction amount for the business relationships with a PEP to serve as a grounds for a person becoming closely related to a PEP. On the other hand, to minimise the number of false negatives, there are transaction limits

recommended for each type of transactions. When designing the PEP status identification model, it is important that transaction types and business areas can be
combined with transaction amount criteria, which can be defined by the user.

The above-discussed challenges show that the PEP identification process will
require a combination of different methods and tools that have to be systematically
organized for achieving the goal of identification of PEPs. To have a systematic view
on the PEP identification process, the PEP status identification model that amalgamates
the methods, algorithms and tools and prescribes their potential sequences of usage is
necessary. Table 1 summarizes the requirements towards PEP status identification

Table 1. Requirements for the PEP status identification model

Area	PEP status identification model shall be able to:
Data sources	1. Extract data from country specific (in this case Latvia) data sources 2. Continue efficient operation irrespective of what data sources are available, i.e. data sources can be added/removed from the model 3. Effectively perform various data renewal strategies from data sources
Data extraction	1. Retrieve and interpret data with language specific diacritical marks, declinations and grammar 2. Assess the reliability of the data source 3. Find, collect and store complete set of personal identification data in various sources to be able to unambiguously identify the person
Data quality	1. Operate with incomplete, erroneous data 2. Analyse information reliability 3. Efficiently involve experts in data review process
Finding PEP related parties	1. Recognize not only the PEPs, which is relatively stable list of persons, but efficiently identifies PEP related parties 2. Discover unregistered relationships (actual cohabitation partners, persons that are substantially considered to be family members in social networks and media (low reliability data sources)
Adding several characteristics/criteria to search values	1. Search and store several person's job place and position combinations (important for correct identification of PEP based on high position in public organisation) 2. Search a combination of person and organisation in related data sources (important for identification of persons with incomplete identification information) 3. Attach time factor to person's status (important for storing the duration of a PEP status due to a maximum term in position and expiry of PEP status after leaving the public position [3, article 25] 4. Link the transaction type of the transaction amount (important for identification or closely related persons to PEPs based on business relationship)
Holistic approach of the model totality	1. Satisfy all PEP definition requirements 2. Provide high reliability of results 1. Provide basis for identifying persons as PEPs 2. Demand only minimal to none involvement of experts 3. Reduce the percentage of false negative results (important as it harms the business of the model users the most – penalties, reputation deterioration, suspension of banking license, etc.)
Model capability to adapt to future changes	1. Add new data sources (e.g. if cohabitation partner information will become available in government officials' income/property declarations as a result of regulatory requirement change) 2. Supplement or change the search/data merge criteria based on PEP definition amendments.

model based on regulatory requirements, the complexity of PEP definition interpretation, and the results of analysis of related work.

It is important to point out that the paper reflects results obtained during the initial stages of the research the final goal of which is to develop an adequate model that satisfies all requirements summarised in Table 1 and provides an optimal sequence of methods, algorithms and tools for processing data about PEPs, their family members and PEP closely related persons. The search for appropriate approaches, methods, algorithms and tools to ensure identification of PEPs with high degree of reliability has been carried out and results are briefly presented in the next section.

5 Multi-agent Model for PEP Identification

To develop the model, the design science principles of obtaining new knowledge and new artefact (the PEP status identification model) were followed. After analysis of the related work, the problem domain was deeply analysed, especially with respect to the data available and reliability of data sources. Data analytics methods and algorithms (potentially applicable in the PEP identification domain) were amalgamated and analysed. Further, candidate approaches from the related work, namely ontology based approaches [13, 14], data fusion based approaches [15, 16] and natural language processing algorithms for text analysis taking into account language specific diacritical marks, declinations and grammar elements [17] were applied to the PEP identification problem [18]. On the basis of the obtained knowledge it was concluded that the identification of PEPs is a complex decision making problem over distributed knowledge domain. Influenced by the contention made by Padgham and Winikoff, who in their book [19] referencing Jennings [20] stated that "agents are 'well suited for developing complex distributed systems' since they provide more natural abstraction and decomposition of complex 'nearly-decomposable' systems", it was chosen to model potential solution with the multi-agent approach. To ensure the production of a rigid agent-oriented solution the Prometheus methodology [19] for modelling was chosen.

The multi-agent approach helps to obtain a natural overview of the planned solution and to identify the potential difficulties of a problem. Before describing the model, it is worth to remind the requirements of the PEP identification. PEPs are those persons who correspond to the PEP features set out in Law [3]. In addition, having regard to the related persons as defined by the Law [3] and the recommendations [5], the model has to identify also the family members and persons closely related to PEP. The PEP family members are visualized in Fig. 1.

Assuming that family links are permanent and the number of PEPs is comprehensible in Latvia (10000–15000 persons [21]), it was found useful to prepare a PEP database containing PEPs and closely related persons (family members and family members placed on the same level to those persons) in advance. Such approach requires compiling a single database of all PEP lists, adding the identification information from various related data sources (to enable unambiguous identification of the person in different data sources) and, for all persons in PEP lists, identification of closely related parties (Fig. 2), thus distinguishing five types of external data sources.

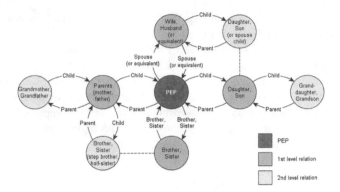

Fig. 1. PEP family members

Definitions of persons closely related to PEP are based on mutual business relations (Fig. 2.). Changes of and transactions related to company ownership structure can be carried out every day, therefore it is beneficial to obtain this information from anew during the PEP status identification request processing.

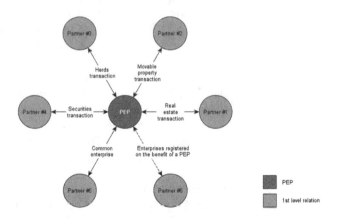

Fig. 2. Persons closely related to a PEP

The system's goals are a natural construct to initiate system specification [19]. This refers also to the building of models. To fulfil the PEP identification requirements, the following two main goals have to be met – *maintain PEP database* and *determine the person's PEP status upon a request*. According to the Prometheus methodology detailed goal models were constructed for both above-mentioned goals (Figs. 3 and 4).

For the PEP database maintenance goal (Fig. 3) four sub-goals were found, namely, maintain data source database, summarize the PEP list from data sources, summarize related family persons from data sources, and identify the persons unequivocally. These sub-goals where further decomposed where appropriate.

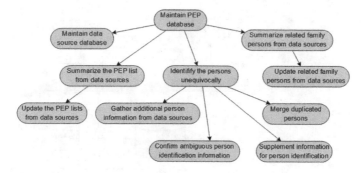

Fig. 3. "PEP database maintenance" goal diagram

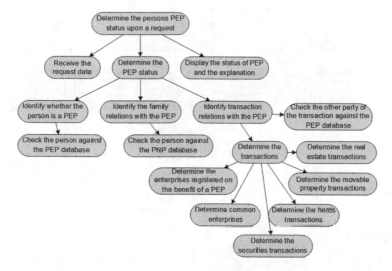

Fig. 4. "Person's PEP status determination upon a request" goal diagram

The diagram for the goal "determine the persons PEP status upon a request" is shown in Fig. 4. To support the goal, it is necessary to handle requests, identify whether person is a PEP, identify the family relations with a PEP, and identify transaction relations with a PEP.

After goal identification, the PEP identification functionalities were established. Conforming to *Prometheus* methodology, the functionality is a term used for "a chunk of behaviour, which includes a grouping of related goals, as well as percepts, actions and data relevant to the behaviour" [19]. Furthermore, the decision about agent classes was obtained by combing the functionalities. According to *Prometheus* methodology "The choice of how functionalities are to be combined is made by considering the functionalities and scenarios and developing possible groupings of functionalities into agents, which are then evaluated according to the standard software engineering criteria of coupling and cohesion" [19]. The obtained agent classes are shown in Fig. 5.

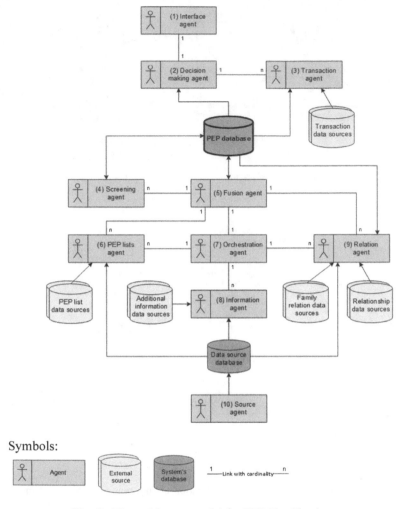

Fig. 5. The multi-agent model for PEP identification

The agent classes are described in Table 2.

To support the identification of PEPs, three main scenarios were established – PEP list maintenance scenario, PEP relation maintenance scenario and request handling scenario. During the setup of the system that will correspond to the above-described model the PEP list maintenance scenario and the PEP relation maintenance scenario are expected to be run sequentially. After the setup any of three scenarios can be run independently, corresponding to the schedule or on a request.

The PEP list maintenance scenario includes data source list update, PEP list renewal from data sources, additional person identification information gathering, data fusion, and, finally, ambiguous data screening for approval. The PEP relation maintenance scenario operates similarly: it starts with the data source list update, then

Table 2. Agent classes

No	Agent class	Realization	Description
1.	Interface agent	Software agent	Implements the user interface for request reception and providing an answer. <u>Specialization:</u> web UI, graph display
2.	Decision making agent	Software agent	Upon receipt of request, examines the person against the PEP database - whether he or she is a PEP or have the family relations with a PEP. Requests the transaction agent for any person's transactions with a PEP. Makes aggregated decision regarding PEP status based on information received. <u>Specialization:</u> decision making, ontology application
3.	Transaction agent	Software agent	Gathers transaction information with the person from multiple data sources. Examines each transaction counter parties against PEP database. Prepares a list of PEP status affecting transactions. <u>Specialization:</u> data source renewal strategy, data crawling, ontology application
4.	Screening agent	Human agent	During local PEP database establishment reviews ambiguous person identification information. <u>Specialization:</u> expert decision
5.	Fusion agent	Software agent	Receives collected information gathered by other agents, such as PEP list agent, Relation agent and Information agent. Performs data fusion on received information. <u>Specialization:</u> data fusion, ontology application, information reliability validation
6.	PEP list agent	Software agent	According to the schedule gathers PEP lists from PEP list data sources. <u>Specialization:</u> data source renewal strategy, data crawling
7.	Orchestration agent	Software agent	Receives person lists for identification information improvement and orchestrates information gathering. <u>Specialization:</u> task orchestration
8.	Relation agent	Software agent	According to the schedule gathers family relationships and close relationship ties from family relationship data sources and close relationship data sources (social networks and news media) in the PEP database. <u>Specialization:</u> data source renewal strategy, data crawling, natural language processing
9.	Information agent	Software agent	Looks for additional identification information for the PEPs and related persons. <u>Specialization:</u> data source renewal strategy, data crawling, natural language processing
10.	Source agent	Human agent	Maintains the data source database, which contains information of data sources for each external data source type and their respective data renewal strategies: PEP list data sources, additional information data sources, family relationship data sources, close relationship data sources and transaction data sources. <u>Specialization:</u> expert decision

continues with PEP family member list renewal from the data sources, the additional person identification information gathering, the data fusion, and, finally, the ambiguous data screening for approval.

The request handling scenario expects that the PEP list maintenance and the PEP relation maintenance scenarios have been executed successfully at least once and the PEP database has been set up. Subsequently, by receiving user request, the request handling scenario checks if requested person can be found in the PEP database, if the person under investigation is related to the persons in the PEP database and if the person under investigation has any transactions with the persons in the PEP database. Finally, complex decision about the requested person's PEP status is made and results are returned to the user.

6 Evaluation of the Proposed Model

From challenges and complexity of the PEP definition and the regulatory requirements discussed in this paper it is evident that for obtaining a holistic and effective PEP identification model no one single approach exists that can be used for satisfying all of these requirements stated in Sect. 4. Instead, a combination of different methods and approaches systematically organized in a model has to be used.

The proposed model is based on the multi-agent paradigm, which allows structuring the complex problem onto several agents. Consequently, each agent is dedicated for solving specific task and it is equipped with selected methods and approaches, such as data fusion, ontology, natural language processing and various information retrieval and data mining algorithms and methods.

In order to verify the proposed model, it will be assessed against the PEP status identification model requirements set out in Sect. 4 of this paper.

During PEP status identification model design, PEP definition requirements were translated into detailed search tasks and possible data sources for each search task were selected. Methods for natural language processing [17] were prescribed by the model to enable search and retrieving of data that contains language specific diacritical marks, declinations and grammar elements, thus ensuring natural language processing capabilities. This is particularly important for handling various unstructured data sources, which is currently the only source for identification of persons closely related to a PEP.

When examining available data sources, it was observed that there was a number of data quality and consistency issues as well as there was a number of areas where the data was not structured and were incomplete. Data-fusion algorithms [15, 16] prescribed by the model are capable of compiling the obtained data, discarding insufficient quality data and involving the expert in the process of ambiguous data review and approval. In order to operate with data of various reliability, the model is able to consider the information reliability factor.

The model provides expert involvement in PEP database preparation process in terms of minimal use of expert time by limiting the expert involvement only to critical assessment functions where human intervention is required in interpretation of the received data. PEP status identification model is built in a way that the expert involvement is not needed in real-time operation, but rather in PEP database establishment and support, which enables to provide PEP status investigation results in real-time.

The proposed model encompasses agents specialised on ontology reasoning methods for rule-based PEP status evaluation. The proposed multi-agent model also assumes maintaining a database, which stores all previously identified PEP persons along with the family relationship and business relationship lists. Addition of an internal database allows faster status identification due to re-using data already obtained and searching the local database only, instead of real time data search in external data sources.

For several agents there are more than one options of how the specific task can be approached. Currently the experiments are carried out to select the most efficient alternatives with respect to better PEP identification, fewer process steps, less time and lesser human expert involvement, and identification of the most efficient sequence of the tasks in the model.

In comparison with related works and analysed patents, the proposed PEP status identification has clearer structure that shows both the main data sources and main functions to be performed over the data, thus, the model has higher potential of reusability than solutions discussed in Sect. 3. It has the ability to cover the totality of regulatory requirements and can be relatively easy changed in case of changes in regulations due to modular structure of the model. The model allows to work with various country specific data sources and language specific diacritic and grammar elements and to retrieve and interpret data from unstructured data sources and, thus, to obtain as complete set of persons identification data as possible, that in turn allows for identification of a person under investigation in various sources and get as precise PEP status identification results as possible with the given sources.

7   Conclusion

This paper focuses on creation of PEP status identification model for the specific case of the Republic of Latvia in accordance with the regulatory requirements set out in the definition of the status of the PEP, as well as the data sources of Latvia. However, since in the Republic of Latvia the PEP status identification and recognition methodology is developed in accordance with the international requirements (FATF definitions) and aligned with European Union directives, the findings of presented work are applicable also for other countries in Europe. For reusing the PEP status identification model, the sources of information and unique parameters should be adjusted to country specific data as well as the local regulatory requirements should be verified to ensure the completeness of the PEP status identification model.

The developed PEP status identification model suggests possible usage sequences of approaches, methods and algorithms for extracting and processing data pertaining to PEPs and their related parties in order to ensure identification of PEPs with a high degree of reliability. Different data analytics methods and their combinations were investigated during the model development process. A multi-agent approach was considered [18, 22] as one of the potential solutions besides the ontology based and data fusion based approaches. The discussion of other approaches as stand-alone solutions is out of the scope of this paper as number of limitations were discovered in their ability to satisfy the PEP status identification model requirements set out in Sect. 4 of this paper. While ontology based and data fusion based approaches proved to be efficient in solving parts of the PEP definition based requirements, the multi-agent approach gave an opportunity to systemically cover all requirements.

The proposed PEP status identification model based on the multi-agent approach demonstrates the suitability for PEP identification task. The model not only allows to incorporate algorithms and methods in a single solution but also leaves space for different algorithm selection for every agent and task, and gives an opportunity to change existing and involve new data sources.

While having developed the multi-agent model for PEP identification further work is to validate different algorithms and methods for each task. Best algorithms and methods will be selected by testing various algorithm and method combinations and sequences and measuring overall solution performance according to the main scenarios of PEP identification.

Acknowledgment. The research leading to these results has received funding from the research project "Competence Centre of Information and Communication Technologies" of EU Structural funds, contract No. 1.2.1.1/16/A/007 signed between IT Competence Centre and Central Finance and Contracting Agency, Research No. 1.14 "Development of Data Processing Algorithm Flow Optimisation Model for Identification of Politically Exposed Persons".

References

1. Johannesson, P., Perjons, E.: A method framework for design science research. In: Johannesson, P., Perjons, E. (eds.) An Introduction to Design Science, pp. 75–89. Springer, Cham (2014). doi:10.1007/978-3-319-10632-8_4
2. Wieringa, R.J.: Design Science Methodology for Information Systems and Software Engineering. Springer, Heidelberg (2014). doi:10.1007/978-3-662-43839-8
3. Law on the Prevention of Money Laundering and Terrorism Financing (in Latvian - Noziedzīgi iegūtu līdzekļu legalizācijas un terorisma finansēšanas novēršanas likums). https://likumi.lv/doc.php?id=178987. Accessed 23 Feb 2017
4. FATF Guidance politically exposed persons (recommendations 12 and 22). http://www.fatf-gafi.org/media/fatf/documents/recommendations/guidance-pep-rec12-22.pdf. Accessed 30 Mar 2017
5. Recommendations for Credit Institutions and Financial Institutions to Establish and Research Politically Exposed Persons, their Family Members, and Closely-related Persons and to Monitor Transactions. http://www.fktk.lv/en/law/credit-institutions/fcmc-regulations/5652-recommendations-for-credit-institutions-and-financial-institutions-to-establish-and-research-politically-exposed-persons-their-family-members-and-closely-related-persons-and-to-monitor-tr. Accessed 30 Mar 2017
6. Reduce Time Spent Screening Politically Exposed Persons. https://www.casewareanalytics.com/events/webinar-reduce-time-spent-screening-politically-exposed-persons. Accessed 30 Mar 2017

7. Reduce Time Spent Screening Politically Exposed Persons, Webinar. https://www.youtube.com/watch?v=10bbVf1pEsI. Accessed 30 Mar 2017
8. Schiffer, M.A.: Method of Ranking Politically Exposed Persons and Other Heightened Risk Persons and Entities, US 8069126 B2, US20080281765, WO2008141161A1 (2008)
9. Lawrence, D.: Automated political risk management, CA2437310A1, EP1358606A2, EP1358606A4, US7181428, US7711637, US8099357, US20020103747, US2007027675, US20100138262, US20120284186, WO 2002061663 A2, WO2002061663A3 (2001)
10. Lawrence, D., Nitze, P., MacDonald, A.: Method, system, apparatus, program code and means for identifying and extracting information, US8996481, US20150278289 (2004)
11. Roland, B., Swim, D.C., Messina, T., Conolly, W.P.: Evaluating customer risk, US20070288355A1 (2006)
12. Regulations on the Latvian Population Registration System Classifier (in Latvian - Noteikumi par Latvijas iedzīvotāju reģistrācijas sistēmas klasifikatoru). https://likumi.lv/doc.php?id=187420&from=off. Accessed 23 Feb 2017
13. Kastrati, Z., Imran, A.S.: Yayilgan, S.Y.: An improved concept vector space model for ontology based classification. In: 2015 11th International Conference on Signal-Image Technology and Internet-Based Systems (SITIS), pp. 240–245 (2015)
14. Protégé. http://protege.stanford.edu/. Accessed 30 Mar 2017
15. Llinas, J., Hall, D.L.: An introduction to multi-sensor data fusion. In: Proceedings of the 1998 IEEE International Symposium on Circuits and Systems, ISCAS 1998 (Cat. No. 98CH36187), vol. 6, pp. 537–540 (1998)
16. Blasch, E., et al.: Issues and challenges in situation assessment (level 2 fusion). J. Adv. Inf. FUSIO 1(2), 122–139 (2006)
17. Ingersoll, G.S., Morton, T.S., Farris, A.L.: Taming Text: How to Find, Organise, and Manipulate It. Manning, Greenwich (2013)
18. Riga Technical University: Deliverable 1 "Data Validation Method and their Algorithm, Statistical and Mathematical Model Evaluation on the Basis of Available Data Sources, Aimed to Assess the Most Appropriate Methods to be Used (including Algorithms) for the Development of Optimal Algorithm Execution Flow Model." of research project "Development of Data Processing Algorithm Flow Optimisation Model for Identification of Politically Exposed Persons" developed for IT Competence Centre and Central Finance and Contracting Agency (2017)
19. Padgham, L., Winikoff, M.: Developing Intelligent Agent Systems: A Practical Guide. Wiley, Hoboken (2004)
20. Jennings, N.R.: An agent-based approach for building complex software systems. Commun. ACM 44(4), 35–41 (2001)
21. With a view to identify politically exposed persons, banks will start customer interrogation (in Latvian - Nolūkā identificēt politiski nozīmīgas personas bankas sāks klientu izvaicāšanu | Financenet | TVNET). http://financenet.tvnet.lv/finansu_zinas/605924-noluka_identificet_politiski_nozimigas_personas_bankas_saks_klientu_izvaicasanu. Accessed 30 Mar 2017
22. Riga Technical University: Deliverable 2 "Selection of the Most Appropriate Methods for the Development of Model for Politically Exposed Persons Identification" of research project "Development of Data Processing Algorithm Flow Optimisation Model for Identification of Politically Exposed Persons" developed for IT Competence Centre and Central Finance and Contracting Agency (2017)

Changing with Grassroots Business Intelligence at a Large Global Manufacturing Firm

Makoto Nakayama[1(✉)], Sebastian Olbrich[2], and Norma Sutcliffe[1]

[1] College of Computing and Digital Media, DePaul University, Chicago, USA
{MNakayama, NSutcliffe}@cdm.depaul.edu
[2] European Business School (EBS), EBS University of Business and Law,
Oestrich-Winkel, Germany
Sebastian.Olbrich@ebs.edu

Abstract. Business intelligence (BI) has attracted considerable attention in the past years with such emerging technologies as predictive analytics, big data, and the Internet of Things (IoT). Despite the hype, BI frequently suffers from broad definitions, unrealistic expectations, and the incongruities of IT needs between headquarters and local business units. We are conducting an exploratory study at a large international manufacturing firm headquartered in the EU. The firm wants to transform itself from a conservative firm with traditional values to a more entrepreneurial and nimble organization with its supply chains driven by Industry 4.0 and the IoT. This research-in-progress paper reports the preliminary findings on how the firm is going through its transformation, focusing on the BI system. The initial findings of our interviews suggest that firms consider BI to be the enabler of change management rather than simply technical tools that extend the traditional systems environment.

Keywords: Business intelligence (BI) · Industry 4.0 · Big data · The Internet of Things · Grassroots BI

1 Introduction

Over the past decade, business intelligence (BI) has drawn considerable attention from both academic and practitioner communities [1]. Indeed, BI systems increasingly include and combine the use of predictive modelling, including (mostly unstructured) big data and sensor data from the so-called Internet of Things (IoT). While BI has become a common term, however, its concept and expectations vary among organizations and individuals; it encompasses the mere description of functionality (e.g. reporting, consolidation) as well as the key elements of information management in large organizations (e.g. creating a corporate memory by means of data warehouses) to constitute a fundamental part of data science (e.g. by including analytical techniques). Hence, BI and analytics are usually referred to as a cornerstone of the digital transformation, which can be broadly defined as IT-enabled major business improvements [2]. As any transformation includes major change management efforts, we are particularly interested in the transformational power of BI in two ways: (1) What impact does

© Springer International Publishing AG 2017
B. Johansson et al. (Eds.): BIR 2017, LNBIP 295, pp. 148–156, 2017.
DOI: 10.1007/978-3-319-64930-6_11

digital transformation have on the roles of BI systems? (2) What transformational effects can BI systems support?

Seeking the answers to these research questions, we currently have an opportunity to observe an organizational transformation project at a large global manufacturing firm aspiring to become a leading Industry-4.0 firm [3]. Our research goal is to learn from this firm's journey towards accomplishing a transformational experience. In particular, it aims to change from a conservative firm with traditional values to a more entrepreneurial and nimble organization with its supply chains driven by Industry 4.0 and the IoT. In this stage, we are focusing on the structuration effects [4] of digital transformation and BI systems at the grassroots level.

2 Literature Review

While a wide range of BI systems can be observed [5], Arnott et al. [6] examined 86 decisions supported by the BI systems used at eight firms. They found that more than 80% of decisions are supported by corporate-wide BI systems, whereas fewer than 20% use departmental or unit-specific BI systems, which IT departments "often [dismiss] as undesirable shadow IT systems" [6]. In other words, current BI systems are predominantly geared towards operational support, not necessarily fostering change and innovation at the grassroots level. For our case study, we briefly review the BI literature regarding terminology, commonly used theoretical/research perspectives, and an underrepresented perspective.

BI Definitions. BI is an umbrella term [1, 7]. The definition of BI can focus on (a) applications, infrastructure, tools, and best practices [7], (b) concepts and methods to improve business decisions [1], (c) the distribution of "the right information to the right people at the right time" [8, p. 22], (d) the purposeful use of data for decision making [9], and (e) the outcomes of information use in the business domain [10]. These different BI focuses may lead to varying expectations among managers and end-users.

BI Perspectives. Given the broad definitions of BI, we must consider a number of contextual factors of a socio-technical nature that affect BI systems [11]. The perspectives put forward in BI review papers include structured vs. unstructured data sources [12], the BI category vs. research strategy [13], socio-technical evolution [14], knowledge management [15], and banking [16]. However, a common perspective is the data-centric approach because "[g]etting data is the most challenging aspect of BI" [17, p. 96].

BI Outcomes. Successful BI implementation provides "analytical tools to present complex internal and competitive information to planners and decision makers" [12, p. 178], self-service and performance measurement capabilities for individual managers [18], decision support, work integration, and improved customer service [19]. BI success also creates operational and strategic business values [20] as well as competitive advantage and stakeholder satisfaction [21].

BI and Change Management. BI is critical for the agility of business processes [22]. Business process change management is a strategy-driven organizational initiative that sets out to achieve competitive advantage by balancing the forces between change and resistance [23]. Although user-oriented change management is regarded as a critical success factor for the implementation of BI systems [24], the maturity and adoption levels of process-centric BI remain low [25].

Underrepresented Perspective. The fundamental outcome of BI is to change the work carried out by individual workers and organizational units by using improved decisions based on timely and relevant information. Because business contexts are usually complex and continuously change, especially with such evolutions as Industry 4.0, we propose that BI users adapt a cognitive approach that "declares knowledge or rules about how to manage activities based on the current state of the environment" [26, p. 181]. From this perspective, we posit that BI should be regarded as the enabler of change management rather than as a technical tool that extends the traditional systems environment.

In sum, BI is often understood in different ways. In particular, because it is heavily data-centric, scholars might have overlooked BI's potential as an agent of organizational change in the socio-technical context.

3   Method

This study is in the pilot phase of an empirical BI study at Strasbourg Industries (the firm name is disguised) headquartered in the European Union (EU). Strasbourg is a traditional manufacturing firm with a long history of global business success, especially in various types of automotive control systems. Recently, the IoT has become a "megatrend" for smart and connected automotive control systems [27]. Given the rise of the IoT, Strasbourg has set the inspiring vision of being a leading Industry-4.0 firm that not only incorporates the IoT into its automotive systems products but also leverages the IoT to create new business models.

The firm's computing vision is heavily headquarters-driven, with the emphasis on developing standardized global templates and then applying those globally with some degree of customization. While it has used multiple ERP systems and data warehousing techniques since the turn of the century, firm-wide BI implementation is still in its formative stage, with the global BI template implemented in its major business units and fine-tuned in North America, the firm's biggest market. This region is regarded as the forerunner of strategic BI initiatives, allowing the firm to establish successful BI templates for the other regions in the world market. We feel the traditional ERP-driven approach at various sites needs adjustment to meet the new vision that emphasizes a more innovative culture. In particular, the firm's leadership must consider BI's role beyond the extension of its ERP systems and data warehousing environment, because business innovations often emerge at the skunkworks level [28].

Because the firm is in the early rollout phase of global BI implementation, it is beneficial that the research team not only observes the process but also shares findings to help managers. We thus use the action research approach that facilitates the resolution of practical problems while gaining scientific knowledge [29]. We are in the diagnostic stage of the action study in which we interviewed a key BI manager in the IT unit and then 10 BI power users, who were chosen based on their business process knowledge and the expectation of leading other users [30] in North America, to assess the state of Strasbourg's BI implementation. The structures of the questions were as follows. For the BI manager, we asked for an overview of the BI strategy as well as of BI programs and projects, progress, and challenges. BI power users were asked about their managerial roles, business needs, BI expectations, communication with the IT unit, and transformational changes before, during, and after certain phase(s) of the BI implementation. The interviews were recorded, transcribed, and coded for analysis. We used descriptive and topic coding to evaluate interviewees' understanding of BI as a concept and tool, communication with IT staff, and current and future expectations. By examining the results (see Sect. 4), we then formulated two dimensions of change management to develop a data-driven management paradigm, as summarized in Fig. 1 in Sect. 5.

4   Tentative Results and Implications

Broad Expectations. We asked the BI power users what BI meant and how they perceived BI functionality. Because the definition of BI is not as clear cut as it is presented in Sect. 2, the responses are, not surprisingly, varied. Some representative answers are as follows:

> "I don't quite understand it." [ERP Coordinator]
> "To me, [BI is] a broad term. I know what it means. It's really the applications – BusinessObjects, Crystal Reporting, and creating dashboards – that basically allow for cockpits, for the organizations to use, and have the information together from the end-user all the way up to the top-level management." [Manufacturing Systems Engineer]
> "[The IT staff in the headquarters] designed canned reports that everyone uses." [Analyst]
> "It is user-driven. It has changed how users interface with data." [ERP Specialist]
> "When I say BI, I think of something that has source data, probably from ERP, feeding the data to cubes to do analytics, especially predictive analytics by using historical data." [Sales Forecasting Staff]

End-users generally perceive BI as a data-driven initiative that extends the scope of ERP systems. However, the expectation of BI goes beyond more standardized, visual reports and explicitly includes the transformation of business and organizational culture. Selected statements are below:

> "[BI] is really for me that you can slice and dice the way you want." [Controlling Manager]
> "There is no IT solution that can fix what I'm doing. It's just not there. I don't think there will ever be a complete IT solution for forecasting; there are too many pieces at play." [Sales Forecasting Staff]
> "[The future of BI is geared towards] developing new business models to provide new revenue streams for Strasbourg [along with the IoT]. ... Yes, there is a big push to change the mindset of employees." [BI IT Manager]

Some end-users anticipate that BI will bring new insights and ideas that go beyond current business practices.

Lateral Communication of the BI Vision. Because BI is contextual to business processes, BI end-users invariably indicate that the communication between business units and IT has been challenging. This raises the question of whether an internal IT department is the right partner for supporting BI.

"Communication is good as long as we are in the same building [with the IT department]." [Sales Forecasting Manager]

"IT groups can tell you the umbrella concepts. But IT is not supposed to understand (the details of) different businesses underneath. They regard themselves as support providers. Being proactive solution providers is not in their scope." [Finance Manager]

"The main challenge has been to have IT staff understand [our] business context. In addition, there are communication barriers when I talk to IT staff [overseas]." [Logistics Analyst]

"To be honest, directly with the IT people, I don't communicate unless we have them on site." [Manufacturing Systems Engineer]

"I use Strasbourg Connect [a collaboration/knowledge-sharing website]. I posted questions four times, but got only one short reply. Strasbourg Connect has not been helpful so far." [Logistics Analyst]

Despite these communication barriers, end-users do not expect their IT colleagues to fully comprehend the details of their operational needs, as seen in the second quote above from the Finance Manager. Recalling the last two quotes from the ERP specialist and Sales Forecasting Manager in the previous section, what end-users implicitly suggested is what we call *grassroots BI*, in which BI end-users drive tool selections and implementation to pioneer ecological grassroots innovation [31]. The term "BI sandbox" [32] refers to the testing environment for BI end-users. *Grassroots BI*, on the contrary, goes beyond analytical solutions to influence work culture and foster innovation.

BI as an Enabler of Change Management. Because the firm has enjoyed long-term business success, its organizational structure and culture appear resistant to changes that may disrupt the status quo. Some users foresee BI as a potential catalyst for organizational change through data-driven innovation.

"The biggest challenge (for BI) is breaking barriers. Our organizational culture is still not into simplicity." [Unit Manager]

"We are nowhere near what technologies can do as far as I can see, for example, at Gartner conferences." [Sales Forecasting]

"There are 'silos' between HR, finance, manufacturing, and operations within [our] division. Great BI applications should help overcome these 'silos.'" [Data Analyst]

The use of analytics is evolving as part of the ongoing transformation. From a technological perspective, changes have occurred with the ever-growing amount of data. However, procedures are needed to analyze and integrate data into the organizational context. Because data analytics is one of the cornerstones of the digital transformation, we are slightly surprised that the organizational transformation towards working with data is still neglected, according to our interview data.

5   Change Management Towards a Data-Driven Paradigm

We borrowed coding elements from the grounded theory approach [33, 34] to investigate the change in the organization in more detail. By coding our sample based on the interview data, we observed two dimensions of change management: a) the need to shift the management culture towards a data-driven work environment and b) the need to facilitate the changes needed to update the systems landscape. Following that logic, we derived a matrix of change management towards a data-driven management paradigm (Fig. 1). In later research, we will use this matrix to guide our investigations.

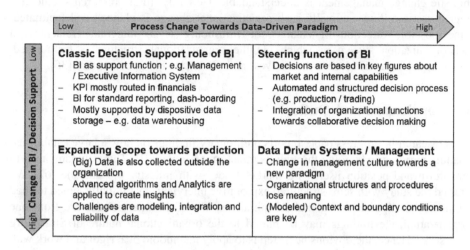

Fig. 1. Change management matrix towards a data-driven paradigm

Traditionally, BI is used to make decisions; some implementations even automate decision making (see the upper left quadrant in Fig. 1). Mostly, Inmon's [35] criteria for data warehousing architecture serve as the design principle. Hence, the classic decision support role of BI is based on a dispositive data logic deeply rooted in financial information and structured standardized reporting.

For many years, the field of BI has been adapting to deal with "bigger" data sources. In addition to the changing design assumptions and system requirements (usually summarized by the three V's of volume, variety, and velocity), the obvious challenge is to integrate data sources into the existing technological stack in order to derive valuable insights for the organization. As the lower left quadrant of Fig. 1 summarizes, only the sound integration of existing and emerging data sources can lead to viable predications.

The second change dimension (leading to the upper right quadrant of the matrix in Fig. 1) addresses the raised expectations of BI users. To modern users accustomed to easily consumable IS services, long procedures of data gathering and siloed analysis are simply no longer acceptable. For instance, many well-known online retailers routinely suggest next best deals. Why not allow BI systems to provide preliminary analysis results based on up-to-date data that could then be incorporated into an established, more traditional organization with sufficient IT resources? Such expectations raise the level of process maturity with fully automated decision making beyond quality reports, churn and fraud analytics, and so forth.

Whether an organization is driven by raised expectations or novel analytical capabilities (Strasbourg tends to be a case of the latter), the result will ultimately be a data-driven organization. Such data-driven modes of working depend on deriving sound figures rather than formal (hierarchical) structures and standardized procedures. By contrast, such legacy structures are often a major obstacle to a data-driven paradigm unleashing its full potential. In that light, the need articulated by our participants for holistic change management is understandable. Certainly, future research should further investigate how optimally such organizational change is planned and facilitated. One possible direction of change for Strasbourg is to integrate Holacracy, a self-organization system in which (1) the organizational structure is team-based, (2) teams design and govern themselves, and (3) leadership is contextual [36].

6   Conclusions and Outlook

This research-in-progress paper reports preliminary findings on how a large established manufacturing firm is going through its transformation with BI. This company aims to transform and position itself as a market leader with Industry 4.0 and the IoT. We started the study with semi-structured explorative interviews that initially aimed to shed light on the alignment of global BI initiatives. Given the interviewees are from one organization, the findings may be biased to the organizational nature of Strasbourg Industries. Hence, the obvious next step is to apply methodological rigor and work with a hypothesis to solidify our results.

Yet, sufficient data were obtained to articulate preliminary findings and postulate a research framework (Fig. 1) for further investigation. During the first phase of our study, we found an interesting and probably under-investigated topic of change management for the digital transformation: changing the current mode of working from operations/procedures towards a data-driven paradigm with what we call grassroots BI. To foster grassroots innovations at the end-user level, we posit BI as the enabler of change management rather than technical tools that extend the traditional systems environment. Taking this fresh look on BI and analytics allows for a novel framing of digital transformation towards a data-driven paradigm.

Our tentative results indicate that such change management for the digital transformation will be a significant challenge, particularly for large, established organizations. In particular, leading tech companies that work with advanced analytics leveraging the IoT and Industry 4.0 will be the cornerstones of the digital transformation. We are grateful to have the opportunity to witness the organizational evolutions of a market leader. Further, we plan to include a second organization in the study to identify and isolate the organizational context as a moderating variable.

References

1. Chen, H., Chiang, R.H., Storey, V.C.: Business intelligence research. MIS Q. **34**, 201–203 (2010)
2. Fitzgerald, M., Kruschwitz, N., Bonnet, D., Welch, M.: Embracing digital technology: a new strategic imperative. MIT Sloan Manag. Rev. **55**, 1–12 (2014)

3. Lee, J., Bagheri, B., Kao, H.A., Welch, M.: A cyber-physical systems architecture for industry 4.0 based manufacturing systems. Manuf. Lett. **3**, 18–23 (2015)
4. Giddens, A.: The Constitution of Society: Outline of the Theory of structuration. University of California Press, Berkeley (1984)
5. Davenport, T.H.: Competing on analytics. Harv. Bus. Rev. **84**, 98–107 (2006)
6. Arnott, D., Lizama, F., Song, Y.: Patterns of business intelligence systems use in organizations. Decis. Support Syst. **97**, 58–68 (2017)
7. Gartner. http://www.gartner.com/it-glossary/business-intelligence-bi/
8. Bogza, R.M., Zaharie, D.: Business intelligence as a competitive differentiator. In: 2008 IEEE International Conference on Automation, Quality and Testing, Robotics, pp. 146–151 (2008)
9. De Leon, L., Rafferty, P.D., Herschel, R.: Replacing the annual budget with business intelligence driver-based forecasts. Intell. Inf. Manag. **4**, 6 (2012)
10. Chung, W., Chen, H., Nunamaker Jr., J.F.: A visual framework for knowledge discovery on the Web: an empirical study of business intelligence exploration. J. Manag. Inf. Syst. **21**, 57–84 (2005)
11. Olbrich, S., Poppelbuß, J., Niehaves, B.: Critical contextual success factors for business intelligence: a Delphi study on their relevance, variability, and controllability. In: 2012 45th Hawaii International Conference on System Science (HICSS), pp. 4148–4157. IEEE (2012)
12. Negash, S.: Business intelligence. Commun. Assoc. Inf. Syst. **13**, 177–195 (2004)
13. Jourdan, Z., Rainer, R.K., Marshall, T.E.: Business intelligence: an analysis of the literature. Inf. Syst. Manag. **25**, 121–131 (2008)
14. Chen, H., Chiang, R.H., Storey, V.C.: Business intelligence and analytics: from big data to big impact. MIS Q. **36**, 1165–1188 (2012)
15. Muhammad, G., Ibrahim, J., Bhatti, Z., Waqas, A.: Business intelligence as a knowledge management tool in providing financial consultancy services. Am. J. Inf. Syst. **2**, 26–32 (2014)
16. Moro, S., Cortez, P., Rita, P.: Business intelligence in banking: a literature analysis from 2002 to 2013 using text mining and latent Dirichlet allocation. Expert Syst. Appl. **42**, 1314–1324 (2015)
17. Watson, H.J., Wixom, B.H.: The current state of business intelligence. Computer **40**, 96–99 (2007)
18. Peters, M.D., Wieder, B., Sutton, S.G., Wakefield, J.: Business intelligence systems use in performance measurement capabilities: implications for enhanced competitive advantage. Int. J. Account. Inf. Syst. **21**, 1–17 (2016)
19. Grublješič, T., Jaklič, J.: Three dimensions of business intelligence systems use behavior. Int. J. Enterp. Inf. Syst. **10**, 62–76 (2014)
20. Fink, L., Yogev, N., Even, A.: Business intelligence and organizational learning: an empirical investigation of value creation processes. Inf. Manag. **54**, 38–56 (2016)
21. Rouhani, S., Ashrafi, A., Zare, A., Afshari, S., Irani, Z., Irani, Z.: The impact model of business intelligence on decision support and organizational benefits. J. Enterp. Inf. Manag. **29**, 19–50 (2016)
22. Krumeich, J., Weis, B., Werth, D., Loos, P.: Event-driven business process management: where are we now?: a comprehensive synthesis and analysis of literature. Bus. Process Manag. J. **20**, 615–633 (2014)
23. Kettinger, W.J., Grover, V.: Special section: toward a theory of business process change management. J. Manag. Inf. Syst. **12**, 9–30 (1995)
24. Yeoh, W., Popovič, A.: Extending the understanding of critical success factors for implementing business intelligence systems. J. Assoc. Inf. Sci. Technol. **67**, 134–147 (2016)

25. Bucher, T., Gericke, A., Sigg, S.: Process-centric business intelligence. Bus. Process Manag. J. **15**, 408–429 (2009)
26. Wang, M., Wang, H.: From process logic to business logic—a cognitive approach to business process management. Inf. Manag. **43**, 179–193 (2006)
27. https://automotivemegatrends.com/interview-elliot-garbus-president-internet-things-solutions-group-general-manager-automotive-solutions-intel-corporation/
28. Rogers, E.M.: Diffusion of Innovations. Free Press, New York (1995)
29. Baskerville, R., Myers, M.D.: Special issue on action research in information systems: making IS research relevant to practice: foreword. MIS Q. **28**, 329–335 (2004)
30. Volkoff, O., Elmes, M.B., Strong, D.M.: Enterprise systems, knowledge transfer and power users. J. Strateg. Inf. Syst. **13**, 279–304 (2004)
31. Jennings, P.D., Zandbergen, P.A.: Ecologically sustainable organizations: an institutional approach. Acad. Manag. Rev. **20**, 1015–1052 (1995)
32. Sallam, R.L., Richardson, J., Hagerty, J., Hostmann, B.: Magic Quadrant for Business Intelligence Platforms (2011)
33. Glaser, B.G., Strauss, A.L.: The discovery of grounded theory: Strategies for qualitative research. Transaction Publishers, Piscataway (2009)
34. Myers, M.D.: Qualitative research in business and management. SAGE Publication, London (2013)
35. Inmon, W.: Building the Data Warehouse. Wiley, New York (1992)
36. Bernstein, E., Bunch, J., Canner, N., Lee, M.: THE BIG IDEA Beyond the Holacracy HYPE. Harv. Bus. Rev. **94**, 38–49 (2016)

Predicting Data Quality Success - The Bullwhip Effect in Data Quality

Mouzhi Ge[1](✉), Tony O'Brien[2], and Markus Helfert[3]

[1] Faculty of Informatics, Masaryk University, Brno, Czech Republic
Mouzhi.Ge@muni.cz
[2] Sheffield Hallam University, Sheffield, UK
tony.obrien@hotmail.com
[3] School of Computing, Dublin City University, Dublin, Ireland
Markus.Helfert@dcu.ie

Abstract. Over the last years many data quality initiatives and suggestions report how to improve and sustain data quality. However, almost all data quality projects and suggestions focus on the assessment and one-time quality improvement, especially, suggestions rarely include how to sustain the continuous data quality improvement. Inspired by the work related to variability in supply chains, also known as the Bullwhip effect, this paper aims to suggest how to sustain data quality improvements and investigate the effects of delays in reporting data quality indicators. Furthermore, we propose that a data quality prediction model can be used as one of countermeasures to reduce the Data Quality Bullwhip Effect. Based on a real-world case study, this paper makes an attempt to show how to reduce this effect. Our results indicate that data quality success is a critical practice, and predicting data quality improvements can be used to decrease the variability of the data quality index in a long run.

Keywords: Data quality · Bullwhip effect · Data quality success · Supply chain · Data quality improvement

1 Introduction

Over the last decade, many researchers and practitioners have emphasised the importance of data quality [3, 4]. Data quality has become a critical concern to the success of organisations. Numerous business initiatives have been delayed or even cancelled, citing poor-quality data as the main reason. Knight and Burn [11] further point out that despite the sizeable body of literature available, relatively few researchers have tackled quantifying the conceptual definitions. The literature provides numerous definitions and taxonomies of data quality dimensions analysing the problem in different contexts [12]. Also, literature provides us with numerous case studies, investigating data quality in practice. Research [7, 9, 14] as well as discussions with practitioners indicate that sustaining and continuously improving data quality in organisations is still challenging. However, most data quality attempts in practice are usually conducted only until the data quality assessment stage or many data quality improvement projects are only executed once.

© Springer International Publishing AG 2017
B. Johansson et al. (Eds.): BIR 2017, LNBIP 295, pp. 157–165, 2017.
DOI: 10.1007/978-3-319-64930-6_12

Continuing the earlier work of [10] in which an approach has been proposed for managing and sustaining data quality in organisation, we expand this work and introduce the concept of Data Quality Bullwhip Effect (DQBE). This paper aims to study the phenomenon and effects of DQBE. It is expected that good data quality prediction models will reduce the observed variability in data quality success indicators, and thus will reduce the DQBE.

In a typical supply chain, consumer's order demand flows up from retailer to wholesaler and in turn goes to distributor, manufacturer and then the raw materials supplier. The bullwhip effect in supply chain occurs when consumer demand indicates a high variability in demand along the levels in the supply chain [13] For example, in order to prevent product shortages and lost sales, the entities in the supply chain tend to order more than they can sell. The extra inventory demand begins from the market fluctuations of supply. When demand increases, the entity like retailer in the lower stream of the supply chain will increase the inventory, likewise, this will amplify the extra inventory on each entity of the supply chain. The Bullwhip effect has been observed across various supply chains in different industries [15].

Following the knowledge from supply chains, the Data Quality Bullwhip Effect is defined as the increase in variability of data quality success over time. Generally, factors that impact the DQBE are related to fuzzy data quality measures and delayed and reluctance to react to the data quality problems [5]. In this paper we considered that the variability of data quality status can be predicted and it helps to reduce the DQBE. We avail of a unique opportunity resulting from a longitudinal case study, in which we observed a data quality programme in a specific organisation. Observing the organisation over time, it revealed variations in the data quality success as well as DQBE. The investigation of this effect and the proposal of forecasting postulates the main contribution of this paper.

The remainder of the paper is organised as follows. Section 2 reviews the related work of data quality success and sustainable data quality improvement. Section 3 describes the Case study of a real-world organisation. Based on the case study, Sect. 4 discusses the data quality prediction model can how it can be used to prevent bullwhip effect. Finally, Sect. 5 concludes the paper and outline the future research work.

2 Related Work

Reducing the DQBE intends to achieve the data quality success, adapted from Delone and Mclean's IS success model, this paper defines data quality success as sustaining data quality efforts over time in terms of improving data quality. DeLone and McLean [2] proposed a comprehensive IS success model that stresses the effects of use and user satisfaction on individual and organizational impact. System quality and data quality are considered as the influencing factors to use and user satisfaction. Importantly, this model brought the attention of data quality to the IS research community and can be considered as one of the pioneering contributions in data quality research. Ten years later, Delone and McLean [1] proposed a revised model that directly focuses on the net benefit instead of organisational impact. As the net benefit can be considered as one form of business value, Delone and McLean' model is not only in line with the model from Gustafsson et al. [8], but also emphasises the importance of data quality and service quality to business value. It can be found that sustainable data quality improvement is an important element in IS success.

DQBE can be observed during continuous data quality improvement. The concept of continuous data quality improvement can be traced back to the 90s. To manage the quality of information products, Wang [16] proposed the total data quality management (TDQM) model to deliver high quality information products. This model is adapted from Deming's plan, do, check and act cycle and consists of four phases: define, measure, analyse and improve. The definition phase is for determining the characteristics of information products, data quality requirements, and how information products are produced in the information manufacturing system. In this phase, we need to identify who assesses the quality of information products and which data quality dimensions are used in such assessment. The measurement phase is for assigning numerical or categorical values to information quality dimensions in a given setting [6]. This phase consists of different measuring methods that can be used to assess data quality. According to the assessment result, the analysis phase is for discovering the root cause of data quality problems and strategizing an effective scheme for data quality improvement. Once the analysis phase is finished, considering budgetary constraints and resource allocation, the improvement phase is concerned with improving the quality of information products for intended use. The four phases constitute a continuous data quality management cycle, indicating that organisations need to continuously implement the TDQM cycle and cultivate data quality concepts into their organisational culture. Although sustainable data quality improvement has been proposed for a long time, there is limited work connecting data quality prediction model and continuous data quality improvement in practice.

Helfert and O'Brien [10] proposed an approach for managing and sustaining data quality in organisation. However, in that work, although the data quality improvement shows significant variabilities, the impact of variations in the data quality success is not investigated. We revisit the important aspects of the case study and use a consolidated case study to show how to reduce the variations in data quality success.

3   Case Study

The case study is related to an UK organisation operating in over sixty individual factories and offices across the entire country. An ERP system was implemented during the latter Nineties and whilst there were many benefits overall it was identified that there was still scope for further improvements especially within the areas of data quality and system complexity. This research study coincided with the commencement of a data quality improvement initiative within the Company during 2005. An initial approach was made across a number of fronts to attempt to promote education and training; documentation of procedures; the acceptance of responsibility, ownership and accountability at all levels for processes and data; together with better management of master data with the identification and implementation of 'quick wins'.

As part of this initiative seven key performance indicators (KPIs) were established around the order fulfilment process, historically the sources of many of the data quality issues. The KPIs were chosen specifically to reflect the salient elements of these essential commercial operations relating to servicing customer needs. The KPIs were designed to reflect the view of the world as seen through the lens of the ERP system, compared with an actual view which could be obtained by direct observation of the actual physical order process. In other words, how closely the 'system' (data within the ERP system) reflects reality (the real world) in the manner described by Wand and Wang [17], whilst also providing a measure of the quality of the actual data and the related processes. From the individual KPIs an aggregated Index was developed weighted to take account of the aging of the various transactions and this was then used as the definitive measurement of the ongoing quality of the data within the KPIs.

3.1   Qualitative Study

The qualitative element of the research took the format of a series of discussion-type focus group meetings sharing experiences, ideas, issues, problems and successes, around a basic flexible agenda, employing an action research approach. This approach attempted to generate discussion and interaction to discover peoples' real feelings and attitudes towards their data. In all, forty-eight of the fifty-four factories and seven business operations and sales teams were covered.

The use of action research in this environment provided the study with a considerable degree of richness in that the researcher had been a member of the organisation for almost twenty years. During this time this 'insider researcher' had worked directly with the majority of the participants and was known to virtually all. This unique approach generated loyalty and trust amongst all parties and not only provided rich material for this study, but also enabled the researcher's colleagues to gain a greater understanding of the significance of quality data and to appreciate the importance of taking ownership of 'their' data. These latter consequences are seen as key to the subsequent improvements that were achieved.

From the outset certain important notions and impressions emerged from the discussions and the analysis and these were subsequently developed as key findings. It was felt that these fell in three broad categories relating to: lessons learnt that should be put in practice at all sites, involving basic quality management principles, ownership, responsibility and support, together with measurement and reporting; positive personal motivational factors which help to engender commitment from individuals, relating to internal competition and targets, an acceptance of best practices and how these relate to one's ideas and principles; together with organizational and cultural environmental elements essentially involving leadership and management issues.

3.2   Measurement and Observation

The importance of measurement, analysis, reporting and feedback was emphasised continually throughout the entire research. Figure 1 below traces the progress of the improvement programme by tracking the Index over the initial three years, highlighting a real trend of improvement over this period, albeit with various explainable fluctuations.

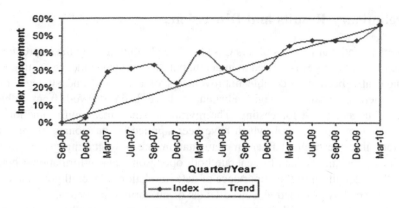

Fig. 1. Data accuracy KPI index improvement tracker

A summary of the progress indicates: 29% improvement in the first six months; 33% improvement in the first year; 16% improvement in the second year; 40% improvement in the first eighteen months; 27% decline in eight months which coincided with the Company's Modernisation Programme; 37% improvement in the year after the modernization; 59% improvement overall within three and a half years. Table 1 below relates the movements in the KPI Index with progression of the site meetings qualitative study both during and following the programme.

Table 1. Data accuracy KPI monthly performance

Month	11	12	01	02	03	04	05	06	07	08	09	10	11
Year	Year 1		Year 2										
No of meetings	0	13	18	3	15	8	0	0	0	0	1	0	0
Index impr. % month	0%	9%	7%	−4%	16%	1%	1%	5%	0%	2%	−3%	7%	2%
Index impr. % cum	0%	9%	15%	12%	26%	27%	27%	31%	31%	32%	30%	35%	37%

It is evident that there was a significant improvement in the Index (27%), following the commencement of the factory and business meeting programme from December to April, in line with the number of meetings carried out. In addition, it may be seen that this level of improvement was maintained immediately following the study and then further improved as the concept of data quality became more established within the organisation.

4   Preliminary Results and Discussion

The direct operational benefits of this Case Study as highlighted by the improved Data Accuracy Index have been referred to in depth, but there is also evidence to suggest that there have also been considerable improvements of a cultural and strategic nature. Further operational and strategic advantages have been derived from enhanced reporting, budgeting and forecasting. The myriad of small meaningful ameliorations, both technical and procedural, which have been applied by passionate people during the period since the original Baan implementation, are now gaining greater maturity alongside higher quality data to generate both operational and informational benefits. Finally, the recognition of the importance of data in relation to overall governance, risk and compliance has provided enhanced levels of authority and control.

Another lessons learned from the case study is how to handle the data quality variability in order to reduce DQBE. Since the data quality variation is featured by the turning points in the prediction curve, we have thus marked some turning points in Fig. 2. Each turning point represent a data quality status at a time, for example, point 1 means that in March 2007 the data quality index will be improved by 30%. This curve shows the data quality improvement in every quarter.

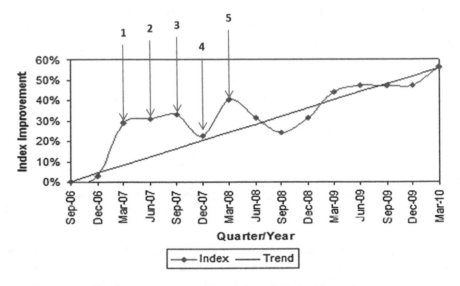

Fig. 2. Data quality turning points marked with numbers

From this case study Figure, we can see that from point 1 to point 3, the data quality improvements are smooth, indicating that there can be limited new data sources or data volumes. In turn, the DQBE can be also limited. However, from point 3 to point 4, there is a significant decrease on the data quality improvement. That means, there might be more data volume or the current data quality improvement cannot handle certain new data source. This fluctuation can possibly cause DQBE. Now the data quality prediction is of significant importance because at point 3 - September 2007, if we know the data quality improvement in the organisation will drop, we could proactively take more data quality improvement actions e.g. shorten the management cycle or include more quality measurements, to prevent the data quality drop. This can then reduce or prevent the DQBE. From point 4 to point 5, if the data quality prediction model indicates that the data quality improvement will be increasing, we could thus release some data quality management resources to reduce the related data quality improvement costs.

Data quality improvement is not just about fixing data or improving quality within a single business application or process, but also about taking a more expansive and forward-looking enterprise-wide approach. This must involve addressing cultural issues, initiating both short and long term process and procedural improvements by a step-by-step, incremental approach, whilst ensuring that the data conforms to appropriate specifications or requirements. In this way any improvement initiative has an opportunity to be sustained. It has to be appreciated that there cannot be a 'one size fits all' remedy to embedding organisational improvements at all levels, but rather to identify appropriate solutions to fit individual situations and circumstances. One accepts that data quality problems are not created intentionally by people, but more by the failure of the surrounding processes whether these are system related or individual related involving lack of education, training, personal developments or purely the person being placed in a position for which they are not suited. There is strong evidence to indicate that solutions exist to improve the quality of data, emanating from both the academic fraternity and the commercial world. This research therefore has not only a strong academic base but also has major practical implications which leads to a further key theme, that of aligning robust theoretical and academic concepts, within the operating environment of a real life organisation, in order to implement sustainable data quality improvements. It is also recognised that research in this specific area may have implications for other functional sectors where process improvements programmes can be applied.

5   Concluding Remarks and Future Research

This research-in-progress paper has conducted a case study from which we have observed the variability in data quality success (index improvement). Inspired from the Bullwhip effect in supply chain, the case study has revealed that there is a similarity between the variability in data quality success and Bullwhip effect in supply chain. Therefore, we termed the variability in data quality success as DQBE. We have used historical data quality improvement as a data quality predication model and discussed that (1) when an organisation should react to which data quality prediction such as increase or decrease. (2) How to proactively react to the data quality prediction in order to reduce the DQBE. Our results further indicate that data quality success is a critical practice, and predicting data quality improvements can be used to decrease the DQBE in a long run.

As future work, we plan to apply the analytical models and frameworks from supply chain research to the data quality domain. As Bullwhip effect is a well-established problem in supply chain, there exists a number of solutions to reduce the Bullwhip effect. These solutions, especially the ones with predication model, may also be used in reducing the data quality bullwhip effect. Another planned work is to validate the DQBE across different contexts in different industries, in which we will simulate the DQBE and use data quality predication model to reduce the DQBE.

One limitation in the paper is that we consider the historical data from the case study as a high quality prediction model, with this model, we can provide the insights to reduce the DQBE. Although the result is limited to the quality of the prediction model, proposing a data prediction model is not in the scope of this paper.

References

1. Delone, W.H., McLean, E.R.: The DeLone and McLean model of information systems success: a ten-year update. J. MIS **19**, 9–30 (2003)
2. DeLone, W.H., McLean, E.R.: Information systems success: the quest for the dependent variable. Inf. Syst. Res. **3**, 60–95 (1992)
3. English, L.P.: Information Quality Applied. Wiley, Indianapolis (2009)
4. Gartner: How to Overcome the Top Four Data Quality Practice Challenges. Gartner, Eghamm, UK (2017). https://www.gartner.com/doc/reprints?id=1-3W2JDZM&ct=170321&st=sb&elqTrackId=6d44157259df451482de51700cca6d36&elqaid=2250&elqat=2. Accessed 18 May 2017
5. Ge, M., Helfert, M.: Impact of information quality on supply chain decisions. J. Comput. Inf. Syst. **53**(4), 59–67 (2013)
6. Ge, M., Helfert, M., Jannach, D.: Information quality assessment: validating measurement dimensions and process. In: Proceedings of 19th European Conference on Information Systems, Helsinki, Finland (2011)
7. Ge, M., Helfert, M.: Effects of information quality on inventory management. Int. J. Inf. Qual. **2**(2), 176–191 (2008)
8. Gustafsson, P., Franke, U., Höök, D., Johnson, P.: Quantifying IT impacts on organizational structure and business value with extended influence diagrams. In: Stirna, J., Persson, A. (eds.) PoEM 2008. LNBIP, vol. 15, pp. 138–152. Springer, Heidelberg (2008). doi:10.1007/978-3-540-89218-2_11
9. Haug, A., Zachariassen, F., van Liempd, D.: The cost of poor data quality. J. Ind. Eng. Manag. **4**(2), 168–193 (2011)
10. Helfert, M., O'Brien, T.: Sustaining data quality – creating and sustaining data quality within diverse enterprise resource planning and information systems. In: Nüttgens, M., Gadatsch, A., Kautz, K., Schirmer, I., Blinn, N. (eds.) TDIT 2011. IAICT, vol. 366, pp. 317–324. Springer, Heidelberg (2011). doi:10.1007/978-3-642-24148-2_25
11. Knight, S., Burn, J.: Developing a framework for assessing information quality on the World Wide Web. Inf. Sci. J. **8**(5), 159–172 (2005)
12. Lukyanenko, R., Parsons, J.: Information quality research challenge: adapting information quality principles to user-generated content. ACM J. Data Inf. Qual. **6**(1), 3 (2015)
13. Lee, H.L., Padmanabhan, V., Whang, S.: Information distortion in a supply chain: the bullwhip effect. Manag. Sci. **43**(4), 546 (1997)
14. O'Brien, T., Sukumar, A., Helfert, M.: The value of good data- a quality perspective. In: International Conference of Enterprise Information Systems, Angers, France (2013)

15. Slack, N., Brandon-Jones, A., Johnston, R.: Operations Management, 8th edn. Pearson Education, Harlow (2016)
16. Wang, R.Y.: A product perspective on total data quality management. Commun. ACM **41** (2), 58–65 (1998)
17. Wand, Y., Wang, R.Y.: Anchoring data quality dimensions in ontological foundations. Commun. ACM **39**(11), 86–95 (1996)

Information Systems Applications

Short Text Classification of Buyer-Initiated Questions in Online Auctions: A Score Assigning Method

Yichen Li, Ananth Srinivasan[✉], and Arvind Tripathi

ISOM Department, University of Auckland Business School, 12 Grafton Road,
Private Bag 92019, Auckland 1142, New Zealand
yli781@aucklanduni.ac.nz, {a.srinivasan,
a.tripathi}@auckland.ac.nz

Abstract. Classification of short text (SMS, reviews, feedback, etc.) presents a unique set of challenges compared to classic text classification. Short texts are characterized by cryptic constructions, poor spelling, improper grammar, etc. that makes the application of traditional methods difficult. Proper classification enables us to use this information for further action. We study this problem in the context of online auctions. The paper presents a score assigning approach which outperforms traditional methods (e.g. Naïve Bayes) in terms of accuracy.

Keywords: Short text classification · Online auctions

1 Introduction

In spite of the considerable work in the area of numerical or categorical data analysis, several challenges remain in the processing of textual data (Losiewicz et al. 2000). Document classification or document categorization is defined as the effort to determine how a document should be categorized under a given heading (Borko and Bernick 1963). With extensive theoretical and empirical studies conducted in this field, currently automatic document classification is widely used in email sorting (Youn and McLeod 2007), spam filtering (Cormack and Lynam 2007), subject categorization (Chuang and Chien 2003), authorship identification (Zheng et al. 2006), and sentiment analysis (Moraes et al. 2013) to name a few areas of enquiry.

Recently, increasing attention has been paid to short text classification, which is a promising and encouraging genre of text document classification with the rapid popularization of e-commerce and online communication. Short texts exist in numerous contexts, such as instant chat messages, microblogs, online product reviews, news comments, intra-transactional Q&A and so on. In this research, our focus is on a particular case of short text occurrences.

Due to its unique characteristics, short text classification is deemed to be demanding and challenging. Firstly, a short text is sparse data which is highly reliant on context (Phan et al. 2008). It is problematic to select powerful language features since shared context and word co-occurrences are insufficient for using valid distance measures. Secondly, short text always appears in large quantity, resulting in

© Springer International Publishing AG 2017
B. Johansson et al. (Eds.): BIR 2017, LNBIP 295, pp. 169–183, 2017.
DOI: 10.1007/978-3-319-64930-6_13

conventional document classification running into problems such as labeling bottle-necks. It is intractable to assign labels manually in a sizable training set while limited tagged instances might not be adequate for machine learning (Song et al. 2014). Secondly, prior efforts in the area of automatic coding of short text failed to guarantee satisfactory accuracy because much of content is only partially related to the coding task (Larkey and Croft 1995). Another difficulty is the common existence of non-standard terms and noise such as misspellings, grammatical errors, abbreviations, slang words or even foul language. An appropriate method should be tolerant of a certain degree of those tough problems (Cavnar and Trenkle 1994). Consequently, how to reasonably represent and choose salient, invariant and discriminatory features, effectively reduce the spatial dimension and noise, and make the best use of those limited hand-labeled instances are stimulating questions for short text classification.

This study looks at a particular type of text, the online auction Q&A, which can be extremely short, cryptic, sparse, and ungrammatical. Moreover, it always fails to provide sufficient term occurrences (Sriram et al. 2010) and it is often complicated to identify the underlying sentiment information. Therefore, conventional classifiers may fail to get high-quality results.

This study uses and compares two methodologies; the first is the classical Naive Bayes algorithm and the other is our newly-developed algorithm which integrates a semi-automated feature selection process and a fully-automated classification according to a set of scores that are assigned to extracted features. The overall objective is broken down into several detailed research questions.

1. How do we define and extract keywords in buyer-posted questions as features to form reasonable category lists?
2. How do we identify question types and sort questions into different categories according to the extracted features?

2   Literature Review

Machine learning for text classification is the cornerstone of efficient document routing (Forman 2003). Unlike automatic text clustering which aims to explore latent structures in a document corpus without exact conceptual classes defined in advance, text classification is supervised learning according to a set of rules based on combinations of words or other features. Normally, group labels are defined beforehand, and the categorization process will be executed by adopting a learned text classifier which works with a training set of human annotated examples. In spite of the effort involved in building and maintaining the rules, supervised text classification still occupies a pre-eminent position in the realm of machine learning since accuracy can be surprisingly high provided that features are cautiously selected and refined by experts. In this section, we delineate the importance and several applications of feature selection and discuss previous investigations on classification of short text.

Automatic feature selection involves the process of filtering redundant attributes based on corpus statistics and collecting relevant terms to construct predictive models using higher-level orthogonal dimensions (Yang and Pedersen 1997). The feature set can be seen as the most informative and indicative subset of the training set. It improves and expedites a certain classifier by reducing the size of powerful vocabulary (John et al. 1994). In addition, it mitigates the risks of over fitting problems and strengthens the categorization performance by disposing of noisy attributes. The extracted features are expected to bear sufficient information to distinguish accurately among patterns when utilized for classifier training. (Dash and Liu 1997; Jain and Zongker 1997). Additionally, in the field of contextual image classification, the selected features should be "insusceptible to distortion, scaling and orientation" (Yao et al. 2012).

In tasks of text classification, feature selection plays an indispensable role in training the text classifiers. Among a variety of techniques, K-Nearest Neighbors (KNN), Naïve Bayes and Support Vector Machine (SVM) are most widely acknowledged and utilized. Chen et al. (2009) compared two different models especially for Naïve Bayesian classifiers used on multi-class text corpus: Multi-class Odds Ratio (MOR) and Class Discriminating Measure (CDM). Through an experimental study, they found that both metrics outperformed other criteria with regard to feature selecting effect for Naïve Bayesian classifiers while the computing of MOR was slightly more complicated and time-consuming (Chen et al. 2009). Zhang and Lee (2003) implemented bag-of-words as well as bag-of-n-grams feature models and a tree kernel function to explore solutions to automatic question classification. They noted that SVM turned out to be the best performer which is capable of exploiting underlying syntactic information of questions (Zhang and Lee 2003).

Apart from employing different metrics individually, hybrid approaches may yield unforeseen outcome development. Rogati and Yang (2002) conducted an empirical study to compare the comprehensive performance of five predominant feature selection metrics and explore whether the synergy of certain criteria would promise higher efficiency or effectiveness using four leading text classifiers, namely, Naïve Bayes, KNN, SVM and Rocchio-style classifiers. Consequently, the chi-square statistic metric coupled with document frequency and information gain criteria have witnessed a distinct increment in performance measure concerning the four classifiers, not to mention the removal of rarely occuring words (Rogati and Yang 2002). Furthermore, the incorporation of several methods have been shown as conducive to optimize the feature selection process by resolving dependency and redundancy problems (Koller and Sahami 1996).

Despite the above-mentioned obstacles in short text classification, some attempts have gained traction. Sun (2012) presented a straightforward but scalable method which achieved favorable categorization accuracy (Sun 2012). The approach starts with a manual extraction of representative word combinations. A Term Frequency and Inverse Document Frequency (TFIDF) weighting scheme was adopted to ensure topic-specificity of the query word sequences that can represent as much content as possible. Then it searched for a limited set of hand-coded texts that are most relevant to the query instances and determined the category heading according to the highest score and vote based on previous search results. In contrast, Li and Qu (2013) subscribed to the view that the classical TFIDF weighting factor is not effective for short text classification. Even the refined TFITF algorithm (ITC) which substitutes term frequency with its logarithmic form has conspicuous imperfections on account of the high dependence on the quality of the training collection (Li amd Qu 2013). Hence, they demonstrated a solution which overcomes the deficiencies to a large extent. The new hybrid functions amalgamated the Document Distribution Entropy algorithm as well as the Position Distribution Weight algorithm together, and it outperformed more conventional methods.

In terms of handling grammatical errors in a document, it is argued that the n-gram-frequency-based classification method is ideal for text documents that come from noisy sources (Cavnar 1995), where N-gram here means N contiguous sequence of letters. Considering that the occurrence rate of any spelling, grammatical or machine recognition errors tend to be relatively low and that every single string is broken down into small pieces, the negative effect of any textual errors is tolerable since only a negligible part of the whole document is affected. One limitation of this method is that the importance of an N-gram profile only depends on its occurrence frequency, ignoring statistics for less frequent N-grams, which might be informative in some circumstances (Cavnar and Trenkle 1994).

3 Data Collection

We examine auction listing data from a widely used online auction platform. A feature of this platform is that it allows interaction among buyers and sellers while an auction is in progress through a Q&A facility. To control for exogenous effects on our results, we restrict our attention to the trading of used cars. This is a product class with sufficient ambiguity to generate a sufficient level of buyer-seller interaction through the Q&A mechanism. Compared to new cars, there exists a higher level of information asymmetry that requires clarification beyond information that is voluntarily disclosed as part of the listing. Such information is typically unique to the particular used car on offer resulting in the exchange. We collected data that consisted of 14812 listings over an 8-month period. This data set represents 42940 instances of short text requiring classification.

4 Pre-determined Categories

Classification involves developing pre-determined categories. Discriminatory and meaningful predetermined categories are an essential prerequisite for classification, whose importance has always been overlooked since a majority of problems are limited to binary classifications. Additionally, for some difficult problems with more than two categories, the categories are determined based on common sense. Nevertheless, for problems that require a new set of categories, reasonable determination and explicit clarification are imperative. In this section, we pre-determined the categorization categories as follows.

Category 1: Product Description and Quality Inspection

Questions and comments regarding asking more/detailed information of used car auction listing and the intention of looking or inspecting the vehicle. Posts in this category tend to concentrate on vehicle's previous usage and maintenance. Depending on the current condition evident in the listing, customers may request more visual information to make better decisions.

Category 2: Seller Information and Credibility

Questions and comments asking for more information of the sellers such as contact number or email address to access the sellers' characteristic and furthermore mitigate the seller uncertainty. This kind of question assists buyers to establish certain relationships with owners and lower the possibilities of seller opportunism.

Category 3: Transaction and Shipment

Questions and comments which involve discussions on payment method and shipment issues. In terms of selecting a payment method, for instance, some customers are only cash buyers while others may require an installment payment rather than pay in full at once. Concerning the handover of a car, some people prefer collecting it themselves whereas others would like it to be delivered. Hence, this kind of questions allows sellers and buyers to discuss what kind of transaction method they are going for and corresponding shipment details if they win the bid.

Category 4: Negotiation

Questions and comments concerning price negotiation and swapping enquiries. Some genuine buyers may inquire if there is a buy now price or reserve price while others may go straight to bargaining with the owner. In addition, a large quantity of people would like to ask if the owner is willing to do a trade-in with their own car even with extra money added. These kinds of questions and comments are dealing with price enquiries and personal swapping negotiation.

Category 5: General Questions and Comments

This category includes all the general questions and comments which cannot be classified into any other categories above. Some questions and comments may include spelling mistakes or abbreviation forms which have no effect on understanding but are hard to be recognized by the machine, whereas some other posts may not appear in proper language. Also, some sellers may add some notes which they want people to know. To ensure the integrity of this research, all the questions in the dataset are included in these five categories, regardless whether the post makes sense.

5   Classification- Naïve Bayes Classifier

Due to the popularity, robustness and widely reported results of the Naive Bayes technique we start with this approach and examine its performance with our data set.

Using a data set of 600 randomly selected questions, we divided the data into two parts, the first 550 made up the training set while the remaining 50 comprised the hold-out set. The program automatically adopts the trained classifier to categorize elements in the hold-out set, then compares the machine-generated results with the human-labelled ones so as to calculate the accuracy. Every time we run the module, the dataset is randomly shuffled, thus a different set of training data is generated to train a new classifier with divergent feature constitutions. Again, this classifier is utilized to cluster the rest of rows, and the performance measure can be computed later. Apart from accuracy percent, it also returns a list of most informative features which has been used in the classifier trained in the last run. For instance, a buyer-initiated question or comment which mentions the feature "number" or "why" is approximately 42 or 14 times more likely to be in the second group (seller information and credibility) than in fourth group (negotiation), which is quite reasonable and justifiable since the second cluster represents people's concern that the seller will act opportunistically. They are more likely to ask for more information of the seller such as phone number and physical address or doubt why the seller wants to sell the car or why the price is extremely low.

In order to estimate how the performance of the Naive Bayes classifier will generalize to other independent classification tasks, a general accuracy percent should be calculated through a certain model validation technique. In this study, the cross validation method is adopted for two reasons. Firstly, this method is easy to be implemented in Python programming language. Secondly, according to trials and experiences in previous research, cross-validation is acclaimed to be adequate for testing hypotheses which are based on data already observed rather than new unknown data, particularly when further observations are expensive, time-consuming or inaccessible (Kohavi 1995). We conducted 12 rounds of cross-validation with different partitions. The graph (Fig. 1) below depicts the accuracy rate recorded in every round. The results fluctuated over the 12 rounds, reaching a peak of somewhere around 75% and a bottom at roughly 55%. Being averaged to approximately 65.13%, we can conclude that the accuracy rate of Naive Bayes classifier on buyer-initiated questions and comments classification is around 65%.

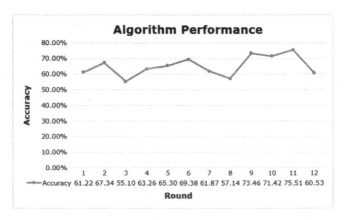

Fig. 1. Accuracy rate recorded in 12 rounds of cross-validation

6 Classification- Score Assigning Approach

Three sets of data are employed in this classification methodology. The first one includes 1000 randomly chosen buyer-initiated questions and comments, which are used to identify and extract clue words and sequences. The second one contains 30000 elements which are prepared for frequency checking. Note that there is no need to pre-process or manually label these two datasets with regard to pre-determined categories, all we want is to keep the original data. The third dataset is identical to the dataset we used in Naïve Bayes classification to enable comparison. 600 buyer-initiated questions are randomly selected and human-labelled with categories. The manually labeled dataset will be the testing set that is utilized to evaluate how the algorithm performs.

6.1 Tokenization and Labeling

The objective of automatic tokenization as well as manual labelling is to extract candidates of clue word and sequence which will be utilized for categorizing. Frequency information provides us with some useful insight to the keywords and phrases since high frequency indicates high-profile areas. However, some words or word combinations that do not appear often can clearly spot which category a question or comment is supposed to belong to. The identification of these clues is mainly based on manual scanning of a randomly chosen sample. Except for some solid principles, the selection of clues depends on how familiar we are with the dataset.

6.2 Automatic N-gram Tokenization

Tokenization is the task of segmenting text in a particular document into required pieces and simultaneously discarding some characters, such as numbers or certain punctuations. Texts saved in electronic form is a linear sequence of characters and white spaces; chopping the whole text up into separate linguistic units is regarded as an initial step before other computational processing can proceed later. An N-gram is defined here as a succession of n single-word utterances. The reason that we conduct N-gram ($N \geq 3$) rather than unigram or bigram tokenization is due to the high dimensionality of the data in the corpus. Since we will filter the tokens afterward by their occurrence frequency, the dimensionality can be largely reduced if we start from trigram tokenization. Additionally, the longer a phrase is, the better it will fit a certain category. R software is utilized to accomplish this task. After removing the numbers and punctuations, R automatically retrieves the three-, four- and five-word combinations and saves them in three term-document-matrices respectively. Large quantities of data will be generated since the algorithm exhausts all the possible word sequences. Therefore, an initial screening is done by setting threshold values of term frequencies. Taking the four-word sequence as an example, setting the thresholds as 2 and 15 generate 289 and 3 word sequences respectively, which leads either to data redundancy or information insufficiency. Therefore, the next step involves selecting an appropriate value by narrowing down the threshold which provides substantial useful information and reduces manual workload. A sensitivity analysis is conducted to confirm the threshold. The final extracted clue word sequences are seen as candidates of the clue words and sequences.

6.3   Manual Labeling

We manually scan a part of the textual data and then trim the short text to obtain words or word sequences as representatives of each query. The representatives should accurately represent the main points of each text. A double scan of the extracted representatives is conducted to remove those that are not topically indicative or are less contributive. The remaining words and sequences are regarded as candidates of the clue words which will be used for categorizing.

The clue word and sequence should be able to:

1. achieve the minimum number of categories that include the maximum range of questions and comments;
2. make a majority of the texts easily and clearly target the group they are supposed to belong to;

6.4   Feature Classification and Frequency Checking

After we obtain the candidates of clue words and sequences, we categorize those features into corresponding pre-determined categories. Therefore, under the name of each group, there will be a list of single words and word combinations. We calculate the frequencies of occurrence of these word combinations.

6.5   Score Assigning

Through manual labeling and automatic retrieving, we obtain an ample chunk of features as well as their corresponding occurrence frequencies. Moreover, these words and combinations are classified into predetermined categories; single words, two-, three- and four- word sequences are listed separately. This section will introduce the functionality and utilization of three kinds of scores, namely thematic scores, impact scores and modification scores, which might be assigned to features.

Thematic Score (TS)

The thematic score is a normalized value which measures how strongly a feature contributes to the determination of a specific theme (category). It has been argued in previous literature that high-frequency words are often more informative and indicative (Callan et al. 1999; Yang and Pedersen 1997). Zipf's Law also suggests that there are some words which overshadow most of the other words in a document corpus with regard to frequency of use (Cavnar and Trenkle 1994). Consequently, we hypothesize that the higher the frequency of a word or word sequence, the more impact it will exert on a categorization task. Therefore, we define the normalized thematic score as the

	word	Frequency	Normalized thematic score 1	Two word sequences	Frequency	Normalized thematic score 1	Three word sequences	Frequency	Normalized thematic score 1	Four word seqences	Frequency	Normalized thematic score 1
	swap	2842	0.424813	my listing	1260	0.329326	swap for my	368	0.253095	a deal with my	124	0.406557
	$	1607	0.240209	how much	1094	0.285938	keen on swap	237	0.162999	keen on a swap	77	0.252459
	Price	1067	0.159492	buy now	965	0.252222	you take $	235	0.161623	will you take $	43	0.140984
Price and trade-in negotiatio n	offer	572	0.085501	trade in	185	0.048353	buy now price	226	0.155433	how much are you after	40	0.131148
	reserve	419	0.062631	trade for	121	0.031626	swap my list	142	0.097662	how much you after	14	0.045902
	bottom	109	0.016293	reserve price	81	0.021171	how much for	134	0.092160	how much u after	7	0.022951
	dollar	74	0.011061	road cost	58	0.015159	will you take	101	0.069464			
				Bottom dollar	35	0.009148	what is reserve	11	0.007565			
				can pay	27	0.007057						
	Column_Sum	6690		Column_Sum	3826		Column_Sum	1454		Column_Sum	305	
	Total	12275										

Fig. 2. Example of the thematic scores that are assigned to features (words and sequences) in Category 4 "Price and trade-in negotiation"

occurrence frequency of a word or word sequence divided by the total frequencies of the whole list. Figure 2 shows an example. The formula and example are displayed as following:

$$TS = \frac{frequency_{(word\ or\ word\ sequence)}}{frequency_{(total)}}$$

Impact Score (IS)

What we are dealing with are short texts which only consist of a few words. Normally the longer the word-sequence, the more information it will include and the more accuracy it will achieve in targeting a predetermined category. Given this, it is appropriate to assign impact scores in order to enhance the influence of word sequences. We define the impact scores of single words, two-, three- and four- word sequences as 3, 9, 27 and 81 respectively, following an exponential (3x) increase.

Modification Score (MS)

1. Modification scores are assigned to the word combinations which consist of other memberships in our clue words and word-combination lists. The score is calculated by the sum of frequencies of the constituent single words as well as word sequences (if any) divided by the frequency of the complete word sequence. We show two examples of the modification score computation (MS) for the word sequence "keen on swap" and "buy now price" (3 word sequences) using the "Frequency" information

$$MS_{(keen\ on\ swap)} = \frac{frequency_{(swap)}}{frequency_{(keen\ on\ swap)}} = 12$$

$$MS_{(buy\ now\ price)} = \frac{frequency_{(buy\ now)} + frequency_{(price)}}{frequency_{(buy\ now\ price)}} = 9$$

2. Due to individual spelling preferences and fuzziness of natural language, some single words are divided into two-word combinations and some word sequences are

merged into a single word, such as "towbar" and "tow bar", "airbag" and "air bag" and so on. Although they have exactly the same meaning, computers will put them in two categories. Since we assign more scores to word sequences than single words, extra modification scores will be assigned to these words so as to balance their influence on categorizing decisions.

3. Some words appear with lower frequencies; nevertheless, they can explicitly target the category that a question or comment should belong to. Owing to rare occurrences, the influence of thematic score is almost negligible. To enhance the accuracy of our classification, extra modification scores are assigned to these words, whose values are based on how indicative those words are. For instance, the word "shipment" only occurs three times in our training set (totally 30000 observations), but sentences with this word can surely be categorized as a member of "transaction and shipment" category. Table 1 shows an example.

4. A few words and word sequences are so recognizable and indicative that they can perfectly categorize a question or comment into the correct category. Taking "how much" as an example, sentences which contain this phrase are undoubtedly asking

Table 1. Low frequency but high informative words and corresponding modification scores

Low frequent word (sequence)	Fr	Cluster	Correctly target No.	Accuracy	Modification score assigned
Image	15	1	15	100%	100
Smoker	19	1	19	100%	100
Defect	13	1	13	100%	100
Modification	21	1	19	90.48%	90
Hide (hiding)	9	2	9	100%	100
Strange	7	2	7	100%	100
Honest	35	2	32	85.71%	80
Money own	6	2	6	100%	100
fishy	7	2	4	100%	100
fake	7	2	7	100%	100
bogus	5	2	5	100%	100
How come	30	2	28	93.33%	90
What happen	34	2	28	82.35%	80
Money owing	35	2	32	91.43%	90
Getting it to	3	3	3	100%	100
Time payment	6	3	6	100%	100
Weekly payment	15	3	15	100%	100
Shipment	3	3	3	100%	100
Ferry	15	3	13	86.67%	80
Freight	50	3	37	74%	50
Can pay	27	4	27	100%	100
Bottom dollar	35	4	35	100%	100
Lowest price	29	4	29	100%	100
Separate	48	4	44	91.67%	90

the price, be it the vehicle price or shipping cost. Accordingly, it is justifiable to assign an extremely high score to these words and phrases to ensure accurate categorizing.

6.6 Automatic Categorizing

Java Programming Language is used to automatically categorize the buyer-posted questions and comments into predetermined categories. After initial processing, we generate an Excel spreadsheet that contains two sheets. The first sheet includes the clue words, scores and the categories to which they belong, while the second one involves the questions and comments to be tested. Each query will be automatically scanned, and all the clue words and sequences in this query will be identified. Note that clue word combination is regarded as an integral part which has higher priorities than the constituent words. We only calculate the score of word sequence if any fraction of it happens to be a clue word or sequence. In addition, if a clue word or sequence appears more than once in a query, repeated accumulation is needed to ensure the quality of categorizing. Scores in each category will be calculated separately by adding together all scores of words and sequences in that category, and the query will be classified into the unique category which achieves the highest score. An example is demonstrated in Table 2. The buyer is trying to deal with his own listing. According to our score assigning rules, clue word sequence "my listing" has obtained the highest score. Consequently, this query is supposed to go to category 4. As a result, an output Excel spreadsheet illustrating queries, total scores in each category and the final categorization outcome will be generated. Queries which fail to belong to any of the first four categories will be regarded as general questions and be assigned to category 5. An example is shown below in Fig. 3.

Table 2. Example of how scores are calculated for each category

"Sweet, text if you need numbers on my listing"		
Category	Clue words	Total score
1. Product description and quality inspection	Text	0.2030
2. Seller information and credibility	Number	2.8940
3. Transaction and shipment issue		
4. Negotiation	My listing	9.0999
5. General questions		

6.7 Performance Evaluation

To assess the performance of our short text classification algorithm, 600 questions and comments are selected randomly and then categorized manually into respective clusters. A coder who was not aware of the purpose of this study was invited to conduct the manual labeling. The outcome of the human labeling is sorted by the categorization number in ascending order and utilized as a reference. In order to compare algorithm

	A	B	C	D	E	F
1	Sentences	Cluster 1 Score	Cluster 2 Score	Cluster 3 Score	Cluster 4 Score	Cluster
2	rego on hold can it be put back on road	13.66721718	0	0	0	1
3	buy now	0	0	0	432.4122479	4
4	good runner engine drivetrain x system all good	0.189731823	0	0	0	1
5	fair enough does it have a towbar	0.024523161	0	0	0	1
6	hi any chance you could post a photo of engine thanks	0.653413165	0	0	0	1
7	seller added photos	0.463681342	0	0	0	1
8	where is the rust	0.114226301	0	0	0	1
9	hi ther wer bouts is pik up from	0	0	0	0	5
10	hi there would you like to swap intex metal frame pool and mgp vx team eddition	0	0	0	3.132255694	4
11	cool thanks for that are you selling because of the condition since the seller was dishonest any other issues that may need addressing have any rust repairs been done thanks is the engine the original cylinder thanks email me answers if you like camlangsford at gmail dot	0.487451599	3.928408443	0	0	2
12	hey guys I am away overseas till nov is it ok to bid an if when pay an pick first weekend home I am from taihape	0	0	0.771872975	0	3
13	hi swap for my plates bluoff and change off ownership cheers	0.097447297	0	0.423849644	43.25479143	4
14	keen for a trade in deal can we have a chat on saturday	0	0	0	2.197908887	4
15	any oil leaks	1.488268156	0	0	0	1
16	am interested would you be in interested in trade for fairmont give me call on	0.202961423	0	0	2.197908887	4
17	would u be interested in a trade cash	0	0	1.82566429	0.360396767	3
18	hi can you please confrim the service history and cost to ship to auckland cheers	0.127133228	0	0.423849644	0.469507715	4
19	hi what would be the buy now for this vehicle thanks	0	0	0	432.4122479	4
20	hi there do you take trade ins at all	0	0	0	2.197908887	4
21	i have a mazda astina lantis hatch its the cc nz new model automatic and about kms on the	1.390853668	0	0	0	1
22	yeah its a great little car just needing something bigger now yes its the lantis shape unsure of price was thinking around $ $ but would be open to working out a deal on this vehicle	0	0	0	4.718221896	4
23	is it turbo or non turbo	0.105621684	0	0	0	1
24	where can i come and view the vehicle please	58.16928159	0	0	0	1
25	would you consider a trade in deal	0	0	0	7.06825838	4

Fig. 3. Example of the output spreadsheet of automatic categorizing

performances with the Naïve Bayes method, we use the same dataset in the method I as our testing set. Subsequently, the algorithm is applied to automatically classify those 600 questions and comments. Then the two sets of results are put together for assessment. We use a score sheet to evaluate the performance of automatic clustering, add one penalty score every time we find an inappropriately grouped text, then accumulate the penalty scores regarding each cluster.

Let P1, P2, P3, P4 and P5 denote the number of incorrect memberships (penalty scores) of each category, let C1, C2, C3, C4 and C5 denote the counts of selected samples in each category, and the performance is calculated by comparing the automatic and manual categorizing: $Performance = 1 - \frac{\sum_{i=1}^{5} \frac{P_i}{C_i}}{5} * 100\%$. Table 3 illustrates performance evaluation.

Table 3. Performance evaluation sheet

Category	Counts (C)	Penalty score (P)	Error rate
1	239	26	0.1088
2	51	6	0.1176
3	27	4	0.1481
4	188	32	0.1702
5	95	18	0.1895
Average error rate	0.1468		
Performance	0.8532		

7 Conclusion

This paper illustrates two different classification methods for textual data. The first one is the Naïve Bayes algorithm which has been broadly used both in theoretical research as well as empirical practices in the field of document classification. For the majority of the time, the performance is surprisingly good considering its naïve independence assumptions. The other algorithm is our self-developed classification method proposed in this study. It is executed by a computer program automatically given a set of scores that are assigned to different clue words and sequences and it clearly outperforms the Naïve Bayes by approximately 20%.

Firstly, rather than only utilizing single-terms as features in Naïve Bayes algorithm, our method also takes into account word combinations which are more informative especially in short text.

Secondly, this categorization approach minimizes misclassification problems which caused by both conceptual and technical reasons. It is the selected features rather than the whole texts that are labeled and put into named categories. Therefore, the meaning of a single term or word combination in a specific context is relatively stable and invariant regarding the group it belongs to, and all the extracted features are exclusive to their particular clusters.

Thirdly, the feature selection process is implemented by both automatic tokenization as well as human labeling, which integrates the merits of the two approaches. On the one hand, machine tokenization is able to effectively identify word sequences that are above the pre-set threshold, extract them efficiently and organize them in descending order, for convenience in recognizing the importance of each word-combination.

Finally, the computational classification program exhibits high flexibility, repeatability and extensibility. This approach does not need a training set, the classification is carried out according to categorized features in advance and corresponding scores assigned to them. Consequently, classification accuracy can be enhanced by optimizing the memberships in the clue words and sequences list as well as the score assigning rules.

A major contribution of this work is to propose a new short text classification method which is based upon s set of scores assigned to different features given their importance and influences in group determination. The objective is to provide accurate and explicit categorizations for subsequent quantitative analyses. The results show that our algorithm outperforms the classical Naïve Bayes classifier regarding online auction buyer-initiated questions and comments classification.

While we have taken some critical initial steps in several directions, we acknowledge that our research is burdened with several limitations, which suggests avenues for further research. Firstly, the classification approach proposed in this study needs a huge collection of texts to conduct frequency checking for the subsequent score assigning process. However, it is hard to ensure that such massive data can be extracted when applying this algorithm to other domains. Future research can refine this approach by improving the way of calculating thematic scores, so that less volume of data is required, and make the performance of this algorithm more rigorous.

Additionally, more work should be done to explore self-learning method which might further decrease the amount of human labelled data. Secondly, the computer program used to conduct the categorization can be upgraded to a system with a friendly graphical user interface.

References

Borko, H., Bernick, M.: Automatic document classification. J. ACM (JACM) **10**(2), 151–162 (1963)

Callan, J., Connell, M., Du, A.: Automatic discovery of language models for text databases. Paper Presented at the ACM SIGMOD Record (1999)

Cavnar, W.: Using an N-gram-based document representation with a vector processing retrieval model, pp. 269–269. NIST Special Publication SP (1995)

Cavnar, W.B., Trenkle, J.M.: N-gram-based text categorization. Ann Arbor MI **48113**(2), 161–175 (1994)

Chen, J., Huang, H., Tian, S., Qu, Y.: Feature selection for text classification with Naïve Bayes. Expert Syst. Appl. **36**(3), 5432–5435 (2009)

Chuang, S.-L., Chien, L.-F.: Enriching web taxonomies through subject categorization of query terms from search engine logs. Decis. Support Syst. **35**(1), 113–127 (2003)

Cormack, G.V., Lynam, T.R.: Online supervised spam filter evaluation. ACM Trans. Inf. Syst. (TOIS) **25**(3), 11 (2007)

Dash, M., Liu, H.: Feature selection for classification. Intell. Data Anal. **1**(3), 131–156 (1997)

Forman, G.: An extensive empirical study of feature selection metrics for text classification. J. Mach. Learn. Res. **3**, 1289–1305 (2003)

Jain, A., Zongker, D.: Feature selection: evaluation, application, and small sample performance. IEEE Trans. Pattern Anal. Mach. Intell. **19**(2), 153–158 (1997)

John, G.H., Kohavi, R., Pfleger, K.: Irrelevant features and the subset selection problem. Paper Presented at the Proceedings of the Eleventh International Conference Machine Learning (1994)

Kohavi, R.A.: Study of cross-validation and bootstrap for accuracy estimation and model selection. Paper Presented at the Ijcai (1995)

Koller, D., Sahami, M.: Toward optimal feature selection (1996)

Larkey, L.S., Croft, W.B.: Automatic assignment of ICD9 codes to discharge summaries. University of Massachusetts (1995)

Li, L., Qu, S.: Short text classification based on improved ITC. J. Comput. Commun. **1**, 22–27 (2013)

Losiewicz, P., Oard, D.W., Kostoff, R.N.: Textual data mining to support science and technology management. J. Intell. Inf. Syst. **15**(2), 99–119 (2000)

Moraes, R., Valiati, J.F., Neto, W.P.G.: Document-level sentiment classification: an empirical comparison between SVM and ANN. Expert Syst. Appl. **40**(2), 621–633 (2013)

Phan, X.-H., Nguyen, L.-M., Horiguchi, S.: Learning to classify short and sparse text & web with hidden topics from large-scale data collections. Paper Presented at the Proceedings of the 17th International Conference on World Wide Web (2008)

Rogati, M., Yang, Y.: High-performing feature selection for text classification. Paper Presented at the Proceedings of the Eleventh International Conference on Information and Knowledge Management (2002)

Song, G., Li, Y., Li, C., Chen, J., Ye, Y.: Mining textual stream with partial labeled instances using ensemble framework. Int. J. Database Theory Appl. 7(4), 47–58 (2014)

Sriram, B., Fuhry, D., Demir, E., Ferhatosmanoglu, H., Demirbas, M.: Short text classification in twitter to improve information filtering. Paper presented at the Proceedings of the 33rd International ACM SIGIR Conference on Research and Development in Information Retrieval (2010)

Sun, A.: Short text classification using very few words. Paper Presented at the Proceedings of the 35th International ACM SIGIR Conference on Research and Development in Information Retrieval (2012)

Yang, Y., Pedersen, J.O.: A comparative study on feature selection in text categorization. Paper Presented at the ICML (1997)

Yao, C., Bai, X., Liu, W., Ma, Y., Tu, Z.: Detecting texts of arbitrary orientations in natural images. Paper Presented at the 2012 IEEE Conference on Computer Vision and Pattern Recognition (CVPR) (2012)

Youn, S., McLeod, D.: A comparative study for email classification. In: Elleithy, K. (ed.) Advances and Innovations in Systems, Computing Sciences and Software Engineering, pp. 387–391. Springer, Dordrecht (2007)

Zhang, D., Lee, W.S.: Question classification using support vector machines. Paper Presented at the Proceedings of the 26th Annual International ACM SIGIR Conference on Research and Development in Informaion Retrieval (2003)

Zheng, R., Li, J., Chen, H., Huang, Z.: A framework for authorship identification of online messages: writing-style features and classification techniques. J. Am. Soc. Inf. Sci. Technol. 57(3), 378–393 (2006)

The Anatomy of Digital Trade Infrastructures

Boriana Rukanova[1], Helle Zinner Henriksen[2($\boxtimes$)],
Stefan Henningsson[2], and Yao-Hua Tan[1]

[1] TU Delft, Delft, The Netherlands
{b.d.rukanova, Y.Tan}@tudelft.nl
[2] Copenhagen Business School, Copenhagen, Denmark
{hzh.digi, sh.digi}@cbs.dk

Abstract. In global supply chains information about transactions resides in fragmented pockets within business and government systems. The introduction of digital trade infrastructures (DTI) that transcend organizational and systems domains is driven by the prospect of reducing this information fragmentation, thereby enabling improved security and efficiency in trade process. To understand the problem at hand and build cumulative knowledge about its resolution a way to conceptualize the different digital trade infrastructure initiatives is needed. This paper develops the Digital Trade Infrastructure Framework that identifies its structural components.

Keywords: International trade · Digital infrastructure · eGovernment

1 Introduction

The global demand for perishable products such as fruits and vegetables [1] and flowers [2] has made the international trade highly dependent on efficient infrastructures. Efficient port administration [3], reliable vessels carrying the goods, and robust mechanisms for coordination of hinterland transport chains [4], as well as digital trade infrastructures (DTI) for handling of data related to the goods are prudent to support a seamless flow of goods. A recent literature review of Information Systems for port administration [3] concludes that integrated systems are crucial for the enhancement of the performance of ports. The review points at the technological advances i.e. cloud computing, sensors and RFID, supporting improvement of the information flow which they observe is confronted with challenges in compliance with regulatory requirements. The complexity of port administration is only one component in the puzzle of moving fruits, vegetables and flowers from producers to the consumers. One fundamental issue in these global supply chains is that information about transactions resides in different business and government systems, which lead to fragmented pockets of information. From an IT perspective this fragmentation can be due to legacy systems [3], different standards and little or none interoperability within and across systems and sectors [5]. Furthermore, non-technical barriers related to strategy and legislation play a central role, parties are often reluctant, or even legally not allowed to share data [2, 6]. As a result, the flow of goods is accompanied with data and information streams of poor quality and end-to-end supply chain visibility is extremely challenging to achieve

© Springer International Publishing AG 2017
B. Johansson et al. (Eds.): BIR 2017, LNBIP 295, pp. 184–198, 2017.
DOI: 10.1007/978-3-319-64930-6_14

[2, 6]. The lack of reliable, accurate and complete data makes it hard to detect risks (such as safety, security, and compliance), which challenges the timeliness of commercial transactions and at the same time makes international trade inefficient.

Governments and interest organizations involved in international trade are increasingly recognizing this information fragmentation across nations and business units as one of the key challenges for improving the conditions for international trade. Information infrastructures for the international trade domain (referred to as Digital Trade Infrastructures/DTI) are considered a key component for the solution. DTI concepts such as Single Window, National Community Hubs, and Data pipelines [7–10] have emerged and recently data pipelines have been conceptualized as Thick or Thin depending on whether documents are exchanged in the data pipeline or only limited event data is exchanged [11]. These initiatives reduce the data fragmentation. They do however not eliminate the need for robust digital infrastructures. A digital infrastructure (DI) has been conceptualized as a Systems-of-Systems [12, 13] that transcends organizational and systems domains. In the trade area specifically, it has been suggested that DTIs that transcends the current information silos can enable more efficient risk assessment, supply chain optimization and cost savings [10, 14–16]. However, accounts from the field suggest that conflicts related to data sharing, standards, financing and benefits distribution make infrastructural initiatives come to a halt [9]. Some of the reported issues correspond to issues of technological complexity and actor enlistment that are known challenges within the digital infrastructure literature. Other issues seem to be specific to the trade domain with its intricate interplay of governments at national and international level to control the flow of goods and in influencing decisions related to infrastructural initiatives [6, 17].

While in the research community there is a growing body of knowledge related to DIs, there is still little understanding about the of DTIs. The highly-regulated domain of international trade, where goods transcend national borders and regulatory regimes set DTI apart from other DIs, such as infrastructures for healthcare at national level [5]. This far, little cumulative knowledge development has been made about the specific challenges of developing DTIs. One important aspect of building an understanding relates to how the many attributes of a DTI are configured. The objective of this paper is to build understanding and provide grounds for cumulative learning regarding DTI. The goal is to conceptualize components of DTIs and map the challenges faced by DTI initiatives. The aim is to address how such initiatives move from initiation to implementation and adoption, thus supporting efficient international trade activities. The specific research question addressed is: What are characteristics related to architecture, process and governance across different types of DTIs? To this end, through an empirically grounded analysis based on four cases of DTIs and using the conceptual lens of DI this paper develops the DTI Framework. This DTI Framework is built around three dimensions identified in the DI literature, i.e. architecture [17, 18], process [5, 13, 19, 20] and governance [21, 22].

The remainder of the paper is organized as follows. The next section briefly presents the three dimensions architecture, process and governance which guide the empirical study. The following section outlines the specific context, the research method, the empirical cases and an analysis of the cases. Section 4 provides a presentation of the elements constituting the anatomy of DTIs. The final section elaborates on a discussion of the possible implications of the framework presented in Sect. 4 and offers some concluding remarks.

2   Digital Infrastructure and Digital Trade Infrastructure Design

The research on the building of infrastructures points to a broad range of challenges. Challenges include the inadequacies of traditional systems development methods [23–26], the inertia of the installed base [27], coordination among stakeholders [21] and political struggles for influence and control [28]. It is widely recognized that infrastructures are built upon existing work practices, human resources, standards, technological artefacts and organizational commitment [13, 21]. This installed base results in, that infrastructures are rarely built from scratch [27], they are rather nurtured and grown involving relevant stakeholder groups [17]. Metaphorically they are cultivated [13]. Consequently, the general conclusion is that effective development of DI requires approaches that are different from the traditional system development methods [13, 29]. Generally, suggestions on how to cultivate a digital infrastructure focus on three design domains: architecture, governance and process.

Architecture refers to the components of the DI and how they are connected. Because DIs are socio-technical, any DI will contain both social and technical components. The social components include stakeholders and practices for using the DI [17]. Drawing on Edwards [17] Gal [18], p. 18 states: "Technically, the construction of an infrastructural system requires the establishment of protocols and standards that enable the system to be used and seamlessly connect with other systems. Socially, its construction necessitates the elaboration of a system of classifications that symbolically represent and organize things in society: people, classes, geographical areas, religions, civil status, and so on."

Regarding governance of DIs there is an extensive body of research demonstrating the shortcomings of traditional IT management strategies, including hierarchical organizational structures and distribution of decision rights, careful planning and execution of plans for the management of DIs [21]. But research on what kind of governance regimes that actually works is largely lacking, with just a few exceptions. One exception is Constantinides' [22] research in which he draws extensively upon Elinor Ostrom's [30] research on "Governing the Commons". It describes three kinds of property or decision rights related to an DI: constitutional, collective choice, and operational. Operational rights refer to rights related to access and contribution and extraction of resources – i.e. rights to access a DI. Collective choice rights refer to rights of removal, management and exclusion of users, while constitutional rights refer to who may or may not participate in making collective choices.

The process design refers to how the DI is being built or how they change into a more complex form [20]. A review of DI cases reported in IS journals identified forty-one different cases were found which focused on the processes in the building of infrastructures [20]. It was assessed that out of the 41 cases 17 were unsuccessful and 24 were successful. A central contribution in this context is the observation that all successful infrastructures started small and evolved into large ones.

The architecture, process and governance design components identified in the DI literature are the starting point for our empirical analysis. In the next section we describe how building on four cases from the trade domain and by using analytical induction [31] we arrived at an anatomy of DTIs.

3 Methodology

We attend to our research objective by an approach similar to analytic induction [31]. An analytic induction approach starts deductively with the formulation of a guiding framework, which is empirically validated and extended by analysis of case data. We use the three design domains of DI (i.e. architecture, governance and process) as general theoretical framework for analyzing cases within international trade to establish the sub-dimensions of each design domain.

3.1 Case Background

During our involvement in different large scale trade projects some general insights have been accumulated which motivate this search for mechanisms which can contribute to effective sea traffic management including onwards processes ensuring more efficient and secure trade. Fundamentally, the observed scenario relate to the increased security requirements carriers are now obliged to follow. They have to send Entry Summary Declaration before the goods are loaded on the vessel at the port of departure, so that Customs at port of entry in EU can make risk analysis. However, in order to do that the carriers have to rely on information earlier in the supply chain. Often the information available in the declaration is not sufficient for Customs at the port of entry to do the proper risk analysis. For example, the Customs may not be able to see based on the declaration who the real seller of the goods is. Sometimes the name of the freight forwarder may appear on the declaration rather than the name of the actual seller.

If Customs is not able to do the risk assessment based on the available information they will request additional information, causing delay in the flow of goods. Any delay has business consequences in terms of costs, i.e. waiting time for the driver at the port, re-planning, calling and e-mailing, which further down the chain can influence the delivery to the customer and cause possible costs of violation of contracts. A delay may also require a change in the on-ward mode of transport, where missing a slot on a cheap on-ward transport via barge may require doing a last minute booking of trucks for road transport at premium prices leading to extra costs. With perishable goods delays can influence the quality of goods and in extreme cases the complete cargo may be damaged. These are just a few examples to sketch the broader context, where the carriers are not only responsible for shipping the goods from port to port but have a large responsibility in terms of information provisioning related to the goods and parties involved in the exchange of goods. The different stakeholders involved in activities related to sea transport such as carriers, terminals, customs administrations, play a key role as users and providers of information and have to deal with inefficiencies of the information fragmentation.

In line with our analytic inductive approach, we searched for cases that would allow us to reveal contextual elements influencing the work with digital infrastructures in international trade. As a basis for our analysis we took four international trade infrastructure initiatives. Each of cases is briefly introduced below:

The Felixstowe Case: focuses on linking a National Hub for information exchange between businesses and the authorities to international, private Thick Data Pipelines. The context of the Felixstowe Case is the Port of Felixstowe which is Britain's biggest and busiest container port, and one of the largest in Europe. The port handles more than 4 million TEUs (Twenty-foot Equivalent Units) and welcomes approximately 3,000 ships each year, including the largest container vessels afloat today (www. portoffelixstowe.co.uk).

The FloraHolland case: focuses on a specific trade lane for importing flowers from Kenya to the Netherlands via Sea and Air by using a Thick Data Pipeline. This trade lane further zooms in the complexities related to coordinated border management involving two different authorities (i.e. Customs and Phyto-sanitary), as well as on mutual recognition of ePhyto certificates. The sea freight trade lane, FloraHolland offers full services to growers from container loading until delivery at the flower auction. Services such as shipment and customs clearance are outsourced to various other parties. This requires high level of control over the supply chain and it is therefore crucial to know where a shipment is, who holds responsibility for the goods and how to anticipate to irregularities such as delays or faulty documentation [2, 6].

The Shipping Information Pipeline (SIP) initiative: SIP is an attempt of one of the largest Global shipping companies MAERSK and the technology provider IBM to develop a global Thin Data Pipeline for international trade. The SIP is like an Internet for shipping. It provides a digital infrastructure in which supply chain partners and authorities can share and access information about events (such as container loading, discharge etc.), as well as links to relevant documents. The shipping information pipeline aims to create end-to-end supply chain transparency and a flow of information that facilitates the flow of goods (www.maersk.com).

The Alpha-initiative (real name is removed due to anonymity): The Alpha-initiative is an attempt to set-up a national digital infrastructure. The aim of the Alpha-initiative is to optimize logistic information-sharing in order to make the sector more efficient and sustainable and to reduce administrative load. The Alpha-initiative focuses on the entire logistics chain, from the public sector to logistic providers and from shippers to main ports, knowledge institutions and system suppliers.

The four cases represent different national contexts (UK and Netherlands) and international relations (FloraHolland). The cases involve interaction between different means of transportation – sea, air and land which all have different requirements (FloreHolland). The cases furthermore involve public sector (Customs, Phyto-Sanitary authorities), private sector (the MAERSK and IBM SIP), and public-private partnerships (the Alpha-initiative). For each of the cases we collected data within the broadly defined streams of digital infrastructure research. The data collection relied on interviews, participation in face-to-face meetings, and used documentation (emails, project reporting and evaluations) for triangulation purposes. The data collection is part of a longitudinal study of a FP7 funded EU project. The direct involvement of the stake-holders from the four cases in the project provides an in-depth insight to the empirical domain and provides an ideal platform for longitudinal involvement and exchange of insights. The data collection took place during the period 2014–2016. An exception is the Alpha-initiative case where data was collected over a longer period from 2012–2016.

3.2   Data Analysis

Data analysis focused on the three dimensions identified in theory (i.e. architecture, process and governance) and we used the "constant comparative analysis" to identify sub-categories, and attempted to link this evolving set of concepts to the higher-level categories [32]. Eventually, the higher-level categories and the sub-categories identified from the cases were consolidated into the emergent DTI characterization framework. During the data analysis we used our own observations accumulated through our continuous engagement in the project, we reviewed project documentation such as deliverables, reports and meeting notes available from the cases. Two of the authors engaged in a number of sessions to discuss the findings from contrasting and comparing the cases. The two other authors played the role of critical reviewers of the findings.

When looking at the architectural component, we compared and contrasted the cases and tried to identify common dimensions that can be used to characterize the DTI initiatives. While the initiatives were quite different they all aimed to facilitate international trade processes, which involved interactions among business and government actors. By comparing and contrasting the cases we also identified actors such as Port Community Systems which played a role in facilitating these interactions. We therefore included the concept of intermediary actors. Next to that when comparing and contrasting the initiatives it was observed that in some cases the actors who were directly involved in supply chain initiatives (such as shippers, freight forwarders, carriers) were driving the DTI development while in other cases trade and business associations were in the lead. We therefore made an explicit distinction among direct and indirect actors.

The analysis of the four cases suggests that some initiatives aimed to introduce National Hubs, while others aimed at Thin or Thick Data Pipelines. To capture that diversity we introduced the concept of DTI type, where we distinguished among Data Pipelines (Thick/Thin) and National Hubs. By doing the continuous comparison and contrasting there appeared to be differences in the scope of the initiatives: while some were focusing on a national level, others had international scope (2 or more countries) and other global ambitions. As such we introduced also the concept of levels under the Architecture dimension in our framework.

Regarding the process dimension, cases were compared and contrasted. There were clear differences, i.e. whereas some initiatives were in the early initiation phases, others were already in operational phase. Next we distinguished new services as a separate phase, as in two of the cases there were prominent discussions about the development of apps as new services that can be offered on top of the infrastructure once the infrastructure is operational. The issues related to these phases were quite different. Therefore we decided to introduce phases and sub-categories of the process dimension. When looking at infrastructure governance it was observed that while in all the cases it was considered as an important dimension, in 3 out of the four cases the governance was informal, and only in one case there as a formal board. We therefore introduced formal/informal as sub-dimensions to indicate a maturity level of the development of governance structures for the DTI initiatives. As governance was considered important but the governance structures in the cases were not well developed further categorization was needed. To give further structure to the governance dimension we introduced the analytical categories of three types of decision rights [22], namely constitutional, collective choice and operational. Lending inspiration from earlier research [9] and empirical observations from the four cases suggest that in all cases cost-benefit sharing, standards and data access are key decision areas. We included these as sub-categories of collective choice rights, as these pointed to specific decision areas related to DTI initiatives.

The brief outline of the components of the DTI framework illustrate that the process of development of the framework utilized empirical insights in a grounded manner by comparing and contrasting the cases and furthermore that we also iteratively went back and forth from the case findings to literature and vice-versa. As a result, we also further sharpened our thoughts and we linked our findings to concepts and findings from literature.

4   Results: Digital Trade Infrastructure (DTI) Framework

Table 1 illustrates the empirically derived DTI Framework. The framework is structured around the three components identified in the DI literature (architecture, process and governance) as overarching dimensions and it further specifies sub-categories of these dimensions based on the four cases and insights from literature.

Table 1. The DTI framework

Dimension	Category	Values
Architecture	Levels	National, international, global
	Actors	Business/Government/Intermediary; Direct/Indirect
	Interactions	Business-to-Business (B2B); Business-to-Government (B2G); Government-to-Government (G2G)
	DTI type	Data pipeline (thick/thin); National hub
Process	DTI development phases	Initiation; Operation and maintenance; New services
Governance	Infrastructure governance	Formal/Informal
	Decision rights	Constitutional rights Collective choice rights • Standards • Cost-benefit sharing • Data access Operational rights

Under architecture, we distinguish among (a) Levels: National, International, Global; (b) Actors: Business, Government, Intermediary; as well as Direct, Indirect; (c) Interactions: Business-to-Business (B2B); Business-to-Government (B2G); Government-to-Government (G2G); (d) DTI types: National Hub, Data Pipeline (Thick/Thin). The Thin and Thick data pipelines support different types of interaction (e.g. Thick Data Pipelines are limited to the Business-to-Business actors), however other configurations are also possible. Furthermore, the analysis suggests three types of National Hubs connecting business and government actors but depending on the scope and ambition of the infrastructure initiative the role and number of National Hubs can also vary. National Hubs are used here as an organizational configuration that enables exchanges among business and government actors on a national level and does not address a technical architecture (i.e. the technical architecture can vary).

Under process we make a distinction among three phases: Initiation, Operation and Maintenance, and New Services. Under governance we distinguish among Infrastructure Governance (Formal/Informal) and Decision Rights (Constitutional, Collective choice, Operational). We further identify Standards, Data Access, and Cost-Benefit Sharing as sub-categories of collective choice rights.

4.1 DTI Architecture

The architectural dimension of the DTI Framework enabled us represent the four different initiatives using the same concepts and visualize them in a similar way.

The analysis of the four cases suggests that the initiatives range from national to international to further to global levels. The cases also differ in terms of the DTI type that they aim at establishing. The Alpha-initiative and the National Hub components of the Felixstowe case (the private Hub Destin 8 and the public attempt the OneGov to establish such a Hub) are all examples of initiatives that try to establish a National Hub to optimize the information exchanges among businesses involved in international trade in a given country along with its relevant government authorities. It is beyond the scope of this particular analysis, but it would be useful to compare these initiatives in order to gain further insights in what are the core drivers behind the setting-up of National Hub infrastructures. In this context it is recognized that these national hubs are important to ensure efficient flow of the goods from the port to the further in-land destination. Better information can facilitate both the processes involving the authorities such as Customs and allow for faster clearance, as well as providing the business parties further in the supply-chain better options for planning of onward transport, supporting reduced waiting times and increase cost savings.

Looking at the Felixstowe, the FloraHolland, and the SIP cases, it is observed that all of them focus on Data Pipeline DTI. We see different choices with respect to the infrastructure type. The Felixstowe case focuses on Thick Data Pipeline, where physical trading documents are exchanged along with the goods which aim at international coverage. The FloraHolland case similarly focusses on a Thick Data Pipeline but is limited to a specific trade lane between Kenya and The Netherlands. The SIP case on the other hand focuses on a Thin Data Pipeline where only event information is exchanged providing links to documents rather than the documents themselves, thus implementing a digital exchange of documents. The SIP case furthermore aims at global reach of the soft documents.

The architectural component of the framework helps us to see how different initiatives fit together. A global Data Pipeline initiative like the SIP aims for global coverage. It relies on existence of and interoperability with other parts of the infrastructure necessary to bring the goods from producers to its final destination. The global coverage requires availability of National Hubs to connect to national governments in the different countries, as well as Thick Data pipelines which can facilitate a physical document exchange among parties if needed.

Thus, the architectural component can be useful for both looking for meaningful comparison cases (e.g. comparison of National Hub DTI initiatives and comparison of Thick Data Pipeline initiatives), as well as for identifying complementarities among different DTI initiatives and how they can be combined as part of a larger DTI.

4.2   DTI Process

The second component of the DTI Framework focuses on the process. As discussed in Section Three, by comparing and contrasting the initiatives we saw the need to conceptually differentiate among three phases, namely: (a) Initiation, (b) Operation and maintenance, and (c) Development of new services. Especially in the SIP demo and the Alpha-initiative we see that a lot of complications arise when it comes to the initial investment and investors willing to invest in the infrastructure. Specifically in the initiation phase, issues related to cost-benefit and infrastructure governance are related to how to get stakeholders on board and make them invest and commit to adopt the DTI.

Once such an infrastructure is up and running (operation phase) the governance issues and the cost benefit issues become quite different, as they relate to development of business models for the operation and maintenance. In the Felixstowe case for example, the initial investments were already done in the past by commercial parties and in the Operation phase the Pipelines are now commercially run with a viable business model behind them. The business model is based on fees for services offered by the infrastructure providers.

In the cases analysed, most of the initiatives are still in Initiation phase, however discussions about the Development of New Services are vividly present. The motivation for new services available on mobile artefacts is driven by a general shift towards apps in society. In the SIP case, a new service App was developed before the infrastructure was in place to gain users' interest and experience. In the Alpha-initiative the parties are eager to develop new planning Apps. However, they are waiting for the infrastructure (the APIs) to be in place so that they can offer their new services. At the same time the initiatives that we analysed are still trying to gain financing for the Initiation phase or are in search for business models for the Operation and Maintenance phase. Such business models are not directly obvious due to the characteristics of the different parties involved and the public and private interests.

The issue of fair cost-benefit sharing (part of the Governance component of DTI Framework) comes repeatedly as a discussion point, especially in the Alpha-initiative.

The DTI is expected to bring savings and efficiency gains to the parties in the chain but it is not obvious how these gains will be redistributed in the chain due to its international dimension. In the cases analysed, substantial efforts are put now in addressing this issue. As we can see, discussing the DTI process immediately links to issues related to DTI governance and this illustrates that the issues are very much inter-linked.

4.3   DTI Governance

Governance is the third dimension of our framework. In the complex multi-actor network of stakeholders governance is very important but remains a challenging issue to address. Data suggests that in only one out of the four cases (the Alpha-initiative) there was a formal governance structure in the form of a governance board. In all the other three cases the governance appeared to be informal. In the Felixstowe case the private providers of Data Pipelines and the private Hub had their governance internally organized and the collaboration among the Pipelines and National Hubs (Destin 8 and OneGov) were managed informally. The FloraHolland case is still in early demonstrator phases but there is a Steering Group of decision-makers from the key partner organizations which oversees the process at the moment. Interview data and interaction with central stakeholders suggest that their role is informally defined. The SIP case is driven mainly by the two established business partners MAERSK and IBM and its formal governance structures still need to evolve. One observation that we can derive regarding the governance dimension is that although theory suggests that it is very important to address the governance is still a complex area that needs to be further understood.

As discussed earlier the allocation of the three categories of rights (i.e. constitutional, collective choice and operational) is central to the governance of DIs [22]. To recall, operational rights refer to rights related to access and contribution and extraction of resources – i.e. rights to access a DI. Collective choice rights refer to rights of removal, management and exclusion of users, while constitutional rights refer to who may or may not participate in making collective choices. These categories can help us to further reflect on the four cases and derive insights for further research.

Reflecting on the four cases and looking at these decision rights in relation to the phases that we identified we can say that the decision rights as defined by Constantinides [22] mostly apply to the Operation and Maintenance phase, as they seem to assume the existence of the DI. It is interesting however to explore the possible links of the conceptual categories of decision rights in relation to the case findings, as well as the other phases we defined.

The constitutional rights refer to who may or may not participate in making the collective choices. If we look at the SIP case, the technology supplier IBM and the shipping company MAERSK are now driving the initiative. Key challenges related to how to mobilize a collective action to secure further funding and ensure wider adoption for this initiative still remain unsolved. To add complexity it is observed that it is likely that the parties who participate in making decisions in the initiation phase are different from those making choices about the Operation and Maintenance phase and when it comes to New Services. It is too early to identify trends on if APIs for New Services are made available and furthermore if external parties take the opportunity to utilize the potential of APIs. If external parties are included into the New Services phase it may be possible that new parties enter and gain decision rights and thus become players in the decision-making process. Thus, it would be meaningful to extend the notion of constitutional rights also to the Initiation and the New Service phase and see what learnings can be derived from that.

The Collective choice rights as discussed earlier refer to rights of removal, management and exclusion of users. This definition is very much centered around the subject of users. If we broaden the view that the parties who have constitutional rights will need to make collective choices related to a number of areas (where users could be one of them for example), then we can further explore and identify which are the specific areas related to the DTI for which collective choices need to be made (i.e. the collective choice rights could be exercised). Our case findings reconfirmed findings from prior research that important choices concerning DTI relate to (a) standards; (b) data access; (c) cost-benefit sharing. The Operational rights as discussed earlier refer to rights related to access and contribution and extraction of resources – i.e. rights to access a DI. Again, this presumes the existence of the DI and the question is what would be the meaning if expanded to the other two phases. For the Initiation Phase it may be linked to investments needed in the set-up of the infrastructure and possible return on investment (in our cases we see that initial investment is crucial and that securing such an initial investment is a difficult process). In the New Services phase it may relate to rights of App providers to the infrastructure and value exchanges related to the use of the infrastructure and the offering of new services.

Another observation that we need to make is that the rights outlined above seem to assume that such rights are easily defined. In our case findings we saw however that most of the initiatives (except one) had informal governance. The rules were not yet explicitly defined. Furthermore, although these categories can help to bring further structure into key decision-making processes, the process dimension of how the actors come together and how constitutional rights are obtained along with the question of who drives and shapes this process is still unclear. Furthermore, the analysis highlights that changes of the actor configuration and evolvement through the different phases of the infrastructure development needs to be further conceptualized and explored. An analysis of collective action processes appears to be a suitable conceptual lens to further examine such processes [33].

5   Discussion and Conclusions

Two big challenges that our society faces today is on the one hand how to increase the safety and security, and at the same time reduce inefficiencies and facilitate trade. Increasing the quality and availability of data is seen as key to achieving that. Governments and businesses are increasingly recognizing it and struggle with establishing the necessary digital infrastructures. Still, as discussed in this paper achieving this digital infrastructure is a difficult task. Over the years we observed different initiatives trying to solve parts of the puzzle but it has so far been difficult to see how the pieces fit together and where the similarities and overlaps are. And while on a demonstrator setting the benefits of initiatives such as the data pipelines have been tested in series of EU projects the scaling-up of these initiatives have turned out to be challenging. Given the importance of these initiatives the need for a framework that will allow comparing and contrasting the initiatives is of utmost importance in order to assess similarities and complementarities. By building on four cases which have different scope and coverage we arrived at a conceptual framework. This framework captured a rich variety of cases, ranging from the Alpha-initiative which aims to optimize a national hub, to the Felixstowe demo which aims to set the link between a national hub and international thick data pipelines for information sharing about goods imported via sea to the UK; to the trade-lane specific data pipeline of FloraHolland and the global Shipping Information Pipeline driven by MAERSK and IBM.

Reflecting on the experience so far the DTI Framework has been useful as a conceptual lens to reason about the architecture, process and governance components of DTI initiatives and their interrelationships. Our analysis illustrates that the architectural, process and governance component are strongly intertwined, and exploring these dependencies is necessary to gain better understanding of the complexities and problems at hand. The DTI framework allows us to characterize a range of components and to look for meaningful comparisons of similar cases, and further to look for complementarities. Understanding better the complex interplay among architectural configurations, processes and governance of DTI will enable us to better understand the complex processes that drive DTI from initiation to operation and further to growth through new services. From all the components, the governance component (and its relations to the other two components) seems to be most complex to address, as it is the complex interplay of actors and decision-making processes that brings DTIs to a halt or drive them to success.

Looking at the process component a possible area of research would be to zoom into the initiation phase and identify factors that block these initiatives and put them on a halt and what are mechanisms that unlock these processes and allow the DTI initiatives to move towards implementation. Regarding the governance, one possible question is to explore the processes of how constitutional rights are obtained and whether and how they change when the infrastructure develops from initiation to operation towards new services. Cost-benefit sharing is another very central area, where further research can focus on identifying cost-benefit sharing models which are useful for supporting the business case in the initiation phase; cost-benefit models for supporting the business model for the operational phase or cost-benefit models for allowing app providers to the infrastructure. Regarding the architecture component possible areas for research is to carry out comparative studies and gain cumulative knowledge on what are complexities related to setting-up a specific DTI type (e.g. National Hub, Thick Data Pipeline or Thin Data Pipeline) and what are lessons learned.

With regards to a general understanding of DI design, three important findings emerge. First, there is a tendency towards archetypical architectural DTI set-ups. That is, in theory, choices in decision points of the infrastructure can be combined freely. In reality, however, it seems like some architectural design choices go more naturally together. These "natural fits" of architectural design choices indicate that there might be possible archetypical infrastructure set-ups of design attributes that align with each other. The implication of this finding is that anyone interested in the shaping of digital infrastructures cannot make independent choices regarding the architectural design but has to recognize the systemic dependencies between the choices. That is, one specific choice will influence the possibility for choices in the other design areas. Second, the different archetypical digital infrastructure set-ups seem to address different problems. Contrasting different set-ups is not about declaring one being better than the other. They are simply different tools, used in different scenarios. The scenario is defined by of the infrastructure set-up. Depending on the set-up (level, actors, scope, etc.) a different archetypical set-up is suitable. For example, for the Felixstowe DTI with a more limited actor and geographical scope it was decided that the best set-up would be to exchange documents within the pipeline (and hence adherence to data standards was of key importance) and offer this as a commercial service. In contrast, the inclusive (geographically and actor) design of the SIP aiming for global scope led to a decision to a minimalist standardization (not standardizing data elements) and a common-good philosophy. Critically, the choice regarding decision points in the Felixstowe case would not be suited for the SIP case, and vice versa. So, the question to answer in a specific case then is: What is the problem to be solved and how to map the connectivity infrastructure set-ups according to that problem. To the extent that an infrastructure set-up design might be flawed, it is because the combination of attribute is not coherent, that the elements for the DTI Framework are misaligned. For example, combining an international ambition with standardization of data elements is likely to be a futile exercise, as no global agreement can be made down to that level. Third, each of the archetypes seems to have their distinct "must win battles", depending on the process (i.e. the phase in which the DTI is in), as well as the governance choices. For the SIP which is currently in its initiation phase, the critical "must win battle" is to mobilize the mass of supply chain actors to join the initiative. Such a design is subject to network effects: the more actors that join the initiative the greater the benefits for all. However, initially, there are no benefits of joining, in the same way that there would be no benefits of being the first (only) one with a telephone or a Facebook account. This is in the infrastructure literature referred to as the "bootstrapping problem" and should be addressed through pre-emptive strategies. This relates to the complexity of governance of DTI in the initiation phase of the initiative. Research on mobilizing collective action can be used as inspiration for further research to address this problem [33].

For future work, it is critical to advance the understanding of DTI architecture set-up archetypes, building knowledge about which choice, and governance decision points, and processes go well together into coherent archetypes, which problems the archetypes can be used to solve, and the particular challenges of each archetype. To this end, what does this research mean for practice? It is important to realize that parties like sea carriers, terminals, port community systems and authorities are well positioned to play a key role in setting up digital trade infrastructures. Some will grasp the opportunities and will try to be the first-movers, others will be forced to reposition their activities to stay in business. Our mapping of the anatomy of DTIs as well as future research in the directions that we identified in this paper can be instrumental for these parties to understand the complexity of the playing field when defining their strategies for action.

Acknowledgements. This research was partially funded by the CORE Project (nr. 603993), which is funded by the FP7 Framework Program of the European Commission. Ideas and opinions expressed by the authors do not necessarily represent those of all partners.

References

1. Jensen, T., Bjørn-Andersen, N., Vatrapu, R.: Avocados crossing borders: the missing common information infrastructure for international trade. In: Yamashita, N., Evers, V., Rosé, C., Watson-Manheim, M.B. (eds.) Proceedings of the 5th ACM International Conference on Collaboration across Boundaries: Culture, Distance & Technology, CABS 2014, pp. 15–24. Association for Computing Machinery, New York (2014)
2. Jensen, T., Vatrapu, R.: Ships & roses: a revelatory case study of affordances in international trade. In: European Conference on Information Systems (ECIS) (2015)
3. Heilig, L., Voß, S.: Information systems in seaports: a categorization and overview. Inf. Technol. Manag. 1–23 (2016)
4. Van Der Horst, M.R., De Langen, P.W.: Coordination in hinterland transport chains: a major challenge for the seaport community. Marit. Econ. Logist. 10(1–2), 108–129 (2008)
5. Aanestad, M., Jensen, T.B.: Building nation-wide information infrastructures in healthcare through modular implementation strategies. J. Strateg. Inf. Syst. 20(2), 161–176 (2011)
6. Jensen, T., Vatrapu, R.: Shipping information pipeline: initial design principles. In: At the Vanguard of Design Science: First Impressions and Early Findings from Ongoing Research Research-in-Progress Papers and Poster Presentations from the 10th International Conference, DESRIST (2015)
7. Hesketh, D.: Weaknesses in the supply chain: who packed the box. World Customs J. 4(2), 3–20 (2010)
8. Rukanova, B., Baida, Z., Liu, J., van Stijn, E., Tan, Y., Hofman, W., Wigand, R., van Ipenburg, F.: Beer living lab – intelligent data sharing. In: Tan, Y., Bjorn-Andersen, N., Klein, S., Rukanova, B. (eds.) Accelerating Global Supply Chains with IT-Innovation, pp. 37–55. Springer, Heidelberg (2011). doi:10.1007/978-3-642-15669-4_3
9. Klievink, A.J., Van Stijn, E., Hesketh, D., Aldewereld, H., Overbeek, S., Heijmann, F., Tan, Y.H.: Enhancing visibility in international supply chains: the data pipeline concept. Int. J. Electron. Gov. Res. 8(4), 14–33 (2012)
10. Tan, Y.H., Bjorn-Andersen, N., Klein, S., Rukanova, B.: Accelerating Global Supply Chains with IT-Innovation. Springer, Heidelberg (2011). Edited Book
11. Janssen, M., van Engelenburg, S., Tan, Y.H.: Comparing a Shipping Information Pipeline with a Thick Flow and a Thin Flow (working paper) (2015)
12. Hanseth, O., Monteiro, E., Hatling, M.: Developing information infrastructure: the tension between standardization and flexibility. Sci. Technol. Hum. Values 21(4), 407–426 (1996)
13. Hanseth, O., Lyytinen, K.: Design theory for dynamic complexity in information infrastructures: the case of building internet. J. Inf. Technol. 25(1), 1–19 (2010)
14. Baida, Z., Rukanova, B., Wigand, R.T., Tan, Y.H.: The story of how heineken's supply chain benefits from tight collaboration with government. Supply Chain Manag. Rev. 11(8), 11–12 (2007)
15. Baida, Z., Rukanova, B., Liu, J., Tan, Y.H.: Rethinking EU trade procedures - the beer living lab. Electron. Mark. 18(1), 53–64 (2008)
16. Rukanova, B., Van Stijn, E., Henriksen, H.Z., Baida, Z., Tan, Y.H.: Understanding the influence of multiple levels of governments on the development of inter-organizational systems. Eur. J. Inf. Syst. 18(5), 387–408 (2009)

17. Edwards, P., Jackson, S., Bowker, G., Knobel, C.: Understanding infrastructure: dynamics, tensions, and design. In: NSF Report of a Workshop: History and Theory of Infrastructure: Lessons for New Scientific Cyberinfrastructures (2007)

18. Gal, U., Lyytinen, K., Youngjin, Y.: The dynamics of IT boundary objects, information infrastructures, and organisational identities: the introduction of 3D modelling technologies into the architecture, engineering, and construction industry. Eur. J. Inf. Syst. **17**, 290–304 (2008)

19. Braa, J., Macome, E., Mavimbe, J.C., Nhampossa, J.L., da Costa, J.L., Manave, A., Sitói, A.: A study of the actual and potential usage of information and communication technology at district and provincial levels in Mozambique with a focus on the health sector. Electron. J. Inf. Syst. Dev. Ctries. **5**, 1–29 (2001)

20. Henfridsson, O., Bygstad, B.: The generative mechanisms of digital infrastructure evolution. MIS Q. **37**(3), 907–931 (2013)

21. Ciborra, C., Hanseth, O.: Introduction: From Control to Drift. In: Ciborra, C. (ed.) From Control to Drift, pp. 1–12. Oxford University Press, Oxford (2000)

22. Constantinides, P.: Perspectives and implications for the development of information infrastructures. Inf. Sci. Ref. (2012)

23. Damsgaard, J., Lyytinen, K.: The role of intermediating institutions in the diffusion of electronic data interchange (EDI): how industry associations intervened in Denmark, Finland, and Hong Kong. Inf. Soc. **17**(3), 195–210 (2001)

24. Sauer, C., Willcocks, L.: Unreasonable expectations - NHS IT, Greek choruses and the games institutions play around mega-programmes. J. Inf. Technol. **22**(3), 195–201 (2007)

25. Hedman, J., Henningsson, S.: The new normal: market cooperation in the mobile payments ecosystem. Electron. Commer. Res. Appl. **14**(5), 305–318 (2015)

26. Rodon, J., Silva, L.: Exploring the formation of a healthcare information infrastructure: hierarchy or meshwork? J. Assoc. Inf. Syst. **16**(5), 1 (2015)

27. Star, S.L.: The ethnography of infrastructure. Am. Behav. Sci. **43**(3), 377–391 (1999)

28. Sanner, T.A., Manda, T.D., Nielsen, P.: Grafting: balancing control and cultivation in information infrastructure innovation. J. Assoc. Inf. Syst. **15**(4), 220–243 (2014)

29. Tilson, D., Lyytinen, K., Sørensen, C.: Research commentary - digital infrastructures: the missing IS research agenda. Inf. Syst. Res. **21**(4), 748–759 (2010)

30. Ostrom, E.: Governing the Commons: The Evolution of Institutions for Collective Action. Cambridge University Press, Cambridge (1990)

31. Patton, M.Q.: Qualitative Evaluation and Research Methods. SAGE Publications Inc., Thousand Oaks (1990)

32. Charmaz, K.: Grounded theory: objectivist and constructivist methods. In: Denzin, N.K., Lincoln, Y.S. (eds.) Handbook of Qualitative Research, pp. 509–536. Sage Publications, Thousand Oaks (2000)

33. Rukanova, B., Henriksen, H.Z., Raesfeld, A.V., Stijn, E.V., Tan, Y.H.: A collective action perspective on technological innovation in business/government networks. In: EIS 2008 Proceedings (2008)

Engaging with Openness Through Common(s) Ground: Healthcare Innovation in the Networked Society

Mark Aakhus[1], Pär J. Ågerfalk[2(✉)], Kanika Samra[1], and Håkan Ozan[3]

[1] Rutgers University, New Brunswick, NJ, USA
aakhus@rutgers.edu, kanikasamra@gmail.com
[2] Uppsala University, Uppsala, Sweden
par.agerfalk@im.uu.se
[3] KPMG, Stockholm, Sweden
hakan.ozan@kpmg.se

Abstract. Hospitals have increasingly embraced their role as centers for innovation and much attention has focused on technology transfer, translational research and even social innovation. Here we explore how open innovation could be a viable strategy for health organizations in contemporary society with its reliance on advanced information and communication technology. The study focuses on (a) innovation centers in hospitals by examining two variables important to open innovation: (i) the direction of value creation and (ii) innovation form, and (b) the development of scenarios for open innovation in healthcare by engaged practitioners in the field. The findings suggest some noteworthy variation in form and direction of innovation for healthcare. Most notably, although innovation is attended to, open initiatives do not loom large today. However, we also see that the future may bring something completely different with a focus on healthcare rather than hospitals. The results suggest direction for future empirical work and strategy development for designing healthcare systems as well as for open innovation practice.

Keywords: Open innovation · Communication · Common ground · Commons · Healthcare

1 Healthcare in Contemporary Society

With this paper, we initiate an exploration of how open innovation could be a viable strategy for health organizations—hospitals, in particular—in the emerging networked society [1] with its reliance on advanced information and communication technology (ICT). Hospitals have increasingly embraced their role as centers for innovation [2] and while much attention has focused on technology transfer, translational research and even social innovation, what is less clear is to what extent open innovation could be a viable part of their innovation strategy. Open innovation traditionally refers to, "the use of purposive inflows and outflows of knowledge to accelerate internal innovation and expand the markets for external use of innovation" [3]. Open innovation thus suggests

© Springer International Publishing AG 2017
B. Johansson et al. (Eds.): BIR 2017, LNBIP 295, pp. 199–211, 2017.
DOI: 10.1007/978-3-319-64930-6_15

a framework for how to leverage contemporary ICT in the healthcare sector for the benefit of both caregivers and caretakers [4]. Yet, a fundamental practical and theoretical puzzle remains for practicing open innovation in the healthcare context—that is, how to create and sustain the required engagement among stakeholders to realize open innovation as a management strategy for hospitals in the networked society? The timeliness and importance of solving this puzzle is highlighted by recent initiatives in both Europe (e.g., the EU eHealth Action Plan) and the United States (e.g., the NSF Smart and Connected Health Program).

A variety of changes in ICT and society have been consequential for the health sector. Through the Internet and social media, for instance, patients have more access to information and opinions about medicine and healthcare than ever before. There is growing interest from healthcare organizations for patient-centered care and a demand to practice evidence based medicine. At the same time, health organizations are exploring the uses of ICTs to create new services for delivering care and reflecting on their role in local communities and society. The promise of ICT to harness the potential of digital innovation, including openness, crowd, scale, participation, and personalization [5–8], is not automatic nor is it guaranteed. It is a matter of design. As a matter of fact, it has long been argued that one should not assume that ICT is the solution, there might be organizational (soft) issues that should rather be addressed [9]. Without a doubt, the emerging networked society is putting pressure on hospitals to adapt to their new information and communication-centered context. The networked society may pose significant challenges to hospitals, however, it may also present an important opportunity for hospitals to increase innovation. Indeed, most of the ingredients that have made open innovation important in other sectors of society are staring hospitals in the face. Leveraging open innovation as strategy by hospitals thus seems both timely and full of potential.

The challenges faced by hospitals also present an important opportunity for developing the concept and practice of open innovation more generally [10]. Open innovation suggests that the most exciting things happen at the boundaries, where diverse competencies, experiences and perspectives meet and cross-pollinate. Open innovation is traditionally described in terms of outbound flows of ideas and information. It was developed primarily as a firm-centric concept concerned with competitors and markets. However, open innovation also happens in other ways, such as flowing from engagements within ecosystems [11]. Benkler [12, 13] made a foundational contribution in this regard, by explaining how innovation is fostered through commons (resources shared among cooperating actors), which entail forms of organizing that are neither market nor management hierarchy based. The crucial point then is how stakeholders engage each other to generate innovation, as each basic form calls out different kinds of communication among stakeholders: markets focus on pricing signals, hierarchies focus on commands, and ecosystems focus on persuasion and dialogue [14]. Thus, successful open innovation depends on rethinking the form and quality of communication among the participants in the innovation process as much as adopting new technological frameworks. Hence, the design and implementation of digital health practices cannot be seen in isolation from organizational context or from the pragmatics of communication [10].

What matters for open innovation engagement, then, are the practices of, and institutions for communication. These are consequential for how participants interact and reason about the problems and opportunities they act upon—that is, for how to think and develop ideas together. Quite simply, these tacit dimensions of organizational and professional practice can mismatch the capacity of ICT in ways that fundamentally challenge the management of open innovation initiatives [15]. In the hospital context, for instance, new, network-based ways of interacting with patients are both threatening and inspiring because these new media can bring the 'outside in' and let the 'inside out'. Thus, the context of the networked society pressures hospitals to address the issue of open innovation—how, when, and to what extent to bring together the outside and the inside? The pressure for open innovation requires decisions about how to introduce new ICT, yet, importantly, these decisions entail crucial matters of designing information systems and associated communication practices [16]. Designing for open innovation must thus be sensitive to two key issues: (1) avoid simply reproducing business-as-usual and (2) anticipate disruptive changes that could far outstrip the capacity of the organization and its practitioners. Thus, successful open innovation depends on rethinking the form, direction, and quality of communication among the participants in the innovation process as much as adopting new technological frameworks.

There is no shortage of models for understanding open innovation [11]. One important model from the healthcare domain, particularly medical technology, is the "technology commodification model" from Philips Healthcare [17], henceforth the Philips model. In this two-dimensional model (see Fig. 1), the x-axis focuses on collaboration forms, ranging from intra-organizational to inter-organizational to completely open.

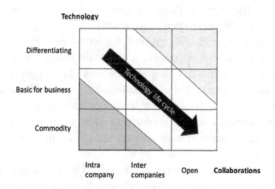

Fig. 1. Technology commodification model from Philips Healthcare [17].

The y-axis focuses on 'technology' features and how the technology in question differentiates from other related technologies on the market. This latter dimension is particularly useful for strategic choices about the uses of engineering resources. The essential question being, how to avoid wasting engineering resources on further development of what have become technology commodities while protecting intellectual property loss from premature sharing of innovations? These are important matters that must be taken into account as organizations make strategic choices and figure out how to use IT in organizational strategy.

The Philips model, however, hides other important matters such as the direction of value creation—that is, who benefits and how from the innovation. Not all goods produced are private goods; some are inherently public or common goods. This is particularly poignant for healthcare. For instance, a strict application of the Philips model in healthcare at large would center innovation strategy by healthcare organizations around commodification but clearly not all innovations in health will be primarily for private benefit. So, to better model open, we include here another dimension to take into account in addition to the innovation form and form of involvement in value creation: the direction of value creation.

Another important model of open innovation [3] views the form and quality of communication for open innovation in terms of inbound and outbound transfers of innovation. In particular, the role of ICT is simply conceived as a conduit that transfers knowledge from one person to another. This unfortunately downplays the ultimate significance of communication for how stakeholders make sense of the innovation context of their collaboration with others in developing innovations and the consequences that follow from the design and implementation of the technological support of communication for open innovation [16, 18, 19]. It is fundamentally problematic for open innovation initiatives to introduce new ICTs with the simplistic hope that new channels will, in and of themselves, foster the necessary connections, creativity, and collaboration [15, 16]. The alternative is to see communication as interactional, 'symbolic activity' that establishes the common(s) ground necessary for diverse actors' joint actions and achievements [15, 20, 21]. Because the form, direction, and quality of communication can vary, such a commons-view of communication and ICT draws attention to the need for creative thinking about designing communication and its technological support to facilitate open innovation.

These matters about common(s) ground for communication in the networked society raise the question of how open innovation could become an explicit strategy for hospitals, rather than a reaction to external pressures. The opportunity for organizational and professional practice is first to consider what communicative practices enable open innovation and then to consider how to design and manage communication for open innovation by hospitals in the networked society. In particular, what kind of communication and information system support should be driving open innovation in healthcare?

We would argue that a not so common, but indeed sensitive to commons approach is needed. In this paper, we report on a project with the dual aim to (a) understand the current state of open innovation in the healthcare sector and (b) actively engage with the sector and develop scenarios for possible ways forward. The findings suggest some noteworthy variation in form and direction of innovation. Most notably, although innovation is attended to, open initiatives do not loom large. The results suggest directions for future empirical work and strategy development for designing common (s) ground as well as for open innovation practice.

2 Research Approach

For this research, we adopted a mixed methods approach [22, 23] that allowed for a combination of descriptive statistics with a qualitative design-oriented focus group approach. First, a survey of U.S. based healthcare innovation centers was devised to gauge how innovation centers were being deployed. Second, the results of the survey provided the basis for developing an interactive workshop that summoned key stakeholders in the sector with the aim to consider future megatrends and to incorporate them into an innovative, but yet realistic, plausible future. The combination of these methods enabled an inquiry into key issues in designing for open innovation—to avoid reproducing business-as-usual and to anticipate disruptive change.

2.1 Healthcare Innovation Center Survey

To take the temperature of the healthcare arena, we first conducted an investigation to explore how hospitals organize their innovation efforts to see if ideas about open were common. Specifically, we were interested in how hospitals orient their innovation and the form their innovation efforts take. Orientation refers to the direction of value creation. For the purpose of this study we defined direction of value creation as primarily for (a) private benefit, that is the hospital, its clients, and investors, or for (b) societal benefit. Innovation form refers to how various stakeholders are engaged in innovation efforts. For present purposes, we defined these forms as internal (self-contained innovation, usually housed within one hospital), open (where the exchange of information, knowledge and expertise is two-way), or hybrid (with inter-organizational, collaborative programs).

The data for this preliminary study focused on the types of programs and initiatives sponsored by hospital innovation centers. The American Hospital Association is a professional body that advocates on behalf of 5,000 healthcare organizations in the USA that has compiled a list of hospital innovation centers. The list contained 126 centers as of April 2015. From those centers we identified 334 innovation programs or initiatives. By examining the descriptions of these initiatives and programs on their websites, we coded them according to the features described above for direction of value creation and innovation form.

2.2 Future Scenarios Workshop

The methodology for the workshop was a combination of (i) trend analysis, (ii) scenario planning and (iii) back casting. A preparatory presentation included areas such as the changing demographics with an aging population, urbanization, increased global mobility, and de-industrialization with a shift of focus toward service innovation, and the changing economic landscape with the rise of emerging markets and digitization. The attendees were then divided into teams that were assigned the task to discuss what the healthcare environment will look like in 10–15 years. The teams were inspired to forecast an envisioned future—a future with few boundaries and most of today's problems innovatively resolved. Each team then presented their envisioned future in a plenary session that focused on identifying possible future scenarios.

Eight people participated in the workshop, in addition to three of the authors of this paper and an appointed rapporteur. The eight participants were handpicked and invited based on their organizational affiliations and documented interest in the area. Two were medical doctors from a local hospital, three represented the local government (community and county councils), one came from a hospital innovation center, and two from the university (a senior researcher and a student). All teamwork was documented, as was the final plenary session.

3   Healthcare Innovation Center Survey Results

3.1   Forms of Innovation

Of the 334 innovation programs analyzed, the majority were categorized as internal (Table 1, Number of Innovation Forms). Hybrid forms were identified in 150 initiatives. Open innovation was evident in 2 programs. Two others could not be coded according to any of the three forms of innovation as these consisted of marketing initiatives publicizing programs run by a hospital. It can be argued that publicity and marketing are directed towards private value creation, but the innovation forms did not adhere to the definitions operationalized for this survey.

Table 1. Number of innovation forms.

Innovation form	N = 334
Internal	180
Hybrid	150
Open	2
No code	2

3.2   Direction of Value Creation by Form of Innovation

Value creation was categorized as private or societal and in certain cases an overlap was found, those programs were coded as both private/societal hybrid (Fig. 2, Value creation by innovation type/form).

The total number of programs with private value creation was 229. This number was further analyzed to differentiate programs according to the form of innovation. Private value creation was the dominant direction in internal innovation forms at 151. Followed by 78 hybrid programs with private value creation direction. Societal value creation was found in 82 initiatives, which included the 2 open innovative forms found in our sample. Sixty of these programs were hybrid in nature while 22 were internal. Some programs displayed elements of both private and societal value creation, of these 9 were. In addition, 3 hybrid programs displayed 0 value creation.

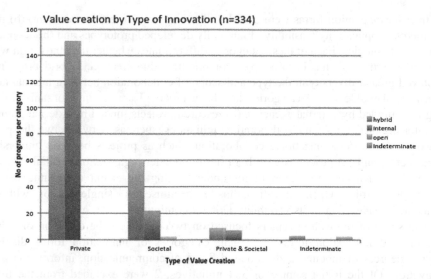

Fig. 2. Value creation by types of innovation. The initial sample of 334 initiatives was categorized according to the innovation forms internal and hybrid and the directions of value creation, private or societal.

3.3 Specifying the Forms of Innovation

The use of an inductive sampling method with emergent categories has expanded the classification of types of innovation. By further examination of the about pages, mission, and vision statements, subtle differences in the innovation forms were identified within each of the main categories. These differences present themselves as points on a continuum of hybridity and internal innovation, as shown in Table 2.

Table 2. Continuum of innovation.

Innovation forms	Definition
1a. Internal	Completely self-contained. Usually housed within one hospital or a network
1b. Internal	Developing a prototype or product with commercial applicability
1c. Internal	Adopting latest technology for private value creation
2a. Hybrid	Inter-organizational, collaborative programs funded by national institutions like U.S. National Institutes of Health
2b. Hybrid	Funded by a grant to carry on with a research project locally at a hospital
2c. Hybrid	Inter-organizational and collaborative programs between two or more hospitals, health networks, outpatient practices or with businesses
2d. Hybrid	Intra organizational collaborative programs such those initiated between university departments
2e. Hybrid	Inter and intra organizational programs
3. Open	Where the exchange of information, knowledge and expertise is two-way or more

Internal innovation forms were coded on the basis of (a) self-containment, (b) the commercial applicability/feasibility of internally developed prototypes and (b) adoption of new technologies. Each of these categories differentiates whether the innovation was initiated internally or has been adopted for private value creation. Hybrid programs displayed greater diversity in the type and scope of collaboration between internal and external stakeholders. The categories that have emerged are (a) inter-organizational programs funded by external agencies, (b) research projects funded by external grants, (c) inter-organizational and collaborative initiatives such as between two hospital networks, (d) intra-organizational collaborations such as projects between university departments, and (e) programs with both intra and inter-organizational collaboration. These slight nuances are important for understanding the extent of openness in a collaborative project. Open innovation, thus far, been used as a single category without sufficient consideration of its variability along a continuum.

The study of innovation centers focused on two variables: the direction of value creation and innovation forms. Emergent categories of innovation forms display varying degrees of inbound and outbound flows of communication, information and innovation. Of the initial sample of 334 initiatives, 2 were excluded from the final analysis due to the indeterminate nature of the programs' value creation direction. The reduced sample of 332 programs (Fig. 3: Types of innovation) were color-coded and show a predominance of self-contained internal initiatives (26%) followed closely by those meant for adopting and implementing cutting edge technology (22%).

When plotted against the direction of value creation (Fig. 4: Value creation by innovation forms), the trend remains true to the initial analysis. Internal programs are predominantly focused on private value creation. The outbound flow in such cases is

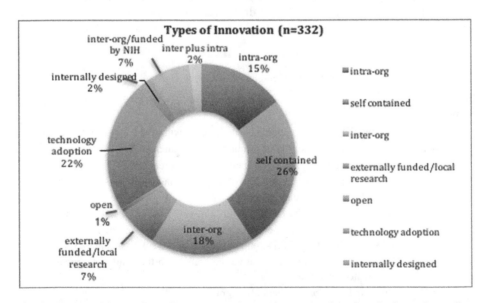

Fig. 3. Types of innovation. The emergent innovation categories plotted after color-coding. (Color figure online)

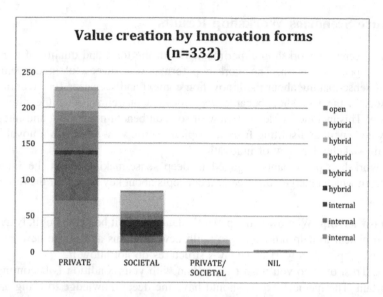

Fig. 4. Innovation forms and value creation. Emergent categories of innovation forms plotted against the value creation direction of the programs. N = 332, excluding two that were indeterminate.

limited. On the other hand, of the 84 programs that are focused on societal value creation, 54% were inter-organizational and collaborative hybrid programs. These initiatives include both, projects funded by external agencies such as the U.S. National Institutes of Health and regional or local level collaborations between hospital networks. The need to communicate and exchange information with an external stakeholder suggests both outbound and inbound flows of communication. However, to what degree the flow of communication impacts the value creation is not given. Vice versa, the aim of societal value creation the force behind a hybrid structure also needs to be investigated. Similarly, open innovation forms are highly collaborative and function only to create societal value. Programs that were found to have both private and societal value (5%) were evenly distributed between internal and hybrid types. But, the hybridity was restricted to inter-organizational collaborations that would perhaps lead to societal gains by virtue of servicing a larger population.

Our observations of innovation initiatives among U.S. hospitals suggests that while there is more variety of innovation forms that anticipated by the Phillip's model, the predominate innovation forms skew toward self-contained innovation approaches that are directed toward private value creation. However, it also appears that inter-organizational collaborations do happen and happen in the context of external funding.

4 Future Scenarios Workshop Results

The future scenarios workshop experimented with the form and quality of communication for open innovation. The workshop format was successful in deepening the quality of sense-making about the innovation context and scenarios for invention. The participants in the workshop became very focused on reimagining the direction of innovation. This included a blended view of societal benefit motivating and integrating with private benefit and shifting from a hospital centric view of health innovation to a more multi-stakeholder view of innovation.

The workshop participants engaged in deep sense-making about the innovation context from which emerged three central concepts about key issues for the direction of innovation:

- **Data ownership**: Who owns the patient's data? Could it be made publicly available by the patient to help innovators to build new solutions and create new cures, the same way open data works? Today's structures do not allow it.
- **Trust**: Trust on who you wish to help you with your condition is becoming more important. The medical expert should have the deep knowledge to bring answers, but many times other **patients** with the same disease have similar – and sometime more – knowledge and understanding of the disease and how it should be treated. So whom do you trust and listen to?
- **Wellness through awareness**: With increased knowledge of what leads to what, such as what food is bad for you, how performing certain actions may cause cancer, etc. it can be better communicated to prevent poor health. By public sharing of experience and data, awareness can be increased and lead to better health conditions for a lot of people.

These directions for innovation were addressed by specific innovation scenarios:

- **Intelligent environments**: The case displayed a city environment with omnipresent sensors that can passively read people's life sensors. It turns into a form of public health monitoring that can alert the medical system whenever an incident of some form occurs.
- **Health prediction systems**: Big data from people's medical journals can be computed on a real-time basis to analyze and predict medical conditions. Imagine that the doorbell rings and outside is a team of medics. When the door opens, they say – "please lay down, you are just about to have a heart attack."
- **Social alarms**: The concept is that everybody has at least some minor knowledge that can be applied as "first level support". If we can find the nearest person who has the most basic competence regarding the disease/condition at hand it may save lives. One person cannot do everything, but many people can do a little.
- **Increased human contact**: Technology is usually regarded as increasing the distance between people. But properly managed, technology can help people to meet. Personal and physical contact is extremely important in overcoming diseases and hard times.
- **The no-hospital environment**: In the future, there may actually not be so many hospitals. Hospitals built on the patient coming to the building. The team was

considering "what if we can skip the buildings and just focus on care". New technology may make it much easier for the doctor to bring "the hospital" – equipment and gear – to the patient instead of the other way around.

One important aspect of the workshop was its experimentation with the form and quality of open innovation communication among a variety of stakeholders in health care. The communicative design of the engagement created common ground among the healthcare professionals and academics by using a combination of techniques: trend analysis, scenario planning, and back casting. The design aimed to generate common ground in terms of both the content and the process of interaction such that no participant had to give up their expertise and identify but the groups could collectively find ways to integrate the different insights relative to the shared interest in better healthcare. While only a microcosm of larger scale interventions, the workshop was instructive for designing collaborative, open engagement around innovation. The participant evaluations pointed to the promise of the model for designing communication to manage open innovation processes. In a final reflection session, some further important results emerged that spoke to this ambition:

- "We need more like this." There was a general feeling that hospital staff and doctors are mostly too occupied with operative work and lack the time, incentives and coordination to strategize on a 10 to 15-year basis. Yet it was seen highly important for the healthcare sector to engage in such discussions.
- There was frustration that "healthcare does not evolve at the same pace as many other industries."
- "Health development becomes supplier-driven, rather than patient-driven." When the hospitals and the medical system are not in charge of driving the development of healthcare based on actual current and future needs, it risks falling into the hands of short-term, profit-driven supplier companies.
- "We need to collaborate more cross-sectional," "The perspectives we gain from discussing with people from other fields are highly valuable when trying to widen our scopes and get new angles of things we thought were carved into stone."

5   Discussion and Conclusion

Our results show that there is indeed attention to innovation in the healthcare sector but it is noteworthy that we found very few instances of open innovation in our survey of hospital innovation centers. At the same time, we found a large number of hybrid forms with a varying degree of openness. If this finding holds upon further investigation, it will need to explain why this is the case. This study contributes another aspect of open innovation by identifying the direction of value creation as key to open innovation engagement. Here we found that open initiatives present themselves only as programs with societal value. This finding could prove to be a crucial insight for creating common(s) ground for innovation in healthcare.

The workshop results confirm the view that the healthcare sector is lagging behind industry and society at large in terms of open innovation. Interestingly, the results show that, although several participants were employed by a hospital, the idea that healthcare is more important than the organizational structure within which healthcare operates today. This calls for an institutional analysis to understand better how openness resonates with existing institutional pressures and tensions in relation 'the hospital' as the traditional archetype for healthcare delivery. In particular, from an institutional point of view, an ecosystem such as healthcare stands in contrast to markets and bureaucratic hierarchies and calls for forms of communication that enable mutual persuasion among a variety of stakeholders in a dialogue. While these forms were not obviously predominate in innovation initiatives from the survey, the workshop was illustrative on a microscale that such forms and qualities of communication are valuable in improving sense-making about innovation contexts among diverse stakeholders in healthcare.

Our survey showed clearly that although innovation is emphasized, open innovation is so far not at the top of the agenda for most hospitals. To better understand innovation and the realization of open innovation requires deeper insight into practices for designing communication for open innovation. In this regard, there is a need for research that frames open innovation in healthcare as a multi-layered opportunity for advancing open innovation practice. Such an effort must engage practitioners and organizations about the practical issues about open innovation strategy in healthcare. This is necessary in order to engage practitioners and academic researchers to explore the complexities of healthcare organizations in the networked society and the prospects for strategic open innovation in healthcare. The workshop conducted as part of this study vindicates both the need for and the potential benefit of such activity.

A possible way forward would be to create a suite of in-depth case studies about designing communication practice for open innovation. This would entail developing theory and method for analysis of institutions for communication and the design of communication practice for open innovation. Ultimately, what is needed is a research agenda for the future of open innovation design practice that can develop applicable core constructs to inform and translate to business practice and also open up research opportunities. To succeed with this ambition, a network of international practitioners and scholars focused on the development of design thinking for open innovation, with a specific focus on healthcare in the networked society will need to be formed. Our hope is that many will see this opportunity and engage with us on this exciting journey.

References

1. Castells, M. (ed.): The Network Society: A Cross-Cultural Perspective. Edward Elgar Publishing, Cheltenham (2004)
2. Edenius, M., Keller, K., Lindblad, S.: Managing knowledge across boundaries in healthcare when innovation is desired. Knowl. Manag. E-Learn.: Int. J. 2(2), 134–153 (2010)
3. Chesbrough, H.: Open Innovation: The New Imperative for Creating and Profiting from Technology. Harvard Business School Publishing, Boston (2006)
4. Chesbrough, H., Di Minin, A.: Open social innovation. In: Chesbrough, H., Vanhaverbeke, W., West, J. (eds.) New Frontiers in Open Innovation, pp. 169–188. Oxford University Press, Oxford (2014)

5. Epstein, R.J.: Digitization and its discontents: future shock in predictive oncology. In: Seminars in Oncology, vol. 37, no. 1, pp. 60–64. WB Saunders (2010)
6. Lapão, L.V.: The future impact of healthcare services digitalization on health workforce: the increasing role of medical informatics. Stud. Health Technol. Inf. **228**, 675–679 (2016)
7. Hood, L., Balling, R., Auffray, C.: Revolutionizing medicine in the 21st century through systems approaches. Biotechnol. J. **7**(8), 992–1001 (2012)
8. Westbrook, J.I., Braithwaite, J., Gibson, K., Paoloni, R., Callen, J., Georgiou, A., Creswick, N., Robertson, L.: Use of information and communication technologies to support effective work practice innovation in the health sector: a multi-site study. BMC Health Serv. Res. **9** (1), 201 (2009)
9. Cresswell, K., Sheikh, A.: Organizational issues in the implementation and adoption of health information technology innovations: an interpretative review. Int. J. Med. Inform. **82** (5), e73–e86 (2013)
10. Vanhaverbeke, W., Chesbrough, H., West, H.: Surfing the new wave of open innovation research. In: Chesbrough, H., Vanhaverbeke, W., West, J. (eds.) New Frontiers in Open Innovation, pp. 281–294. Oxford University Press, Oxford (2014). Chap. 15
11. Remneland Wikhamn, B., Wikhamn, W.: Structuring of the open innovation field. J. Technol. Manag. Innov. **8**(3), 173–185 (2013)
12. Benkler, Y.: Coase's penguin, or, Linux and the nature of the firm. Yale Law J. **112**(3), 369–446 (2002)
13. Benkler, Y.: The Wealth of Networks: How Social Production Transforms Markets and Freedom. Yale University Press, New Haven (2006)
14. Powell, W.W., DiMaggio, P.J. (eds.): The New Institutionalism in Organizational Analysis. University of Chicago Press, Chicago (1991)
15. Aakhus, M., Ågerfalk, P.J., Lyytinen, K.: Te'eni, D.: Symbolic action research in information systems: introduction to the special issue. MIS Q. **38**(4), 1187–1200 (2014)
16. Aakhus, M.: Deliberation digitized: designing disagreement space through communication-information services. J. Argum. Context **2**(1), 101–126 (2013)
17. Lundell, B., van der Linden, F.: Open source software as open innovation: experiences from the medical domain. In: Eriksson Lundström, J.S.Z., Wiberg, M., Hrastinski, S., Edenius, M., Ågerfalk, P.J. (eds.) Managing Open Innovation Technologies, pp. 3–16. Springer, Heidelberg (2013). doi:10.1007/978-3-642-31650-0_1
18. Thorén, C., Ågerfalk, P.J., Edenius, M.: Through the printing press: an account of open practices in the swedish newspaper industry. J. Assoc. Inf. Syst. **15**(11), 779–804 (2014). Special Issue on Open Innovation
19. Aakhus, M.: Communication as design. Commun. Monogr. **74**(1), 112–117 (2007)
20. Jackson, S., Aakhus, M.: Becoming more reflective about the role of design in communication. J. Appl. Commun. Res. **42**(2), 125–134 (2014)
21. Clarke, H.H.: Using Language. Cambridge University Press, Cambridge (1996)
22. Venkatesh, V., Brown, S.A., Bala, H.: Bridging the qualitative–quantitative divide: guidelines for conducting mixed methods research in information systems. MIS Q. **36**(1), 21–54 (2013)
23. Ågerfalk, P.J.: Embracing diversity through mixed methods research. Eur. J. Inf. Syst. **22**(3), 251–256 (2013)

Finance Information Systems Usage in Universities in a Developing Country: Implementing Factors and Their Influence on Use

David Kiwana(✉) and Björn Johansson

Department of Informatics, School of Economics and Management,
Lund University, Ole Römers Väg 6, Lund, Sweden
{David.kiwana,bjorn.johansson}@ics.lu.se

Abstract. Finance information systems (FISs) store and provide timely, accurate and consistent financial data for management and decision-making. Many organizations especially in developing world however fail to attain desired success during implementation and usage of the FISs despite the fact that many success factors for implementation have been suggested. This study thus investigated the usage of FISs with the aim of finding out how factors presumed to influence implementation impact usage. The presumed factors included; top management support, effective communication, evaluation of staff performance, technical support, project management, change management program, effectiveness of IT unit and flexibility of consultants. The study focused on universities in Uganda which is a developing country. Of the nine factors that were investigated only top management support, technical training and flexibility of consultants exhibited a positive impact with only top management support being significant. The rest of the factors exhibited negative impact and only effective IT unit being significant.

Keywords: CSFs · Critical success factors · Developing countries · Finance information systems · Implementation · Usage

1 Introduction

A finance information system (FIS) can be described as a set of automation solutions that enables users to plan, execute and monitor budgets by assisting in prioritization, execution, and reporting of expenditures and revenues [1]. FISs are usually comprised of many accounting modules and according to Khemani and Diamond [2] they consist of; General ledger, Budgetary accounting, accounts payables, accounts receivables and noncore modules can include; payroll system, budget development, procurement operating and capital budgets, working capital reports, cash flow forecast and project ledgers.

Contextually while FISs have many benefits, it has been found that putting them in place can be costly and in most cases requires a lot of training and commitment by the people involved [3]. As a result, many organizations find difficulties to attain the

© Springer International Publishing AG 2017
B. Johansson et al. (Eds.): BIR 2017, LNBIP 295, pp. 212–230, 2017.
DOI: 10.1007/978-3-319-64930-6_16

desired success when implementation is done. Pan et al. [4] say that there is still a significant body of evidence that many information systems implementation projects end in failure. Also Mulira [3] says that many critical success factors for IS implementation have been suggested, however actual evidence to devise solutions for failed projects has not been clearly established. This paper presents research done that aims at answering the research question: How factors involved in implementation of a FIS later on impact usage of the system.

The next section shortly presents the factors investigated. Section 3 then presents the two different phases of the study, first the quantitative study done among 7 universities in Uganda and then the follow-up qualitative validation study among 4 of these universities. The results of the quantitative study are also presented in that section which then is discussed in relation to the findings in the qualitative study in Sect. 5. The final section then presents conclusions in relation to the 9 factors and the research question investigated.

2 Factors Influencing Implementation

In a study on usage of finance information systems in developing countries Kiwana et al. [5] presented nine factors which were perceived to be of influence to implementation of FISs in Ugandan Universities. These included; top management support, effective communication, evaluation of staff performance, technical support, project management, change management program, effectiveness of IT unit and flexibility of consultants. These factors are described shortly below.

Top management support: Conceptually, Hansen et al. employees and all [6] describes top management support as the extent to which top managers in the organization provide direction, authority, and resources during and after acquisitions of IT systems. vom Brocke [7] Illustrates that top management support is the degree to which senior management understands the importance of the information systems function and the extent to which they get involved in the information system activities.

Effective communication: Communication in respect to information systems implementations includes formal promotion of project teams and advertisement of the project progress in the rest of the organization [8]. According to Sajady et al. [9] employees and all other stakeholders should be told in advance about the scope, objectives, activities and updates, and they should admit that change would occur.

Education and training: According to James [10] the basis of education and training in implementation of FIS relies on creating awareness on the 'to do' part of the software. James argues that employees need training and re-skilling to understand how a system can change business processes.

Evaluation of staff performance: Dhillon [11] posits that regular evaluation of staff performance today should be used as a vital tool to identify the work potential of an employee, instead of choosing the best individual in the organization. And Easttom II [12] argues that it is important that the performance of employees in using FIS is continually assessed.

Project management: According to Rosario [13] Project management is about minding the scope and the overall engineering process of an organization programs.

Fui-Hoon Nah et al. [14] state that the scope must be clearly defined and should include the amount of systems to be implemented, the involvement of business units and amount of business process reengineering that is needed.

Change management program and FIS implementation: Fui-Hoon Nahet et al. [14] say that at the beginning of a project it is important to start change management and continue with it throughout the entire system life cycle. Fui-Hoon Nahet et al. [14] argue that a culture with shared values and common aims is conducive for success and organizations should have a strong corporate identity that is open to change.

Effective IT unit: Literally an IT unit is a department in an organization that is mandated with managing information systems. Judge et al. [15] argue that one of the biggest challenges of implementation of information systems especially in developing worlds is lack of IT units in organizations.

Technical support: Technical expertise refers to the extent to which internal and external mediating entities such as vendors and consultants provide knowledge, training, maintenance, and other technical support to the adopting organization [16].

Flexibility of consultants: Consultants are very important in the process of implementing and using Information Systems in an organization [17]. Paston and Grabski further indicate that the most commonly-cited impact of flexibility in consultation towards success of FIS has been that of more effective organizational change management.

In this paper we present results from a study that investigated how the above mentioned factors impact usage of the FISs and the circumstances in which this happens.

3   Research Methodology

This research employed a combination of qualitative and quantitative approaches in collecting and verification of the study findings, thus constituting a mixed-model research [18]. The rationale of this approach as argued by Eisenhardt and Graebner [19] is that triangulation made possible by multiple data collection methods provides stronger substantiation of constructs.

As a first step, an exploratory study was undertaken at a single university namely Makerere University to find out factors that influence implementation of FISs and this took a qualitative approach. The emergent results were compared with extant literature and hypotheses were developed, then a quantitative field study was conducted to find out the extent at which the found results through the exploratory study could be confirmed to be true or galvanized and also to find out the relationship between implementation and use of FISs. And lastly a qualitative validation study was conducted to explain the findings from the quantitative survey.

In employing mixed methods, it is possible to overcome a number of challenges that would be faced by single based studies like limited knowledge, biases, and inflexibilities, but rather, it would become imperative to integrate qualitative and quantitative data, sampling techniques [20]. Quantitative and qualitative research methods made it easier to apply differing designs, sampling techniques, data collection methods and validity studies to capture a detailed understanding of the study objectives and components. The mixed methods was advantageous because it helped to complement the strengths of a single design, to overcome weaknesses of a single design, to address the questions at different levels and to address the theoretical perspective at different levels also.

3.1   Quantitative Study Design

The quantitative study was carried out in seven Ugandan universities with the aim of finding out how factors perceived to influence FIS implementation later on impact its usage. A construct of Use was borrowed from DeLone and McLean [21] and the above mentioned factors were brought together into a framework that would help to explain the impact of the factors on the use of the FISs.

It was hypothesized that the nine factors that influence the implementation of FIS impact positively the usage of the FIS, as shown in Fig. 1.

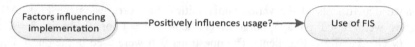

Fig. 1. Conceptual framework

The impact is assumed to be in terms of; Dependency, Frequency of use, Amount of use and, Nature of use, [21]. To test this, the following nine hypotheses were formulated:

- **H1:** Top Management support during implementation influences positively the use of FIS systems.
- **H2:** Effective Communication within the organization during implementation influences positively the use of FIS systems.
- **H3:** Evaluation of Staff Performances during implementation influences positively the use of FIS systems.
- **H4:** Education and Training of staff during implementation influences positively the use of FIS systems.
- **H5:** Technical Support for staff during implementation influences positively the use of FIS systems.
- **H6:** Project Management during implementation influences positively the use of FIS systems.
- **H7:** A Change Management Program during implementation influences positively the use of FIS systems.
- **H8:** Effective IT Unit during implementation influences positively the use of FIS systems.
- **H9:** Flexible Consultants during implementation influences positively the use of FIS systems.

Table 1 presents background information on the seven universities that were included in the quantitative study. The study used a structured questionnaire consisting of a series of closed-ended questions to collect data. The questionnaires were issued to staff

Table 1. Background information about investigated universities

University		System being used	Duration (years)	No of staff	No of students'
Makerere University	Mak	Integrated Tirtiary System (ITS)	7	5000	40000
Kyambogo University	KYA	Navision and e-compus for foes collection	5	2000	20000
Makerere University Business School	MUBS	Sage Accounting plus other internally developed system	5	1000	15000
Uganda Management Institute	UMI	Navision	6	800	5000
Mbarara University	MUST	Patel	4	1500	10000
Busitema University	BUSI	Pastel	4	900	12000
Uganda Christian University	UCU	Focus and SAP	6	1000	10000

in finance departments of the various universities that were using the FISs. All the questions were based on a 5 point Likert scale: (1 = Poor, 2 = Fair, 3 = Good, 4 = Very Good and 5 = Excellent). The questions that were used in the questionnaire and their sources are presented in Table 2.

Table 2. Investigated implementation factors and its related survey questions

Construct	Measure	Source
Top management support	Through participation in implementation process. e.g. attending implementation meetings	Ragu-Nathan et al. [22]
	Through Swift Decisions making	
	Through Demand for regular implementation progress reports	
Effective communication	There is a clear communication channel on all issues that pertain to the system	Amoako-Gyampah and Salam [23]
Evaluation of staff performance	There are regular Staff performance evaluations on system use	
Education and training	There was adequate training on FIS use	Amoako-Gyampah and Salam [23]
	Refresher training on FIS use is provided from time to time	
Technical support	Quick support service is provided	Amoroso and Cheney [24]
Project management	There is a clear mechanism of addressing issues and problems that arise	
Change management program	I was taken through a change management/sensitization program before using the system	
Effective IT unit	The institution has an IT unit responsible to support the IT system operations including the FIS	Antony et al. [25]
Flexible consultants	The suppliers/consultants are always willing to incorporate desired new changes into the system without much difficulty	

To understand the level of usage, the respondents were introduced to different items for them to have their say. These were; Dependency on the system, Frequency of Use, Amount of use and Nature of use of the system and a 5 point Likert scale was used to measure the responses (1 = Strongly Disagree, 2 = Disagree, 3 = uncertain, 4 = Agree and 5 = Strongly Agree). The following Table 3 details the questions that were asked in order to measure usage of the implemented FIS.

Table 3. Questions included in the questionnaire investigating usage

Rate the following statements with regard to the use of your FIS	Source
Dependency: My work fully depends on the system	Petter et al. [26]
Frequency of use: I use the system all the time	
Amount of use: I generate and prepare all my financial reports form the system	
Nature of use: The system is used almost by everybody in the accounts department	

The questionnaire was piloted amongst selected judges who were seasoned researchers and experts in the field of information systems, after which they were modified to improve their validity and reliability [27].

The convergent validity of the scale items was assessed using three criteria. First, the factor loadings which should be greater than 0.50 as proposed by Hair et al. [28]. Secondly, the composite reliability for each construct which should exceed 0.70. And lastly, the Average variance extracted (AVE) for each construct should be above the recommended cut-off of 0.50 [29].

In the study, the factor loadings revealed support for convergent validity for the nine constructs. All loadings were greater than 0.50 with most loadings exceeding 0.60. The factor loadings ranged from 0.54 to 1.0. Items with loadings less than 0.70 can still be considered significant, but more of the variance in the measure is attributed to error [28]. The high factor loadings give reason to conclude that the measures have convergent validity. All constructs factor loading exceeded the 0.50 cut-off as indicated in Table 5 under column heading "AVE", with the exception of use (AVE = 0.5404). This therefore, meant that all variables considered for this study were convergent or similarly related and valid to be used. However, the use dimensions were found to have adequate convergent validity based on their high composite reliability (>0.70) [30]. See Table 4 below.

The next step in investigating construct validity was to determine the reliability of the construct items. A measure of internal consistency or composite reliability is a composite alpha value. This value was used to assess the reliability of the nine constructs. Construct reliability coefficients should all exceed the 0.70 lower limits (Hair et al. [28]; Rossiter [31]). However, Nunnally et al. [32] and Srinivasan (1985) suggest that values as low as 0.50 are acceptable for initial construct development. The composite reliability and Cronbach's alpha values for the studied constructs were computed by Smart PLS and ranged from 0.8196 to 1 and 0.6054 to 1.0, respectively as indicated in Table 4.

Table 4. Summary of PLS quality

	AVE	Composite reliability	R Square	Cronbach's alpha
Evaluation of staff performance	1	1	0	1
Change management	1	1	0	1
Flexibility of consultants	1	1	0	1
Effective communication	1	1	0	1
Effective IT unit	1	1	0	1
Project management	1	1	0	1
Top management support	0.6863	0.8658	0	0.7815
Training and education	0.7064	0.8265	0	0.6054
Technical support	1	1	0	1
USE	0.5404	0.8196	0.5038	0.7043

Table 5. Details of Informants Interviewed

Uni	People interviewed	FIS found
KYA	4 people were interviewed and they included: two Administrative Assistants, one Accounts Assistant and one Revenue Collection Assistant	Navision being used for recording of payments and e-Campus and academic records being used for fees collection. Integration of the 2 systems is being done. For final reports they use Excel.
MUBS	2 people were interviewed, both working as Assistant Directors of Finance	Internally developed system for especially recording fees collections
UCU	4 people were interviewed and they included: two Administrative Assistants, one Accounts Assistant and one Revenue Collection Assistant	Focus being used for all accounts transactions and then a new system SAP being implemented.
UMI	4 people were interviewed and they included: one Senior Accounts Assistants, one Accounts Assistant, One Payroll Officer and one Stores Assistant	Navision being used for all accounts functions

As per Table 4 it can clearly be seen that almost all the variables used in this research were reliable since it obtained the Composite Reliability and Cronbach's Alpha values more than 0.7. All values fall within the acceptable range to conclude good reliability. The data that was collected was analysed using PLS and the process involved summarizing the information collected so as to establish the relationships between the factors that influence implementation and the use of the FIS.

The last step in the construct validation process was to assess discriminant validity. Discriminate validity was assessed by examining the cross loadings of each item in the constructs and the square root of AVE calculated for each construct. All the items should have higher loading on their corresponding construct than the cross loadings on the other constructs in the model. The square root of AVE for all factors should be greater than all the correlations between that construct and other constructs.

In regard to data analysis and outputs it was descriptive statistics and then relationships between each of the nine factors and the use construct that were generated. And this paper presents results for only the relationships which were generated through structural equation modelling (SEM) with use of PLS.

3.2 Qualitative Validation Study Design

The qualitative validation study was carried out in four out of the seven universities that participated in the quantitative study. Data was gathered through focus group interviews based on results that were obtained from the quantitative study. Four sets of interviews were conducted in four universities, as presented in Table 5. The focus group interviews were done to explore and understand the meaning of quantitative study results that could not be explained statistically. The interviews were based on results from the quantitative study presented in Table 6.

Table 6. Path coefficients along with their bootstrap values, 'T' values

Factors	β – values	T statistics (|O/STERR|)	p values	Relationship
Top management support	0.6451	7.081	0.00001	Positive and significant
Effective communication	−0.0359	0.3448	0.730815	Negative and not significant
Evaluation of staff performance	−0.1462	1.5473	0.124279	Negative and not significant
Education and training	−0.1729	0.9534	0.342199	Negative and not significant
Technical support	0.1923	1.8743	0.063187	Positive and not significant
Project management	−0.1155	1.2964	0.197188	Negative and not significant
Change management program	−0.0063	0.0667	0.946925	Negative and not significant
Effective IT unit	−0.2254	2.4276	0.016601	Negative and significant
Flexible consultants	0.0115	0.1364	0.891721	Positive and not significant

4 Results

This section presents results from both the quantitative study and validation study and these are presented in Subsects. 4.1 and 4.2 respectively.

4.1 Quantitative Field Study Results

The model was assessed using three criteria: (1) path coefficients (β); (2) path significant (p-value); and (3) variance explain (R). Following Chin and Newsted [33], bootstrap re-sampling method was employed to test the statistical significance of each path coefficient. One hundred and twenty-eight (128) randomly selected sub-samples were performed to estimate the theoretical model and hypothesized relationships.

The criterion put forward by Rossiter [31] states that for the structural model all paths should result in a t-statistic value greater than 1.96 and latent variable R- Squares (R^2) greater than 50%. Significance was considered at 0.05. In Table 6 the column for β values represents the impact of the factor on use of the FIS. The range is from -1 to 1 whereby a negative figure means that the impact is negative whereas a positive figure that the impact is positive. And the columns for T statistics and P values each represent the levels of significance. For an item to be significant the value of the T statistic had to be greater than 1.96 or the P value had to be less than 0.005. The results that are shown in the column label "Relationship" indicate that only two factors were significant, that is top management support and effective IT unit. The rest of the factors were not significant.

4.2 Validation Study Results

Findings from the validation study are presented here below. The presentation is given per factors beginning with top management support.

Top Management Support
It was found that in all four universities that were visited, top management would support the implementation processes of the FISs by for example; participating in needs identifications, sourcing for consultants, coordinating the development of system updates with consultants, pushing the adoption of FISs across all the university departments, ensuring effectiveness of controls in the system such that no other system could be used. It was found though that Kyambogo University top management was not very keen at providing financial support towards the implementation task.

Effective Communication
It was found that in Kyambogo University communication on issues of implementation was not there at all during their FIS implementation such that people had to find their own ways around issues. But also in the other universities where communication was reported to have always been effective it was found that at times this would negatively affect usage of the FISs. This was the case especially in places where users were experiencing difficulties in using the FISs. In such places whenever users would receive instructions like for example to generate some reports they would instead use other software tools which would be simpler for them to use to do the work within the given time frames. This would therefore affect the usage of the actual FISs.

Staff Performance Evaluation
At Kyambogo University it was reported that they did not have a performance evaluation system for staff. At Makerere University Business School staff evaluations

would be conducted, and during the exercises people would get opportunity to speak out and discuss their challenges, and this would help boost the use rate of the system. At Uganda Christian University, they had two systems and supervisors would focus more on the users' abilities to perform duties given to them irrespective of the system being used. A person would therefore only use a system that he or she is most comfortable with. At Uganda Management Institute they had an appraisal system but they had a feeling that the FIS itself would evaluate a user basing on the extent at which he or she would be using it.

Education and Training
It was found out that at Kyambogo University users took too long to start using the FIS after doing training and that affected their abilities to use the systems. At Makerere University Business School training was done off station which turned out to be inadequate to users because with this method user were trained on examples as opposed to doing actual work. At Uganda Christian University it was found that the more users would be trained the more they would discover short comings in the system, and as a consequence the less they would want to rely on the system. At Makerere University Business School it was found that the system they were using at the time of the interview had been developed internally so people were being trained progressively as the system was being developed. The informants also said that new staff would be trained by old staff and all problems would be solved within the department through knowledge sharing. At Uganda Management Institute it was reported that training did boost the use rate of the system significantly. It was also reported that users would get refresher training and new staff members would always also be trained.

Technical Support
Two universities that is Uganda Management Institute and Uganda Christian University had consultants who would offer technical support and users would contact them only through the IT units. At both Kyambogo University and Makerere University Business School they had some people in their respective finance departments who had technical skills such that they would always help their colleagues whenever they would get problems. In addition, at Makerere University Business School they had at least one person with such skills in each department.

Project Management
It was found that by virtue of working under a project management environment implementation teams would try to work within the set timelines but many times this would compromise on the use rate of the system because when timelines are set many times users resort to using other tools that can deliver results much more quickly. And in some universities it would be difficult for people to work within set schedules and timelines because of problems like absenteeism from duty by some people during execution of various critical activities and therefore the use rate of the FISs would be affected.

Change Management
At Kyambogo University and Uganda Christian University they had a problem with the change management program in that in many cases people would equate a new system to loss of job. On the other hand, Uganda Management Institute information that was

picked was that if a university was strict on staff performance then with or without change management the use rate of the FIS would not be affected.

Effective IT Unit

In Makerere University Business School it was found that in order to achieve and ensure maximum effectiveness of the IT unit one of the IT staff was stationed right in the finance department. At Uganda Christian University people in the IT unit were not very conversant with the user functions of the system. This would frustrate the users and as a consequence they would keep trying to get other systems. At Kyambogo University it was found that staff in the IT unit had a conflict of interest that would affect their performance because the university was using two systems, one developed by the IT unit itself and another that had been outsourced. At Uganda Management Institute it was found that the IT unit was essential because the people in the unit had been trained by the consultants during implementation.

Flexibility of Consultants

It was found that Kyambogo University, Uganda Christian University and Uganda Management Institute that consultants who were always willing to work on needs of users in coordination with the IT units. And at Makerere University Business School the university had a contract with the consultants so they were never reluctant to work on any issues, the informants said.

5 Discussion

This section presents a discussion of the study results in relation to available literature and as discussions are made findings from the validation study are incorporated as well.

In regard to Top management support the result for impact on FIS use is positive. This was in line with the earlier hypothesis stated. This suggests that support, commitment, authority, and direction from top management for the system and for the various people affected by the system's implementation is necessary in ensuring overall use of the system. In context of the study, this result permits the suggestion that FIS use would continue to be enhanced not only at the implementation phase, but also at latter stages in the software's lifecycle as long as top management support and commitment is high during implementation. This is in congruence with Hansen and Mowen [34] who ascertained that FIS projects success or failure relies heavily on top management willingness and commitment. Furthermore, Motwani et al. [35] also in-line with the above scholars indicate that top management is very critical since it is the top managers who set the direction in which the organization runs as well as controlling funds utilization. This means that they would always have a decisive role on whether they support the system implementation or not. These are complemented by what Wee [36] found out that the role of top managers is fundamental since they have the duty to publicly and explicitly identify the project as a top priority.

In respect to effective communication the result from the quantitative study indicated this factor as not being significant. This result is contrary to earlier literature. Burt [37] for example, argues that effective communication is key and is the basis for realizing success in any IT project because it lies in the powers of communication or message that flows from the top to the implementers, to have the job well-done in time, efficiency and effectively. Mintzberg [38] shares the same opinion and says that that the primary onus of ensuring effective internal communication lies with the project's managers. The reason of this contradiction can be picked from the results of the validation study which showed that in for example Kyambogo University communication was minimal during the FIS implementation and each user would find his or her own way around the issues. Also in some universities where communication was said to have been very evident at times this turned out to have no impact or negative impact on the usage of the FISs. This was the case especially in places where users were experiencing difficulties in using the FISs. In such situations it was found that whenever users would be instructed to generate certain reports within some timelines they would in some instances resort to using other software tools which would be simpler for them to use and be able to do the work within the given timelines.

In respect to evaluation of staff performance the result from the quantitative indicated this factor as non-significant. This result however is contrary with what earlier studies. Barlow et al. [39] for example, ascertains that regular evaluation of staff performance is regarded widely as a necessary attribute for improving the usage of information systems, and part of an over-riding value set of efficiency. Congruently, Qureshi and Hassan [40] support the above view while arguing that regular evaluation of staff performance forms a baseline for setting the objectives and helps in giving a clear picture to employees and clearly explains, what is expected from them. On the other hand, during the validation study it was found that at Kyambogo University staff appraisals were not being conducted. At Uganda Christian University staff appraisals were being conducted but results would never be produced. At Makerere University Business School staff appraisals were optional, although according to the informants the exercise would give opportunity to people to speak out and discuss their challenges At Uganda Christian University, they had two systems and the supervisors would focus more on the individual's ability to perform duties given to them irrespective of the system they would be using. People would therefore end up using only a system they were most conversant with. At Uganda Management Institute it was found that appraisals were being conducted although the informants believed that it was the FIS itself that would evaluate a user basing on the extent or level at which that person would be using it.

With training and education, the result from the quantitative indicated this as a non-significant factor. This was found to be contrary to some of the previous literature. Hall [41] for example indicated that educating employees should be considered as top priority at the beginning of the project to ensure successful implementation of the new system. Kumar and van Hillegersberg [42], says that introduction and on board training in software facilitate easy socialization of new employees in an organisation and implementation of FIS, It prepares employees on how to use and implement FISs and it also establishes work relations. Aceituno [43] in a further illustration asserts that training of employees in financial information systems provides receivable management solutions to financial service institutions both in the government and private sector. On the other hand, picking from what was found during the validation study, in some universities users would take too long to start using the FISs after training and this would affect their abilities to use the systems. It was also found that in some universities the training was done while staff was off their desks which would turn out to be inadequate because with this method the users would be trained on examples as opposed to being shown how to use the system to do actual work. Also in some universities it was found that the more the users would be trained the more they would discover short comings in the system, and therefore the less they would want to rely on the system.

With respect to technical support the result from the quantitative study indicated this as a non-significant factor. However, what was gathered during the validation study was that all universities had arrangements for technical support and in one university namely, Kyambogo University it was found that even some members of staff would offer support to their fellow colleagues. This affirms that the systems' benefits tend to be highly realized when quality vendors/consultants are engaged as argued by Ridings et al. [44] and Gefen [45]. This information can be interpreted to mean that the engagement of quality external sources of expertise (i.e., vendors/consultants) for FIS acquisitions can compensate for an organization's inability to fully understand how the system supports its business vision (i.e., organizational goals and mission) and where top managers show low support for the software. Two possible explanations can be put forward in support of the foregoing proposition: (1) Attewell [46] who says that the diffusion (and subsequent success) of complex IT systems hinges upon the elimination of knowledge barriers between the adopting organization and the providers of the software. It is logical to expect that organizational members would want to attach more importance to the external sources of expertise that are capable of providing them with the knowledge and support needed for getting most out of the acquired systems, (2) Vendors and consultants of specialized, complex systems such as FIS are usually versed about how their products can be used to support business objectives across the vast number of industries and may provide such information to organizational members, including top managers who may in turn use it for organizational planning purposes [47].

Regarding project management, the result from the quantitative study indicated this as non-significant factor. This was found to be contrary to some earlier literature. Mullins [48] for example, argues that project management is a critical component in determining the success of FIS projects. He ascertained that there must be enough consideration of project plans, controls, monitoring and evaluation. These must be adhered to, if success of such projects is to be realized. Howard [49] adds that projects executed in the software industry are characterized by high uncertainty, need to use state-of-the-art system, rapid changes, a high need for interpersonal skills; high importance of organizational structure, large number of request changes during the project life cycle, high use of virtual teams, high importance of group learning and high influence of matrix organizational structure if they are to succeed. Bondarouk [50] concludes by confirming that project stakeholders must be consulted in the project management process to ensure that the quality of a project is enhanced. The contradiction between this discussion and the fact that project management was found not to be significant can be explained by picking on what was found during the validation study. For example, at Uganda Management Institute, it was mentioned that in some cases it was difficult to administer the project management function because some activities that would strictly need to be done when everybody was around would fail to take off because it would not be easy to get all people around at the same time to work on a given task.

In regard to change management program the result from the quantitative study indicated this as non-significant factor. This result resonates very well with what was found during the validation study. The informants at Kyambogo University for instance said that they never had a clear change management program. They said that the problem they had with a change management program was that in many cases people would equate the new system with loss of jobs. At Uganda Management Institute the informants said that it was an administrative policy that with or without a change management program people had to use the FIS otherwise they would risk losing their jobs. On the other hand Fui-Hoon Nahet et al. [14] say that change management is an important starting point at the project phase and should continue throughout the entire life cycle and further argues that a culture with shared values and common aims is conducive to success and organizations should have a strong corporate identity that is open to change. In this context, this argument brings out the fact that organizations should possess cultural values that are not static and that do not promote resistance to change. Oliver et al. [51] further argues that users must be trained, and concerns must be addressed through regular communication, working with change agents, leveraging corporate culture and identifying job aids for different users if the implementation of FIS is to be successful. Wallace et al. [52] also asserts that the development of a new system must be carefully managed and orchestrated, and the way a project is executed is likely to be the most important factor influencing its outcome.

Regarding effective IT unit, the result from the quantitative study indicated that this factor had a negative impact on usage. Contrary to this Robbins and Coulter [53] indicate IT units act as leaders of implementing information system and this kind of leadership becomes instrumental and accountability to change management.

And on the other hand Kwena [54] agitates that some organizations in developing world do have IT units but they are not effective and this has had a negative effect on usage of FIS. And also picking on what was found during the validation study there are two reasons that can be used to explain why the effective IT unit was found to have a negative impact. The first reason was based on the issue of some universities having more than one finance management applications and more so when the IT units have preferences amongst those applications. In this kind of situation, the IT unit could decide to favour and promote some particular applications at the detriment of others. This would become more pronounced when some of the applications are developed by staff in the IT unit as the issue of conflict of interest would very strongly set in. The second reason comes from the fact that many users have a perception that IT units by themselves can solve all IT problems including user problems which is not necessarily true because user problems usually are issues for the software providers. So when a user with such a perception contacts the IT unit for help on some user problem issue and the unit fails to handle, it would not go well in the user's mind.

In regard to flexible consultants the result from the quantitative study indicated this to impact positively on usage but not significant. There are two arguments picked from the validation study that can be used to explain why the impact would be positive. Firstly, the experience that many actors have in implementing and using FIS systems in the Ugandan universities is still relatively low because most of these technologies are new to many people and at the same time most of the universities are new as well. Therefore, it is not easy for many of the decision makers and IT managers in these institutions to develop complete and comprehensive FIS requirements specifications at a single time. Many times it is during the time of using the systems that people discover deviations and missing gaps that would have to be sorted out before the systems become usable. Also because of limited experience most people are unable to under-stand and fully comprehend the capabilities of the new systems before they themselves start using them. This therefore means that the need to adjust the systems from time to time while being used is inevitable. This is what exactly necessitates the need to have consultants who are easy to work with, who are flexible and who are committed to their work otherwise the implementation and use of the systems could fail. Secondly, considering how the business of IT items is conducted in many developing countries including Uganda where almost all items have to come from outside the country and with a lot of bureaucratic formalities involved, many times the procurement processes of items like FISs take too long to be concluded and in many cases this occurs when already some of the supporting technologies like the hardware and operating systems have changed. This would in many cases require for adjustments to be made on the items before they could be installed. With such challenges if the consultants are not flexible enough and corporative the entire project could fail. These observations are in congruence with Hussein et al. [55] who argue that the most commonly-cited benefit being derived from flexibility in consultation mechanisms has been that of more effective organizational change management and implementation of financial infor-mation systems. This is based on the fact that organizations need to hold employee workshops which can identify problems and develop solutions focused on providing the workforce with a much fuller awareness of the implementation of FIS by supplying information on what is required [56].

6   Conclusions

In this section we present conclusions on the research question: How factors involved in implementation of a FIS later on influences the usage of the system? from the study on the nine factors perceived as important during implementation of FIS in developing countries.

In the virtue to explain the circumstances under which top management support impact the usage of FISs, it is clear that the role of top management lies more in initiating the idea and supporting the implementation of FIS in the primary stages, sourcing for consultants, coordinating the development of system updates with the consultants, pushing for adoption of the FISs across all departments, ensuring the effectiveness of controls in the system such that for example no other system could be used.

Regarding effective communication, it can be deduced that where users were not very conversant with the system or when the system itself was not easy to use, effective communication would affect the usage rate of the FISs because users would instead look for simpler ways of producing what was being demanded from them, meaning that they to some extent actually select to use other systems.

In relation to the factor staff evaluation two scenarios can be deduced from the findings, one was that through the process of staff evaluation, users would get opportunity to discuss and get solutions about issues regarding their system use. Secondly for universities that had more than one system it was found that performance evaluation would be based on the system that a user would be most conversant with. This would mean that for purpose of aiming to get high scores the users would end up concentrating on a single particular system and ignoring others which could also include the main FIS.

When it comes to training and education it can be concluded that in some universities there were prolonged delays between the times when people would be trained and the times when they would start using the systems. This would negatively affect the use rate of the systems because people would forget what they would have been trained on. Secondly training that would be done when people are not doing actual work would not benefit much because at the end of training people would get difficulties in relating what they actually do with the functionalities in the system. Thirdly if the system was not thoroughly tested before acceptance some faults could surface while people would be using the system and when this would persist, the use rate would drop. Therefore, it is worthwhile to understand that until education and training is practiced in an effective real-life style, there would not be impact on usage.

From the study it can be concluded that regarding technical support all universities had arrangements for technical support and while some universities had consultants others had staff amongst themselves that would handle the technical issues in addition to doing their own work. From this it can be claimed that it is actually unclear, if there exist or not exist technical support which ordinarily would be expected to be given by hired consultants, if there is any effect on usage.

Regarding the factor project management, it can be deduced that in some universities project management was not adequately done. In universities where they attempted to do it, it would be difficult for people to work within the set schedules and timelines because of problems like frequent absenteeism from duty by some users during the execution of the various critical activities. This would happen especially in places where supervisors would have laxities. This could probably explain why the relationship is shown as having a negative impact, but it is important to say that it was not significant.

From the change management factor, it can be concluded that the idea of change management itself would not have an impact on usage because some people would equate a new system with job loss. And also it was found that when the university administration would get strict on people's performance then with or without change management the use rate of the FIS would not be affected.

Regarding effective IT unit, it can be concluded that the impact on FIS usage would get affected when staff in the unit are not conversant with the user functionalities in the system. The usage rate would also be affected when in addition to the FIS the institution had other parallel systems and more so if some of the parallel systems were developed by staff in the IT unit. From this it can be said that if the IT unit is more effective they might influence the user to use other systems which explains that there could be a negative impact on usage of a specific system.

Finally, from the factor flexible consultants it can be concluded that it is very important for universities in Uganda to take seriously into consideration the issue of flexibility when soliciting for suppliers. This is mainly because of the fact that IT experience by many of the actors in the country especially in systems implementations is still relatively low. Secondly being dependent on imported technologies and when the procurement processes are not efficient because of many bureaucracies usually involved many imported items arrive for installation when already some of the supporting technologies like operating systems have changed. These kind of challenges would require a lot of flexibility from consultants if these challenges should have a chance to be resolved quickly.

References

1. Dener, C., Watkins, J., Dorotinsky, W.L.: Financial Management Information Systems: 25 Years of World Bank Experience on What Works and What Doesn't. World Bank Publications, Washington DC (2011)
2. Khemani, P., Diamond, M.J.: Introducing Financial Management Information Systems in Developing Countries (EPub). International Monetary Fund, Washington DC (2005)
3. Mulira, N.K.: Implementing Inter-Organisational Service Systems: An Approach for Emerging Networks in Volatile Contexts. TU Delft, Delft University of Technology, Delft (2007)
4. Pan, G., Hackney, R., Pan, S.L.: Information Systems implementation failure: insights from prism. Int. J. Inf. Manage. 28(4), 259–269 (2008)
5. Kiwana, D., Johansson, B., Carlsson, S.: Usage of finance information systems in developing countries: identifying factors during implementation that impact use. In: Khalil, I., Neuhold, E., Tjoa, A.M., Da Xu, L., You, I. (eds.) CONFENIS/ICT-EurAsia -2015. LNCS, vol. 9357, pp. 333–342. Springer, Cham (2015). doi:10.1007/978-3-319-24315-3_34
6. Hansen, D., Mowen, M., Guan, L.: Cost Management: Accounting and Control. Cengage Learning, Boston (2007)
7. vom Brocke, J.: Design principles for reference modeling: reusing information models by means of aggregation, specialisation, instantiation, and analogy. In: Reference Modeling for Business Systems Analysis, pp. 47–75 (2007)
8. Gerdin, J.: Management accounting system design in manufacturing departments: an empirical investigation using a multiple contingencies approach. Acc. Organ. Soc. 30(2), 99–126 (2005)
9. Sajady, H., Dastgir, M., Nejad, H.H.: Evaluation of the effectiveness of accounting information systems. Int. J. Inf. Sci. Manage. (IJISM) 6(2), 49–59 (2012)
10. James, H.A.: Accounting Information System. Seven Edition, Singapore (2011)
11. Dhillon, G.: Principles of Information Systems Security: Text and Cases. Wiley, New York (2007)
12. Easttom II, W.C.: Computer Security Fundamentals. Pearson Education, Upper Saddle River (2011)
13. Rosario, J.: On the leading edge: critical success factors in ERP implementation projects. Bus. World 17(May), 15–29 (2000)
14. Fui-Hoon Nah, F., Lee-Shang Lau, J., Kuang, J.: Critical factors for successful implementation of enterprise systems. Bus. Process Manage. J. 7(3), 285–296 (2001)

15. Judge, T.A., et al.: Self-efficacy and work-related performance: the integral role of individual differences. J. Appl. Psychol. **92**(1), 107 (2007)
16. McShane, S., Von Glinow, M.: Perception and learning in organizations. Organ. Behav. **4**, 68–100 (2008)
17. Poston, R., Grabski, S.: Financial impacts of enterprise resource planning implementations. Int. Journal Acc. Inf. Syst. **2**(4), 271–294 (2001)
18. Saunders, M.L., Lewis, P., Thornhill, A.: Research Methods for Business Students, vol. 4. Prentice Hall, Upper Saddle River (2009)
19. Eisenhardt, K.M., Graebner, M.E.: Theory building from cases: opportunities and challenges. Acad. Manage. J. **50**(1), 25–32 (2007)
20. Greene, J.C.: Is mixed methods social inquiry a distinctive methodology? J. Mixed Meth. Res. **2**(1), 7–22 (2008)
21. DeLone, W.H., McLean, E.R.: The DeLone and McLean model of information systems success: a ten-year update. J. Manage. Inf. syst. **19**, 9–30 (2003)
22. Ragu-Nathan, B.S., et al.: A path analytic study of the effect of top management support for information systems performance. Omega **32**(6), 459–471 (2004)
23. Amoako-Gyampah, K., Salam, A.F.: An extension of the technology acceptance model in an ERP implementation environment. Inf. Manage. **41**(6), 731–745 (2004)
24. Amoroso, D.L., Cheney, P.H.: Testing a causal model of end-user application effectiveness. J. Manage. Inf. Syst. **8**, 63–89 (1991)
25. Antony, J., et al.: Critical success factors of TQM implementation in Hong Kong industries. Int. J. Qual. Reliab. Manage. **19**(5), 551–566 (2002)
26. Petter, S., DeLone, W., McLean, E.: Measuring information systems success: models, dimensions, measures, and interrelationships. Eur. J. Inf. Syst. **17**(3), 236–263 (2008)
27. Amin, M.E.: Social Science Research: Conception, Methodology and Analysis. Makerere University, Kampala (2005)
28. Hair, J.F., et al.: Multivariate Data Analysis, vol. 6. Pearson Prentice Hall, Upper Saddle River (2006)
29. Fornell, C., Larcker, D.F.: Evaluating structural equation models with unobservable variables and measurement error. J. Mark. Res. **18**, 39–50 (1981)
30. Anderson, J.C., Gerbing, D.W.: Structural equation modeling in practice: a review and recommended two-step approach. Psychol. Bull. **103**(3), 411 (1988)
31. Rossiter, J.R.: The C-OAR-SE procedure for scale development in marketing. Int. J. Res. Mark. **19**(4), 305–335 (2002)
32. Nunnally, J.C., Bernstein, I.H., Berge, J.M.F.T.: Psychometric Theory, vol. 226. McGraw-Hill, New York (1967)
33. Chin, W.W., Newsted, P.R.: Structural equation modeling analysis with small samples using partial least squares (1999)
34. Hansen, D.R., Mowen, M.M.: Managerial Accounting, 8th edn. Thomson South Western, USA (2007)
35. Motwani, J., Subramanian, R., Gopalakrishna, P.: Critical factors for successful ERP implementation: exploratory findings from four case studies. Comput. Ind. **56**(6), 529–544 (2005)
36. Wee, S.: Juggling toward ERP success: keep key success factors high. ERP News, February 2000
37. Burt, R.S.: The network structure of social capital. Res. Organ. Beh. **22**, 345–423 (2000)
38. Mintzberg, H.: Mintzberg über Management: Führung und Organisation Mythos und Realität. Springer, Heidelberg (2013)
39. Barlow, D.H.N., et al.: Single Case Experimental Designs: Strategies for Studying Behavior for Change. Prentice Hall, Upper Saddle River (2009)

40. Qureshi, A., Hassan, M.: Impact of performance management on the organisational performance: an analytical investigation of the business model of McDonalds. Int. J. Acad. Res. Econ. Manage. Sci. 2(5), 54–76 (2013)
41. Hall, J.: Accounting Information Systems. Cengage Learning, Boston (2012)
42. Kumar, K., van Hillegersberg, J.: Enterprise resource planning: introduction. Commun. ACM 43(4), 22–26 (2000)
43. Aceituno, V.: On information security paradigms. ISSA J. 24, 225–229 (2005)
44. Ridings, C.M., Gefen, D., Arinze, B.: Some antecedents and effects of trust in virtual communities. J. Strateg. Inf. Syst. 11(3), 271–295 (2002)
45. Gefen, D.: TAM or just plain habit. Adv. Top. End User Comput. 3(1) 2004
46. Attewell, P.: Technology diffusion and organizational learning: the case of business computing. Organ. Sci. 3(1), 1–19 (1992)
47. Davenport, T.H.: Putting the enterprise into the enterprise system. Harvard Bus. Rev. 76, 121–131 (1998)
48. Mullins, R.: Anaphylaxis: risk factors for recurrence. Clin. Exp. Allergy 33(8), 1033–1040 (2003)
49. Howard, Y.: Routine Technology, Social Structure, and Organization Goals. Adm. Sci. Q. 14(1), 366–376 (2001)
50. Bondarouk, T.V.: Action-oriented group learning in the implementation of information technologies: results from three case studies. Eur. J. Inf. Syst. 15(1), 42–53 (2006)
51. Oliver, N.M., Rosario, B., Pentland, A.P.: A Bayesian computer vision system for modeling human interactions. IEEE Trans. Pattern Anal. Mach. Intell. 22(8), 831–843 (2000)
52. Wallace, L., Keil, M., Rai, A.: How software project risk affects project performance: an investigation of the dimensions of risk and an exploratory model*. Decis. Sci. 35(2), 289–321 (2004)
53. Robbins, S.P. Coulter, M.: Pearson Education Inc., publishing as Prentice Hall (2012)
54. Kwena, F.I.: Factors influencing the use of integrated financial management and information systems in public sector. In: A case of selected government ministries in Kenya (2013)
55. Hussein, R., et al.: The impact of organizational factors on information Systems success: an empirical investigation in The Malaysian electronicgovernment agencies (2005). kmap2005. vuw.ac.nz/papers/The%20Impact%20of%20Org.Factors%20on.pdf
56. Sedera, D., Gable, G., Chan, T.: Knowledge management for ERP success. In: PACIS 2003 Proceedings, p. 97 (2003)

Information Systems Development

Ontology and DSL Co-evolution Using Graph Transformations Methods

Boris Ulitin[✉] and Eduard Babkin

National Research University Higher School of Economics,
Nizhny Novgorod, Russia
{bulitin, eababkin}@hse.ru

Abstract. The article is related to the problem of implementing consistent changes in the model of some subject area and in the syntax of domain specific language (DSL), dealing with problems in that domain. In our research, we explore an opportunity to provide the method of co-evolution of the ontology, used as a model of the subject area, and DSL. This method combines graph representation of the ontology and DSL with the set of rules, formulated in terms of an automated graph-transformation language. Applicability of the proposed approach is demonstrated using a real-life example of co-evolution of the ontology and DSL in the railway transportation domain.

Keywords: Domain-specific language · Ontology · Evolution · Graph transformation · Railway transportation

1 Introduction

Currently, domain-specific languages (DSL) become more and more widespread. Such popularity can be explained by the fact, that DSL is a fairly simple and convenient way of organizing work in a certain subject area. DSLs contain only the required set of terms of the domain, representing some kind of its reflection, because every DSL uses as its basis some model of the current subject area [1]. As a result, the effectiveness of DSL actually depends on the degree of correspondence between the subject area and its model: a greater level of consistency results in greater flexibility of the language.

The ontological approach can provide such a degree of accuracy in the description of the subject area, because an ontology reflects a set of concepts of the target domain and the connections between them [2]. Consequently, application of the ontology as a model of DSL guarantees that DSL is identical to the corresponding domain, thereby allows interacting with it more effectively.

Any domain demonstrates a tendency to changes over time (evolution, in other words). In accordance with the evolution of the subject area, the evolution of its ontological representation also occurs [3, 4]. However, DSL frequently remains unchanged, since it is built on a snapshot of the domain (and the ontology) and reflects only the fixed state, without reacting to subsequent changes. This specificity in the process of DSL design results in the emerging the problem of maintaining co-evolution of DSL and its domain and, accordingly, co-evolution of DSL and the ontology. At worst, uncoordinated changes can lead to the situation, when DSL, being fixed in its

© Springer International Publishing AG 2017
B. Johansson et al. (Eds.): BIR 2017, LNBIP 295, pp. 233–247, 2017.
DOI: 10.1007/978-3-319-64930-6_17

original state, loses its relevance for the significantly changed domain. As a result, the language becomes inapplicable for solving practically important tasks in the subject area. In [15] Challenger, et al. describe a case of DSL, which could not create entities, unspecified in the original ontology model.

We also need to note that the sceneries of working with DSL may vary due to considerable differences in experience of information needs of different DSL users. As a result, in parallel to the development of the skills and knowledge of the user, the set of DSL terms, that he/she operates with, can also change. It means, that every user defines his own model of DSL and, because every DSL is connected with the domain, creates own domain representation, which may differ from the one originally used in the DSL. In these circumstances, we also face the evolution of the DSL and the subject area, which leads to the inconsistencies between the domain and the DSL model, and have to resolve them through the use of interconnected transformations.

In order to avoid such problems, automated methods of conflict detection that may arise in the course of the co-evolution of the domain ontology and DSL are needed. An important addition to such methods can be the ability to resolve emerging contradictions. We believe that a new approach is needed which combines the formal ontology mechanism with modern mathematical models of graph transformation [3, 5].

That ontology-based approach seems to be more effective in comparison with similar ones, for example, described by Cleenewerck or by Challenger. In [14] Cleenewerck tries to use the mechanism of graph transformation without prior establishing a correspondence between the ontology and DSL. It leads to the need to define a whole complex of disparate transformation rules for each component of the language. Furthermore, this system of transformations has to be changed every time, when DSL modifications are required. In contrast to Cleenewerck, Challenger in [15] proposes to abandon the dynamic matching of the subject area and DSL, but to redefine the DSL model whenever the ontology is changed. This approach is also not optimal, since, in fact, it offers not to adapt the existing DSL to changes in the domain, and each time to create a new language.

In this article, we concentrate on the object level co-evolution and only to a certain extent on co-evolution in a functional sense, primarily because of the complexity of developing a universal description for the set of operations in any domain.

The article describes our proposed approach as follows. In Sect. 2 we give some facts from the theory of design of ontologies and domain-specific languages and some principles of processes of model evolution. Section 3 describes a universal graph-model for DSL and also contains the analysis of using graph-transformation techniques in presence of different types of evolution. Section 4 demonstrates advantages of our approach in the case of the railway transportation domain instead of applying graph transformations without establishing a correspondence between the ontology and DSL. We conclude the article with analysis of the results and specification of the future researches.

2   Background

2.1   Definition and Classification of Ontologies

Ontology is a representational artifact, comprising a taxonomy as proper part, whose representations are intended to designate some combination of universals, defined classes, and certain relations between them [2]. In accordance with formalization framework [6] the ontology can be naturally perceived as a graph (O, R), with a set of functions of constraints F.

On the other hand, the ontology is some kind of representation, created by the designer [7] which has a certain goal. As a result, in [2, 6] the following ontology kinds are detected: *top-level ontologies*, *domain (task) ontologies*, and *application ontologies*, which describe concepts that depend both on a particular domain and a task, and often combine specializations of both the corresponding domain and task ontologies.

In the current research, we pay attention only to the Application ontologies, especially in the domain of railway processes – the railway resource allocation procedure. But as the Domain ontology contains only the necessary concepts of a subject area, applied ontology operates with a subset of these concepts necessary to achieve a certain goal. That allows us to consider the Application ontology as the reduced Domain ontology.

2.2   Definition and Structure of DSL

A domain-specific language (DSL) is a computer language specialized to a particular application domain. This is in contrast to a general-purpose language, which is broadly applicable across domains, and lacks specialized features for a particular domain [1]. In [8] two parts of the DSL are identified: (1) a syntactic part, which defines the constructions of DSL; and (2) a semantic part, which manifests itself in the semantic model. The first part allows defining the context for working with the second one, which defines meaning of DSL commands in terms of the target domain.

In addition, a syntactic part of DSL can be separated into two levels: the level of objects and the level of functions. The object-level is equivalent to the set of objects of the ontological model of the target domain. The functional level contains operations, which allow to specify the context for the objects. The combination of these two levels determines the meta-model of DSL, which identifies the entities, used in DSL, and relations between them.

This two-level division of the DSL terms into objects and commands allows not only to achieve the maximum correspondence between the ontological model of the target domain and the DSL model, but also to construct the most convenient way of organizing conversions between them. In order to provide such transformations, it is sufficient to adjust the system of matching rules between the components of the ontological model of the target domain and the components of the DSL model. One of the solutions to this problem can be the mechanism of graph transformations between the graph representation of the ontology and the DSL model. In such mechanism, formal specification of transformations is defined by one of specialized graph-transformation languages such as

ATL Transformation Language [9], GReAT (Graph REwriting And Transformation) [10, 11], AGG (Attributed Graph Grammar) (http://www.user.tu-berlin.de/o.runge/agg/), etc.

In our research, we propose to use ATL, because this language allows to describe the transformation rules from any original model into any target model, conducting a transformation at the level of meta-models. ATL has a simple scheme for defining the transformation rules with only 4 components: the name of the rule, the type of the element of the original model, the type of the equivalent element of the target model and the block for definition of the additional actions with transforming and corresponding components of the original and the target model (Fig. 1).

```
rule     rule_name {
from     type_of_the_element_of_original_model (conditions_expression)
to       action or type_of_ the_element_of_target_model
do {     additional_actions    }
}
```

Fig. 1. The scheme for definition the transformation rules in ATL

2.3 Definition and Classification of Model Evolution

As already mentioned above, the ontology is some kind of a model of the certain area and DSL, which is created for working with some specific domain, contains inside some model of this domain. However, the subject area can evolve. In this connection, the models created within the given domain should be changed accordingly. These assumptions lead to the idea, that instead of the concept of co-evolution of ontologies and DSL, we can consider a single concept of the model evolution.

From the formal point of view, the structure of every model is a combination (E, R) of some entities (each entity is a set of its attributes $e_i = \{attr_{i_1}, attr_{i_2}, \ldots, attr_{i_M}\}, M \in \mathbb{N}, i = 1, N)$ in the certain domain and relations between them correspondingly. In these terms, evolution of the model is a process of changes in structure of this model. However, structure means not only entities, used in some specific model, but and relations between them. As follows, model evolution can be separated into two classes [4]: vertical evolution and horizontal evolution.

Vertical evolution means the change in level of conceptualization (perspective) of the model. In this case of evolution new entities are added into the model (with(out) changes in the set of relations). It means, that vertical evolution can be formalized by the following manner: (E^1, R^1) is a result of vertical evolution of the model (E, R) if $|E| \neq |E^1|$ and $|R| \neq |R^1|$. In terms of ontologies it means, that new objects (universals and/or classes) can be added or some previously created objects can be deleted, with corresponding changes in the set of relations. In terms of DSLs it means, that the object level will be changed: some objects will be introduced, some will be removed from the language – alongside with the corresponding changes on the functional level.

Horizontal evolution means preserving the level of conceptualization, but changing the sets of attributes for some entities, or changing the set of relations. It means, that vertical evolution can be formalized as follows: (E^1, R^1) is a result of horizontal evolution of the model (E, R) if $|E| = |E^1|$ and $\exists e_i \in E, e_i^1 \in E^1 : Attr_i \cap Attr_i^1 = Attr_i \bigwedge |Attr_i| \neq |Attr_i^1|$ and $\exists r_i \in R, r_j \in R^1 : r_i \notin R^1 \vee r_j \notin R$. In terms of ontologies it means, that the set of objects (universals and classes) will be the same, but some of them can be specified by adding new (or deleting old) attributes. In addition, the set of relations can be changed. In terms of DSL it means, that the object level will be changed only in terms of objects attributes with corresponding changes on the functional level (so-called constructors of objects) or in terms of connections between them (in this case changes on the functional level depend on the nature of changed connections).

In these circumstances, the question is how to synchronize changes in the onto-logical model of the domain and in the DSL model. To answer this the graph-model of DSL have to be introduced.

3   Problem of Co-evolution of the Ontology and DSL

3.1   The Graph-Based Model of DSL

In order to organize the transformation rules between the graph representation of the ontology and the DSL meta-model, we need to specify rules in terms of the graph transformation formalism. According to principles described in [12, 13], we will use the following concepts:

- A **set of entities** of the meta-model $Set = \{set_i\}, i \in \mathbb{N}, i < \infty$, where every entity $set_i = \{SName_i, SICount_i, Attr_i, Opp_i, SRest_i\}$ is characterized by its name ($SName_i$, which is unique within the current model), available amount of exemplars of this entity   ($SICount_i \in \mathbb{N}, SICount_i \geq 0$),   a   set   of   attributes ($Attr_i = \{attr_{j_i}\}, j_i \in \mathbb{N}, j_i < \infty$), a set of operation on exemplars of this entity ($Opp_i = \{opp_{j_i}\}, j_i \in \mathbb{N}, j_i < \infty$)   and   a   set   of   restrictions ($SRest_i = \{srest_{j_i}\}, j_i \in \mathbb{N}, j_i < \infty$).
- A **set of relations** between the entities $Rel = \{rel_i\}, i \in \mathbb{N}, i < \infty$, where every relation $rel_i = \{RName_i, RType_i, RMult_i, RRest_i\}$ is identified by its name ($RName_i$, which is unique within the current model), type ($RType_i \in \mathbb{N}, RType_i \geq 0$), defining the nature of the relation, the multiplicity ($RMult_i \in \mathbb{N}, RMult_i \geq 0$), which defines, how many exemplars of entities, participating in current relation, can be used, and a set of restrictions ($RRest_i = \{rrest_{j_i}\}, j_i \in \mathbb{N}, j_i < \infty$).

In this case, the graph of the meta-model can be characterized as an oriented pseudo-metagraph GMM = (V, E), for which the following constraint holds:

$$V = Set \bigcup_{i=1}^{|Set|} Attr_i \bigcup_{i=1}^{|Set|} Opp_i \bigcup_{i=1}^{|Set|} SRest_i \bigcup Rel \bigcup_{i=1}^{|Set|} RRest_i$$

$$E = ESA \bigcup ESO \bigcup ESR \bigcup ERR \bigcup ESRR$$

where

- $ESA = \{esa_i\}, \overline{\imath = 1, |Set|}$ – a set of arcs connecting each entity with a set of its attributes;
- $ESO = \{eso_i\}, \overline{\imath = 1, |Set|}$ – a set of arcs connecting each entity with a set of operations on it;
- $ESR = \{esr_i\}, \overline{\imath = 1, |Set|}$ – a set of arcs connecting each entity with a set of restrictions imposed on it;
- $ERR = \{err_i\}, \overline{\imath = 1, |Rel|}$ – a set of arcs connecting each relation with a set of restrictions imposed on it;
- $ESRR = \{esrr_i\}, i \in \mathbb{N}, i < \infty$ – a set of arcs connecting between the entity and relations, in which it is involved.

Simplifying this model, the set of attributes of entities can be considered within a set of entities. Moreover, we can say that the sets of restrictions, both for entities and relations, also can be combined in one set. Accordingly we propose to consider the structure of the DSL model as $(Obj, Rel, Rest, Opp)$, where the first two $Obj = Set \bigcup_{i=1}^{|Set|} Attr_i$, and Rel are responsible for the object-level of DSL, and other $Rest = \bigcup_{i=1}^{|Set|} SRest_i \bigcup_{i=1}^{|Set|} RRest_i$, Opp represent the functional structure of DSL. Interpreting the set Obj as the set of objects in some domain, Rel as a set of relations between them and $Rest, Opp$ as a set of operations on entities and restrictions to them, we argue that the structure of the ontological model of some domain and the structure of DSL can be related by some correspondence. That means, that there is a way for organizing automated co-evolution of them.

3.2   Vertical Evolution of Domain

In order to identify this type of evolution we have to create a set of rules, which transform new entities of the ontology into entities of the DSL model. The first assumption is that the DSL meta-model has the following structure scheme (Table 1).

The second assumption is that an initial correspondence exists between the ontology and the DSL model. It means, when DSL was created, the rules of correspondence between the ontology elements and the elements of the DSL model were determined.

Table 1. Description of DSL scheme components

Element	Meaning
SchemeName	Defines the name of the current DSL model
Class	Defines the class/type of objects (with some attributes inside)
Function	Defines the function (with a set of classes, instances of which are used in the function)
Constructor	Defines the constructor for creation of the current object with the list of attributes and its values

Considering these, we identify two classes of ATL rules for vertical transformation between elements of the OWL ontology representation and the DSL model (Fig. 2).

```
rule    OWLClass2DSLClass {
from    a: OWL!OWLClass (not exists (select b|
                                    b.isTypeOf (DSL!DSLClass)
                                    and a.name = b.name))
to      b: DSL!DSLClass,
        c:DSL!Constructor
}
rule    DropDeletedOWLClassInDSLClass {
from    b: DSL! DSL Class (not exists (select a|
                                    a.isTypeOf (OWL!OWLClass)
                                    and a.name = b.name))
to      drop
do    { drop c: DSL!Constructor (c.name = b.name) }
}
```

Fig. 2. ATL rules for synchronizing added and deleted elements between the ontology and DSL

According to the these ATL rules, OWLClass have to be replaced with specific OWL class, and DSLClass – with a corresponding DSL class. The first rule provides the reflection of all new elements in the ontology, which are absent in the DSL model, and creates corresponding constructor-procedures. The second one drops all elements in the DSL model, removed from the ontology.

Of course, there are situations, when these two rules are not enough. For example, if new entity in the ontology is associated with one of the previously created. In this case, additional rule has to be identified to create all needed relations between the DSL model entities (Fig. 3).

```
rule    OWLClassWithParents2DSLClassWithParents {
from    a: OWL!OWLClass (a.parent->exists())
to      b: DSL!DSLClass (b.name = a.name)
do    { b.parent.name = a.parent.name }
}
```

Fig. 3. ATL rules for reflecting connected elements from the ontology into DSL

Three designed ATL rules (Figs. 2, 3) are sufficient to organize basic vertical co-evolution of the ontology and the DSL model, because they cover all possible changes, which are peculiar to this kind of transformation.

3.3 Horizontal Evolution of the Domain

Following the assumptions established in the previous section and taking into account the fact that horizontal transformation includes changes in terms of entity's attributes and/or relations, the following variants to organize the horizontal co-evolution of the ontology and the DSL model are possible: (1) changes occurred in the attributes of entities or (2) in the relations between entities.

The first situation (1) means, that some attributes of entities in the ontology were deleted, or new ones were added. In terms of formal rules in ATL language, these cases can be identified by the next rules (Fig. 4).

```
rule    OWLClassAttributes2DSLClassAttributes {
from    a: OWL!OWLClass!OWLObjectProperty (
                not exists (select b|
                            b.isTypeOf (DSL!DSLClass!DSLObjectProperty)
                            and a.name = b.name))
to      b: DSL!DSLClass!DSLObjectProperty (b.owner.name = a.owner.name),
        c: DSL!Constructor!DSLObjectProperty (b.owner.name =
c.owner.name)
}
rule    DropDeletedOWLClassAttributesInDSLClassAttributes {
from    b: DSL!DSLClass!DSLObjectProperty (
                not exists (select a|
                            a.isTypeOf (OWL!OWLClass!OWLObjectProperty)
                            and a.name = b.name))
to      drop
do    { drop c: DSL!Constructor!DSLObjectProperty (c.name = b.name) }
}
```

Fig. 4. ATL rules for synchronizing changes in attributes of elements in the ontology and DSL

The first rule transforms new attributes from entities in the ontology into corresponding entities attributes in the DSL model and adds these attributes as arguments into constructors of corresponding entities. The second one drops attributes, deleted in the ontology, from the corresponding entities and constructors in the DSL model.

The second situation (2) means, that a set of relations in the ontology was changed. To support it the next rules can be used (Fig. 5).

```
rule    OWLClassWithParents2DSLClassWithParents {
from    a: OWL!OWLClass (a.parent->exists())
to      b: DSL!DSLClass (b.name = a.name),
do    { b.parent.name = a.parent.name }
}
rule    DropDeletedOWLClassParentsInDSLClasses {
from    b: DSL!DSLClass (
                not exists (select a|
                a.isTypeOf (OWL!OWLClass)
                and a.name = b.name and a.parent.name = b.parent.name))
to      drop b.parent
do  { drop c: DSL!Function!DSLObjectProperty(
                                c->getProperties()->contains(b.parent)) }
}
```

Fig. 5. ATL rules for reflecting changes of relations in the ontology and DSL

The first rule is the same with vertical evolution. The second one provides the opportunity to drop all relations, deleted in the ontology, with corresponding reduction of the list of arguments of the functions, which are used for initialization of corresponding relations.

3.4 Using ATL IDE for Co-evolution of the Ontology and DSL

After description of all possible variants of the model evolution, we have to identify all important stages, used for identification of the process of co-evolution of the ontology and DSL. In other words, we have to define the mechanism, which connects changes between two models: the ontology and DSL meta-model. For this goal, we use ATL Integrated Environment (IDE) [9], which allows to transform the ontology into the target model (DSL model in this case), using the system of defined rules. In order to create the whole consistency between the ontology and DSL meta-model we perform the following steps.

Step 1: Identification of the ontology. On this stage, we formulate the original state of the ontology in terms of one of available formats. In our case, we use the OWL format for this propose.

Step 2: Identification of the DSL meta-model. We define a set of entities that form the basis of the DSL object-level. For this propose we use the KM3 language (http://wiki. eclipse.org/KM3), which is an implementation-independent language to write meta-models and thus to define abstract syntaxes of DSLs.

Step 3: Definition of transformation rules. We introduce the system of the transformation rules, which are responsible for establishing the correspondence between them. Examples of such rules were given in Sects. 3.2 and 3.3.

Step 4: Applying the transformation rules to the ontology. We initialize the transformation procedure – apply defined earlier transformation rules to the current ontology. As output, we have the ready DSL model, which corresponds to the structure of the ontology and is a complete description of the object level of the DSL. After the DSL structure is ready, we need only to (re)configure the syntactic analyzer, which transforms the terms of DSL into the terms of some general programming language.

4 A Use Case: Co-evolution of the Ontology and DSL in the Railway Allocation Domain

4.1 Ontology-Part and DSL Description

In the current research, we will consider the ontology of railway transportation. A fragment of the application ontology of this domain is represented in Fig. 6 in the form of a generic semantic network, whose vertices are basic concepts, and arcs express relations between them (part-whole, gender-type, reservation, etc.).

According to this ontology the structure of DSL's object-level was designed (Fig. 7). This structure contains all needed elements of the ontology, which are used in the process of allocation railway station resources. Some ontology entities are transformed into equivalent entities, other (connected between each other) become the attributes for entities of higher level. Also, the relations were transformed into the corresponding fields of classes or into separate classes of connectedness, which contains links to the connected classes. In addition, we need to include into DSL some helper classes to finalize the syntax of DSL.

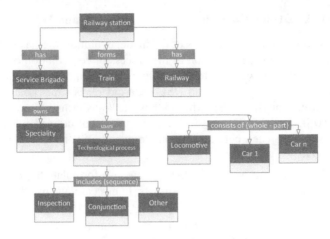

Fig. 6. A part of the railway transportation ontology

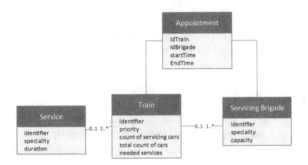

Fig. 7. The structure of DSL: the object level

In order to work with the designed structure of main and helper classes, the next structure of DSL constructors on the functional level is developed (Fig. 8).

On Fig. 8 the meta-symbol '*' means, that a preceding sequence of objects can be written multiple times. The meta-symbols '[' and ']' specify a list of single-typed entities.

```
Trains
({id priority length timeArrival timeDeparture [services]
   wagonsToService})*
EndTrainsBlock;
Services
   ({name mayBeInParallel [speciality] standartDuration [equipment]})*
endServiceBlock;
Servicing Brigades ({id [ speciality ] capacity})*endBrigadeBlock;
Appointments
   ({idBrigade->idTrain timeStart timeEnd})*
endAppointmentBlock;
```

Fig. 8. Constructors for DSL objects

The ontology and DSL above are used in order to appoint servicing brigades between arriving trains. Both contains only terms, which are used throw this process. Other objects and relations ignore, since they have no effect on the procedure under consideration.

4.2   Sceneries of Evolution and Solving Conflicts

In Sect. 4.1 we introduced the ontology for the railway transportation domain and the corresponding DSL. During their design, we assumed that both are universal and can be used for the allocation servicing brigades between trains on any types of stations. However, as can be seen, the original ontology has no whole consistence with the DSL meta-model: some entities of the ontology have no equivalent entities in DSL (or has, but with differences in names) and vice versa. This means that in addition to the previously defined in Sects. 3.2 and 3.3 universal rules, which transforms only equivalent entities of the ontology and DSL, we have to create an additional system of specific rules. The specific rules allow to treat all the differences between the ontology and DSL. Below we consider two situations of evolution scenarios of the ontology and DSL.

The first scenario is that starting in 2018 all servicing brigades will become universal. It means, that all brigades will have no unique skills, providing all types of services. Due to these modifications, the ontology has to be changed. We delete from it such an entity, as Speciality and the corresponding relation as well.

But DSL lefts unchanged and ceases to fully comply with the subject area. Because now such attribute as skills has no equivalent in the ontology. From the pragmatic point of view, it means, that user will continue operate with this term of DSL language and fill the value of this attribute for every brigade. But now he/she will have to input all values of the skills list, otherwise there may be a situation when a brigade cannot be allocated to the maintenance of the train due to an incomplete list of skills. That contradicts the actual state of the subject area. To solve this conflict between the target domain (ontology) and DSL we have to add to the universal rules and apply the next ATL rule (Fig. 9). That rule deletes one particular class 'Speciality' and transforms the new state of the ontology into the updated DSL model.

```
Rule    DropSpecialityOWLClassInDSLClassAttributes {
From    b: DSL!DSLClass!DSLObjectProperty("Speciality" = b.name)
to      drop
do { drop c: DSL!Constructor!DSLObjectProperty("Speciality" =c.name)}}
```

Fig. 9. The ATL rule for DSL correction after deleting entity Speciality from the ontology

We have to use this rule because changes in the ontology are vertical: one entity should be deleted. But we need no other rules, since entity Speciality has no other children entities and requires to delete only corresponding attributes in DSL objects and Constructors. After applying this rule, the new scheme of DSL objects will be the following (Fig. 10).

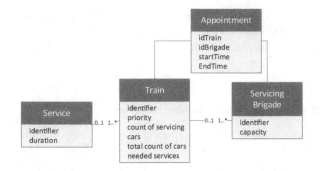

Fig. 10. The structure of DSL after corrections: the object level

As we see, the attribute speciality, which was the equivalent to the entity Speciality in the ontology, is absent. Corresponding changes will be done in the Constructor of the Servicing Brigades and Services on the functional level of DSL (Fig. 11).

```
Services
   ({name mayBeInParallel standartDuration [equipment]})*
endServiceBlock;
ServicingBrigades ({id [ speciality ] capacity})* endBrigadesBlock;
```

Fig. 11. Constructor for DSL objects Servicing Brigades after corrections

The second scenario is caused by the fact, that there are some types of trains, which need organizing services not within the whole train, but for each car separately. It means, that in terms of the ontology, our relation between Services and Trains have to be expanded on Cars. And this change is not so trial, as a first one. Here we have a combination of the vertical and horizontal transformation.

The former transformation is needed because of creation a new type of relation between Service and Car. And the later transformation is the result of DSL earlier structure: because we had no need to operate every Car separately, this entity of the ontology was replaced with the attribute 'total count of cars' in Trains. But now this concept is incorrect. To resolve these contradictions, we extend the previously created rules by the following system (Fig. 12).

The first rule deletes the property 'total count of cars' from DSL. Other rules add skipped entities and relations from the ontology into DSL. But we see, that all rules are specific and are caused by the fact that the structure of the DSL was not originally adapted to the structure of the ontology.

Summarizing two given scenarios of co-evolution, it can be argued that in the case, when the ontology and DSL has no whole coherence, we need to complete the system of universal transformation rules with a set of specific rules, which aims to resolve differences between the ontology and DSL. Furthermore, this system of rules extends every time, when the ontology changes. This significantly complicates the procedure for the organization of co-evolution of the ontology and DSL.

```
rule    DropCarsPropertyInDSLClassAttributes {
from    b: DSL!DSLClass!DSLObjectProperty (b.name = "total count of
cars"))
to      drop
do {
        drop c: DSL!Constructor!DSLObjectProperty (c.name ="total count
of cars")
    }
}
rule    OWLClassCars2DSLClass {
from    a: OWL!OWLClass (a.nam->contains("Car"))
to      b: DSL!DSLClass, c:DSL!Constructor
}
rule    OWLClassServiceCars2DSLClassServiceCars {
from    a: OWL!OWLClass (a.parent->exists() and a.name->contains("Car"))
to      b: DSL!DSLClass (b.name = a.name),
do      { b.parent.name = a.parent.name }
}
```

Fig. 12. The rule for DSL correction after adding the relation between services and cars

In order to avoid the above problems, we have to build a DSL model as a complete reflection of the ontology when the latter is designed for the first time. For this purpose, we proceed through all the stages, described in Sect. 3.4. In this case, we don't create the structure of the DSL model manually, but automatically obtain it from the ontology. As a result, the structure of DSL can be updated every time, when the structure of the ontology is changed – we need only to identify the principle for running the previously created system of universal rules of correspondence between the ontology and DSL.

As a result of this approach, the model of DSL will be described as follows (Fig. 13).

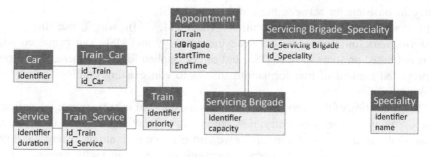

Fig. 13. Structure of DSL in the case of co-evolution with the ontology

Of course, in a manner, such a structure of DSL may seem superfluous. But in fact, from the point of view of designing further changes, this structure of DSL guarantees the simplicity of correspondence with ontology updates, because co-evolution needs only universal rules, described in Sects. 3.2 and 3.3. To optimize this structure of DSL we can use the level of functions, which is not so trivial from the position of establishing equivalent transformations with the ontology, because this level of DSL can differ from the similar one in the ontology because of the limitations of the latter.

5 Conclusion

To summarize, we can say that DSL is an effective tool for working with the subject area. At the same time, it is necessary to control all the changes that occur in the target domain and reflect them in the DSL structure, because otherwise there can be a contradiction between the model of DSL and the subject domain, thus DSL may become completely inapplicable.

To solve this problem, mechanisms for the organizing the co-evolution of the domain ontology and the DSL model can be used. We believe that it is very important to consider what kind of evolution occurs: vertical or horizontal. The first one means changes in the level of the abstraction with affection of the amount of entities in the ontology. The second one happens, when only relations between an object in the ontology or their attributes are modified. Vertical changes can be solved by a simple mechanism of finding differences in the set of entities in DSL and the ontology and organizing corresponding transformations of them. The horizontal evolution is more complicated, because it requires not only mirror changes in the system of relations between entities, but also transformations in terms of the functional level of DSL.

The proposed approach allows to simplify the needed procedures for achieving the correspondence between the ontology and DSL. This approach uses the graph-based definition of the ontology and the DSL model and allows to create the universal system of rules, which provides all needed changes in objects and constructors of the functional level of DSL.

In the paper, it was shown that the proposed approach can be applied also in the case when the designer of DSL only informally relied on the domain ontology in the development of the DSL, and in the case when DSL is constructed as a complete reflection of the ontology. In both cases a system of universal transformation rules has to be used, but in the first case we need to extend it with a set of specific rules, which resolve inconsistencies between the ontology and DSL.

In comparison to existing solutions (like [14, 15]), which use the graph-transformations for conversions between the ontology and DSL, our proposed solution is not based on some specific DSL, but can be applied for any of them. In addition, the proposed method of transformations allows to edit existing ontologies and DSL without recreating them.

The application of the proposed approach is most useful in areas where the structure of the ontology changes frequently: new entities or connections between them appear. For example, in the areas of administrative and economic planning, where the ontology, used in the process of resource allocation, changes constantly because of the emergence of new regulatory documents. Another sphere of potential usage of co-evolution mechanism is the sphere of modelling DSLs, which are used for creation of some models – in this case the changes in components of model have to be reflected in terms of DSL, otherwise DSL is not useful for updated version of the model specification.

In the future, we expect to modify this approach by adding opportunity to change the functional level of DSL model in accordance with the ontology. In addition, such concept of ontologies as Roles have to be examine.

References

1. Fowler, M.: Domain Specific Languages. Addison Wesley, Boston (2010)
2. Arp, R., Smith, B., Spear, A.D.: Building Ontologies with Basic Formal Ontology. The MIT Press, Cambridge (2015)
3. Kosar, T., Bohra, B., Mernik, M.: Domain-specific languages: a systematic mapping study. In: Information and Software Technology, pp. 77–90. Elsevier (2016)
4. Cleenewerck, T., Czarnecki, K., Striegnitz, J., Völter, M.: Evolution and reuse of language specifications for DSLs (ERLS). In: Malenfant, J., Østvold, Bjarte M. (eds.) ECOOP 2004. LNCS, vol. 3344, pp. 187–201. Springer, Heidelberg (2005). doi:10.1007/978-3-540-30554-5_18
5. Pereira, M., Fonseca, J., Henriques, P.: Ontological approach for DSL development. In: Computer Languages, Systems & Structures, pp. 35–52. Elsevier (2016)
6. Guizzardi, G.: Ontological foundations for structural conceptual models, vol. 15. Telematica Instituut Fundamental Research Series, The Netherlands (2005). ISBN 90-75176-81-3
7. Guizzardi, G., Halpin, T.: Ontological foundations for conceptual modeling. Appl. Ontol. **3**, 91–110 (2008)
8. Parr, T.: Language Implementation Patterns: Create Your Own Domain-Specific and General Programming Languages. Pragmatic Bookshelf, Raleigh (2012)
9. ATL Transformation Language. http://www.eclipse.org/atl/
10. Agrawal, A., Karsai, G., Shi, F.: Graph transformations on domain-specific models. Int. J. Softw. Syst. Model. **37**, 1–43 (2003). Vanderbilt University Press, Nashville
11. GReAT: Graph Rewriting and Transformation. http://www.isis.vanderbilt.edu/tools/great
12. Sprinkle, J.: A domain-specific visual language for domain model evolution. J. Vis. Lang. Comput. **15**, 291–307 (2004)
13. Bell, P.: Automated transformation of statements within evolving domain specific languages. In: Computer Science and Information System Reports, pp. 172–177 (2007)
14. Cleenewerck, T.: Component-based DSL development. In: Software Language Engineering, pp. 245–264 (2003)
15. Challenger, M., Demirkol, S., Getir, S., Mernik, M., Kardas, G., Kosar, T.: On the use of a domain-specific modeling language in the development of multiagent systems. In: Engineering Applications of Artificial Intelligence, pp. 111–141 (2014)

Evaluation of Capability Delivery Capacity Requirements

Jānis Grabis[1]([⊠]), Tania González Cardona[2], and Lauma Jokste[1]

[1] Institute of Information Technology,
Riga Technical University, Kalku 1, Riga, Latvia
{grabis,lauma.jokste}@rtu.lv
[2] Everis, Avda. Cortes Valencianas, 39-9 C, 46015 Valencia, Spain
tania.gonzalez.cardona@everis.com

Abstract. Capabilities characterize ability and capacity to provide business services in different circumstance in accordance to performance requirements. The Capability Driven Development methodology provides means for designing and evaluating such capabilities. This paper specifically focuses on the capacity aspect of capability design. It assumes that every capability is delivered by using a specific set of resources and delivery performance directly depends upon availability of appropriate resources. A method for evaluation of capacity requirements is proposed in the paper. Its application is illustrated using an example of design of information technology management services.

Keywords: Capability · Capacity · Resource requirements · Context

1 Introduction

The capability characterizes an ability and capacity to provide business services [1]. From the strategic planning point of view, it is very important for digital enterprises to evaluate whether they possess a certain capacity and if this capacity is sufficient for addressing various context situations. This paper proposes a capacity evaluation method, which allows to evaluate capacity availability. Capacity availability is one of the factors determining suitability of the capability for all stakeholders involved. It is assumed that a capability is possessed by a company providing services to various consumers in a collaborative manner. The collaboration implies that all parties commit some resources for enabling the services and the capacity evaluation method is used to appraise capacity availability.

This setting is motivated by a case observed at a company providing information technology and eGovernment services to municipalities [2]. These services are managed by Portfolio Management Office (PMO). Besides capacity evaluation at the service provider side, capacity availability also should be evaluated for all municipalities involved. Given that there is large number of municipalities, the capacity evaluation procedure should be streamlined. The capacity evaluation method provides a systematic approach to capability evaluation and can be applied to all entities involved in capability delivery. It is a constituent part of the Capability Driven Development

© Springer International Publishing AG 2017
B. Johansson et al. (Eds.): BIR 2017, LNBIP 295, pp. 248–259, 2017.
DOI: 10.1007/978-3-319-64930-6_18

Methodology (CDD) [3]. The method component is the part of the capability design cycle and deals with capability evaluation prior to its deployment.

A capability model is developed during the capability design cycle. Deployment of the capability requires development of supporting information systems as well as enterprise's commitment to delivering this capability to its customers. In order to invest in new capability delivery and the development activities, capability evaluation is required. The purpose of the method is: (1) to evaluate capacity availability in different context situations; and (2) to evaluate expected efficiency of the capacity design.

An important precondition for this method is that parties involved are able to calculate resource requirements for the capability design. It is also assumed that the capacity requirements depend upon the context values. The capacity evaluation is performed during the capability design cycle and the actual values of measurable properties are not known.

The rest of the paper is organized as follows. Section 2 describes background information and related research. The capacity evaluation method is described in Sect. 3. An application example is provided in Sect. 4. Section 5 concludes.

2 Background

This section discusses the PMO case motivating development of the method. It briefly recaps the CDD meta-model and methodology to extent relevant to capacity evaluation and summarizes related work on capacity evaluation.

2.1 Motivational Case

The PMO scenario consists of a project management tool used to manage incoming project incidents from the moment they are created to the moment they are solved or closed. Depending on the type of the incident and the skills to resolve it, every project incident has the possibility to be assigned to three resolution groups: PMO, Municipality and External Company.

When a new incident is created, the application is able to automatically assign a user from a given group to the incident. This assignation is based on data from the incident as well as data from the members of each group, which leads to an optimum decision making. The data can vary from the type of incident to the members' knowledge and availability. If the chosen member is capable of solving the incident, it proceeds to work on the resolution until it is successfully solved. Otherwise, a supervisor of the group evaluates the incident and decides whether to reallocate it to another member from the current group or from a different one. Depending on the supervisor's choice, the application makes the appropriate evaluations and reallocates the incident.

When an incident is assigned to a member from the External Company group the process has a slight variation. Incidents assigned to this group entail new programming implementations for features, bugs, etc. There needs to be a previous evaluation of the budget and the hours available for the resolution of the incident to be accepted or denied. The application handles this evaluation automatically. If the evaluation is negative, a supervisor's evaluation is made and the incident is properly reassigned. If the evaluation is positive, the member begins to work on the resolution until the incident is solved.

2.2 Capability Modeling

The capability model defines ability and capacity to provide services to clients facing specific circumstances. Figure 1 provides a simplified overview of the key elements used in capability modeling. Goals are business objectives the capability allows to achieve. The capability is designed for delivery in a specific context as defined using context elements. The context elements name factors affecting the capability delivery while context situations refer to combinations of context element values. The process element specifies a capability delivery solution. Process variants describe the capability delivery process for a specific context situation. Resources are used in process execution. In this case, the resources included those provided by the service company as well as those possessed by service consumers. Capability is delivered by so called Capability Delivery Application (CDA). In order to ensure that capability is delivered as expected in different contextual situations, adjustments are used to adapt capability delivery [4]. The adjustments take context data and goals as input and evaluate potential changes in capability delivery. The evaluation results are passed to CDA to alter its behavior. This concept is also used to specify context dependent calculations of resources requirements. Technically, that allows for separating resource requirements calculation from other parts of capability delivery application and enables specification of unique calculations for specific context.

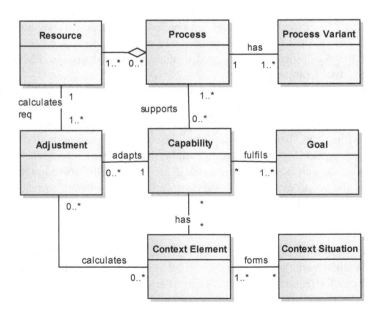

Fig. 1. Key concepts of capability modeling.

The capability modeling meta-model forms a backbone of the CDD methodology. The main features of the CDD methodology are:

- Enterprise modelling phase, which defines information about the digital enterprise necessary to specify requirements for development of capable information systems. It allows involving business people in information system development;
- Design phase, where the capable information systems is designed on the basis of the existing knowledge in a model-driven manner;
- Delivery phase, where the capable information system is executed, monitored and adjusted to changes in the operating environment if necessary;
- Feedback phase, where the system delivery experiences are accumulated and changes in the design are requested.

The capacity evaluation method primarily concerns the design phase.

2.3   Related Work

Capability evaluation is a major challenge faced by companies seeking to understand their competitive advantages. Existing enterprise architecture based methods focus on internal perspective of capability evaluation taking into account only a limited number of influencers [5] and judgmental methods such AHP [6] are usually used for these purposes. The proposed capacity evaluation method allows for quantitative evaluation of capabilities and explicitly accounts for external factors affecting capability delivery (i.e., context elements).

Quantitative aspects of capacity planning and evaluation have been evaluated in various other domains such as operations management and business process management. Olhager et al. [7] shows that capacity planning should be considered as a cross-disciplinary problem and at multiple planning levels. Formalization of resource management in business processes has been investigated in [8] by introducing notation for explicitly representing resources in business process diagrams. Similarly, resource related aspects in relation to business processes are modeled using object-role modeling [9]. This approach allows for modeling of different types of resources and their complex allocation to business process tasks. Simulation together with analytical tools is also used for evaluation of resource-constrained business processes [10]. This paper defines basic building blocks of the resource-constrained business processes and derives expressions for analytical calculation of the performance measures. Resource planning in risk-aware business processes is investigated in [11] and risk can be perceived as one specific context factor. Statistical models and machine learning have been used to predict resource requirements in customized manufacturing systems, where customer demand is an external factor influencing the resource requirements [12]. Dorsch and Häckel [13] demonstrate the positive impact of collaborative capacity planning in relation to cloud service delivery. Quantitative models such as queuing and simulation models have been applied for capacity planning in area of information technology management and incident management in particular [14, 15]. These models could be used to estimate resource requirements in capability design and specified in a form of adjustments.

3 Method

The capacity evaluation is a part of the capability design cycle. It is one of the capability evaluation activities. It consists of five main steps shown in Fig. 2. It takes the capability design as an input and provides information necessary for approving further development of the capability delivery application. The key steps of the method component are:

- Defines resources and their capacity available for capability delivery – if the capability design does not yet specify resources needed for capability delivery, the necessary resources are defined in the capability model using the Resource concept from the capability meta-model. Capacity of every resource is specified.
- Generate potential context situations – the capability design includes specification of all context elements and their ranges. At design time, context values are not known and context situations are generated by drawing and combining values from the context element range.
- Specify calculation of resource requirements depending on the context situation – the Calculation element of the capability meta-model is used to specify calculation of resource requirements. These calculations can have an arbitrary degree of complexity ranging from simple expressions to complex mathematical models, which take the context situation as a primary input.
- Create capacity evaluation matrix – the evaluation matrix is the main artifact for analyzing capacity availability. It shows availability of capability delivery resources according to context situations.
- Analyze capacity availability in different context situations – a capability analyst uses information in the evaluation matrix to identify cases of insufficient capacity and uses decision analysis methods to investigate sensitivity and robustness of the evaluation results.

Fig. 2. Steps of the capacity evaluation method.

3.1 Step 1: Definition of Resources and Their Capacity

Resources available for capability delivery are used to evaluate capability delivery capacity. They are defined by their name and attributes. The typical attributes are resource capacity, capacity unit and resource type (see [16] for definitions of resource attributes and types). These attributes are used in calculations involving the resources. The objective of Step 1 is to define resources available for capability delivery. That includes definition of human resources as well as material resources. The main activities of this step are:

- Definition of resources R_j. Resources used in capability delivery are named in the capability design.
- Definition of resource capacity RC_j and assignment of appropriate numeric values. Every resource has its capacity expressed in appropriate units. The capacity of human resources is defined by the number of time units (e.g., hours) available. The capacity of limited material resources is defined as the number of items/units available. Some of the resources can have infinite capacity.
- Definition of constants affecting calculation of resource availability and requirements. Resource availability and requirements are calculated using appropriate expressions, and the calculations are affected by parameters $A = (a_1, \ldots, a_K)$. These parameters are defined in the capability design.

The result of these steps is definition of resources involved in capability delivery including their capacity.

3.2 Step 2: Generation of Context Situations

The context model defines context elements and context element ranges. The context element value is determined during capability delivery and combinations of these values form a context situation. In order to perform capacity evaluation, the context situation also needs to be initialized at the design time. That is achieved by generating context situations out of the context element ranges. All possible context situations or only the most significant ones are generated. The objective of this step is to define context situations requiring capability delivery capacity evaluation.

The main activities are:

- Generation of context situations out of context element ranges.
- Selection of context situations relevant for the evaluation. The selection is performed to reduce the number of context situations generated. The selection can be performed manually according to business-oriented considerations or using principles of design of experiments [17].

The result of this step is a set of plausible context situations to be considered for further evaluation.

3.3 Step 3: Calculation of Resource Requirements

The resource model defines resources available for capability delivery. Capacity requirements depend upon the capability delivery solution, context situation and other factors. The capacity requirements evaluation is specified using the Calculation element. It can be a simple numerical expression or an advanced evaluation model.

The objective of this step is to define the calculation element for evaluation of resource requirements for a given context situation. To achieve this objective, the following activities are performed:

- For each resource define calculation adjustment of the resource requirements.
- For each calculation specify the expression and bindings.

The resource requirements generally are computed using numeric measurable properties though these are not available in the design-time. Therefore, a probabilistic calculation of the design time measurable property is used. The default evaluation is an inverse function of measurable property to context element calculation in the case of continuous, monotomic and inversable function.

The resource requirements calculation expression is:

$$RR_j^s = \varphi(\mathbf{P}, A).$$ (1)

The design-time estimates of the measurable properties are obtained as:

$$P_m^* = f^{-1}(CV_i)$$ (2)

In the case of continuous and monotomic f, the measurable property's estimates also can be obtained using a triangle distribution approximation

$$P_m^* = \frac{1}{6}\left(b_{il}^L + 4b_{il}^M + b_{il}^U\right)$$ (3)

where b_{il}^L is low, b_{il}^M is most likely and b_{il}^U is high value of the context range value definition used in the context calculation. The most likely value is either specified by an expert or assumed as a mid-point of the range.

The calculated value is used as an expected value of the measurable property in the case of a given context situation.

If resource requirements can be computed directly from the context situation then computation of the design time measurable property value is not necessary.

3.4   Step 4: Creation of Capacity Evaluation Matrix

The capacity evaluation matrix is a major tool for the evaluation of capability feasibility. The matrix rows are context situations. The matrix columns are resources. The cells contain comparisons between resource capacity and resource requirements for the given capability. Initially, it is assumed that resource capacity is independent of context situation. The capacity context dependency later on can be introduced as capability run-time adjustments. The objective of this step is to provide a demonstrative representation of comparison between resource availability and requirements in the context situations under consideration.

During this step the capacity evaluation matrix is created. The capacity evaluation matrix is automatically generated by taking all context situations under evaluation and computation of resource availability and resource requirements measures for every resource specified in the capability model. Each cell evaluates either true or false. The true value indicates that the capacity is sufficient for the given context situation while the false value indicates that the capacity is insufficient. The evaluation results are conditionally formatted for highlighting purposes. The capability capacity index (CI) is evaluated as a ratio of cells evaluated as TRUE and total number of cells. A sample layout of the evaluation matrix with is given in Table 1.

Table 1. Layout of the capacity evaluation matrix.

	R_1	...	R_J
CS_1	$RC_1 > RR_1^1$	...	$RC_J > RR_J^1$
...	...	...	...
$CS_{|CS|}$	$RC_1 > RR_1^{|CS|}$	...	$RC_J > RR_J^{|CS|}$

3.5   Step 5: Analysis of Capability Delivery Capacity

The capacity evaluation results shown in the capacity evaluation matrix depend upon several controllable factors including resource capacity, attributes and categorization of context ranges. The analysis is performed to discover the most significant factors and to investigate ways for expanding the capability delivery capacity. The objective of this step is to test factors substantially affecting capability delivery capacity and to identify ways for expanding capability delivery capacity.

Several types of studies could be performed by changing values and concepts in the capability design and reevaluating the capacity evaluation matrix.

- Study of relationships between resource capacity availability and capability delivery capacity
- Study of relationships between the constants and capability delivery capacity
- Redefinition of context element range

In the first study, the resource capacity is modified in a structured manner to identify resources having the most substantial impact on the capability delivery capacity. The results of this study would suggest potential changes in resource capacity to expand the capability delivery capacity.

In the second study, the constants used in capacity requirements calculation are modified in a structured manner to quantify their impact on the capability delivery capacity. It is assumed that these constants characterize efficiency on the capability delivery solution and capability delivery capacity can be expanded by improving this efficiency.

In the third study, calculation of context ranges is redefined. If capability delivery capacity is insufficient for some of the range values, the range definition could be refined.

The capacity evaluation matrix can be perceived as a kind of decision table [18] as methods used in the analysis of a decision table can be adopted for usage in capacity evaluation. The results of this step are (1) list of factors substantially affecting capability delivery capacity; and (2) analysis of observations and suggestions for potential adjustments.

4 Example

In the case of the PMO's capability, incident message processing is performed by the technical support staff. The resources requirements, i.e., number of technical support specialists depend upon a number of requests received as well as complexity of the requests in this case characterized by their priority. The context model data is given in Table 2 and the resource model data is given in Table 3. The complexity of incidents is a qualitative variable and fixed numeric values of 0.8 and 1.2 are assigned to the context elements range elements Low and High, respectively.

Table 2. Context elements.

Context element	Context element range	Measurable property
Number of incidents (NI)	(low, high)	Number of incidents (numeric) (MNI)
Complexity of incidents (CI)	(low, high)	Complexity of incidents (numeric) (MCI)

Table 3. Resource data.

Resource	Number of resource units (α)	Incident processing rate per hour (ρ)	Total capacity (RC_{TS}), incidents per hour
Technical support specialist (TS)	5	10	50

The evaluation objective is to evaluate capability delivery capacity depending on the context situation. The context element value is calculated as defined in (4) (indices refer to context elements and measurable properties as defined in the tables above)

$$CV_{NI} = \begin{cases} low, 0 \leq p_{MNI} < 10 \\ high, 10 \leq p_{MNI} < 50 \end{cases}. \tag{4}$$

The resource requirements are calculated as

$$RR_{TS}^s = p_{MNI} \times p_{MCI} \times \rho, \tag{5}$$

where ρ is the incident processing rate per hour. The resource requirements depend upon the estimated average complexity of incidents and more complex messages require more processing time. The resource capacity in this case is expressed as

$$RC_{TC} = \alpha \times \rho, \tag{6}$$

where α is a multiplier indicated reduction of the processing rate due to increasing complexity of incidents. The parameters α and ρ can be defined as adjustment constants in the capability model. The design time measurable property value is estimated by inversing (4) using (3) and the range mid-point as the most likely value. The capability capacity evaluation matrix is given in Table 4. It can be observed that the capability delivery capacity is insufficient for the context situations $CS_3 = $ (High, Low) and $CS_4 = $ (High, High).

Table 4. The capability capacity evaluation matrix example, $RC_{TS} = 50$.

CS	NI	CI	MNI*	MCI*	RR^s_{TS}	Are resources sufficient?
1	Low	Low	5	0.8	40	TRUE
2		High	5	1.2	60	FALSE
3	High	Low	30	0.8	240	FALSE
4		High	30	1.2	360	FALSE

*Indicates the design time estimate of the measurable properties.

To perform analysis of capability delivery capacity, the resource capacity is changed and capacity evaluation matrix is regenerated to study the impact of potential resource increases. Figure 3 shows capacity index dependency upon available resources. The increase of resource availability leads to an expansion of capability capacity. However, there is still a context situation for which sufficient capacity cannot be ensured. That implies changing the capability design to exclude unsupported context situations. In this case, it is context situation (High, High).

The constant α referring to the effort multiplier describing additional effort needed to process complex incidents also could be improved (e.g., by having better qualified support specialists) to reduce capacity requirements.

During the analysis, calculation of context ranges also could be redefined. If capability delivery capacity is insufficient for some of the range values, the range definition could be refined. For instance, if the context element Number of Incidents

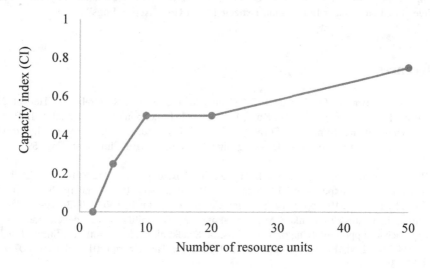

Fig. 3. Capacity index as function of MNI*.

Received has a range value $CR_{NumberOfIncidentsReceived} = (low, high)$ and the capability delivery capacity is insufficient, then the range can split into $CR'_{NumberOfIncidentsReceived} = (low, high, very high)$ and the reevaluation could show that there are sufficient resources for the high level while an insufficient capacity for the very high level. If a lack of capability delivery capacity cannot be resolved by adjustments or other means, the capability design should be changed to exclude the corresponding range value because the company should be able to deliver capability for all context situations defined in the capability model.

5 Conclusion

The paper has introduced a method for capacity evaluation as a part of the CDD methodology. The method specifically focusses on collaborative capability delivery where resources should be committed by both service provider and service consumers.

The capability meta-model provides a reusable framework for evaluation of capability requirements for a large group of potential service consumers. Adjustments allow to specify capacity requirements calculations of an arbitrary complexity. The method also provides a systematical approach for evaluating resource requirements for all applicable context situations.

Further investigations are necessary to evaluate ability of the adjustments to handle complex capacity planning logics and to assess performance and limitation of the method in practical use cases.

Acknowledgments.   This work has been funded in parts by the EU-FP7 project no: 611351 CaaS – Capability as a Service in Digital Enterprises and from the research project "Competence Centre of Information and Communication Technologies" of EU Structural funds, contract No. 1.2.1.1/16/A/007 signed between IT Competence Centre and Central Finance and Contracting Agency, Research No. 1.6 "Development of Software Adaptation Algorithms and Module Based on Context Information Extracted from Users Action Logs".

References

1. Bērziša, S., Bravos, G., González, T., Czubayko, U., España, S., Grabis, J., Henkel, M., Jokste, L., Kampars, J., Koç, H., Kuhr, J., Llorca, C., Loucopoulos, P., Pascual, R.J., Pastor, O., Sandkuhl, K., Simic, H., Stirna, J., Giromé, F.V., Zdravkovic, J.: Capability driven development: an approach to designing digital enterprises. Bus. Inf. Syst. Eng. **57**, 15–25 (2015)
2. Bravos, G., González, T., Grabis, J., Henkel, M., Jokste, L., Koc, H., Stirna, J.: Capability modeling: initial experiences. In: Johansson, B., Andersson, B., Holmberg, N. (eds.) BIR 2014. LNBIP, vol. 194, pp. 1–14. Springer, Cham (2014). doi:10.1007/978-3-319-11370-8_1
3. Stirna, J., Grabis, J., Henkel, M., Zdravkovic, J.: Capability driven development – an approach to support evolving organizations. In: Sandkuhl, K., Seigerroth, U., Stirna, J. (eds.) PoEM 2012. LNBIP, vol. 134, pp. 117–131. Springer, Heidelberg (2012). doi:10.1007/978-3-642-34549-4_9

4. Grabis, J., Kampars, J.: Design of capability delivery adjustments. In: Krogstie, J., Mouratidis, H., Su, J. (eds.) CAiSE 2016. LNBIP, vol. 249, pp. 52–62. Springer, Cham (2016). doi:10.1007/978-3-319-39564-7_5

5. Azevedo, C.L.B., Sinderen, M., Pires, L.F., Almeida, J.P.A.: Aligning enterprise architecture with strategic planning. In: Persson, A., Stirna, J. (eds.) CAiSE 2015. LNBIP, vol. 215, pp. 426–437. Springer, Cham (2015). doi:10.1007/978-3-319-19243-7_39

6. Lekurwale, R.R., Akarte, M.M., Raut, D.N.: Framework to evaluate manufacturing capability using analytical hierarchy process. Int. J. Adv. Manufact. Technol. **76**(1–4), 565–576 (2014)

7. Olhager, J., Rudberg, M., Wikner, J.: Long-term capacity management: linking the perspectives from manufacturing strategy and sales and operations planning. Int. J. Prod. Econ. **69**(2), 215–225 (2001)

8. Vasilecas, O., Laureckas, E., Rima, A.: Analysis of using resources in business process modeling and simulation. Appl. Comput. Syst. **16**, 19–25 (2014)

9. Ouyang, C., Wynn, M.T., Fidge, C., ter Hofstede, A.H.M., Kuhr, J.C.: Modelling complex resource requirements in business process management systems. In: Rosemann, M., Green, P., Rohde, F. (eds.) ACIS 2010 Proceedings (2010)

10. Oliveira, C.A.L., Lima, R.M.F., Reijers, H.A., Ribeiro, J.T.S.: Quantitative analysis of resource-constrained BP. IEEE Trans. Syst. Man Cybern. Part A: Syst. Hum. **42**, 669–684 (2012)

11. Jakoubi, S., Goluch, G., Tjoa, S., Quirchmayr, G.: Deriving resource requirements applying risk-aware business process modeling and simulation. In: 16th European Conference on Information Systems, ECIS 2008 (2008)

12. Dean, P.R., Xue, D., Tu, Y.L.: Prediction of manufacturing resource requirements from customer demands in mass-customisation production. Int. J. Prod. Res. **47**(5), 1245–1268 (2009)

13. Dorsch, C., Häckel, B.: Combining models of capacity supply to handle volatile demand: the economic impact of surplus capacity in cloud service environments. Decis. Support Syst. **58**(1), 3–14 (2014)

14. Li, T., Lee, J.: Capacity planning and management of IT incident management services based on queuing models. In: Maximizing Management Performance and Quality with Service Analytics, pp. 1–32 (2015)

15. Li, Y., Li, T., Katircioglu, K.: Estimating and applying service request effort data in application management services. Int. J. Bus. Process Integr. Manag. **7**(1), 22–33 (2014)

16. Stroppi, L.R.J.: A BPMN 2.0 extension to define the resource perspective of business process models (2011)

17. Montgomery, D.C.: Design and Analysis of Experiments. Wiley, Hoboken (2012)

18. Triantaphyllou, E.: Multi-Criteria Decision Making Methods: A Comparative Study. Kluwer, Dordrecht and Boston (2000)

Triple-Agile: Cloud Solutions for SMEs

Marite Kirikova[1(✉)] and Edgars Salna[2]

[1] Department of Artificial Intelligence and Systems Engineering, Riga Technical
University, 1 Kalku, Riga LV-1658, Latvia
marite.kirikova@rtu.lv
[2] Datorzinību Centrs, 4 Pulkveza Brieza, Riga LV-1010, Latvia
edgars.salna@dzc.lv

Abstract. Agility has become the must have feature for small and medium
sized companies (SMEs). One of the enablers of agility is the use of appropriate
information technology solutions. In turn, cloud solutions have been advocated
as the ones well suited to SMEs. Agility as a concept includes the fast reaction to
changes. So, for supporting agile SMEs, the providers of cloud solutions have to
be able to produce their products and services in an agile manner, so that agile
adoption or acquisition of these solutions is possible. The Triple-Agile paradigm
is proposed to address all three aforementioned issues of agility by stating that in
a business ecosystem of SMEs and cloud service providers three types of processes should be agile: the SME processes, the service development and maintenance processes, and the service adoption/provision processes. This research
in progress paper reports on the first step in the use of this paradigm, namely, it
shows the conceptual outlook of the Triple-Agile paradigm applied to cloud
solutions dedicated to SMEs. The conceptual outlook is illustrated by the
ArchiMate language of enterprise architecture representation.

Keywords: SME · Cloud computing · Agile

1 Introduction

Enterprise agility (ability to change quickly and easily) has nowadays become an
important aspect of organizational design [1]. It is common to infer that the enterprise
agility depends on the agility of IT solutions; and cloud solutions are advocated as one
of the IT options for agility. However, there is an interesting observation in [2] showing
that software as a service (SaaS) alone does not impact the agility of the enterprise.
Therefore the goal of this paper is to introduce the paradigm that would be helpful in
supporting small and medium sized enterprises (SMEs) in their agility with cloud
solutions including SaaS; and to provide a conceptual outlook of this paradigm.

We propose a Triple-Agile paradigm that is created on the basis of the following
assumption: for (1) agile business processes of SMEs, the (2) agile development and
maintenance of cloud services, and (3) agile adoption or acquisition of (e.g. migration
to) cloud services is necessary. The proposed paradigm is illustrated in Fig. 1.

In the paper we refer to agility as the capability to act agilely and consider three
ways of acting agilely (or three levels of agility), i.e. being agile by being versatile,
being agile by reconfiguration, and being agile by reconstruction as discussed in [3].

© Springer International Publishing AG 2017
B. Johansson et al. (Eds.): BIR 2017, LNBIP 295, pp. 260–267, 2017.
DOI: 10.1007/978-3-319-64930-6_19

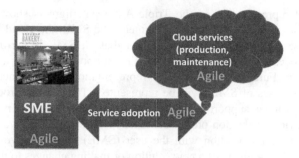

Fig. 1. Triple-Agile paradigm

Versatility is thus the highest level of agility while reconstruction is the lowest. Thus, according to the Triple-Agile paradigm all three agilities (namely, SME processes, service adoption or acquisition, and service development and maintenance) can have any of three levels of agility. The challenge here is how to combine different levels of agility of all three components of the Triple-Agile paradigm.

This research in progress paper addresses this challenge by the development of conceptual outlook of the Triple-Agile paradigm. The conceptual outlook of the paradigm is presented in Sect. 2. It has to be noted here that the project, inside of which the paradigm and its conceptual outlook were developed, specifically addresses non-core processes of SMEs. So the rest of the paper will focus on those SME processes which are not the life-blood (core or operational processes) of the enterprise. Further, in the paper, the non-core processes are called "support processes" of SMEs. While the proposed conceptual outlook might be applicable also to agile core (operational) processes of SMEs, additional research is needed to prove it. Related works are briefly considered in Sect. 3. Section 4 concludes the paper and points to the agenda for further research.

2 A Conceptual Outlook of the Triple-Agile Paradigm

To realize the Triple-Agile paradigm it was necessary to build a conceptual outlook of the paradigm and visualize how the paradigm could be used in the chosen context: cloud solution provision for non-core process (i.e., support processes, e.g. document management, security management, etc.) of SMEs. The ArchiMate language [4, 5] was chosen for the representation because it provides the elements that are easily understandable for different groups of stakeholders. The following method was applied for constructing the visualization:

1. The high abstraction level representation of the paradigm was created.
2. The detailed representations were created, based on the abstract one, so that for each way of acting agilely (i.e. agility level) [3] of SME non-core processes, there would be corresponding service provisions (service development and maintenance and service adoption/acquisition) represented.

The abstract representation of the Triple-Agile paradigm is shown in Fig. 2. It involves processes of three generic roles, namely: the SME, the cloud service broker, and the cloud service producer. It is assumed that an SME is performing its core (operational) processes agilely and therefore its support processes also have to be performed agilely. Further, in the detailed representation of the conceptual outlook, only support processes of SMEs will be represented. The service producer produces (cloud) services that can support the support processes of SMEs. The model prescribes two types of service production processes: reactive ones and proactive ones. Reactive processes are run in cooperation with the user (SME) representatives; reactive processes can be the development of a new solution or making changes to the existing one. Proactive processes can be performed solely by the service producer (i.e. on the basis of research, innovations, or other activities), thus, the service is available without the user requesting it. This is in contrast to what would happen in a traditional agile systems development project [6].

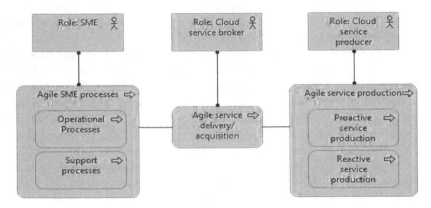

Fig. 2. Conceptual outlook of the Triple-Agile paradigm at a high level of abstraction

The mission of the broker is to enable the usage of the services. This role mainly refers to the services that are developed by proactive processes. It can refer to both traditional service brokers in service oriented architectures [6] and brokers in multi-cloud environments [7]. The brokers can have several sub-roles such as aggregator, integrator, controller, adapter, etc. [7]. In the Triple-Agile paradigm, the service provider can be simultaneously in the role of "producer" and in the role of "broker". So, in the detailed representation of the conceptual outlook, both roles will be attached to the service provider.

In the detailed description of the conceptual outlook of the Triple-Agile paradigm we distinguish between two stages: (1) the stage of initiation of the cooperation between an SME and a service provider and (2) the stage of continuous cooperation between an SME and a service provider. In the initiation stage we can further distinguish between automatic initiation of the cooperation (Fig. 3), manual initiation of the cooperation (Fig. 4), and initiation of the cooperation through a project (Fig. 5). In the first two cases the service provider already has the ready-made services; in the third case a service development process takes place.

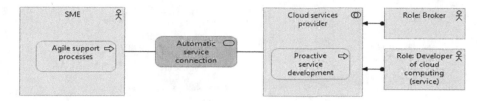

Fig. 3. Automatic initiation of cooperation

Automatic initiation of the cooperation (Fig. 3) can start without direct communication between employees of the SME and the service provider before the start of the use of the service. For this to occur, the provided services should be either at a configurable level or a versatile level of agility. However, the level of agility of the service is not exactly the same thing as the agility of the processes that are used for the development of the service; and thus different options of achieving configurable or versatile services are possible.

Manual initiation of cooperation (Fig. 4) requires direct communication between employees of an SME and a service provider. There can be several communication options: the service configuration can be done by the service provider based on the SME needs analysis, the configuration can be done at the SME's side after some learning process, etc. The cooperation initiation through the service development project (Fig. 5) corresponds to the "traditional" project development and does not require proactively built services.

The service provider can also take care of initiating the cooperation by providing particular marketing activities (also using corresponding marketing software) to promote all three above-mentioned options of initiation of cooperation between the SME and the service provider.

In the initiation stage we did not distinguish between the levels of agility of SMEs. For the continuous cooperation stage the difference between the levels of agility will be taken into account. The following types of continuous cooperation are considered: (1) cloud services for versatile SME processes, (2) cloud services for configurable SME processes; and (3) reconstruction of SME processes.

Versatile business processes can be understood as adaptive processes that can change without external involvement. For versatile business processes, services of the same agility level are needed (see Fig. 6). For versatile services proactive service development is necessary.

For configurable business processes, support has four different possible variants: (1) supported by versatile cloud services; (2) supported by configurable services equipped with additional configuration services – in this case the configuration can be done on the SME side; (3) supported by configurable services with manual configuration on the service provider side; (4) supported by configurable service and configuration service that can be invoked by cooperating between the SME and the service provider (see Fig. 7). In all these cases proactive service development processes are necessary.

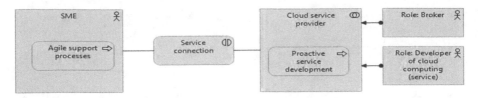

Fig. 4. Manual initiation of cooperation

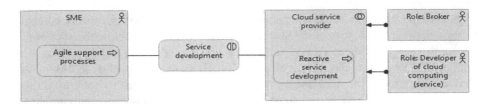

Fig. 5. Initiation of cooperation through the project

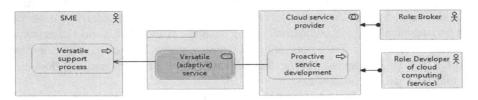

Fig. 6. Supporting versatile SME's processes with versatile services

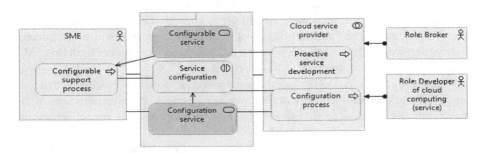

Fig. 7. Configurable SME's business process supported by configurable service and configuration service that can be invoked together by the SME and the service provider

If the SME's processes have to be reconstructed – the corresponding service reconstruction process has to be initiated unless, in the SME, the reconstructed process is such that it can use services that have already been developed. If the service is to be reconstructed, it can be done by reactive processes, so that in this case, proactive service development is not required.

In the above description 10 different types of SME and service provider cooperation were mentioned (4 types for initiation of cooperation and 6 types for continuous cooperation). The types of cooperation can change from one to another over time. So the detailed models of the conceptual overview can be organized in potential sequences as it is done in situational methods engineering [8]. Each move from one type of cooperation to another (e.g. changing from automatic initiation (Fig. 3) to versatile (adaptive) support of versatile SME processes (Fig. 6)) can be considered as a strategy [8] that can be chosen according to the current type of cooperation and the intentions of stakeholders. All combinations of detailed cooperation models that lead from a lower level of agility to a higher level of agility, of at least one of the process types in the abstract model represented in Fig. 2, form 20 main strategies in the conceptual outlook of the Triple-Agile paradigm.

While there are different ways that SMEs can cooperate with service providers, it is worth emphasizing that only two cases (initiation through the project and support of SME process reconfiguration via the project) correspond to common practice in agile systems development, i.e. reactive systems development. In other cases the methods for proactive development of services should be defined and appropriate software and technological requirements considered. The next section ponders the possibilities of populating technologically the conceptual outlook of the Triple-Agile paradigm by considering related work of several research areas.

3 Related Work

Agile systems development is usually related to software development; however, it has been extrapolated also to other areas of activity, such as information systems development [3] and enterprise management [1]. Cloud computing has been mentioned as one of the enablers of information systems agility [2]. The outlook of the Triple-Agile paradigm suggests structuring the related work into three mutually related areas, namely: agility of SME processes, service brokering agility, and service development and maintenance agility.

While it is commonly acknowledged that SMEs should be agile, there is not much work that discusses the SME agility in detail. However, there are works that relate SME agility to the usage of cloud services [9]. When looking at the statistics about how well SMEs are using cloud services, we can see that, in countries with a well developed network infrastructure, a high percentage of SMEs use cloud services. However, looking more deeply, these are mainly such services as e-mails and data storage, i.e. these services are not dedicated to specific business processes. For instance in Latvia 24% of SMEs use storage cloud services, 21% of SMEs use e-mail services, 18% of SMEs use different SaaS, and all other cloud usage types (including dedicated process support services) do not exceed 10% [10]. This shows that there is room for improvement for supporting SME business processes. From the theoretical viewpoint, there are attempts to establish the theory for supporting agility of business processes [11]. However, the theory is quite generic and there are not many reports on its usage. To sum up this area of focus, the related work affirms the necessity of supporting SME agility and provides a number of particular solutions for this support in terms of theory and solution architectures. The related work does not distinguish between the levels of agility of SME business processes. There are also differences in the use of terminology, e.g. [9] refers to adaptive processes, which could be understood as the processes of a versatile level of agility, but, when looking more deeply into the content, it rather applies to a configurable level of agility (when user involvement is required to change the processes).

Agile service brokers have been considered in the related research [6, 7]. They address both single cloud and multi-cloud solutions. A brokering function is analyzed in depth in [12]. It distinguishes between explicit and implicit broker functions. The following explicit functions are mentioned: initiation of the virtual enterprise, focused marking of resource creation (resource identification), resource selection, resource systems integration, resource integration scheduling, resource systems reconfiguration, resource monitoring and reliability analysis, resource control, information dissemination, virtual environment provision between the client and server levels. The list of implicit functions includes interaction with other brokers, resource market /virtual net creation, resource market maintenance, resource selection, negotiation, guaranteeing confidentiality between client and supplier, and creating mechanisms that support transaction lists. While [12] does not directly address the three levels of agility of the Triple-Agile paradigm; still, the set of functions discussed, can be useful in populating technologically the conceptual outlook of the Triple-Agile paradigm.

Agile service development is the most broadly and deeply researched focus area. It includes the work on agile software development with its reactive nature in terms of availability of on-site users and their requirements [13]. There is also the work that especially concentrates on how to best cooperate between IT solution developers and the rest of the enterprise [14]. This knowledge can also be extrapolated to the setting of the Triple-Agile paradigm. The knowledge of agile software development can be reused for populating those detailed models of the conceptual outlook of the Triple-Agile paradigm that involve reactive processes on the side of the service provider. However, there is much less research on agile pro-active service development.

4   Conclusions

The paper proposes the Triple-Agile paradigm and its conceptual outlook that have a business eco-systemic view on agile SMEs processes, cloud service adoption/ acquisition (or brokering) processes, and service development and maintenance processes. The conceptual outlook also distinguishes between three different levels of agility for each of the three abovementioned types of processes. As (1) the conceptual outlook reveals that traditional agile software development methods cover only two of ten agility level combinations and (2) the related works do not directly distinguish between the agility levels, further research is needed for incorporating existing business and technological knowledge in the Triple-Agile paradigm and developing new solutions for populating, technologically, the conceptual outlook of the paradigm.

Acknowledgement. This research is part of the project "Competence Centre of Information and Communication Technologies" run by IT Competence Centre, contract No. 1.2.1.1/16/A/007, co-financed by European Regional Development Fund, Research No. 1.3 "Agile paradigm application in small and medium enterprises business support processes management". More information at http://www.itkc.lv/.

References

1. Burton, M.: The future of organization design: an interpretative synthesis in three themes. J. Organ. Des. **2**(1), 42–44 (2013)
2. Sawas, M.S., Watfa, M.K.: The impact of cloud computing on information systems agility. Australas. J. Inf. Syst. **19**, 97–112 (2015)
3. Martenson, A.: Produsing and consuming agility. In: Desouza, K.C. (ed.) Agile Information Systems, pp. 41–51 (2007)
4. ArchiMate 2.1. ArchiMate 2.1 specification. Open Group (2013). http://pubs.opengroup.org/architecture/archimate2-doc/
5. ArchiMate 3.0 ArchiMate 3.0 specification. Open Group (2016). http://pubs.opengroup.org/architecture/archimate3-doc/
6. Dillon, T.S., Wu, C., Chang, E.: Reference architectural styles for service-oriented computing. In: Li, K., Jesshope, C., Jin, H., Gaudiot, J.-L. (eds.) NPC 2007. LNCS, vol. 4672, pp. 543–555. Springer, Heidelberg (2007). doi:10.1007/978-3-540-74784-0_57
7. Wadhwa, B., Jaitly, A., Hasija, N., Suri, B.: Cloud service brokers: addressing the new cloud phenomenon. In: Rajsingh, E.B., Bhojan, A., Peter, J.D. (eds.) Informatics and Communication Technologies for Societal Development, pp. 29–40. Springer, New Delhi (2015). doi:10.1007/978-81-322-1916-3_4
8. Ralyté, J., Deneckère, R., Rolland, C.: Towards a generic model for situational method engineering. In: Eder, J., Missikoff, M. (eds.) CAiSE 2003. LNCS, vol. 2681, pp. 95–110. Springer, Heidelberg (2003). doi:10.1007/3-540-45017-3_9
9. Feld, T., Hoffmann, M.: Process on demand: planning and control of adaptive business processes. In: Brunetti, G., Feld, T., Heuser, L., Schnitter, J., Webel, C. (eds.) Future Business Software. PI, pp. 55–66. Springer, Cham (2014). doi:10.1007/978-3-319-04144-5_5
10. Vasiljeva, T., Shaikhulina, S., Kreslins, K.: Cloud computing: business perspectives, benefits and challenges for small and medium enterprises (Case of Latvia). Procedia Eng. **178**, 443–451 (2017)
11. Uluhan, E., Aydin, M.N.: Complex adaptive systems theory in the context of business process management. In: Zehbold, C. (ed.) S-BPM ONE 2014. CCIS, vol. 422, pp. 147–156. Springer, Cham (2014). doi:10.1007/978-3-319-06191-7_10
12. Ávila, P., Putnik, G.D., Cunha, M.M.: Brokerage function in agile virtual enterprise integration — a literature review. In: Camarinha-Matos, L.M. (ed.) PRO-VE 2002. ITIFIP, vol. 85, pp. 65–72. Springer, Boston, MA (2002). doi:10.1007/978-0-387-35585-6_8
13. Hoda, R., Salleh, N., Grundy, J., Tee, H.M.: Systematic literature reviews in agile software development: a tertiary study. Inf. Softw. Technol. **85**, 60–70 (2017)
14. Martini, A., Pareto, L., Bosch, J.: A framework for speeding up interactions between agile teams and other parts of the organization. In: Bosch, J. (ed.) Continuous Software Engineering, pp. 67–82. Springer, Cham (2014). doi:10.1007/978-3-319-11283-1_6

Organizational Structures for an Implementation of Virtual Teamwork - A Case Study Analysis

Birgit Großer[✉] and Ulrike Baumöl

FernUniversität, Hagen, Germany
{birgit.grosser,ulrike.baumoel}@fernuni-hagen.de

Abstract. In many successful companies, teams work together virtually instead of face to face. These teams are supported by technology, allowing effective virtual teamwork across the globe. Some companies are even successful in business without any offices at all. The ways of working in virtual teams appear to be ingrained in these companies' cultures. The paper at hand performs a case study analysis synthesizing individual patterns found in companies that are built on virtual teamwork to a generic organizational pattern. This generic pattern can be deployed to support changes due to virtuality and digitalization in more traditional companies. The case study analysis provides a holistic view on virtual teamwork and contributes to research on this evolution.

Keywords: Virtual team · Teamwork · Case study analysis

1 Introduction

Digitalization as a socio-technical phenomenon bears the potential to change how people live and work. The way people are socialized and decide to live and work impacts the development of new technological solutions as well as technological innovation enable certain ways of life. Megatrends, like globalization, urbanization, sustainability, and flexibilization, further drive the fundamental change in how we live and work. Companies that make use of virtual teams (VTs) working across the globe are one of the many manifestations of this development in society and organizational design. Obviously, these concepts introduce an advancing degree of virtuality. People spend time with their friends in virtual networks and introduce virtuality into their work life. Companies use virtual teamwork to acquire qualified employees and save costs on expenses or real estate.

Many different aspects of how and why VTs work successfully are addressed in scientific literature. Answers are e.g. sought on how "identification develops in hybrid and pure virtual settings" [1] or on "how communication with Millennials will affect organizations" [2]. For these very narrow aspects, guidance is derived that is also offered to practice. The case study analysis at hand seeks to provide further insights and a holistic view on organizational structures of companies deploying VTs in order to contribute to the body of knowledge. The research objective is thus to present a generic organizational pattern as synthesis of the identified individual patterns found in

© Springer International Publishing AG 2017
B. Johansson et al. (Eds.): BIR 2017, LNBIP 295, pp. 268–278, 2017.
DOI: 10.1007/978-3-319-64930-6_20

companies. This can be used to plan change for less virtualized companies, based on the analysis of enterprises that are mainly built of VTs.

A case study analysis is performed as this research approach allows identifying patterns while acknowledging the context [3]. The analyzed companies are chosen due to their high degree of virtuality. Virtuality in this context means that the companies consist of teams that work together asynchronously and geographically dispersed (see Sect. 2). The revealed patterns can in turn be used to derive hints for established traditional companies on how to adopt or intensify virtual teamwork.

The relevant concepts show how to define virtuality of teams and how to identify patterns in Sect. 2. Section 3 introduces the research method and provides details on how data was collected and analyzed. The context and findings of the case study analysis are shown in Sect. 4, closing with a discussion towards open research ideas in Sect. 5. [4] proposes five key components of case study design. These components are shown in Table 1 which also illustrates the approach of this paper.

Table 1. Key components and action plan [4]

Component of case study design	Implementation and section
1. Research question	What are patterns in organizational structure of companies with a high degree of virtuality in teamwork? Sect. 2
2. Theoretical propositions	The scope is limited to companies with a high degree of virtuality in teamwork. Concepts for virtuality and for patterns are derived in Sect. 2
3. Units of analysis and data	Questionnaires, websites of and articles about organizational structures of four companies are analyzed in Sect. 3
4. Linking data to propositions	The findings are mapped to an integrated framework in Sect. 4
5. Criteria for interpreting findings	Criteria and their manifestation are proposed in Sect. 3

2 Virtual Teams and Organizational Patterns in Work Settings

Research topics concerning many aspects of virtual teamwork have been and still are analyzed in scientific literature [5]. These works mostly focus rather narrow topics, as described above (e.g. [1, 2]). More holistic views on VTs, their processes, how they work and are embedded in companies are mostly built on practical experience and do not follow a scientific approach (e.g. [6]). The paper at hand contributes to the current aim [7] for substantial and more comprehensive scientific research on VTs by focusing on the organizational structures which enable VTs in successfully operating companies.

Companies with a high degree of virtuality in teamwork are to be chosen for this case study analysis as role model. Therefore, a concept for defining and comparing the degree of virtuality is needed in order to decide which companies fit into the sample. Yet, there is no consensus on how virtuality in teams is defined or even measured [8].

Typically, different aspects are in- or excluded in order to discriminate VTs from traditional teams [5]. Even though a common definition does not exist so far, current concepts tend to abandon the strictly dichotomous approach of virtual versus traditional team [8]. Teams are regarded to be located in between these two poles [8].

VTs, communities, offshore development etc. are overlapping concepts derived in scientific discourse. [9] analyze criteria that are used in literature to define the virtuality of teams. Following the synthesis of this literature study, virtuality of teams is determined by the two criteria *asynchrony* and *geographic dispersion*. This concept of VTs is viable for the study at hand, as it focuses on the main properties analyzed here. VTs in this context use information and communication technology (ICT) for actually being able to work as a team. The deployed ICT include e.g. software solutions, such as project management tools, virtual meeting rooms and video call applications. However, this technology use can be regarded as a result of the need for virtual teamwork rather than as criterion for defining and measuring virtuality [9]. The concept of "asynchrony" is explained as teams which work at the same location with different schedules or at different locations with different time zones, both leading to mostly asynchronous communication. Geographic dispersion defines the actual distance of team members. Both criteria alone are sufficient to define a team as virtual and can be used to measure the degree of virtuality of a team according to [9]. Criteria such as cultural diversity and lifespan of the teamwork are also often used for defining the virtuality of teams, but as shown by [9] cannot alone define virtuality satisfactorily. The degree of virtuality can be located on a continuum between completely virtual and not virtual at all [9] as shown in Fig. 1.

Fig. 1. Degree of virtuality

[9] propose to measure the degree based on the definition of virtuality as shown in Fig. 1 above, and additionally aim at teamwork time and team characteristics. Thus, in order to check the degree of a companies' teamwork virtuality, two questions are asked:

- What proportion of teamwork time is performed virtually?
- What proportion of team members work virtually?

Further dimensions that do not constitute, but are found to correlate with virtuality of teams (e.g. [5]) are shown in Fig. 2.

In order to identify patterns in enterprise structure and processes, a suitable framework has to be introduced. The framework (Fig. 3) allows creating a holistic overview of a company in its context. The existing conditions concerning the VTs are

virtual team		traditional team
heterogenous	. . . . culture and socialization	homogenous
intense	. . . . ICT use	minor
media based	. . . . communication channel	face to face

Fig. 2. Dimensions that correlate with team virtuality

analyzed based on this framework in order to derive similarities and differences. These serve to evolve patterns and create a generic model. As the goal of this study is create a single model of relevant patterns, this resulting generic model can in turn be used to plan possible paths of development for other companies, especially less virtualized ones (Sect. 4). The components of the different layers of the framework and their relations are shown in Fig. 3. The layers are described in the following and in further detail in [10, 11].

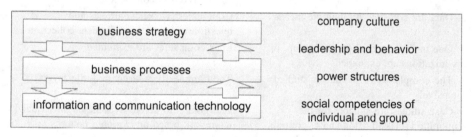

Fig. 3. Framework with functional and emotional-culturally-oriented layers

Business strategy, processes and deployed ICT are defined, as well as their interrelationship. These layers of the model can be regarded as functional layers [10]. Information on company culture, leadership and power structures are gathered and relevant social competencies compiled [11, 12]. These model layers are emotional-culturally-oriented. Perspectives on governance, context and external factors can be included in subsequent research. The functional layers are codependent. The strategy influences the processes, which influence the choice and use of ICT and vice versa. The emotional-culturally-oriented layers are also codependent [12] and are strongly related to the design of the functional layers. Thus the functional layers are represented to be embedded in the environment of the emotional-culturally-oriented layers [13] in Figs. 3 and 4.

The analyzed organizational patterns are based on these layers. The presented layers have been applied for change management in practice [14] and their validity is supported by case studies [12]. The framework presents a holistic view on the company and allows recognizing main structures and dependencies. Thus, these layers are used for analyzing the selected cases in Sects. 3 and 4. The layers show individual manifestations in the analyzed companies along this framework. The identified manifestations are used to derive the final artefact, the generic organizational pattern (Sect. 4).

3 Analysis Design and Procedure

Case study analyses allow collecting rich data on current events and entities. The studies can be of explanatory, exploratory or descriptive type [4]. As the objective of this study is to reveal existing patterns, it can be regarded to be of exploratory type. The selection of more than one case results in a multiple-case design [3]. Thus the recognition of patterns is facilitated and theory building is enabled. Adapting the conceptualization of case studies by [3], Table 2 shows the characteristics of the case study analysis at hand.

Table 2. The analysis' characteristics and their implementation

Characteristics by [3]	Implementation
1. Phenomenon is examined in a natural setting	Organizational patterns of virtual teamwork are analyzed in companies
2. Data are collected by multiple means	Companies' websites, articles and questionnaires are used for data collection
3. One or few entities (person, group, or organization) are examined	Four companies are examined
4. The complexity of the unit is studied intensively	The complexity is structured into layers
5. Case studies are suitable for the exploration, classification and hypothesis development stages of the knowledge building process	The goal is to derive hypotheses on virtual teamwork based on explored patterns
6. No experimental controls or manipulations are involved	Data is collected following scientific standards for case study research
7. The investigator may not specify the set of independent and dependent variables in advance	The variables are not set, yet the hypothesis induces virtuality as context for the independent variables
8. The results derived depend heavily on the integrative powers of the investigator	The conceptualization of the topic and derived research process support the integrative potential
9. Changes in site selection and data collection methods could take place as the investigator develops new hypotheses	Changes in site selection or collection methods will be noted for future research
10. Case research is useful in the study of "why" and "how" questions because these deal with operational links to be traced over time rather than with frequency or incidence	"Why" and "how" questions are implemented in search for patterns. The synthesis of individual patterns found among the units of analysis supports the exclusion of arbitrariness
11. The focus in on contemporary events	The focus is on currently operating companies

3.1   Data Collection

For the case study analysis, Basecamp, Fire Engine RED, 10up, and Zapier were chosen as unit of analysis. All four analyzed companies have been operating successfully for several years. Following the definitions from above (Sect. 2), each company is characterized by a high degree of virtuality and the correlating dimensions. The companies are thus selected as patterns are predicted to exist among them [3, 4]. Due to the exploratory character of this case study analysis, a small set of cases is selected [3]. Many more companies exist that fit the profile for this study. These can be included in future research for validating the findings. The selection of the companies analyzed here and the exclusion of others is furthermore based on the availability of information documented on their websites.

Multiple data collection methods are used in order to provide a rich set of data. These include documentation (journalistic articles) and archival records (companies' websites) [4]. The companies' websites were used as primary source for data collection. Especially the "about" - and the career-sections provided information for the model elements of the integrated framework. Additionally, online articles were used for data collection. These articles are mainly blog articles by founders or members of the companies, interviews with company founders or further material provided by the companies, such as the guidelines by [6]. Furthermore, the companies were contacted via email. The emails contained a short introduction into the topic and open questions, one regarding each layer of the framework and allowed short and precise answers. The set of questions and the answers received can be obtained from the authors.

3.2   Data Analysis

The integrated framework was used to structure the data as described above (Sect. 2). The following Table 3 presents the central findings for the single layers of the framework. These are synthesized and dependencies between the layers are explained in Sect. 4. Table 3 contains summaries by the author and quotes from the websites, related articles and questionnaires sent via email.

Table 3. Patterns of companies based on virtual teamwork

Integrated framework	Basecamp[1, 2]	Fire engine RED[3]	10up[4]	Zapier[5]
Business strategy	One product, less is more, simplicity, clarity, ease-of-use, and honesty	Innovation, easily accessible software solution, four services provided	Customized web services, craftsmanship, innovation, openness, ownership	Create processes and systems that let computers do what they are best at doing and let humans do what they are best at doing
Business processes	Regular work/task cycles (6 weeks), emergent idea	Customer care, online meetings, face-to-face once a year, no	Weekly metric based reports, core sets of	Every employee works in customer support, weekly online meetings

(continued)

Table 3. (*continued*)

Integrated framework	Basecamp[1,2]	Fire engine RED[3]	10up[4]	Zapier[5]
	development, big believers in asynchronous communication, no formal marketing role	micromanagement of employees	standards for each discipline	
ICT	Self-developed tool for unified documentation, communication, idea pitches	Variety of free and payed collaborative tools	Variety of free and payed collaborative tools	Variety of free and payed collaborative tools
Company culture	Sustainability, long-term growth	Employee retention first, client retention second	Equal perspective on clients, employees and community	Transparency (e.g. hiring process)
Leadership and behavior	Coworkers, company as a product, teams stay together for whole cycle, teams max. 3p, no project manager, no time tracking, strict deadline	Value employees by providing promotions and raises	Teams of 6–8p plus manager, serve team through encouragement and support	Small teams, supportive/positive/inclusive workplace (code of conduct), buddy system, regular structured feedback calls, weekly result update
Power structures	50 employees worldwide, headquarter	40 employees from US and Canada	120 + employees worldwide, headquarter	20 + worldwide, supervisor hierarchy
Social competencies of individual and group	"Treat people right"	Value and recognize employees	Culture built on empathy and teamwork, collaboration, self-management	Code of conduct promotes guidelines for communication, teamwork, face-to-face-meetings

[1]https://basecamp.com
[2]https://m.signalvnoise.com/how-we-set-up-our-work-cbce3d3d9cae#.bp3n8tjd1
[3]http://www.inc.com/winning-workplaces/articles/201105/where-virtual-is-the-best-policy.html
[4]https://10up.com/
[5]https://zapier.com/

4 Discussion

The results of the case study analysis allow identifying certain similar instantiations of the patterns and creating a generic model (see Fig. 4 below).

While researching the companies' websites, two main aspects were eminently prominent: the emphasis on selling one main product and the focus on the companies' employees. This impression is supported by the findings as shown in detail in Table 3 above. The generic pattern is outlined in Fig. 4 and explained below.

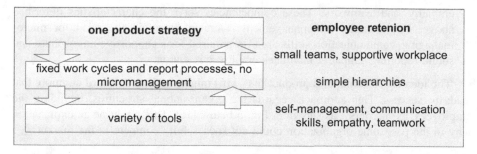

Fig. 4. Generic organizational pattern as synthesis of the identified individual instantiation

- All companies focus on *one main product*. Additional services are offered, but no company promotes a wide range of different products or services. Especially the characteristic to provide a simple and clear solution that fits the customers' individual needs was found on all sites.
- This strategy is mirrored in the *business processes*. Examples are fixed work cycles and report processes. The employees are not micromanaged. On the other hand, rather rigid framework conditions are set. As shared mental models are found to be essential for virtual team success [15], these set conditions can support the consistency of the team members' mental models.
- Three out of the four analyzed companies use a *variety of tools* for communication, documentation, project management, etc. The companies have established the use of a certain tool for each task. Thus, the tools are not selected based on the employee's individual preferences but mostly standardized across the company for each process. One exception with respect to the choice of tools is Basecamp. Basecamp develops the project management software of the same name and states to use its own software for all management and communication related processes.
- All companies show strong focus on *employee retention*, this can be regarded as a main finding concerning company culture. Some companies state that their employees' needs are in focus first and their clients' needs come only second. This can be regarded as major difference to traditional companies, at least the fact that this priority is stated in public.
- Characteristics regarding *leadership and behavior* are also employee-centered and serve the processes as described above. The teams are small and self-managed. A supportive workplace is regarded to enhance performance and employee retention. Guidelines for behavior are described on the companies' websites, in detail even as code of conduct.
- The *power structures* are also in line with the ideas about the product and processes. Hierarchies do exist but are structured to avoid confusion or complexity. Two or maximally three hierarchy levels are found in the analyzed companies. Roles and responsibilities for e.g. reporting are clearly defined.
- The last analyzed layer of the framework regards *social competencies of individual and group*. The companies focus on self-management, communication skills,

empathy, and teamwork. These competencies serve the characteristics described above. For example, self-management is crucial to avoid the need for micro-managing, communication skills are also required for a supportive atmosphere and sound reporting, empathy facilitates employee retention.

The idea of 'customer and product first' [16] might not be a standard anymore that leads to success. This approach regards the organizational structures, including the employees, as "barriers", as shown in Fig. 5 below [16]. This might be an explanation why in the past some organization could not successfully compete in the market.

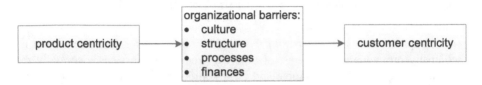

Fig. 5. Organizational structures as barriers on the way to customer centricity [16]

However, the changes we found based on the analysis might change that. Factors such as competition for an adequate workforce and changes in the organizational culture are examples of dynamics that impact organizational structures in companies and might be the reasons for the observations of this study: the *one-product-strategy* and focus on *employee retention* (Fig. 6).

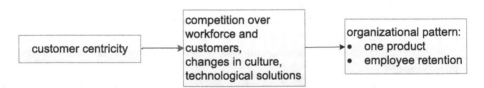

Fig. 6. From customer centricity to the new organizational pattern

Reviewing scientific literature shows that this employee-centric culture of virtual companies - and also currently active companies of less virtual degree - needs yet to be put in the focus of research.

There are some limitations concerning the interpretation of the results of the study at hand. The main sources of the gathered information about the companics are their websites. These are designed to promote the companies to clients and potential employees, as a consequence, these information probably have a bias with respect to an "over" positive presentation. In fact, less biased data would add to the validity of the results of this study. However, they nonetheless give some indications how the orga-nizational structures of these companies are meant to be working and that allows for an interpretation not only of the intention, but also of the actual representation.

5   Conclusion

The impact virtualization has on people and companies introduces change in our everyday (work-)lives. The companies presented in this study are vivid examples of how to successfully live this change. This study contributes to scientific guidance for how to learn from these companies. Individual patterns of these companies that operate virtually to a high degree are extracted and synthesized to form a generic organizational pattern as shown in Sect. 4. This pattern can be applied to plan change for less virtualized companies that seek to establish the use of VTs. Noticeable shifts towards employees and a strategic focus on one main product are main findings that contribute to the insights on how virtuality changes individuals, companies and vice versa. These results are first steps to actually understand how companies work today and where an ongoing virtualization can lead us.

Subsequent empirical studies that include a higher number of companies with different degrees of virtuality could be used to validate the found patterns. Further data collection methods, such as direct observations and physical artefacts [3] could be included in future research for refining the revealed characteristics and define the patterns in further detail. The processes of companies deploying VTs will be mapped in detail in subsequent studies based on the insights of the study at hand.

References

1. Fiol, C., O'Connor, E.: Identification in face-to-face, hybrid, and pure virtual teams: untangling the contradictions. Organ. Sci. **16**(1), 19–32 (2005)
2. Myers, K., Sadaghiani, K.: Millenials in the workplace: a communication perspective on millenials' organizational relationships an performance. J. Bus Psychol. **25**(2), 225–238 (2010)
3. Benbasat, I., Goldstein, D., Mead, M.: The case research strategy in studies of information systems. MIS Q. **11**(3), 369–386 (1987)
4. Yin, R.: Case Study Research. Design and Methods. Sage, Thousand Oaks (2014)
5. Gilson, L., Maynard, M., Young, N., Vartiainen, M., Hakonen, M.: Virtual teams research: 10 years, 10 themes, and 10 opportunities. J. Manag. **41**(5), 1313–1337 (2015)
6. Foster, W.: The Ultimate Guide To Remote Work. Zapier (2015)
7. Dulebohn, J., Hoch, J.: Virtual teams in organizations, Hum. Resour. Manag. Rev. Spec. Issue. Elsevier (2017)
8. Hosseini, M., Zuo, J., Chileshe, N., Baroudi, B.: Evaluating virtuality in teams: a conceptual model. Technol. Anal. Strateg. Manag. **27**(4), 385–404 (2015)
9. Schweitzer, L., Duxbury, L.: Conceptualizing and measuring the virtuality of teams. Inf. Syst. J. **20**(3), 267–295 (2010)
10. Österle, H., Blessing, D.: Business engineering modell. In: Österle, H., Winter, R. (eds.) Business Engineering, pp. 61–81. Springer, Berlin (2000). doi:10.1007/978-3-642-19003-2_4
11. Österle, H., Winter, R.: Business engineering. In: Österle, H., Winter, R. (eds.) Business Engineering, pp. 3–20. Springer, Berlin (2000). doi:10.1007/978-3-642-98097-8_1
12. Salminen-Karlsson, M.: Enabling virtual communities of practice: a case-study of swedish-indian collaboration in it development. Electron. J. Inf. Syst. Eval. **17**(1), 60–70 (2014)

13. Baumöl, U.: Change Management in Organisationen - Situative Methodenkonstruktion für flexible Veränderungsprozesse. Gabler, Wiesbaden (2008)
14. Friedel, D., Back, A.: Determination of enterprise 2.0 development levels with a maturity model. In: Nunes, M., Peng, G., Roth, J., Weghorn, H. (eds.) Proceedings of the IADIS International Conferences, pp. 3–9, Lisbon (2012)
15. Maynard, M., Gilson, L.: The role of shared mental model development in understanding virtual team effectiveness. Group Organ. Manage. **39**(1), 3–32 (2014)
16. Shah, D., Rust, R., Parasuraman, A., Staelin, R., Day, G.: The path to customer centricity. J. Serv. Res. **9**(2), 113–124 (2006)

Author Index

Printed in the United States
by XXXX information services

Printed in the United States
By Bookmasters